D1198993

GENDER

GENDER
A GENEALOGY OF AN IDEA

Jennifer Germon

palgrave
macmillan

GENDER
Copyright © Jennifer Germon 2009

All rights reserved.

First published in 2009 by PALGRAVE MACMILLAN® in the United States - a division of St. Martin's Press LLC, 175 Fifth Avenue, New York, NY 10010.

Where this book is distributed in the UK, Europe and the rest of the world, this is by Palgrave Macmillan, a division of Macmillan Publishers Limited, registered in England, company number 785998, of Houndmills, Basingstoke, Hampshire RG21 6XS.

Palgrave Macmillan is the global academic imprint of the above companies and has companies and representatives throughout the world.

Palgrave® and Macmillan® are registered trademarks in the United States, the United Kingdom, Europe and other countries.

ISBN: 978–0–230–60827–6

Library of Congress Cataloging-in-Publication Data

Germon, Jennifer.
    Gender : a genealogy of an idea / Jennifer Germon.
       p.   cm.
    ISBN 978–0–230–60827–6 (alk. paper)
    1. Gender identity.   2. Feminism.   I. Title.
    HQ1075.G4687 2009
    306.7082—dc22   2009015738

Design by Integra Software Services

First edition: December 2009

10 9 8 7 6 5 4 3 2 1

Printed in the United States of America

For N. A.

Contents

ACKNOWLEDGMENTS

I pay tribute to the tenacity and courage of the people who participated in the original research on which this book is based. Thank you for sharing your insights and your stories with such generosity and eloquence. Most especially I pay tribute to Yann, whose journey through uncharted waters provided inspiration for this project.

The writing of this book was made possible by the support of many people. To each of you I am extremely grateful. To all my fine friends and fabulous colleagues, near and far, who have been so generous with encouragement and all sorts of practical assistance, what is there to say except, *couldn't have done it without you. Mwah!* Especially you, Sam.

I pay tribute as well to Alpha House, a cooperative housing initiative for artists, writers, and musicians—and my home since 2006. Living in this extraordinary social experiment amid so many talented people propelled the writing of this book. For that I offer my heartfelt thanks.

Last but not least I offer my gratitude to the editorial and production staff at Palgrave. Thank you Brigitte Shull, Farida Koohi-Kamali, Julia Cohen, Kristy Lilas, Lee Norton, Niranjana Harikrishnan, and everyone else who has contributed to the production of this book.

INTRODUCTION

CIRCUMNAVIGATING PLANET GENDER

It is a handicap in the study of sexually dimorphic behaviour that, for all the millennia in which men and women have existed, no one yet has an exhaustive list of what to look for.[1]

CIRCUMNAVIGATING PLANET GENDER

Imagine a world without "gender." How would we make sense of our social worlds? How would we think about or theorize relations between and among the sexes? How would we account for what it means to be a boy or a girl, a man or a woman? There can be little argument that the concept of gender has become essential to the way that English speakers understand what it is to be a sexed subject. Yet gender did not exist 60 years ago—at least not in the way we understand it today. Gender as an *ontological* concept has so thoroughly naturalized into the English language that today it seems indispensable. A lack of attention to gender's origins has led to the common assumption that it has always been available, an assumption due in no small part to gender's formidable conceptual, analytical, and explanatory power. Yet gender does indeed have a history, and a controversial one at that. Until the 1950s, gender served to mark relations between words rather than people. While there is evidence that it was used sporadically during the nineteenth and twentieth centuries, the mid-1950s stands as the historical moment in which gender was codified into the English language as a personal and social category and so began its ascent as a potent new conceptual realm of sex.

The story begins in the late 1940s, when a young John Money undertook his doctoral research on human hermaphroditism at Harvard University. Less than two years after graduating, Money offered the term *gender*" as part of a framework for understanding hermaphroditism, as a rationale for clinical practices, and as a conceptual device for understanding human subjectivity. Money's ideas have come to have a profound effect on how people in English-speaking contexts understand subjectivity as masculine and feminine. This is because he extended his theories of gender from the intersexed to the wider population to offer an account of how everybody acquires their gender. That extension is representative of a common turn in the biological and medical sciences, where phenomena that deviate from a norm are used to demonstrate and explain the course of normal development.[2]

For all of the above reasons this book offers a critical intervention into gender that proceeds along two interconnected trajectories. The first situates the production and reproduction of the concept of gender in its historical context while the second explores the intricate relation that the intersexed had—and continue to have—to gender. While that relation may not be at once obvious the links are, as I demonstrate, inextricable. That is to say, if it were not for sexology's fascination with those of us who are "otherly sexed," the concept of gender as understood today might well not exist. The intersexed have historically provided medical science with the means to generate particular truths about what it is to be a sexed subject, and what it means to be human. The intersexed can rightfully claim to be the basis for many of our ideas about what is considered normal in bodily sex, but more importantly they represent the basis for what is considered normal in gender.

Since the early 1990s, both Money and his work have come under increasing scrutiny and have been attacked from various quarters. He has been accused of callous self-interest, of privileging nurture over nature, and of concealing the truth regarding the outcome of his best-publicized "experiment," which he used for a time to evidence the efficacy of his theories of gender acquisition.[3] As a consequence, his work has been roundly dismissed by detractors outside of sexology and by rivals from within the field, as if his ideas were of no value.[4] Such outright dismissal constitutes—in the vernacular—"throwing the baby out with the bathwater." This is shown by the fact that many of the counterclaims of Money's critics are unwittingly saturated with elements of his theories that have become axiomatic over the past 50 years. This all adds considerable weight to my claim that Money's influence on how and what we know about gender is today seriously underestimated. Against his detractors I propose that Money's gender offers a third wave of productive potential, one that differs from the second (as in second-wave feminism), precisely because his theories presuppose an interactive relation of cells to environment and to experience(s). To make such a claim is not to elide the problematic aspects of his ideas, however this in itself does not diminish their overall usefulness. Unharnessed from the tyranny of dimorphism, Money's theories of sex-gender[5] are among the most sophisticated we have available and for that reason, opportunities abound to critically reinvigorate Money's gender.

In Conversation(s)

This text is in conversation with other histories of the concept of gender. Most accounts are to be found in John Money's own corpus of work and in the feminist literature. While gender's origins are vaguely acknowledged in some feminist accounts, its intimate relation to the intersexed and to intersex case management practices is not.[6] While linguistics is identified correctly as the original home of gender in English, many feminist accounts remain blind to the precise context in which gender was transformed from language tool to human attribute.[7]

Feminist genealogies of gender that emerged from the poststructuralist moment of the 1980s drew on a poststructuralist emphasis on language, particularly in the work of Michel Foucault, Jacques Derrida, and Roland Barthes. These accounts focused their attention on the semantic differences between *grammatical* gender in the Romance and Germanic languages and *natural* gender, a classification unique to the English language.[8] However in doing so, many such accounts privilege the linguistic significance of gender over its ontological bearing.

Over the past two and half decades, the origins of gender in sexology have, almost without exception, been elided. While Bernice Hausman[9] has provided a detailed account of the centrality of Money and of the intersexed to the production of ontological gender, the lack of attention to historical accuracy has resulted in gender being variously framed as the invention of sociology;[10] of Robert Stoller;[11] as the legacy of Simone de Beauvoir;[12] and as the invention (through its appropriation from linguistics) of feminism.[13] It seems that from the moment that gender settled into the lexicon, the idea that it was a feminist invention spread rapidly to become part of feminist folklore.

The fact that this idea became received wisdom may be explained in part by the way that knowledge has traditionally circulated within feminism. But more than this, it is an effect of the efficacy of gender as both an analytical and an explanatory tool. That the history of such a recent conceptual device should elude so many with so much invested in it surely warrants attention.

This book seeks to reintroduce the work of Money and in doing so, disrupt previous feminist genealogies of gender. The occlusion of Money's work has had a number of consequences. First, it has allowed earlier poststructuralist analyses to remain firmly fixed on the discursive rather than the material production of sex, since it sustains the idea that gender is at heart a category of signification constituted through discourse. Second, it serves to thoroughly ahistoricize gender as if, as a concept, it has always been available. Third, it supports and sustains an epistemological investment in sexual difference—to the order of two. Fourth, it serves to entrench feminism firmly into a series of binary logics (sex/gender, male/female, man/woman, straight/gay). Fifth it contributes, however unwittingly, to the ongoing status of hermaphrodites as abject: as the impossible Other. As a critical historical intervention into gender, this text seeks to demonstrate that the intersexed have always had an intricate relation to the concept and were there at the beginning.

Since 1990 growing numbers of cultural critics have turned the spotlight on intersex case management (ICM) in order to examine the ethics and efficacy of the clinical practices used to mediate the births of intersexed infants.[14] This growing body of literature is one that this text is very much in conversation with because the production of the concept of gender is intricately linked to intersex research and clinical practices. The different forms of analysis employed in these critical approaches vary considerably: they range from historical, ethnomethodological and rhetorical approaches; bio-ethical and "insider" critiques; and philosophical, sociological, semiotic, and cultural analyses. It is notable however that a significant amount of this literature straddles disciplinary boundaries.[15]

The historical accounts offer fascinating insights into the various means by which medical and biological investigators have sought to stabilize sex in and on the body—both materially and discursively. This is part of what my project is concerned with. Others explore medicine's relation to the law. While the links between medical and legal perceptions of sexual ambiguity are said to extend back centuries, critics point out that the former understands sex quite differently than the latter. While medical science has long understood that the complexity of sexual development produces a spectacular array of human bodily forms, the law assumes a straightforward oppositional relation between two sexes. For that reason critics argue that medical technologies play a significant role in permitting the maintenance of a "legal fiction of binary gender as an absolute."[16]

A considerable number of the critiques tackle the issue of medical ethics. Of central concern is the continued deployment of a treatment model designed well before the implementation of contemporary ethical standards in medical care. Intersex case management procedures are seen by some as a throwback to the nineteenth-century project of teratology.[17] While individuals are today permitted to live,[18] their particular forms of somatic difference are rendered invisible because physicians consider intersex conditions as "social stigmata to be excised in the operating room."[19] Critics roundly condemn (and rightly so) those doctors who recommend to parents that their intersexed children be kept in the dark about their medical histories. The same applies to the (still) widespread practice of withholding diagnostic information from adult intersexed individuals.

After almost two decades of intellectual and political engagement with the medical practices of ICM, certain lines of argument weave through this burgeoning body of knowledge. A number of these have now gained hegemonic status within the field. The most dominant of these discourses have gained significant currency outside the field as evidenced by numerous other sites (theoretical and political) that have increasingly become inflected with considerations and explorations of intersex.[20]

Four of the key arguments serve as points of departure for my analysis, arguments that this text seeks to complicate in order to open up a conceptual space to think differently about some of these issues. In the following section I describe and then problematize each of these in turn. The first point of departure turns on the ahistoricizing of gender. The second is the idea that ICM represents a disciplinary practice that enforces a heteronormative social order. The third position I seek to complicate is what I refer to as the "erasure analysis," where the eradication of the intersexed is seen as something already achieved. Finally, I seek to disrupt the idea that the intact bodies of the intersexed do not matter, or put differently, the idea that bodies matter only *after* they have been sexed/gendered.

AHISTORICISING GENDER

There is a tendency in the critical literature on ICM to ahistoricize gender as if it had always been available in the way that it is today. This practice, an instance of presentism, serves to universalize the concept of gender and so homogenize both the meanings and experiences of being a sexed subject across time and place. As many of these accounts reveal, even as Money's relation to ICM is writ large, his role as the "creator" of ontological gender is often overlooked.[21] Historical accounts that deal with the more recent past also overlook the concept's intricate relation to ICM. As one example, Deborah Findlay offers an analysis of the way that Canadian physicians mapped their understandings of dichotomous sex onto the bodies of the intersexed during the 1950s. While she acknowledges that Canadian medical theory and practice was influenced by the international literature, nowhere in her account is the work of Money mentioned. Given the prestige and wide circulation of medical journals such as the *Bulletin of the Johns Hopkins Hospital* and *Pediatrics* in which Money published, this oversight has a decontextualizing effect on the overall study.[22]

Even when gender's historical specificity is acknowledged, the term is often used liberally to reference historical periods prior to the mid-1950s. As a result, all "sex" becomes "gender" and so analyses of how perceptions of sex difference came to be understood precisely as gender remain under- or uninterrogated.[23] Gender is also ahistoricized when employed as a referent for both the social and the biological aspects of sex.[24] Such an approach is intended to highlight the constructedness of all aspects of maleness and femaleness, and while it does have theoretical utility, it nonetheless qualifies as what Eve Kofosky Sedgwick might call a significant but expensive leap. This leap is expensive precisely because the specificity of gender's history becomes obscured and opportunities to explore the production of the concept are foreclosed. When all sex is gender, the fact that physicians quite literally work with the material signifiers of sex is subsumed within larger debates about ideology. Privileging ideology over technological considerations overdetermines the former and at the same time diminishes the body's resistance to "ideological captation."[25] Similarly, when medical technologies are read as patriarchal tools of exploitation and degradation, the degree of bodily resistance to those technologies is overlooked or at the very least downplayed.

COMPULSORY HETEROSEXUALITY

Perhaps the line of argument that has most achieved hegemonic proportions within these critical discourses is the idea that ICM is a disciplinary practice used (after Butler) to enforce a heteronormative social order.[26] The image of doctors actively engaged in enforcing heterosexuality is evident in a multitude of critiques, each offering variations of the same theme.[27] Doctors are represented as the metaphorical princes of darkness charged with upholding the status quo by violent, coercive, and deceptive means. The heteronormativity argument tends to work in tandem with what Elizabeth Wilson identifies as one of the conventionalisms of feminist studies of the sciences. Wilson suggests that this conventionalism manifests in the idea that the biological sciences are inept both conceptually and politically and thus "the goal of feminist analysis of the sciences is to correct ideological error, rather than to learn from the data that have been produced."[28]

Heteronormative analyses tend to slide into an explanatory mode even as they are invoked for their analytical power (a tendency they surely share with the concept of gender). The application of a heteronormative analysis to ICM represents what might be called a soft analysis that carries with it some rather expensive consequences. By soft I mean the relative ease with which it is possible to find evidential support; expensive because it serves to obscure more than it makes visible. As an explanation, heteronormativity is compelling precisely because of the wealth of evidence that exists to support the claim. Yet there is something disquieting about it at the same time.

Heteronormativity has surely become as monolithic a concept as patriarchy. By purporting to explain everything, it forecloses investigations of what intersex—and indeed gender—mean for *all* sexual identities. A political economy of sexual difference has a very broad-based constituency, since those who are invested in gay and lesbian identities have a particularly keen interest in being able to demarcate between male and female bodies. As Dreger wryly notes, "if you don't know who is a male and who is a female, how will you know if what you have is a case of heterosexuality or homosexuality?"[29] In the twenty-first century, sexual variation not only raises the specter of homosexuality, it also raises the specter of heterosexuality, and bisexuality.

Borrowing from Teresa de Lauretis but reversing the terms of her argument, I propose that gender (currently) operates as a technology of dimorphic sexual difference. This allows us to see that the normative order at issue is sexuality per se, not just a heteronormative order. To put it another way, ICM supports and upholds *monosexuality* as normative.[30] The concept of monosexuality allows us to shift the terms of the debate away from the privileged homo/hetero coupling. As a category of analysis, it has a critical valence that extends beyond the reach of heteronormativity. As a conceptual tool, it makes visible those forms of sexed and sexual subjectivities whose materiality is constantly elided from the "real" and from the present. The intersexed, for example, are rendered pathological because they defy monosexual categories at a somatic level. From this angle the spectrum of interest groups invested in binary gender are brought into focus. So too is gender's standing as the most recent historical apparatus to legitimate all those social and sexual practices that rely on a distinction between two sexes.

ERASING ALL TRACE

A number of the cultural critiques argue that over the course of the twentieth century medical professionals have completed what the legal system had originally set out to do: to completely *erase* of any form of somatic sex that does not conform to a binary (hetero)sexual model.[31] This idea is made manifest in Epstein's assertion that "suppression achieves its perfect form in 'excision,' and the Other's potential for subversive social arrangements is eradicated altogether."[32] It is a strong claim although one that leaves people who are intersexed with little room for agency, whether they would choose subversive social arrangements, or otherwise.[33]

In medical discourses, surgical and hormonal interventions serve to relieve intersexed patients of their "condition" so they are no longer intersexed. This makes possible the argument that the intersexed are subject to a form of erasure, since they cease to exist in their own right, in the present. At a material level, case management practices have certainly rendered intersexed people all but invisible outside of the medical literature because their bodies are reconfigured to resemble male and female bodies.[34] The idea that ICM represents a return to medicine's teratological roots frames eradication as something already achieved.[35] Yet even if that were possible to prove, it would tell only part of the story.

In the following chapters I make the case that it was not in fact Money's gender or ICM that fully apprehended the hermaphrodite subject. That work had already been accomplished a decade earlier by psychologist Albert Ellis. It was he who categorized hermaphrodites' erotosexual status as heterosexual, homosexual, or bisexual. In apprehending hermaphrodites' sexuality in this way, a third or differently sexed Other was instantly made redundant. The idea of a third sex had loomed large in early sexual scientific thought but disappeared in a flash, since within the logic of a normative bipolar erotosexual order there is no place for a third or Other sex.[36]

As I discuss in detail in Chapter 5, intersex advocacy groups and many individuals seek an end to mandatory genital surgery on newborns. For some, the logical end of that goal is the obsolescence of intersex identities. This adds a whole other dimension to the issue of erasure. From this perspective intersex is a condition produced by surgery and hormonal therapies rather than an identity. Therefore it is not a subject position. Canadian activist and scholar Morgan Holmes, for example, has been quoted as saying the intersex movement is a "utopian project which can envision its own obsolescence."[37] By this account, bringing mandatory surgery to an end would render intersex identities moot, leaving in its wake men and women with penises and clitorises of differing sizes. In other words, genitalia would represent "phenotypes with no particular clinical meaning."[38]

But does this not also constitute a form of erasure? Does it not, by its privileging of maleness and femaleness, reinforce the supposed naturalness of existing binary categories? And in so doing, does it not banish the intersexed from the present, relegating them once more to mythical realms?[39]

THESE BODIES DON'T MATTER?

A further line of argument draws on the analysis Judith Butler put forward in *Bodies That Matter* where she suggested that bodies had to be sexed in order to matter. For Butler the materiality of the body does not exist *a priori*, or prediscursively. Rather it is coextensive with its degree of cultural intelligibility—as gender. By this account intersexed bodies matter only *after* they have been sexed and after receipt of what Iain Morland has called the "idealized" and "authorized version" of genitals.[40] Epstein asserts that "armed with the heaviest artillery available medical science attempts to enforce a binary sex differentiation that is known not to exist in biomedicine."[41]

Certainly the birth of an intersex infant elicits what can be described only as an extreme response by clinicians. This suggests that intersexed bodies do indeed matter. Intersexed bodies require mediation because they are excessive at a somatic level and because they exceed cultural intelligibility. ICM happens because human subjectivity is understood on the basis of twos, pairs, and opposites. The intersexed do not fit this way of seeing the world, and that is why and that is how they are perceived as a "problem." When all is said and done, it would appear that the bodies of the intersexed matter even more than those of the non-intersexed.

THEORETICAL FRAMEWORK

Thomas Kuhn was one of the first to highlight the way that scientific observations can never be "pure" since they are always shaped by concepts. In other words, our vision of what is possible in sex is limited by the reach of our ideas such that we are unable to see that for which we have no words or concepts. In this sense, there are no facts independent of the ideas available to describe them since concepts shape perception. An underlying premise of this book is that the conceptual framework of dimorphic sexual difference is an interpretation of natural properties rather than facts of nature. Having just two legitimate sex (and two gender) categories prevents us from seeing the variety of types that a different conceptualization might reveal, as James Parsons noted over two and a half centuries ago:

If there was not so absolute a Law, with respect to the being of only one Sex in one Body, we might then, indeed, expect to find every Day many preposterous digressions from our present Standard.[42]

Over the past 50 years gender has become *the* interpretive framework for making sense of human bodies and subjectivities such that "one begins with the activities and presumptions about gender and works backwards as it were, toward the body."[43] Recognizing the limitations of relying on binary concepts to interpret bodies, identities, and behaviors provides an impetus to think differently about each of these aspects of selfhood. It also opens up opportunities to examine just what kinds of understandings are allowed, what are refused, and what are obscured by the binary.[44]

Georges Canguilhem's analysis of the relation between physiology (the science of living organisms) and pathology (the science of disease) provides a useful way of shedding light on the processes involved in medical science's bounding of "the normal." Nowhere is this more salient, it would seem, than with respect to what is normal in sex. An anomaly, according to Canguilhem, becomes pathological only at the point that it begins to stimulate scientific study, since neither diversity nor anomaly are, in and of themselves, disorders or diseases. By exploring the "relations between the determination of statistical norms and the evaluation of the degree of normality or abnormality" of any particular divergence, Canguilhem demonstrated that the concept of a norm is not so much a judgment of reality but rather one of value.[45] John Money said as much in his own research.[46] Once a cause of an anomaly is identified, the anomalous becomes pathological; from that point on, the pathological serves to substantiate that which is deemed to be normal. This is certainly the case for contemporary understandings of so-called normal (or unremarkable) fetal development which came directly from studies of the intersexed, just as Money's theories of gender acquisition did.

At a semantic level, the term *abnormal* follows from the definition of normal because it functions as the latter's logical negation. Canguilhem believed that because the relation between the normal and the abnormal is always one of exclusion, it is not paradoxical to claim that "the abnormal, while logically second, is existentially first."[47] Normality is that which goes unmarked precisely because its boundaries are delineated by what it is not. The normal, even when understood in terms of a continuum, remains little more than a rudimentary "conception of a lack of difference, of conformity, of the capacity to blend in invisibly."[48] In effect, normality cannot be apprehended on its own terms. By extending the concept of gender beyond the context of hermaphrodite research, Money was able to use it to substantiate "normal" development: in this case the development of masculine and feminine identities.

Hermaphrodites once fell under the rubric of teratology—the study of monsters. Within the logic of that field,[49] characteristics deemed monstrous are explained as the products of faulty embryological development and so take on the significance of disease. This is precisely the process by which the intersexed have come to be considered pathological. The concept of monsters has traditionally involved all kinds of duplication of the human form, or its component parts. Excess at the level of the body generates both curiosity and anxiety in medical science, not least because, as Grosz has noted, an excess of bodily parts seem somehow much more "discomforting than a shortage or diminution of limbs or organs."[50] The anxiety of which I speak is invoked by the specter of a monstrous chimera, a creature capable of transcending species boundaries. In this way the "monstrous hermaphrodite Other" stands as "both liminal and structurally central" to what we perceive as normal human subjectivity.[51] That structural centrality does not merely demarcate between normal and abnormal because

without the monstrous body to demarcate the borders of the generic, . . . and without the pathological to give form to the normal, the taxonomies of bodily value that underlie political, social, and economic arrangements would collapse.[52]

At the same time medical science turns to natural biological variation to define normality, it also attempts to neutralise that variation.[53] As I demonstrate in subsequent chapters, the work of John Money (and Robert Stoller) falls squarely within that tradition.

Rosemarie Garland Thomson's analysis of the (ongoing) project of modernity makes clear the ways that it has "effected a standard-ization of everyday life [one] that saturates the entire social fabric producing and reinforcing the concept of the unmarked normative, level body as the dominant subject of democracy."[54] Since moder-nity is characterized by "mechanized practices such as standardization, mass production, and interchangeable parts," the autonomous subject of modernity is grounded in a body that is required to be consis-tent in both form and in function.[55] That is why biomedicine as a form of modernist scientific discourse valorizes regularity and uni-formity as the supposedly objective grounds for its epistemological claims. The conventions of health care insist on constituting all bodies—including those marked by radical difference—as stable and predictable. That reliance on the predictable compels scientific dis-courses to depreciate particularity. Any variation from an idealized standardized body requires "corrective" intervention(s). Peculiarity—in whatever configuration—so threatens to interrupt "the paradigms of sameness and difference on which western epistemology, ontology and ethics are founded" that it is received as something that *must* be managed into neutrality.[56]

The idea that hermaphrodites require medical intervention tends to go without question; indeed medical mediation is sold on the grounds that hermaphrodite individuals are doomed to a life of misery and dejection without it.[57] The underlying premise of Money's research assumes that intersexed individuals would have been born as normal males or normal females if something hadn't gone wrong. At the same time the intersexed are considered to have *bodies* that are unfinished. This particular logic has two effects: on the one hand it justifies a medical response and provides a mandate to manage or more pre-cisely to "correct" these so-called disordered bodies; on the other hand it serves to uphold the apparent truth of dimorphic sexual dif-ference. Humans really do, after all, consist of just two sexes. But understandings of bodies are, of course, always representations.

Neither scientific nor popular modes of representing bodies can ever be innocent because they always tie bodies into larger systems of knowledge production.[58] John Money's production of gender is exemplary in this regard. Working under the transdisciplinary umbrella of sexology, he drew upon bodies of knowledge that extended far beyond the medical sciences, for example zoology, lin-guistics, and anthropology. At the same time his work fed back into those and other institutionalized bodies of knowledge by informing and shaping the concepts generated from them. Money's concepts have also informed other bodies of knowledge including feminism, sexuality scholarship, and intersex activism and scholarship. His influence on what one might call everyday understandings or local cultural knowledge of what it means to be a gendered or sexed subject is evident everywhere.[59]

Nonetheless, the hegemonic truths of gender and of sex are—like all dominant discourses—inherently unstable. The project of many poststructuralist analyses has been to demonstrate the way that gender's discursive production operates through constant reiteration and a continual referencing to its own "essential-ness." These are the conditions under which a sense of stability is bestowed on gender in such accounts. However gender does not merely function on a discursive level; it also functions relationally, as sociologist Erving Goffman and others have noted.[60]

While Goffman never offered a direct critique of the work of Money, his analysis speaks well to many aspects of the latter's project.[61] In *The Arrangement Between the Sexes*, Goffman offered a twofold analysis of gender relations that in many respects echoed the ideas of Money, as will become apparent in the chapters that follow.[62] Goffman's analysis functioned at two levels: the micro and the macro. At a micro level, his analysis offered a particularly nuanced account of the processes by which sex-specific modes of appearances, behaviors, and emotions come to be assimilated into embodied and psychic experience.[63]

It is the macro component of Goffman's analysis that most assists my investigation into the concept of gender. Goffman's refusal of the body as the (*a priori*) natural ground for gender allowed him to analyse gendered social arrangements as power relations. His analysis is notable for, among other things, the way that he explored gender's intersectional relation to class, race, and ethnicity. Gender, by his account, was nothing less than "a remarkable organizational device" for arranging humans into one of two (sex) classes from birth onward, despite its often tenuous relation to the body. He believed it paradoxical that something so inherently unstable as gender was able to function as such an effective "opiate of the masses."[64] In Goffman's view, to speak of *the sexes* or of the *other sex* in oppositional terms, as Money did, was a "dangerous economy" precisely because it so neatly tied into cultural stereotypes.[65] He argued strongly, and persuasively, that sex should be regarded only as the property of organisms, not as a class.

Goffman also stressed the importance of examining the various means by which medicoscientific understandings of gender shape and substantiate the normative understandings of local cultural knowledge. By his account those normative understandings about gender are empowered by medicoscientific beliefs about dimorphic sexual difference. Thus empowered, they have a self-fulfilling effect on gendered behavior. In this way, Goffman understood gender to operate tautologically.

METHODOLOGICAL NOTES

Gender: A Genealogy of an Idea approaches its subject matter by drawing on aspects of a genealogical method in the Foucauldian sense. Such an approach seeks not to discover any truth in gender, but rather to unsettle and disrupt assumptions of a continuity of meaning and, moreover, to disrupt the idea of fixed essences. A genealogy aims to reveal that what appears to be the truth is but an interpretation or series of interpretations of, in this context, bodies and subjectivities that each have their own historical specificity.

As I demonstrate throughout the book, gender is an incredibly dynamic concept. It has been subject to a series of transformations since first being offered as an ontological category 50-odd years ago and has thrived in the process. A genealogical approach provides the tools to look at the conditions under which each of the following phenomena was made possible: gender's transformation from grammatical tool to ontological attribute, the institutionalization of surgical responses to intersexed infants, the conceptual split between sex and gender, and gender's privileged status as the central organizing concept of feminism. Finally, it allows for an examination of the most recent political domain to be concerned with gender: intersex politics.

The research upon which this book is based employed a mixed method that combined textual analyses of different bodies of knowledge and qualitative face-to-face interviews. A critical textual analysis of the published sexological literature was selected as the most appropriate method for exploring the early work of Money and that of Robert Stoller. This approach was also my method of choice for examining the published feminist literature of the late 1960s and 1970s. These published works form the basis of many ideas about gender circulating (past and present) in the public domain.

The primary historical material this text engages includes the work of John Money, Robert Stoller, and a number of feminist scholars of the 1970s. They serve most obviously as *objects of analysis*, since my approach is a critical one. Yet that critique is not intended to be an end in itself but rather a means to an end, and that end is to contribute toward further dialogue. Nor do I have an interest in negating or diminishing the theoretical contributions offered by the same material. In fact some of these primary texts also function as *analytical tools.* They do so because, as theoretical texts, they offer concepts that are particularly useful to my project. This is especially the case with the work of Money. The material around which Chapter 5 is organized comes from two primary sources. The first includes organizational texts produced by intersex advocacy groups, which are publicly available on Web sites; published first-person narratives; and a range of journal articles and essays by activists/scholars. Those texts are juxtaposed with material generated from a small number of in-person interviews conducted with intersexed persons residing in various locations in Australia, New Zealand, India, and North America between December 2001 and February 2002. A total of six interviews yielded some 17 hours of recorded material that is rich and insightful and, at the same time, poignant. Subsequent dialogue over the intervening years with some of those who so generously agreed to participate in my research works both with and against the original material as it addresses subsequent turns in mainstream North American intersex politics and in medical discourse.

The initial fieldwork for this project was motivated in no small part by the question of what might constitute an intersex or hermaphrodite subjectivity as opposed to an intersexed condition—in contemporary parlance, a "disorder." In the sexological, biological, and medical literature[66] the adjectives *intersexed* and *hermaphroditic* refer to particular types of bodies, never to subjectivities. My interest lay in what people had to say about their embodied relation to gender, to sexuality, and to erotic desire. Making a distinction between sexuality and desire was intended, for I suspected that the available framework for making sense of the erotic might well be inadequate to the task of accounting for the desires and practices of the people I spoke with. Finally, the questions I asked were "how" questions rather than "why" questions, because "how" questions invite people to identify what is most central to their own narrative accounts and to do so in a context where there are no right or wrong answers.[67]

NOTES ON TERMINOLOGY AND DEFINITIONS

Against convention, I have chosen not to offer a fixed, delimited definition of the central organizing concept, gender. To do so would in fact defeat one of the primary objectives of this project: to make plain the dynamic nature of gender as a concept, since it is that very dynamism that makes it such a potent conceptual device. Yet at the same time I am cognizant of the need for researchers to elucidate their key concepts and so for that reason I draw upon John Money's original conceptualization of gender rather than more recent alternatives that assume and so reproduce a clear distinction between sex and gender.

Money's version of gender is especially useful to my project because it refuses the sex/gender distinction and so refuses the false but compelling dichotomy that informs the nature/nurture debates. For Money a person's gender is produced by the interaction between the corporeal, the sensorial, and the social. In other words, it is through this interactive relation that we become gendered. While I certainly have no argument about their interaction, I want to suspend the notion of becoming and replace it instead with the idea that Money's account provides us with a way of understanding the mechanisms involved in *learning to be* gendered.[68] While this distinction is a subtle one it is, I believe, important, since it grants a certain vitality to ontological experience and recognizes the fact that our concepts of what it means to be a gender are not static across different historical moments.

One of my aims is to try where possible to refuse the sex/gender distinction. In order to signify that refusal I use a hyphenated form that appears on the page as *sex-gender*. For Money, gender was not separate or distinct from sex, since he devised the former as an overarching term that included the erotic. Moreover he assumed a fully interactive relation between physiologies and experiences, since the latter are always mediated through the central nervous system.[69] Money's refusal predated the making of the distinction between sex and gender in the mid-1960s, since his first published book offered a strong critique of Cartesian dualism, the foundational principle upon which that distinction is based.[70] The only real sense in which sex can be said to be distinct from gender is in terms of its own history and historical legacy; the former long preceded the latter as an ontological category.

Using historically specific terminology randomly or in an ill-considered manner constitutes what Dreyfus and Rabinow refer to as *presentism*: the projection of contemporary meanings onto earlier historical periods in the attempt to locate and identify parallel meanings.[71] This has the effect of ahistoricizing terms and concepts that would have made no sense at the time to which they are applied. Prior to the introduction of an ontological form of gender into discourse, the term *sex* encoded biological *and* social categories. This is not to suggest that what we today know as gender was any less operative in social relations; rather, it did not signify a separate component of "being a sex".[72] Since one of the central aims of this book is to highlight gender's historical specificity, I refrain from using gender when referring to historical periods that predate its introduction into the English language as an ontological category. Instead I use the term *sex* and/or its derivatives. The term *intersex* is treated similarly.

Intersex is a relatively recent historical term that entered the medical diagnostic lexicon during the early twentieth century.[73] Its subsequent popularity in that domain throughout the twentieth century may well have stemmed from its earlier liberal use as a referent for both same-sex desire and the desire to "embody the body" of the other (sex). Intersex now came to signify bodily difference and served to define a population in a way that naturalized the privileged status of male and female. Until very recently the terms *intersex* and *hermaphrodite* were used interchangeably in the contemporary medical literature. The latter was generally modified by the terms *true* and *pseudo-* and by the qualifiers *male* and *female*. For this reason many intersexed people spurn the term hermaphrodite, as I discuss in Chapter 5.

The history of the term hermaphrodite can be traced back to classical antiquity and so predates medical scientific thought by centuries. There are points throughout this book at which I use the term *hermaphrodite*. I do so to honor the historical persistence of a people whose existence long precedes their medicalization. Debates have raged for years within the intersex (IS) political movement about what is appropriate and acceptable with respect to terminology. For many activists the term hermaphrodite is stigmatizing and misleading since it is believed to imply duplicate sexual organs and has mythical connotations. There are others for whom the term intersex is equally problematic because of its inextricable link to medical pathology on the one hand, and its literal meaning—between (the "real") sexes—on the other. This latter objection is particularly salient for those who claim an ontological status *as* hermaphrodite. In connection with those whose words are reproduced in this text, I respectfully use *their* term of choice.

More recently a radical turn in the domain of mainstream intersex politics has propelled the development of a revised medical nomenclature and a new paradigmatic frame through which intersex is understood in clinical contexts. Where once the truth of sex was to be found in the gonads (late eighteenth century), then later in hormones (early to mid-twentieth century), and still later in "genital potential" (mid- to late twentieth century), today that truth is to be found in our genes. We need look no further than the latest classification system for intersex which privileges genetic sex over all other bodily signifiers of sex: each diagnostic category is prefaced by a karyotype. This shift has reinstitutionalized intersex as pathology and reinstitutionalized a developmental and determinist framework as indicated by the acronym DSD (disorders of sex development).

The passion behind the terminology debates give one pause for thought about how to use language so as to "do no harm." Throughout this text I use the term *the intersexed* as a way of calling attention to the fact that those who of us who are differently sexed are *rendered* intersexed by their lived environments: socioculturally, legally (with few exceptions), politically, and of course above all medically. This understanding draws on the British social model of disability.[74] Disability is understood in this context not as something possessed; but rather, an effect of environments that are *disabling*. This is not to suggest that the bodies of the intersexed, or the intersexed themselves, are simply passive objects of clinical, cultural, and discursive practices.[75] Bodies have agency, they have a life of their own so to speak. They are active in and necessary to the creation of selfhood.

CHAPTER OUTLINE

Tracing the history of the concept of gender requires a mapping forward in a temporal sense, yet also backward at times. In Chapter 1, I begin mapping the concept of gender through a close reading of the early work of Money. In 1955 he, along with colleagues Joan and John Hampson, presented their research at international pediatric conferences and published their findings in a series of articles that effectively extended the ideas contained within Money's doctoral research. In those articles, Money and colleagues described their hermaphrodite research, laid out their theories of gender acquisition, promoted a set of guidelines for the clinical mediation of hermaphrodite bodies, and offered a measurement tool for assessing the degree of a person's adaptation to a gender. Effectively, Money provided a complete package that included a theory that served as a rationale for a set of clinical practices and a means of measuring not the efficacy of those practices but rather people's capacity to *be* the gender to which they were assigned.

The analysis in Chapter 1 extends beyond Money's earliest theorizing of gender to examine the various ways in which he refined his ideas after extending them to the wider population. Money's work serves as an exemplar of the way that medical science turns to biological variation in order to demarcate "normality." Elaborating Money's theories of gender acquisition and the assumptions that underpin them offers opportunities to explore their implications, not just for the intesexed but indeed for the population at large.

Chapter 2 is concerned with the ideas of Robert Stoller, who was the first to intervene in gender in the mid-1960s following Money's introduction of the concept a decade earlier. Stoller made what was (for him) a relatively benign conceptual turn when he divested gender of its interactive relation to sex. In a metaphorical sense, Stoller placed that relation in a state of suspended animation so that he could get on with the (seemingly) not so messy business of developing a theory to explain male to female transsexualism. Stoller placed everything that he was not going to be concerned with under the rubric of sex, which he interpellated as the natural, the material, and the carnal. The things that Stoller was interested in became gender, specifically the psychical or psychological elements of sexed subjectivity.[76] This conceptual turn effectively sanitized gender by removing from it any association to body lust and the "dirty business" of sex.

The sex/gender split offered a contemporary expression of the age-old mind/body distinction. Cartesian dualist logic demands, of course, that gender not merely be contrasted to sex, but framed in opposition to it. Stoller's conceptual bracketing left the production of knowledge about sex above or beyond analysis. The effects of that theoretical suspension were soon made manifest. Yielding to the compelling simplicity of either/or propositions, the sex/gender distinction began to assume a life of its own and before long became thoroughly institutionalized in sexological, medical, and social discourses.[77] It is unlikely that Stoller would or could have predicted that a convenient conceptual bracketing would lead to the institutionalization of a desexualized gender, so desexualized, in fact, that gender would be transformed into something akin to that orifice-free space between the legs of the otherwise highly sexualized Ken and Barbie dolls.[78]

Chapter 3 takes as its focus gender as it related to the feminist project of the late twentieth century. Gender was appropriated from the sexual sciences by a number of early academic feminists and put to work to argue against women's inferior social, political, and economic standing. The significant and powerful interventions into gender by feminism over the past 30 years have contributed much to augment gender's axiomatic status. Yet for the most part, that appropriation happened without a clear analysis of the assumptions that underpinned the concept—nor where those assumptions had taken sexological theory and clinical practice.

For two reasons the scope of Chapter 3 is limited primarily to material produced during the 1970s. The first is entirely pragmatic, given the huge corpus of literature and the multiple nodes of analytical and political strategies generated by the feminist project. Second, as I demonstrate, gender—the central organizing concept of feminism—took an entire decade to settle into that lexicon. Gender was not embraced by many of the earliest and most influential feminist theorists of the day, and indeed there was considerable debate about its conceptual merits for the best part of a decade. That finding has guided my exploration of "feminist gender" since little recognition is given in the literature to just how contentious the concept once was within that domain. In light of this I offer a detailed examination of when and how gender was first used in English-speaking feminism and the key issues around which the terminological debates centered.[79]

Chapter 3 also continues the parallel task of mapping the ongoing relation of hermaphrodites to gender. Within the feminist scholarship of the 1970s there is considerable evidence of early feminist engagement with hermaphrodite research. And it was to the work of John Money and Robert Stoller that they turned.

By the 1980s gender was embedded in the feminist lexicon and, with two notable exceptions, feminist scholars ceased to engage with hermaphrodite research—and with the intersexed—although androgyny was being promoted as an idealized state in that domain during the same time period.

In Chapter 4 I turn to John Money's theories of sexuality and desire. This chapter draws primarily on Money's 1988 text *Gay Straight and In-Between*, since in it Money elaborated his theories of sexuality through gender.[80] In order to place Money's ideas regarding the sexual into context, I explore in detail five methodological hallmarks and four key suppositions that have marked sexology since it emerged as a field of inquiry in the late nineteenth century. That provides the context for the examination of Money's theories of sexuality and desire and at the same time permits an exploration of precisely how those themes and methodologies play out in his work, and the consequences of his ideas for contemporary sexual subjects.

Chapter 5 focuses on the discourses of contemporary intersexed people in order to explore the ways in which gender is understood and negotiated by those from whom the concept was originally derived. It examines the official discourses of intersex advocacy groups along with the narrative accounts of intersexed individuals. This chapter is therefore concerned with a different type of expertise on gender. While much of the work of intersex advocacy groups centers on the fate of newborns and children, I am interested in the various ways that adults make sense of the relation between their experiences as differently embodied and their ways of being in the world. Among the more controversial ideas generated by this material are an ontological hermaphroditism and a form of eroticism that exceeds one-dimensional constructs of sexuality that rely upon gender as their reference points and homosexuality and heterosexuality as their endpoints.

The concluding chapter draws upon the insights offered in Chapter 5 to consider a framework that might enable the development of nuanced and responsive models to further enrich our understandings of sex-gender and sexuality. The quest to comprehend what it means to be sexual, social, and corporeal continues unabated and will do so with or without responsive models. Those of us who take issue with what is currently available have a responsibility, if not an obligation, to make some contribution toward the development of frameworks that build upon the best of that which has come before.

* * *

Gender: A Genealogy represents a necessary historical project that contextualizes the production and reproduction of gender as an ontological concept in order to highlight the power and the efficacy of a simple six-letter word. What the reader will gain in the chapters that follow is a sense of the extraordinary contribution that John Money has made to academic and lay understandings—in English-speaking contexts—of what it means to be a sexed subject. By offering gender as a new conceptual realm of sex, Money provided medicine and the sexual sciences with a rationale for a particular set of clinical practices. He also provided feminism, sexuality studies, and the social sciences with a vehicle through which to articulate a range of theoretical and political projects. Finally he provided the wider culture with a terminology through which to make sense of what it means to be a man, a woman, a girl, a boy. Concepts by their very nature must generate ideas that are useful, and in this regard gender has proved to be exemplary. The ongoing "desire for gender" indicates there is some life left in "the old girl" yet. The question is, how might we harness gender's conceptual dynamism as a means of restoring the dignity and humanity of those who have historically been most marginalized by it?

CHAPTER 1

MONEY AND THE PRODUCTION
OF GENDER

INTRODUCTION

John Money offered "gender" as a new conceptual realm of sex in the mid-1950s. He initially did so as part of a framework for understanding the phenomenon of human hermaphroditism. That framework was first and foremost a rationale for clinical practices designed to habilitate the intersexed into girlhood and boyhood, womanhood and manhood. It would become so much more. To contextualize Money's ideas I begin by tracing his early academic training; the professional context in which he first became interested in the subject of hermaphroditism; and some of the key theoretical influences on his work. His research stands within a long tradition in sexology and medical science but was also heavily influenced by the then-dominant paradigm of the social sciences. What began as a doctoral research project became a life's work for Money as he built his oeuvre over the next 50 years. Following the completion of his doctoral studies, Money was invited by the esteemed pediatric endocrinologist Lawson Wilkins to take up a position as codirector of a newly created research unit at the Johns Hopkins University Hospital in Baltimore. Under the auspices of that unit Money continued his research, gathering increasing numbers of case reports and data with which to evidence his claims. It was in that context that Money identified a need for a single overarching term that would enable him to discuss the masculinity and femininity of the intersexed. The term he eventually settled on was *gender*.

As part of his broader project, Money recodified "sex" by adding two psychosocial signifiers to the already recognized bodily markers. While five physiological signifiers had long been recognized in medical science, Money's innovation led to a profound shift in medical approaches to the bodies of the intersexed. No longer were clinicians compelled to discover a person's *true* sex; now their job involved determining a *best* sex for each of their patients. This had specific consequences—epistemological *and* material—for those in whose name gender was initially put to work.

Money and his colleagues began presenting their ideas at pediatric conferences in the United States and in Europe prior to publishing their work in the *Bulletin of the John Hopkins Hospital*[1] and other medical journals between 1955 and 1957. The choice of publications ensured the dissemination of his ideas to a broad medical audience. The articles provided a vehicle for Money to elaborate the theories he had begun to formulate in his doctoral research and they mark the beginning of his ascent as a leading authority on hermaphroditism during the second half of the twentieth century.

The articles argued forcefully that the long-recognized biological markers of sex were not reliable determinants of a person's psychosocial or psychosexual orientation. This allowed them to accord primary status to social signifiers and provided a philosophical basis for a treatment regime designed to ensure that future generations of intersexed infants developed unambiguously masculine or feminine identities. I offer a close reading of those articles that examines the ways that Money and his colleagues discredited the reliability of the physiological signifiers of sex; their prescription for training parents to manage their child's gender; their recommendations for habilitating intersexed individuals into an assigned gender; and the key performance indicators they used to determine whether a person had successfully habilitated into the assigned gender. The proof of that success demanded what can only be described as excessive or hyperbolic displays of masculinity or femininity.

While Money initially offered his gender theory to account for a relatively small segment of the population, it soon became a compelling explanation of identity formation per se. In the tradition of the great metatheoretical projects of the late nineteenth and twentieth centuries,[2] Money extended his ideas beyond intersexed populations to explain how everybody acquired an identity as masculine or feminine. As will become clear, many of those ideas have achieved axiomatic status over the past 50 years although some of them rest on rather shaky foundations.

* * *

SECTION I
Academic and Professional History

John Money graduated from Victoria University in Wellington, New Zealand in 1944 with a double master's degree (psychology/philosophy[3] and education) and a teaching qualification before heading to the United States in 1947.[4] Since it was not possible to undertake a PhD in psychology in New Zealand in those days, Money had to go offshore to pursue postgraduate studies. While many of his contemporaries pursued postgraduate education in the United Kingdom, Money chose to go instead to North America. That choice was determined in part by his engagement with the scholarly material coming out of North America at the time, and by the influence of one of Money's former teachers at Victoria University, the social anthropologist Ernest Beaglehole.[5] Once in the United States, Money secured a place in the graduate program of the Psychological Clinic and Department of Social Relations at Harvard University, where his teachers included the social theorist Talcott Parsons, whose *role theory* dominated the social sciences throughout the 1950s, 1960s, and 1970s.[6]

Toward the end of 1949 Money attended a presentation by faculty member George Gardner, an event he would later describe as serendipitous. Gardner presented a case study of an intersexed individual who had been reared male and identified as such, despite possessing a phallus that more resembled a clitoris than a penis and despite developing female secondary sex characteristics at puberty.[7] Money had been working on a review of psychosexual theory from pre-Freud through to the present day for a term paper but had begun to realize that the enormous nature of the task was beyond the scope of an essay.[8] Inspired by Gardner's presentation, Money reconfigured the project into a critique of Freud's first essay on sexuality.

Money realized fully the significance that the intersexed living as men and as women held for psychosexual theories of instinct and drive. Just as Freud and countless other sexologists had done, Money drew on hermaphrodite research to argue his case. He reviewed the mid-twentieth-century medical literature on the psychology of hermaphroditism,[9] adding four of his own detailed case reports, to argue that there was no instinctual basis for masculinity and femininity. For Freud, an individual's sexual outlook—as masculine or feminine—and the direction and goal of the libido were directly related to unlearned determinants and thus represented constitutional or instinctive elements of subjectivity. Money strongly refuted that idea, since the intersexed who identified as men or women provided clear evidence that "psychosexual orientation bears a very strong relationship to teaching and the lessons of experience and should be conceived as a psychological phenomenon."[10] That someone who was neither obviously male nor obviously female could establish an identity as a man or a woman provided substantial weight to Money's claim. His innovation was not to deny that masculinity and femininity were grounded in the psyche, but rather how it happened and when.

The term paper proved foundational to Money's entire career, laying the ground for his ascent as a leading authority on human hermaphroditism. It provided the basis for his doctoral thesis, which involved a comparative study of medical case reports written between 1895 and 1951. More importantly, Money's critique of Freud was the first step toward gender's ascent as *the* signifier for human characteristics and behaviors commonly attributed as masculine and/or feminine. The rest, as they say, is history.

Money's review turned up 248 reports written in English that he supplemented with an additional 10 detailed case studies of his own. Gaining access to his informants through their physicians, Money conducted interviews and performed a range of psychological tests on each of them. From the data, Money ordered the cases into a range of categories on the basis of morphological and physiological status using criteria and terminology established in the late 1870s. Money's nomenclature included the following diagnostic types:

1. Female pseudohermaphrodites with the adrenogenital syndrome, characterized by precocious virile development
2. Female pseudohermaphrodites with ovogenesis and without postnatal virilization
3. True hermaphrodites with ovarian and testicular structures
4. Male pseudohermaphrodites with mullerian organs differentiated and developed
5. Male pseudohermaphrodites with atrophic, undescended testes, but simulant females in their morphology

6. Pseudohermaphroditic males with hypospadias and breasts, resembling Klinefelter's syndrome
7. Pseudohermaphroditic males with penoscrotal or perineal hypospadias
8. Miscellaneous cases, unclassifiable owing to insufficient data[11]

Some background to these classifications is warranted. At the time that the earliest case studies in Money's review were written, the dominant theory in medical circles about sex and particularly about hermaphrodites centered on Theodor Albrecht Klebs's notion that the truth of sex was to be found in the gonads.[12] Improvements in anesthesia and medical hygiene during the late 1800s had made laparotomy a viable technique for examining the internal gonadal tissue (or "sex glands") of living patients, where previously such examinations had been possible only postmortem. It was in this context that Klebs was able to make a distinction between so-called true hermaphroditism and pseudohermaphroditism.[13] According to Klebs's schema, a true hermaphrodite was someone who possessed both testicular and ovarian gonadal tissue—either in the form of one ovary and one testis or as a single ovotestis. A diagnosis of pseudohermaphroditism took one of two forms: male psuedo-hermaphroditism was the diagnostic category accorded to those who possessed two gonadal testes and female secondary sex characteristics, whereas female pseudohermaphroditism was the diagnosis given to individuals with two ovaries who displayed male secondary sex characters at puberty.[14]

Mining the historical record has a long tradition in medical and biological research. Throughout the course of the nineteenth century, a number of clinicians who worked with sexually ambiguous subjects turned to the historical medical literature. According to Alice Dreger, this type of historical review was conducted for comparative purposes throughout the 1800s, but toward the end of the century was increasingly used to *re*classify forms of hermaphroditism.[15] This process of reclassifying was variously used to reduce or to extend the range of hermaphroditic bodily types. The work of Franz von Neugebauer provides an example of reclassification for reductive purposes. He collected over 900 case reports of hermaphroditism (including 38 of his own) and on the basis of his analysis determined that there was no such thing as true hermaphroditism. That an individual could possess both ovarian and testicular gonads was in his view impossible, despite his noting microscopically proven instances of ovotestes in the literature. Von Neugebauer insisted that *all* hermaphroditic individuals were in fact pseudohermaphrodites and thus for diagnostic and therapeutic purposes, that was the only category worth considering.[16]

In more recent times the trend has been toward extending classifications, which is arguably a by-product of developments in medical technologies that have allowed for greater access to the internal workings of the body. Money's nomenclature is an example of this expansive trend. Yet despite his increasing the number of categories and subcategories of hermaphroditism, Money's schema was just as thoroughly grounded in Klebs's discursive legacy as von Neugebauer's was. In fact, Klebs's legacy remains evident in much of the contemporary medical literature produced on the subject.[17] The gonadal sex criterion remained the cornerstone of Money's classificatory system for some years even as he dismissed its relevance for diagnostic purposes. His rationale for retaining that criterion was purely expedient, because it was convenient for medical taxonomy and discussion.[18]

Once Money had organized each of the case reports into the above categories, he set about answering two primary research questions. The first was how people with intersexed bodies adapted to their sex of assignment and rearing. This generated a set of secondary questions about the relative influences of physiological functioning and socialization (vis à vis nature versus nurture) and how enduring the impact of each of these was. Second, he was—as a psychologist—interested in the mental health of his sample population. This would prove crucial to the establishment and routinization of a set of clinical practices that collectively are known as intersex case management (ICM). Money asked:

> Do they, with such manifest sexual problems to contend with, break down under the strain, as psychiatric theory may lead one to believe; or do they make an adequate adjustment to the demands of life?[19]

It is hard to ignore the dramatic tone with which he framed his questions and their already loaded nature. Money scrutinized his data sources (case reports, interview data, and test results) for the following information: sex of rearing, including any subsequent change of assignment; nonlibidinal orientation and demeanor, including congruity with sex of rearing or lack thereof (gender); libidinal orientation, including congruity with sex of rearing or lack thereof (sexuality); and psychological adjustment.[20] The third and fourth items are particularly relevant.

In terms of libidinal orientation it is clear that Money's investigation of the data assumed that congruency equated to a heteronormative orientation. This is evident in his declaration that he was examining the data for possible links between a reassignment of sex after infancy and the relative incidence of bisexual inclinations across the total sample.[21] This apparently straightforward and unproblematic link between masculinity, femininity, and normative desire would remain at the heart of Money's subsequent theorizing of gender and sexuality despite the increasingly radical tenor of his later work on human sexuality.

"Psychological adjustment," the fourth and final variable he was interested in, was haunted by another assumption, one that must surely have influenced Money's interpretation of the data he had gathered. That assumption is writ large in the following three-point scale:

1. Adequate
2. Disheartened and/or guardedly reticent
3. Manifesting symptoms of psychopathology—psychoneurosis, organic and nonorganic psychosis[22]

Notable by its absence was any point on the scale that approximated to psychological health. From the outset, the best Money could envisage was an adequate form of adjustment. These ideas did not of course develop in a vacuum but reflected a long-standing tradition in the medical and sexological literature regarding clinical concepts of normality and abnormality. Importantly, the findings of Money's own research failed to support such pessimism. In his doctoral dissertation he had written:

The incidence of so-called functional psychoses in [even] the most ambisexual of the hermaphrodites was extraordinarily low . . . apparently, therefore, sexual conflicts and problems are not in themselves sufficient to induce psychosis or neurosis.[23]

In other words, the findings of Money's research contested rather than supported the assumptions that underpinned the scale he devised to measure psychological adjustment. Despite this, Money was adamant that without medical interventions the intersexed would be unable to function as "normal" individuals, a point I return to repeatedly throughout the text.

Money's doctoral thesis was significant for collating a sizeable body of data from the preceding half century into a single text, but more importantly, it offered four distinct innovations. It provided a new and expanded codification of hermaphroditic types based on bodily morphology; offered data that challenged psychological and psychiatric theories positing masculinity and femininity in terms of instinct and drive; provided compelling evidence against the idea that an individual's erotic preferences bore any relationship to unlearned determinants; and finally, offered an (alternative) theory of acquisition, although initially without the concept of gender. While Money went on to refine and elaborate particular aspects of his gender acquisition theory, the essence of it remains true to the ideas presented in his doctoral dissertation.

Toward Authority

The post–World War II period in North America tends to be seen today as an era of moral and political conservatism that reinforced a rigid sexual division of labor and equally rigid social roles for both men and women—including the veneration of a cult of domesticity for women. This was an era haunted by the double perils of communism and homosexuality, yet at the same time it proved a particularly fruitful period for sex research, as evidenced by Alfred Kinsey's groundbreaking works, *Sexual Behavior in the Human Male* and *Sexual Behavior in the Human Female*;[24] Evelyn Hooker's studies of homosexual men;[25] and Masters and Johnson's research that led to the publication of *Human Sexual Response*.[26] In fact, sex research flourished during the period despite the enormous pressures exerted on funding agencies by politicians and conservative lobbyists who demanded the withdrawal of financial support from projects they believed threatened the moral fiber of the nation. Significantly, much of the sex research produced during that time was carried out under the umbrella of medicine and the biological sciences, which provided an element of safety in authority, a point not lost on Money. The scientific method also provided sex researchers with a form of legitimacy—its language, postures, and costumes provided, in the words of William Simon, "conceptual rubber gloves" with which to examine the dirty business of sex.[27]

Money's interest in hermaphroditism led him to develop close working relationships with urologists, pediatricians, gynecologists, endocrinologists, and other medics involved in the diagnosis and treatment of hermaphroditism, no mean feat for a relatively young psychology graduate. Indeed, Money began his career working under the aegis of luminaries such as Lawson Wilkins, whose own research was concerned with the role of hormones in fetal development. Their first meeting had taken place at a pediatric seminar in Boston (ca. 1950), where Money asked to visit the clinic established by Wilkins a few years earlier at Johns Hopkins University Hospital. The request was met favorably. At the clinic Money was given access to unpublished case studies of Wilkins's patients and archival material belonging to the renowned urologist Hugh Hampton Young. More importantly, Wilkins allowed Money to interview some of his patients and use the resulting data in his doctoral research.[28]

This association with Wilkins led to the offer of a position at the newly established Psycho-Hormonal Research Unit at John Hopkins in 1951 after Money completed his doctoral studies. Wilkins teamed him up with a psychiatrist by the name of Joan Hampson, appointing the pair codirectors in a gesture that bears testament to Wilkins's confidence in Money. The collaboration between the pair, who were later joined by Hampson's husband, John, yielded a series of articles published in consecutive issues of *The Bulletin* in 1955. The articles crystallized the ideas Money had articulated in his doctoral dissertation.

While *The Bulletin* was the primary text through which Money and his colleagues presented their early work, they also published in other medical, psychological, and sexological journals, ensuring wide dissemination of their ideas in medical and scientific circles.[29] The tone of the articles was assured and authoritative. By incorporating embryological and endocrinological concepts, their claims had added gravity—as did the authors' association with Wilkins, whose support extended beyond mere association. In 1955, for instance, he published an article in the journal *Pediatrics* endorsing Money's theory of gender acquisition.[30]

The need for an umbrella term had become increasingly clear to Money during his early years at Johns Hopkins when he was writing about the manliness or womanliness of people who had been born with the delicately termed "indeterminate genitals."[31] At that time the only readily available term was *sex*, which Money found unsatisfactory because of its conceptual overload. Sex referred not only to bodies status (of the *female/male* sex), it also referred to erotic acts and behaviors (to *have* sex), a person's psychological status as masculine or feminine (sexual *identity*),[32] and (after Parsons) to patterns of social and intimate behaviors deemed appropriate to men and to women (sex *roles*).[33] Money would later write of his frustration at having to use statements such as "a male sex role except that his sex role with the sex organs was not male, and his genetic sex was female."[34] After some deliberation, Money found the term he was looking for. He borrowed *gender* from linguistics (philology), where historically it had been used to signify relations between words rather than between people. Linguistic gender denotes the status of nouns and pronouns as masculine, feminine, common (e.g., child, neighbor, friend), or neuter (neutral) and determines which pronouns go with which nouns.

So while the term *gender* was not new to the English language, Money's innovation was to apply it in a different context—as a human attribute—while maintaining its traditional denotations. Thus gender provided a conceptual tool to discuss the masculinity or femininity of those who were born neither male nor female. In the first of the *Bulletin* articles Money defined gender as a referent for a person's outlook, demeanor, and orientation.[35] In those days he used the term *gender role* and *gender* interchangeably but accorded the former a more elaborate definition. Gender role signified "all those things that a person does or says to disclose himself as having the status of a boy or man, girl or woman, respectively. It includes, but is not restricted to sexuality in the sense of eroticism."[36] The use of the term *role* here is worthy of scrutiny. At Harvard, Money had studied under Talcott Parsons, the sociologist often referred to as the founding father of functionalism in the United States. Parsons's role theory dominated the social sciences for over 30 years, effectively setting the parameters for sociological theorizing in North America during that period.

In sociological functionalism, the social life of people is framed holistically as a "functional unity."[37] Sociological functionalism assumes and seeks to explain the interconnectedness of all forms of human activity and so lends itself well to biological and organicist analogies. Indeed, the most used heuristic device in functionalist theory is the organic analogy that is used to draw comparisons between the social body and human bodies. By this account, the body contains a number of different organs that perform specific tasks and contribute toward the maintenance of a homeostasis or equilibrium. Analogously, social institutions perform particular functions that serve to sustain the larger whole. The family, for example, is the primary site for the socialization of children, since human personality is not something that individuals are born with but rather something to be *made*. Parsons himself referred to the family as "factories which produce human personalities."[38]

The relation between functionalism and medicine is one that extends far beyond any relative abstractions of social theory, since a functionalist paradigm fully saturates biomedical understandings of the body—particularly the ways in which it understands penises and vaginas (as indicated by the common referent, reproductive organs). The dominance of functionalist paradigms in both the social and medical sciences would account for Money's early use of the term *gender role*, despite his academic training in psychology with its emphasis on personality and identity. In Money's formulation, gender and gender role were referents of a unitary concept that incorporated an individual's sense of self as masculine or feminine (identity), along with the public manifestations of that identity (social role).

Recodifying "Sex"

In addition to offering the concept of gender, Money was also responsible for codifying seven signifiers of sex. Five of these were grounded in the body and had long been recognized in medical circles while the remaining two were of psychological and social origin. The five physiological signifiers included chromosomes (X and Y), gonads (ovaries and testes), hormones (relative levels of androgenic and estrogenic substances), internal accessory structures (uterus and prostate), and external genitals (penis/clitoris, scrotum/vulva). To these Money added sex of assignment and rearing, and adaptation to assigned sex. These last two indicators represent what is now commonly referred to as gender. The significance of this intervention should not be underestimated.

During the previous century, the internal gonads had been privileged as the definitive marker of sex in medical and sexological discourse, but by the twentieth century, advanced medical technologies revealed that things were considerably more complicated.[39] Together, the emergence of embryology as a branch of medicine; the discovery and isolation of estrogen, testosterone, and other hormones through the field of endocrinology; and the consolidation of genetics as a field of biology produced evidence that the various physiological markers of sex could no longer be assumed to be unilateral. Nor could a person's somatic sex be relied upon as an absolute.[40] That lack of certainty would prove fortuitous for Money because it allowed him to privilege the psychosocial signifiers of sex.

The refinement of plastic surgical techniques during WWII further increased physicians' capacity to mediate hermaphroditism with surgical and hormonal treatment regimes.[41] Those developments went hand in hand with a growing concern among clinicians for the psychological well-being of their patients. There is evidence of a hesitation running through the medical literature between the 1920s and 1940s regarding which sex to assign to hermaphroditic individuals, particularly those diagnosed as "true hermaphrodites." Assigning a sex on physiological grounds alone became increasingly harder to justify when the body offered little certainty of revealing a single true sex.[42] As a result, clinicians began to rely more and more on psychosocial factors as the primary grounds for (re)assigning a sex, particularly in older subjects.[43]

Psychologist Albert Ellis, for example, had conducted a review of the literature on hermaphroditism a decade earlier, in order to determine if "the physiological factors which disturbed the soma of the hermaphrodite so drastically [could] equally affect his or her psyche."[44] Foreshadowing Money, Ellis concluded that biological factors were not decisive determinants of masculinity or femininity of either so-called true hermaphrodites or pseudohermaphrodites. Rather it was Ellis's view that a person's sex role was more likely to be a consequence of his or her upbringing. Ellis was particularly interested in the erotic inclinations and orientations of those he studied, since he believed eroticism to be indivisible from a person's psychosexual masculinity and femininity. He concurred that while the power of human sex drive might very well depend on physiological factors, its direction appeared to have no direct connection to constitutional elements.[45] Ellis suggested that this held true for all hermaphrodites regardless of whether their libidinal orientations were "normal" (that is, heterosexual) or "deviate" (homosexual or bisexual) in relation to their sex of rearing. That Money's work is saturated by Ellis's ideas is without question, as will become evident when I turn to Money's conceptualization of desire.

It is clear that many of the conceptual frameworks Money used in his doctoral thesis and later work were by no means original. Rather they had an established history and reflected an existing train of sexological thought. Money's contribution was to offer a concept that allowed him to make a number of important interventions in discourse and clinical practices. The innovation of gender operated symbolically *and* pragmatically.

The addition of two psychosocial signifiers of sex increased the status of the noncorporeal markers of sex among medical professionals who worked primarily with flesh and blood. Clinicians had grown increasingly anxious about the psychological health of their patients. Post-Freudian psychoanalysis and psychology had gained a significant foothold in North America by the time Money extended sex to gender. Not only was he instrumental in securing an increased legitimacy for social and environmental factors in sex assignment decisions, he was instrumental in their attaining primacy over the physiological markers in treatment decisions.

At a pragmatic level, gender provided a solution to the uncertainty of any absolute somatic sex. Gender served to stabilize what advances in medical technology had rendered more and more unstable during the first half of the twentieth century. It was no longer so important that the somatic signifiers of sex failed to align; what increasingly mattered were the psychosocial and cultural signifiers of masculinity and femininity. Where once clinicians sought to discover a true sex hidden within an ambiguous body, now it was a matter of determining a best sex for any given individual—that is, whichever sex seemed most appropriate in light of the person's genital appearance, psychological makeup, and familial environment.[46] The promise was that a best sex would give a person the best kind of life. In this way gender provided a solution to an unintended consequence of technological advancement and, at the same time, to the sociocultural problem of "excessive" sexual difference.[47] As to whether it has lived up to its promise to provide a better life for the intersexed, the jury is still out.

*   *   *

SECTION II

Spreading the Word

The series of articles Money and colleagues published in *The Bulletin* during the mid-1950s laid out the theories they developed under the auspices of the Psycho-Hormonal Research Unit. Their early research focused exclusively on the intersexed, although that focus later broadened to include a diverse range of individuals diagnosed with what today we know as gender dysphoria or gender identity disorder.[48] The first two articles in the series—written by Money and Joan Hampson respectively—were offered as companion papers, and it is here that we find Money's first articulation of gender as an ontological concept. The third and fourth in the series (penned by Money and both Hampsons) consolidated Money's framework further.

Together the articles do a number of things. They provide a vehicle for the articulation of a theory and terminology; they offer "hard" biological evidence to back the theory; they lay out recommendations that would become institutionalized as intersex case management (ICM) protocols; they address a number of ethical conundrums relating to future sexual function and fertility and the removal (partial or otherwise) of clitoral tissue; they also provide the intellectual context for Money's ideas; and they strike at the foundations of psychological theories that seek to explain what it means to be a sexed subject. What is more, they mark the beginning of Money's ascent as a world authority on hermaphroditism and, for a time at least, *the* authority on gender.

Let's begin with the theory. Long a critic of Cartesian dualism with its legacy of binary oppositional concepts of mind and body, Money proposed a model of gender acquisition that was composed of three rather than two elements. To nature and nurture, Money added a *critical period* in order to mediate the gaping chasm of the nature-nurture divide.[49] The concept of a critical period originated in embryology. Charles Stockard devised the term in the 1920s to describe prenatal events whose effects manifested postnatally. A critical period is understood as a specific time span (in contemporary terms, a window of opportunity) of heightened sensitivity to environmental stimuli that has irreversible developmental consequences.[50] The addition of a critical period to the theoretically opposed poles of nature and nurture allowed Money to transform them into elements of a single theory. But Money didn't stop there.

Money extended Stockard's innovation by taking the concept beyond fetal life to the postnatal period from birth to 18 months of age. This he said was *the* major critical period for gender acquisition when sensory stimuli—mediated through the central nervous system—mapped onto preestablished neural pathways. On the basis of rodent and primate studies, Money proposed that hormone production[51] from the fetal gonads primed a cognitive schema or neural template in utero that coded for masculinity, femininity, and androgyny and lay dormant until stimulated postnatally by "matching input stimulus [that] releases a highly specific output response."[52] He later coined this schema a "gendermap," and it was here that the interaction of nature and nurture at a critical period produced a "permanent sequela that, in turn, may react at another critical period with a new facet of nurture."[53]

Money's commitment to the idea that gender became hardwired into the brain provided the ultimate rationale for swift interventions on infants and newborns in order to assure a stable gendered identity. Articulating this idea in typically dramatic fashion, Money wrote, "when the gender identity gate closed behind you, it locked tight.

You knew in the very core of your consciousness that you were male or female. Nothing short of disaster could ever again shake that conviction."[54] Little wonder he considered the postnatal period to be the more important of the two critical phases. Like Stockard and Konrad Lorenz before him, Money understood the imprinting process to be irreversible, and this added further impetus to his recommendation for early interventions on intersexed infants.

To add force to his argument, Money asserted that the critical period for gender identity differentiation was linked to the critical period for language acquisition, since both derived from the origins of conceptual language. He had long held that learning (and remembering) was a function of biology because all stimuli are mediated through the central nervous system.[55] If an individual's gender had not established unequivocally during this period there was likely to be a mismatch between neural template and genital appearance that would result in a faulty or spoiled identity. This was likely to express itself through an incomplete coding of the positive and negative poles of the template.[56]

The Identification/Complementation Component of Gender Acquisition

In the Freudian tradition, identification is the means by which individuals become aware of their own masculinity or femininity. That is, children learn through imitation, modeling the behavior of the same-sexed parent (in simple terms, boys identify with their fathers and girls with their mothers).[57] For Money, this model told only part of the story. Turning again to language acquisition, Money suggested that the phenomenon of bilingualism offered a useful analogy. Just as the bilingual child was exposed to two different language systems that required two different sets of responses, the acquisition of a gendered identity/role required exposure to what he referred to as "bi-genderism."[58]

By this account children receive and respond to two sets of gender stimuli—male behaviors and female behaviors. Not only do children imitate the behavior of their same-sexed parent and peers, they also learn to behave in a *complementary* fashion to the other sex.[59] Learning and remembering which behaviors are appropriate for one's sex-gender is an effect of the continual reinforcement (positive and negative) of parents and peers. Hence Money stressed how important it was that children received consistent signals from both of their parents and/or caregivers.

Money's identification/complementation thesis turned on the idea of reciprocal learning schemas in the brain, one coding positively and the other negatively. Money suggested that the positive pole coded for "me," and the negative for "thee."[60] Once locked into the brain, the schemas were said to govern sex-dimorphic behavior. In other words they became hardwired.[61] Money described the process thus:

> For the ordinary little boy growing up, everything pertaining to the female gender role is brain-coded as negative and *unfit for use*. The opposite holds for little girls. The negatively coded system in both instances is not a void, however. It serves as a template . . . of what not to do and also as a guide of what to expect in the behavior of the opposite sex, when one's own behavior must be complemental.[62]

Money certainly did not rule out the possibility of overlap; indeed the more overlap, the more likely androgynous behavior would result. Conversely, less overlap would result in an individual rigidly adhering to and investing in sexual stereotyping. While he was willing to allow for a degree of change over the lifespan, it was Money's view that a person's identification/complementation quotient remained relatively stable.

Show Me the Money

The first article in the series lays out the findings of the team's three-year study of 60 people who ranged in age from a few weeks to 50 years.[63] Drawing on the nomenclature he devised as part of his doctoral research, Money compared the three dominant corporeal markers of "sex"—internal gonads, hormones, and chromosomes— to sex of assignment and rearing for their efficacy as predictors. He wanted to demonstrate that none could be relied upon to indicate a person's (future) gender. This allowed him to position the sex of assignment as the most reliable and consistent predictor.

In order to make his case, Money split his sample population into three subsets: those whose *gonadal sex* (ovaries or testes) contradicted their sex of assignment and rearing as male and female respectively; those whose *hormonal functioning* contradicted sex of assignment and rearing; and those whose *chromosomal makeup* contradicted their assigned sex. Of the first group all but three were said to have "disclosed themselves in the gender role fully concordant with their rearing," despite their gonads being out of step with their gender.[64] With assigned sex and gender matching for almost

80 percent of this group, gonadal sex was declared another unreliable indicator of a person's gender.

Of the second group all but four were reported to be fully adapted to their assigned sex. Money was at pains to point out that hormonal sex had to be distinguished from the structure of the gonads or sex glands, since the testes of some hermaphrodites produced estrogens (designated female hormone) rather than androgens (designated male sex hormone). Similarly, the possession of ovaries offered no guarantee of estrogen production.[65] Since all but the four in the second subset reported full adaptation to their sex of assignment and rearing, Money categorically dismissed the significance of hormones on a person's orientation as masculine or feminine. It is important to note that Money was not contesting the role of hormones in embryonic sexual differentiation, development of secondary sex characteristics, and/or eroticism. Rather he was contesting the role of hormones with respect to *gender*. Despite these disclaimers it is likely that a significant number of children with testes reared as girls *would* produce testosterone both from their testes and from their adrenal glands as we all do, since both hormones are germane to the species human.[66]

In addressing the third dominant marker of sex—chromosomes— Money acknowledged that testing had not been routinely undertaken across the sample. Of course, since chromatin testing was in still in its infancy in the 1950s this is hardly surprising. Nonetheless Money maintained that "preliminary evidence *clearly* indicates that chromosomes bear as little relationship to sexual orientation as do gonads."[67] To support his assertion, Money pointed to the then-recent discovery that people diagnosed with a condition known as gonadal (ovarian) agenesis possessed a Y chromosome.[68] The femininity of such individuals, he said, could hardly be disputed since it had never been questioned by any of the medical professionals who had had dealings with the 23 individuals in his sample accorded this diagnosis.

To this day chromatin testing is undertaken only where there is a question mark over a person's sex or fertility. Despite the weight attached to chromosomes as markers of sex, most of us have no idea of our actual chromosomal makeup. In other words, the idea that we "know" women possess two X chromosomes and men an X and a Y is little more than an article of faith, one that is currently being tested by contemporary findings in genetic research that suggest sexual variation is far more common than we imagine.[69] What if significant numbers of the population, if tested, warranted a diagnosis as intersexed? What if sexual difference is far more prevalent in the population than we currently imagine? I revisit this issue in the final chapter.

To return to the articles, the authors considered where else an innate masculinity or femininity might reside in the body. The authors asked if the brain might hold the answer. The late-nineteenth-century forensic psychiatrist Richard von Krafft-Ebing had hypothesized special centers in the brain. Money. dismissed the idea, not because he disagreed with the idea of neural centers, but because he took issue with the idea of *innateness*.[70] He and his colleagues had evidence that intersexed individuals with identical diagnoses had been successfully raised as girls and as boys. This bolstered their ability to discredit the notion of an instinctive gender on the one hand, and laid the ground for an alternative explanation on the other. They argued that the capacity for intersexed individuals to establish an identity as male or as female provided support for the view that

psychologically, sexuality is undifferentiated at birth and it becomes differentiated as masculine or feminine in the course of the various experiences of growing up.... Our studies have pointed very strongly to the significance of life experiences encountered and transacted in the establishment of gender role and orientation.[71]

They went on to caution that this was not to be read as an endorsement of a simplistic social or environmental determinist approach, because central to their theory was the concomitance of the terms *encountered* and *transacted*. They argued that "encounters do not automatically dictate predictable transactions [because] there is ample place for novelty and the unexpected in cerebral and cognitive processes in human beings."[72] But lest the reader interpret this as an argument for an infinite field of possibilities in gender, Money and colleagues turned immediately to the evidence offered by intersexed people who had been subject to a sex *re*assignment after infancy and who were said to have been inadequately (read uneasily) adjusted to their assigned gender. These people demonstrated that gender was not infinitely modifiable because once established, it became *indelibly* imprinted in the brain. It was on this point that the authors argued most forcefully for routinized medical interventions on hermaphrodite infants.

On Fertile Ground?

After dealing with the big three markers of sex, Money and his team turned their attention to the remaining biological signifiers: the internal accessory organs—uterus and prostate—and genitalia. Like the others, these failed miserably in Money and the Hampsons' analysis. The failure of these final two biological markers was used as further evidence against Freud's claim of an innate and instinctive basis for masculinity and femininity. Yet while genital appearance might have been a poor predictor it did have a central role in sex assignment decisions.

Of all the physiological markers of sex, Money et al. privileged the genitalia in assignment decisions. The use of a single criterion such as gonadal structure or chromosomal patterning was extremely unwise according to Money and his colleagues, since it was known that in the intersexed there were commonly contradictions between the various markers of sex.[73] Undeterred by their own advice, the researchers argued that just as external genital morphology served as the key indicator for sexing regular male and female neonates, they should also be given prime consideration in ICM. The key point of difference with hermaphrodite infants was that external genital structures were to be appraised on how well they would lend themselves to surgery.

If the external organs are so predominantly male, or so predominantly female that no amount of surgical reconstruction will convert them to serviceably and erotically sensitive organs of the other sex, then the sex of assignment should be dictated by the external genitals alone.[74]

After sexing, all subsequent surgical and hormonal interventions were to be directed toward maintaining the assigned sex in order to ensure successful adaptation to a gender. Money and his colleagues believed that the only time it was ever appropriate to give weight to hormonal (and perhaps gonadal) sex was in cases of extreme ambiguity when surgical reconstruction options were equally "promising" in either direction.

Money et al. acknowledged how contentious this recommendation was because it had implications for future fertility. Addressing the criticism that it was ethically flawed to privilege genital appearance over reproductive potential, the authors argued that actual childbearing was a completely different issue than potential fertility. In keeping with the ideological framework set up throughout the four articles, actual childbearing was said to be contingent upon not just biological capacity but also "the social encounters and cultural transactions of mating and marrying, which are inextricably bound up with gender role and orientation."[75] It is worth noting that when Money et al. referred to actual childbearing, they were not referring to biological or physiological capacity but to social context. This turn is particularly curious given the amount of attention paid to morphological structures and formations in the discussion that preceded this advice. Moreover, the creation, removal, and/or reorganization of genital structures involves the material, not the social, for it quite literally involves working with flesh.

Reproduction within the context of this discussion was located firmly within the institution of normative heterosexual relations, which during the 1950s meant within the context of marriage. What remained unspoken by this assertion was the conviction that without medical and pharmaceutical intervention(s), hermaphrodite individuals would be unlikely to establish intimate relationships that might lead to marriage. Yet the *majority* of adults in their own sample had reported engaging in sexual relationships of a heterosexual nature and indeed some were, or had been, married.

This type of disjuncture between the recommendations and the evidence has further fueled criticism that intersex case management is driven by a heterosexist imperative. While it is hard to deny such a claim, again it is important to keep in mind the political context in which these ideas were being articulated. During the 1950s, homosexual practices were criminalized by the legal system and pathologized by medicine and psychiatry. In such an environment it would have been irresponsible, even unethical, for clinicians to do anything other than try to facilitate a heterosexual outcome in their patients.[76]

But what of those four people from the sample of 60 (6.6 percent) who were assessed as having a gender that was discordant with their sex of assignment? All had been raised as girls and, while tomboyish behavior was noted in each, tomboyishness was not enough to warrant the assessment, of a gender "mismatch" since it was understood then as it is today as "just a phase" that many girls traverse. Rather it was their expressed attraction to girls and women that rendered three of the four discordant, while the fourth had sought a change of sex at the age of 16. Normative gender then was intricately tied to normative sexual expression. I take up this issue in detail in Chapter 4.

Producing Gender

Ultimately Money discredited the reliability of each of the biological markers of sex to corroborate his own claim that the sex of assignment and rearing was *the* best predictor of a hermaphroditic person's gender. He was not denying the workings of the body in gender, but he was suggesting that body could in turn be worked upon—surgically and socially—to produce a gender, indeed an exemplary gender. Their studies had shown a clear "advantage to rearing an intersexed child so that its gender role was clearly defined and consistently maintained from the beginning."[77]

But, the authors cautioned, the capacity for sex of assignment and rearing to be the best predictor was contingent on two factors: clinicians had to be unequivocal in deciding a sex and parents had to be vigilant in reinforcing that decision at every turn.[78] That was because children grew into their gender "against a background of myriad experiences encountered and transacted"[79] Those experiences included everything they learned, assimilated, and interpreted regarding their own status as boys or girls from their parents, siblings, and peers, and importantly, how they interpreted their own body. Little wonder the authors emphasized the importance of the postnatal critical period to gender acquisition.

Money and colleagues conceded that it was entirely possible for a hermaphrodite to establish a gender role that aligned fully with their sex of rearing "despite a paradoxical appearance of the external genitals."[80] Yet nowhere is there an indication that the authors considered what this might mean for the promotion of mandatory surgical interventions. In an extraordinary sleight of hand, Money and the Hampsons managed to co-opt the very idea that surgery was *not necessary* to the establishment of a gendered identity into a case for surgery *as necessary*. That maneuver passed unnoticed, buried in a discussion about the predictive power of bodily signifiers.

What exactly did all this mean for the intersexed? Put differently, what impact did the institutionalization of Money's model have on the material reality of the intersexed in Western liberal democracies? There is no doubt that it did have an impact. Money hadn't set out to debunk the historical assumption that biological sex determined one's psychosexual orientation for any kind of abstract theoretical reason. He did so to promote a rationale and a framework for clinical practices designed to manage the intersexed. At that time surgical interventions were not as customary as they are today. The very fact that they *are* customary today is a direct result of the recommendations of Money and his colleagues.

Carving Gender

So what were the recommendations? While the clinical practices were certainly vital to Money's treatment model, managing the intersexed extended far beyond the walls of the clinic. The 1955 articles also contain the first published expression of the protocols known as intersex case management (ICM). Those recommendations included strategies to psychologically manage parents into their role as gender coaches and allay their anxieties about *producing* sexually deviant offspring; strategies for psychologically managing the children into a gender using genital appearance to guide (rather than determine) sex assignment decisions; and "appropriate" types of surgical interventions. The articles also raised two particularly vexatious issues with respect to surgery from an ethical and a material perspective. Those issues were clitoridectomy and whether or not fertility would be preserved.

Until the mid-1950s it was not uncommon for a change of sex to be imposed on preschoolers and young children if they were discovered to have gonadal structures that contradicted the sex they were originally assigned—a legacy of Klebs's true sex model. Joan Hampson had noted in her article that historically even those old enough to have an opinion were seldom consulted about their own preferences. It is little wonder that some individuals were reported to have manifested mild forms of neuroticism of one kind or another. While the impact of imposing a sex was acknowledged by Hampson to be less than ideal, it would remain conspicuous by its absence as a potential cause of neuroses under the terms of their model.

Money and colleagues stressed the central role of clinicians in assuring a well-developed gender identity in their patients. It was incumbent upon clinicians, they said, to be meticulous about "settl[ing] the sex of a hermaphroditic infant once and for all, within the first few weeks of life, before establishment of a gender role gets far advanced."[81] Money stressed that the earlier a sex was assigned and the more consistently it was reinforced, the greater the likelihood that a hermaphroditic child would develop a positive gendered identity as male or as female. Hence it was the responsibility of clinicians and physicians to show clear and unwavering leadership to ensure the successful habilitation of hermaphrodite individuals (and their families) into a gender.

Perilous Ambiguity

If physicians had doubts about the sex of their patients, those doubts could easily be transmitted into the minds of parents and generate misgivings about the sex of their children. This in turn would enhance the risk of the children sensing there was something wrong with them. The transmission of doubt could also compromise parents' ability to rear their children in a "gender-appropriate" manner. The degree of parents' conviction as to whether they were raising a girl or a boy represented another risk factor for Money et al. Parental misgivings about their child's sex increased the risk of the child developing a spoiled identity because equivocation was, for them, a potent factor that contributed to an unstable gender identity.

Money and colleagues offered counsel on how best to manage the parents of hermaphroditic children. They recommended that parents *always* be told frankly about any doubts concerning the sex of their child. The authors believed that it was far better for parents to remain doubtful about the sex of their child than for the original announcement of a child's sex to be renounced and another sex assigned. They offered a stern warning that attempts to impose a change of sex after 18 months of age were doomed to result in a corrupted gender identity that would be psychologically hazardous for the child. The term *frankly* is especially worthy of scrutiny since clinicians were advised to set parents straight that they had a child whose genitals were *unfinished* (including infants whose assigned sex rendered their phallic tissue, enlarged clitorises), a point taken up below when I discuss Money and colleagues' recommendations for managing children into a gender.

To illustrate their point, for educative purposes the researchers used diagrams of male and female sexual differentiation that included what could be read as a hermaphroditic stage of development. But this is not the way that the earliest stages of fetal development are understood and thus signified by medical science, even today. The initial undifferentiated stage of sexual development is generally signified as "male and female identical." This particular signification substantiates the idea that hermaphrodite bodies are unfinished, since it suggests an implicit link to a presexually dimorphic state. Yet these representations offer possibilities for thinking otherwise since they clearly indicate that all human bodies contain the elements of both recognized sexes. Using illustrations of male and female sexual differentiation represents a doubling back of the normal/pathological relation discussed in the Introduction. Medical science uses the so-called abnormal (read infrequent) to understand and substantiate so-called normal (frequent) development, but here the relation is upended so that "normal" development becomes the vehicle through which "abnormal" development is understood.

Parental fears regarding a child's future sexuality—specifically, that the child might grow up to be sexually deviant[82]—were also addressed by Money and colleagues. The authors recommended educating parents to alleviate their concerns. In a statement dripping with irony to twenty-first-century eyes, they advised, "most parents need to be told that their child is not destined to grow up with *abnormal and perverse desires*, for they get hermaphroditism and homosexuality hopelessly confused."[83] Statements like this provide convincing evidence in support of a heteronormative critique, but I intend to resist such an analysis. As discussed in the introductory chapter, global analyses obscure opportunities to explore the wide range of investments in gender as a binary concept.

A more fruitful approach lies in an examination of the epistemological context in which Money and his colleagues produced their theories. Money had of course undertaken his postgraduate training during the period that Parsonsian functionalism dominated the social sciences in the United States. To have remained impervious to the influence of that paradigm was unlikely, since Money had studied directly under Parsons at Harvard in the department the latter had founded during the 1940s.[84] Critics of functionalism highlight its propensity for circular reasoning by pointing to the way that the effects produced by social institutions come to be perceived as their raison d'être. Indeed this is how functionalism works to legitimate rather than contest prevailing social orders. Two other factors are relevant. Money's early academic training was in the field of psychology, a discipline that has historically focused its lens upon the individual outside of broader social contexts, and of course, Money conducted his research in a medical facility alongside an interdisciplinary team of clinicians whose understandings of the body were also thoroughly imbued in a functionalist paradigm.

In functionalist terms, the clitoris has been of little interest. Like the appendix it has historically been considered redundant anatomy. With pleasure as its sole (known) function, the clitoris failed functionalism's use-value demands. Little wonder that its removal could be perceived as unproblematic. Joan Hampson was the first to publish the team's position on the procedure. Referring to the historical record that formed the basis of Money's doctoral thesis, Hampson noted that until mid-century there had been no surgical options available to people reared as female who possessed phallic structures that were larger than clinically acceptable clitorises. While a few such individuals were known to have adopted a masculine persona and lived as men—with the accompanying social status—many lived as women in keeping with their sex assignment. Hampson argued that a frequently erect phallus was a source of immense distress, not least because it drove some to frequent and desperate masturbation despite personal propriety.

For Hampson, twentieth-century technological advances provided the means to not merely alleviate this kind of distress, but avoid it altogether. The most effective treatment in her view was to surgically create "normal looking" female genitals by reducing the size of the clitoris or removing it altogether. As if this were not alarming enough, Hampson went on to assert that there were little grounds for assuming orgasmic function would be compromised or lost as a result.[85] The assertion was made on the basis of just six individuals from the sample group who had undergone clitoridectomy as adults. All six were reported as being orgasmic postoperatively, with one of the six said to have experienced her very first orgasm following the more radical of the two procedures—that is, the complete removal of the clitoral tissue. That point was specifically made to reassure surgeons who might have concerns about depriving their patients of the most significant erotic zone of the body. As the discussion in subsequent chapters will show, contemporary critics of ICM have rather a different story to tell. It is noteworthy that Hampson made no mention of whether the achievement of orgasm by this group was clitoral or vaginal despite extensive debates about the issue in both psychoanalytic and sexological circles during the 1950s, debates Hampson was clearly cognizant of at the time she penned her article.

Money and colleagues acknowledged that the procedure aroused vigorous debate in expert circles because of the risks it posed to erotic sensation. Nonetheless, the third article in the series reiterated Hampson's claim that none of the sexually experienced women they surveyed had reported deleterious effects following the loss of their clitoris.[86] The authors were also at pains to point out that none of the women under discussion had resisted *the idea* of clitoridectomy, since each regarded herself unequivocally as a woman with a concomitant gender role. This point was made to add weight to the "correctness" of the recommendation. Money would later describe female orgasm rather chillingly as "nature's reproduction insurance . . . so intent is nature on maintaining it that surprisingly large amounts of sexual tissue can be removed or relocated without destroying the capacity for orgasm."[87]

Offering a disclaimer regarding the finer points of extirpation versus amputation (that is, a complete excision versus a reduction), Money et al. suggested that since the discovery of cortisone, it was sufficient just to amputate. They had earlier considered complete extirpation necessary to avoid priapism of the amputated clitoral stump (that is, prolonged and painful erection), which some of their patients had reported.[88] Prior to the availability of cortisone, the only remedy for priapism was further surgery to remove any remaining (visible) phallic tissue. At no point did the authors give consideration to the idea that priapism might itself be a direct result of nerve damage caused by the surgery.[89]

Demonstrating a cautionary approach rarely found elsewhere in these articles, the authors went on to state:

> Though there is considerable evidence that an amputated clitoris is erotically sensitive, enough uncertainty remains to require conservativism in recommending clitoridectomy for hermaphrodites living as women in whom there is neither a blind vaginal pouch nor a vagina opening into a urogenital sinus.[90]

The considerable evidence of which they spoke equated to the reports of just 12 women. While this was twice the number cited in Hampson's article, it remained a very small sample on which to recommend such a radical and irreversible intervention.[91] What we can see here is an acknowledgement of a role for the intact phallic structure in female sexual pleasure, albeit as a consolation prize for those without a penetrable vagina.

As to the timing of what can only be described as an extreme and thoroughly controversial procedure, Hampson recommended that clitoridectomy be carried out as early as possible after birth and for older individuals as soon as possible after diagnosis. While reluctant to commit to an exact timeline, Hampson suggested that since gender was indelibly established by two years of age, clinicians should use that as their guiding principle and not wait until the child was of preschool age. Other surgical procedures such as vaginal extension or construction could be delayed until the child was older. Once the intersexed child's body was "fixed," the fixing of gender could begin in earnest.

Gender Immersion

For Money, the education of hermaphroditic youngsters was essential to the effective management of their gender, and this is reflected in the original case management model. Yet it would appear that over the years clinicians responsible for implementing the protocols have been unable to reconcile the educative component with the need to ensure the development of an unambiguous gendered identity.[92] While Money and the Hampsons argued strongly that both the parents and the child's interests were best served by undertaking surgical interventions as early in the child's life as possible, they conceded that so long as children were told about future medical and surgical plans they were fully capable of accommodating any impositions that resulted from their nonnormative-appearing genitalia. Without that information children were likely to construe themselves as freakish, whereas with it they had the means to develop strategies to deal with "interim emergencies [like] school urinary habits" in the case of assigned males.[93] It was also said to provide the child with a buffer against teasing or intrusive questioning by other children.

Clinicians were advised that children be told what to expect of proposed surgical procedures in simple terms. "A 3 yr old girl about to be clitoridectomized, for example, should be well informed that the doctors will make her look like all other girls and women."[94] Simple terms indeed, for this type of explanation perpetuates the idea that there is a single standard in female genitalia: a standard that any pediatrician, gynecologist, or obstetrician can attest is a complete misnomer.[95] And as British scholar Iain Morland so poignantly notes, "no child can actually look like all the other girls without becoming a polymorphous, *monstrous* chimera."[96]

Money and colleagues were adamant that keeping patients informed of their condition(s) in age-appropriate language would facilitate an understanding of the circumstances of their birth and that this would have a positive impact on their sense of self:

It is preferable that . . . a child know, from the time when she can first begin to comprehend it, that she has a clitoris like all other girls but that it is too big and will be made smaller sucrgically. With little boys, the simplest comprehensible explanation is that one day the surgeons will finish off the penis so that the boy can stand up to urinate.[97]

Such instruction was intended to facilitate in the children an understanding that they were not a "half girl and half boy but rather girls or boys who were *not finished* genitally."[98] Yet this advice begs the question of how children assigned as female are supposed to make sense of the information that their genitals are on the one hand, "too big" and on the other "not finished"? In developmental terms, the advice makes no sense, since a clitoris deemed to be too big can hardly be said to be either *under*-developed or unfinished.

Money also stressed the importance of children being given basic instruction in prenatal development as part of their training into a gender. Take, for example, his recommendations for the types of discourse clinicians should use to that end: "Girls should also know, incidentally, that whereas boys have a penis, girls have a vagina—in juvenile vocabulary, a baby tunnel—as a double insurance agains childish theories of surgical mutilation and maiming."[99] Three points are worthy of note in this advice. In the first instance, to interpret diagrammatic representations of sex differentiation in this way is not only misleading, it is factually incorrect. There is *no* relationship between a penis and a vagina prenatally since the homologue of penis is clitoris. This advice does not equate to basic instruction in prenatal development, it is more of a primer for (hetero)sex education. Little wonder, then, that many cultural critics accuse Money of being an agent of compulsory heterosexuality.

In the second instance, the type of language used begs scrutiny in light of Money's views on potential versus actual fertility (see below) and his views on the importance of managing the psychological well-being of his patients. For what are the implications of telling a child she is a girl and that girls have "baby tunnels" if the child does not have a vagina or, for whatever reason, is unable to bear children? This would seem to create the very conditions for trauma that Money sought to avoid.

In the third instance, the advice serves to infantilize a child's apprehensions and fears regarding what can only be described as radical and invasive surgical procedures that involve body parts tainted by taboo and shame within Western (as well as many other) cultures.[100] Money and colleagues recommended that children be told about pre- and postoperative procedures (including anesthesia), because he recognized that what might seem to be trivial details to medical professionals could be the source of "intense anticipatory terrors and misconceptions" for children.[101] Yet the idea that children might be traumatized by their clinical and surgical experiences (including repeated genital examinations often carried out by teams of doctors and/or repeated genital surgeries) is conspicuous by its absence in the authors' consideration of potential causes of "maladaptation" to an assigned gender. Such trauma is said to be one of the main reasons that so many people have become lost to follow-up as adults, a situation lamented by ICM clinicians and their critics alike because without long-term follow-up, the efficacy or otherwise of ICM procedures remains difficult if not impossible to determine.

There is considerable evidence in the medical literature (and in the narrative accounts of intersex individuals) that genital reconstructive surgeries almost never involve a single procedure but in fact require multiple interventions over extended periods. This is particularly the case when first surgeries are undertaken on infants and young children, a commonplace occurrence even today.[102] Money and colleagues stressed that decisions about the timing of operations should always be contingent on estimates of safety and optimal outcomes; however—clitoridectomy excepted—surgical success was better achieved after the organs had grown some. Surgical success in this context referred to both form and function. Form related to genital appearance and function meant for assigned females a receptive vagina and for assigned males the ability to engage in penetrative (vaginal) sex and to urinate from a standing position.

The idea that children needed a grasp of basic anatomy so they would not think of themselves as half female and half male is crucial on another level. Despite having firsthand knowledge that humans come in more varieties than $n = 2$, these researchers were unable to conceive of a healthy hermaphrodite or interexed subjectivity. When male and female are the only legitimate legally and socially sanctioned options, the intersexed can only ever be unfinished. This point is exemplified in the premise that if something had not gone wrong in utero, the intersexed would have been born as normal males or normal females, a point that is particularly relevant to the discussion and analysis of Chapters 5 and 6.

By the account of Money and the Hampsons, any form of gender ambivalence on the part of a child had to be the result of prevarication on the part of clinicians and/or parents. Prevarication often led to a child's original sex assignment being revoked and was considered harmful for both the child and the parents—particularly after the child had reached the age of two. After infancy children were said to be virtually incapable of coping with a change of sex. Such changes were "fraught with severe psychologic hazard for the child" according to Joan Hampson.[103] There is a clear contradiction between this and the idea that educating children about their medical history and plans for future surgical and other medical interventions would enable them to accommodate any impositions that might be brought to bear by so-called anomalous genitalia. Hampson's claim was made on the evidence of ten individuals whose sex had been reassigned after the neonatal period. Four had been reassigned prior to their first birthday and were reported to be free of psychological disturbance, while all but one of the remaining six were said to be "inadequately adjusted" in one way or another. In the concluding passage of Hampson's article the dangers of reassignment after infancy were reiterated in considerably more strident terms. Reassignment with or without genital surgery represented, she said, an *extreme* psychological hazard, although no indication was given as to what that might constitute. In light of her earlier statement that psychosis was conspicuous by its absence across the entire sample, there is a clear disjuncture here. The same warning resonated in all of the subsequent material produced by the trio and in Money's work more generally.

For individuals who had not been surgically mediated as infants, Money et al. recommended that reassignment decisions be guided by the degree to which a gender role was already established. This population, they believed was most at risk of a spoiled gender identity and presented the "most perplexing and difficult of problems."[104] That was because parents would assign even the most ambiguous child a sex before long, since the English language demands that a child be referred to as a he or a she and parents would be compelled to announce that their child was a son or a daughter. Once that announcement was made, parents would begin to raise the child accordingly and so facilitate the process of gender acquisition. In cases where the original assignment was deemed to be incorrect, it was vital that the child be reassigned sooner rather than later because it was far too difficult for parents to have to relinquish a son in favor of a daughter, or a daughter in favor of a son. Effectively, then, Money and his colleagues were promoting a prophylactic approach to managing ambiguity in order to help parents cope with having a child who was not—in the statistical sense of the term—normal.

Measuring Success: Key Performance Indicators

Money's theory of gender acquisition also codified a set of variables by which to measure a person's adjustment as masculine or feminine at a time when there were few uniform or coherent measuring tools available. Perhaps the best-known and most widely used scale prior to Money's intervention was that devised by Lewis Terman and Catherine Miles during the 1930s. The Terman-Miles test consisted of a written questionnaire designed to measure "mental masculinity and femininity" and was designed to allow clinicians to quantify the degree and direction of an individual's "deviation from the mean of his or her sex."[105] It was also designed to allow quantitative comparisons between groups. Money's interest, however, extended beyond the psychological or "mental" since he wanted to be able to measure the extent to which individuals *executed* their masculinity and femininity. Terman and Miles's test, like others available at that time, could not do the work that Money and his colleagues required. Undeterred, they developed their own set of measurements.

So how did these researchers gauge a person's success in adapting to the sex of assignment, that is, to a gender? They devised an inventory of variables to evaluate the degree of a person's masculinity or femininity. Their inventory included the following indicators:

[G]eneral mannerisms, deportment and demeanor, play preferences and recreational interests, spontaneous topics of talk in unprompted conversation and casual comment; content of dreams, daydreams and fantasies; replies to oblique inquiries and projective tests; evidence of erotic practices; and the individual's own replies to direct inquiry.[106]

What is problematic about these indicators is that they rely so heavily on the subjective judgment of those making the assessment. I remind the reader once more that a functionalist approach begins from the premise that something exists because it performs a function.[107] When one knows, for instance, what feminine behavior is and what masculine behavior is, all that is required is to assert its function in order to provide an explanation.[108] Much as we remain bound by stereotypical notions of what is gender appropriate in the twenty-first century, there have been significant attitudinal and behavioral shifts over the past 50 years, particularly with respect to the feminine. What remains constant is the oversimplification of complex multidimensional phenomena that serve to convey "a sense of stability and permanence to [that which is] inherently flexible."[109] The concepts of masculinity and femininity put forward by Money were in many respects oversimplified accounts of unstable and complex phenomena.

Hampson noted that almost 30 percent of the people in their sample had lived for more than two-thirds of their lives with a contradiction between genital appearance and sex of assignment and rearing, and this indicated how incredibly adaptive the human organism is. With one exception, all of the individuals discussed by Hampson were reported to have grown up with an orientation (as male or female) wholly consistent with their assigned sex and rearing. While some had disclosed feelings of shame and shyness at feeling different, in very few instances was *any* form of neuroticism evident, and psychotic symptoms were simply "conspicuous by their absence."[110] Moreover, most children were said to be resilient enough to deal with their genital appearance and even grew up with a sexual orientation that was "appropriate" to their assigned sex sans surgery.

Even those who believed an error had been made were reported by Hampson to have adapted to their assigned sex with little more than an uneasy kind of adjustment; perhaps the very mildest forms of neuroses. Money had reported in his doctoral research that a contradiction between a person's identity as male or female and his or her physical appearance did not in itself lead to psychoses or even neurotic symptomology. Yet he and his colleagues persisted with the idea that medical interventions designed to normalize their bodies were essential to the psychological health and well-being of the intersexed.[110]

*   *   *

SECTION III

Beyond Dichotomous Sex and Dichotomous Gender?

In an article published many years later in the *Journal of Sex and Marital Therapy*, Money wrote that his early studies had led him to realize that there was no absolute dichotomy of male versus female.[111] Again this statement cannot be read as an endorsement of the idea that there might be more than two sexes, for Money's point was made with reference to variables, not individuals. Within the framework he devised to codify the markers of sex, intersex constituted a series of contradictions between two or more of the seven variables. Thus assignment decisions had to be made on the basis of multidimensional factors rather than any single criterion.

Money suggested that for those of us who might be described as unremarkable females and males, it was entirely feasible to assume that sex was univariate in character because theoretically all seven signifiers of sex—physiological and social—were concordant with one another. However, concordance was and remains to this day assumed for most people because, as discussed in the preceding section, chromatin testing is undertaken only when there is a question about a person's sex or fertility. Since this is not the case for the majority of people, the assertion of a general concordance is speculative at best because it is without empirical support.[112]

Money's hermaphrodite research and the clinical guidelines he and the Hampsons developed in the 1950s stand as exemplars of the normative medicoscientific traditions discussed in the Introduction. That tradition tends to substantiate the statistically frequent by rendering the statistically infrequent as anomalous and as pathological. This provides the mandate for clinicians to rectify the bodies of the intersexed—ultimately to ensure that their gender becomes fixed.

The idea that medical intervention is necessary was completely unquestioned for half a century. Indeed, intervention is sold on the grounds that without it, the intersexed are doomed to a life of misery and dejection. While there has been considerable debate in the medical literature around what form interventions should take, the option of nonintervention *as* an option has only recently been on the table.

The underlying premise of Money's research is that intersexed individuals would have been born as normal males or females if something hadn't gone *wrong*. When perceived as unfinished—or disordered—in a context where interventions are possible, medical science is compelled to make an intervention, to make things right, to "finish what nature failed to do," to bring order. It is a compulsion through which the ideological is quite literally made material. By situating the intersexed as both unfinished and finish-able, the apparent truth of dimorphic sexual difference is not merely upheld, it is "proven." In other words, the human species properly consists of two (and just two) sexes. This is a poignant example of the is/ought distinction, since doctors' interpretations of *what is* are fully informed by their beliefs about *what ought to be*.

When Money extended the concept of gender beyond the intersexed population, gender came to substantiate the development of so-called normal masculine and feminine identities. He continued to refine and complicate his earliest ideas but never strayed too far from his original premises. Yet something significant happened in the transposing. At the moment at which gender came to signify the normative, the intersexed who had been so central to the concept disappeared from the frame, banished from the here and now by the very concept that owed its existence to them.

Imprinting and Native Language

Just as intersexed children acquired an identity as masculine or feminine during the first 18 months of life, so too did everybody else. Money's explanation of the *mechanism* of gender acquisition seems particularly persuasive. Humans are born with a template in the mind that primes for *both* masculinity and femininity. This enables children to learn which behaviors are appropriate for their gender and which are appropriate for the "other"—and by extension, *in*appropriate for them. This point is crucial. Money insisted that once acquired, an identity as male or female became permanently hardwired into the brain in exactly the same way that native language did.

The link between native language and gender acquisition represents one of Money's most powerful articulations. In his view:

Once ingrained, a person's native language may fall into disuse and be supplanted by another, but it is never entirely eradicated. So also a gender role may be changed or, resembling native bi-linguilism may be ambiguous, but it may also become so deeply ingrained that not even flagrant contradictions of body functioning and morphology may displace it.[113]

The potency of this link should not be underestimated. Linking gender with language served to ground the former in a significant and persuasive way. Money did not just propose similarity in terms of process; he also proposed that native language and gender acquisition were temporally simultaneous. Both occurred prior to two years of age, a point that was reiterated in many of his subsequent writings on gender. Of course there can be no denying that language acquisition occurs in response to external postnatal stimuli. To suggest that once established, a person's native language(s) could be *un*learned is of course, a specious claim.

Money was fully aware that mainstream psychological theories of the day gave little credence to the idea that psychological functions established postnatally might resist eradication, despite a number of powerful medical analogies that would support such a notion.[114] Indeed, the idea struck at the heart of the philosophical framework of psychotherapy and behavior modification therapies. Yet this is precisely what Money was proposing with his theory of gender. With no precedent in their own fields of psychology and psychiatry, Money and his colleagues had turned to the work of Austrian embryologist Konrad Lorenz to support their assertions.

Lorenz claimed to have successfully established himself as a "mother figure" to a clutch of mallard ducklings by imitating the adult female's quacking for a half day after the birds had hatched. From then on the young birds had continued to respond to him as if he were their mother.[115] Money used this analogy to argue that learned responses and behaviors were as resistant to elimination as those of genetic or hormonal influence. Native language offered a prime example of how permanence at a neural level was not synonymous with innateness. Questions about whether gender was innate or acquired, established prenatally or postnatally, or the product of nature or nurture, for Money were completely separate from the issue of whether gender was immutable or changeable.

Sexual Signatures was the first of Money's publications explicitly directed toward a lay audience. In it Money and his coauthor Patricia Tucker offered a fascinating account of the history and politics of language development. They linked language development to relations of power and suggested that when written language came into being, generalization had already become an effective tool for ruling elites to augment their power. Once accepted, generalizations became what Money described as "eternal verities" that assume a life of their own. For Money, because generalizations about gender were "embalmed in language and custom" they weighed heavily on understandings of what it means to be human, since our capacity for thought is both constrained and shaped by language.[116] He suggested that the legacy of those generalizations serves to distort our thinking. In fact he went so far as to state that while arbitrary gender-based distinctions were in and of themselves relatively harmless, "their cumulative effect is to polarize the sexes, [and] to so overstress sex differences that the *human similarities* are overlooked."[117] That Money was fully aware of the cumulative effects of such distinctions is paradoxical in light of the multiple ways that his own work contributed toward maintaining stereotypical notions of what it means to be a girl or a boy, a woman or a man. Money's theories of gender have reinforced rather than contested the very distortion and limited thinking of which he spoke, by overstressing sex differences—as oppositional—and ignoring or underplaying similarities.

Gender Identity/Role: A Dimensional Account

In teasing out and refining his gender theory over the course of the 1970s and 1980s, Money developed a four-dimensional schema of gender differences, most of which were based on social and cultural stereotypes. Each dimension was in the first instance classified as either irreducible or reducible. The sole irreducible category covered the reproductive capacities of males and females: that is, men's capacity to impregnate and women's capacity to ovulate, menstruate, gestate, and lactate. The operative word here is capacity, since for Money there was no imperative that men actually impregnate or that women menstruate and so on to qualify as male or female respectively.[118] What mattered was that these elements of sexual difference formed the basis upon which all others were built.[119]

The reducible categories were all said to be influenced to some degree by the release of prenatal hormones. In making an explicit link between the prenatal critical period and behaviors, Money was not arguing that the latter were a direct product of the former, nor that any behavior could be said to be the exclusive property of one sex or the other. Rather he was referring to the threshold for the release or manifestation of particular behaviors. The examples he gave included kinetic energy expenditure (particularly with respect to sports); competitive rivalry; roaming; territorialism; defense against intruders; guarding and defense of the young; nesting behaviors; care-giving; active and passive forms of sexual behavior; and erotic arousal to visual or tactile stimuli.[120] In my reading of these categories (and to a degree in Money's also), at stake are a range of *human* behaviors and characteristics that may (or may not) be subject in any given historical period to classification as masculine or feminine. Yet the three reducible categories or dimensions included more than behaviors, for they also incorporated aspects of physicality.

The second dimension in Money's schema he called sex-derivative. This category referred to secondary sex characteristics and to physiological features such as bone structure, muscularity, and fat distribution. At a behavioral level, he included characteristics that have been linked to hormones, such as aggression, and to urinary posture.[121] Money also speculated that any sex differences in morbidity and mortality might one day be found to have an underlying hormonal cause and, if so, would also qualify for inclusion in this category.

The third dimension—sex-adjunctive—referred to socially ascribed roles manifested through the sexual division of labor and occupational stereotyping. Money proposed that this category superimposed on the second (sex-derivative) one. What distinguished this and the fourth category from those discussed above was their very loose association to the body and to capacity. The elements of the sex-adjunctive dimension were, he said, the effects of the differential treatment accorded boys and girls from the moment they were born. Drawing on the anthropological record, Money associated women's historical responsibility for food preparation and other domestic duties with the constraints of pregnancy and breast-feeding in the prehistorical context. While hard physical labor was gender-coded for both men and women, Money argued that men's generally larger muscular build and relative strength (sex-derivative characteristics) were compatible with distance and long absences from the domestic sphere. Invoking the hunter-gatherer thesis, Money suggested rather curiously that men's ancient predisposition to territorial roaming extended contemporarily to truck driving. Yet at the same time he declared that in the contemporary context rigid divisions of labor were anachronistic, since no definitive or incontrovertible evidence existed to support the phyletic destiny of male dominance in humans at an erotic or a domestic level.[122]

The fourth dimension of Money's schema was designated sex-arbitrary. Included in this category were recreational, educational, and vocational interests and accomplishments, as well as grooming styles, adornment, body language, and social etiquette. Money also included sex differences in vocabulary and speech patterns within this dimension, although he did note the influence of social class in vocal intonation. The very arbitrariness of this category, he said, provided ammunition for those invested in the nurture side of the nature/ nurture debates because they lent a superficial credence to the idea that all gender roles were the product of arbitrary social constructs.[123]

Money argued that women's increased participation in the work-force was often interpreted by conservatives as a threat to the very fabric of social life and a challenge to those sex-irreducible components of gender relations. It was his argument that the four dimensions of gender coding represented a "pervasive unity" and so any threat—perceived or real—to one component was experienced as a threat to the whole. Women's liberation provided a perfect example. The liberation of women would not, as many feared, lead to anarchy in the bedroom or require women or men to forfeit their erotic and procreative roles. Rather its benefits would extend to everyone, in his view.[124] In the late 1970s he wrote:

The stereotype says that the ideal woman is not a very good human being. If a woman is feminine she's incompetent, if she's competent she's not feminine, and the value of whatever she does except procreate will be downgraded because it was done by a woman. Protesting such systematic erosion of their pride of gender is anything but a rejection of female gender identity/role, yet that is how a great many men and some women view the women's liberation movement.[125]

The various controversies generated by women's liberation were something of a wonder, he suggested, given that all that was really at stake were "historically arbitrary decisions regarding the decorative, recreational, educational, vocational, and legal roles of men and women."[126] In other words, what he perceived to be at issue were those historically contingent elements of the third and fourth dimensions of his schema: dimensions with only the very loosest association to the body.

In Money's view, behind every biologically determinist explanation of sex differences lay a deep-seated anxiety of those invested in preserving the power differential between men and women. Proponents of biological determinism were, he said, as politically motivated as their nurturist or social constructionist counterparts:

[N]ature is a political strategy of those committed to the status quo of sex differences. They use reductionist biology to maintain the biological inevitability of sex differences and to exclude the possibility of their being historically stereotyped.[127]

Yet this was not an argument in support of nurturism. Money had little time for those invested in the false dichotomy of nature or nurture, irrespective of what side of the fence their allegiances lay.

Money's emphasis on the greater importance of postnatal stimuli has been interpreted by many over the years as evidence that he privileged nurture over nature in gender acquisition. However the framework he offered was infinitely more complex than any simplistic nurture versus nature (vis à vis constructionist versus essentialist) argument can sustain.[128] From the outset Money had articulated an enormous frustration with the Cartesian dualism inherent in the nature/nurture debates. The approach he consistently employed throughout his career is known as interactionism, a theoretical position that attempts to bridge the divide between the nature/culture debates without reifying either. Acutely aware of the complex interactive relation between cells, environment, and experience, Money repeatedly stressed that "at every stage of development, nothing is purely nature and nothing is purely nurture. There is always a collaboration between the two."[129]

I would suggest that Money's dimensional account of sex differences was not, then, an argument for the maintenance of the status quo. From this perspective his account of sex role differences reads as descriptive rather than prescriptive, since he recognized the rigidity of the sexual division of labor across societies: a division as subject to the "force of custom and the weight of religion [as it was to] the power of the law."[130]

Indeed, the loosening up of the sexual division of labor over the course of the twentieth century was in Money's view a thoroughly positive development that could be attributed to three factors: the impact of the second wave of feminism; automation in the workplace; and the increasing computerization of many occupational tasks. In this regard Money's analysis and theory making are infinitely more complex than any straightforward vilification or valorization of the man and his work can offer.

Of course Money accorded the non-intersexed a much greater degree of latitude with respect to culturally sanctioned stereotypes than he extended to the intersexed. The latter were expected to demonstrate through their words, deeds, and social presentation the epitome of manliness and womanliness. Nothing less would satisfy the demands of those who measured and recorded the adaptation of the intersexed to their assigned sex-gender. In other words, it was incumbent upon the intersexed to identify with and display a type of hypermasculinity or hyperfemininity.[131] Take, for example, the following assessment of the results of a survey of ten of Money's patients diagnosed with Androgen Insensitivity Syndrome (AIS) from the early 1970s:

With respect to marriage and maternalism, the girls and women showed a high incidence of preference for being a wife with no outside job; of enjoying homecraft; ... of having played primarily with dolls and other girl's toys; of having a positive and genuine interest in infant care.[132]

He went on to assert that 80 percent of this sample reported "a strong interest in personal adornment which *clearly* tell[s] a story of women whose genetic status as males was utterly irrelevant to their psycho-sexual status as women."[133] These statements indicate equally clearly that the proof of successful adaptation lay in how closely individuals conformed to rigid (yet arbitrary) stereotypes. At a time of profound social change in the United States brought about by the sexual revolution, the rise of counterculture, gains made by the American civil rights movement, and the burgeoning women's movement, one must ask why he relied so heavily on such static, inflexible concepts. Perhaps the answer lies in the remark about genetic status. As I have demonstrated in the preceding pages, Money insisted from the outset that there was no necessary one-to-one relation between the bodily signifiers of sex and a person's social and personal status as a man or a woman. Hypermasculine and hyperfeminine hermaphrodites, then, provided proof positive of that idea and also provided proof of the veracity of his treatment model.

CONCLUSION

In the preceding pages I have laid out the central elements of Money's theories of gender from his earliest articulations through to their fuller elaborations over the course of his career. I make no claim to have offered a full and complete representation of Money's theories about gender: that is a task well beyond the scope of this text. Rather I have endeavored to capture the central elements of a significant and substantive body of work in order to pursue two (nonbinary) lines of argument that are woven through the entire book. The first concerns the historical and ongoing relation that the intersexed have to gender. It is a relation obscured—almost to the point of invisibility—by the very theories that Money devised, by the case management protocols he and his early collaborators developed, and by the interventions of others who have found the concept of gender useful to their theoretical and political projects. My second line of argument is that gender represents one of the great conceptual devices of the late twentieth century. I base that claim on the fact that gender has fully naturalised into the English lexicon in just 50 years so that today it seems almost indispensable to thinking about, writing about and speaking about what it means to be a woman or a man.

This chapter began with an examination of the intellectual and historical context in which Money embarked upon what would become his lifework. Much of the discussion has turned on his earliest published material. For it was in those articles that Money initially offered the term *gender* to explain how someone who was neither male nor female was able to acquire an identity as masculine or feminine. In a clinical context gender proved to be a powerful stabilizing factor at a time when technology was increasingly undermining the long-held medicoscientific assumption that the bodily signifiers of sex aligned unilaterally. And then it became a stabilizing factor in a broader social context. Gender served to substantiate the idea that one's identity and behaviors were natural and inevitable products of one of two natural and inevitable types of bodies: male and female. In this way, gender can be read as the most recent historical apparatus to contain the body within a political economy of dimorphic sexual difference.

In the following chapter, I continue to trace the history of gender through the work of Robert Stoller, who picked up the concept during the mid-1960s, some 11 years after it was initially offered by Money. Stoller made a number of important interventions into gender that have had, as I demonstrate, significant ramifications for the way it has become possible to think about and talk about gendered and sexed subjectivity since. They also had significant ramifications for the intersexed.

CHAPTER 2

STOLLER'S SEDUCTIVE
DUALISMS

INTRODUCTION

Money and colleagues' work was especially profitable to psychoanalysts and others who were dealing with transsexed subjects in their clinical practices and theorizing transsexuality as a phenomenon. A prominent figure in United States psychoanalytic circles from the early 1960s onward was analyst and MD Robert Stoller. His work determined to a significant degree, gender's history as an ontological concept. Stoller's role in this history is commonly recognized, in fact more so than Money's. He was responsible for reconfiguring some of Money's fundamental maxims concerning gender. As will become clear in the following pages, Stoller's idea of what gender might mean was very different from Money's.

While the sex/gender distinction was without doubt Stoller's best-known contribution to gender theory, he actually did a great deal more than this. In fact he made not one but three significant interventions that each shaped the way that sexed subjectivity came to be talked about and understood by psychologists, medical professionals, social scientists, feminists, and, in time, by the wider population. In the following pages I explore those interventions and in the course of doing so examine the often tenuous relation between Stoller's ideas and his evidence base, just as I did with Money.

In a paper published in 1964, Stoller elaborated on Money's more generalized concept of gender, which had originally been defined in terms of role and orientation.[1] The "Contribution" paper is remarkable for its refinement of Money's original concepts through a number of distinct though not unrelated interventions. I want to begin with an examination of the distinction that Stoller made between one's identification as a gender (gender identity) and its behavioral manifestations on the basis of social expectations (gender role). This distinction enabled Stoller to develop an account of the psychological status of those whose identifications and behaviors were at odds with their morphological status. His second intervention was to name the outcome of the imprinting process as described by Money. Framing this outcome as a "core" gender identity enabled Stoller to devise a theory to account for so-called aberrant gender identifications in both the intersexed and male transsexuals. These interventions provided the ground that enabled Stoller to separate out the concept of sex, his most well known contribution to gender.

In the tradition of biomedicine, Stoller developed a theory of "normal" development by turning to the so-called abnormal: those "experiments of nature" as the intersexed are so often referred to in the medical literature.[2] Much of the focus of this chapter concerns the way that Stoller put hermaphroditism to work to both reinforce understandings of normative gender identity formation and to cement his claims about how that process became distorted in some individuals. The legacy of his work remains with us to this day, a legacy that was as reductive as it was productive. On the one hand it opened up the theoretical possibilities for an emergent second-wave feminist movement and on the other it circumscribed the ways in which it was possible to think about gender. This point is central because, as I demonstrate in this and subsequent chapters, it reproduced and reinforced the status of the intersexed as abject Other.

Each of Stoller's interventions had significant consequences for the way in which sexed subjectivity has come to be understood. Money's more general concept of gender relied upon the binary logic of dimorphic sexual difference, and the theoretical work done by Stoller served to entrench gender even further into that logic. It did so by returning to and reinforcing an imagined nature/nurture divide, rendering sex the property of the former and gender the property of the latter. Over the past 30 years, in the feminist literature particularly, it has been the received wisdom that Stoller's contribution to understandings of sexed subjectivity was the sex/gender split.[3] What I intend to reveal in the following pages is a greater level of complexity to Stoller's theoretical and conceptual contributions than such received wisdom allows.

OF BEING AND DOING

Robert Stoller's early academic training had, like Money's, been in the field of psychology.[4] Unlike Money, who had rejected Freud's theories of instinct and drive, Stoller embraced psychoanalysis, going on to become a practitioner after training at the Los Angeles Psychoanalytic Institute. In the mid-1950s he joined the faculty of the Department of Psychiatry at the newly established UCLA medical school where he remained on staff until his sudden death in 1991. Stoller was one of a group of psychoanalysts from the Los Angeles region who set up the Gender Identity Project in 1958 specifically to study transsexualism.[5] Among his collaborators was fellow psychoanalyst Ralph Greenson, whose research was concerned with masculine identity formation; endocrinologist Harry Benjamin; and later, a former student of Money's by the name of Richard Green.[6] Four years later the Gender Identity Research Clinic was formed under the auspices of the School of Medicine at UCLA.[7] This was the first such clinic on the West Coast of the United States and it was from there that the Gender Identity Project continued.[8]

Stoller's earliest intervention into Money's gender theory was to unpack the original concept, partitioning gender identity and gender role. He did so in order to make a clear distinction between one's self-awareness as male or female and the behavioral manifestations and social expectations associated with belonging to a gender. This allowed him to focus on gender as a psychological rather than a cultural phenomenon. Stoller offered the term *gender identity*[9] in order to talk about the psychological sense of knowing "to which sex one belongs, that is, the awareness 'I am a male' or 'I am a female.' "[10] Stoller credited the introduction of the term to himself and Ralph Greenson after they had used it in their presentation at a psychoanalytic conference in Stockholm in 1963.[11] Gender identity was offered as a working term to account for all those psychological phenomena "related to the sexes but without direct biological connotations."[12] Recall that historically, a range of terms had been used interchangeably in English to refer to what we now understand as gender, the most common being "sexuality," "sexual outlook," "sexual identity," and "psycho-sexual identity."

The term gender identity offered a number of advantages for Stoller over its predecessors because they were all haunted by ambiguity. Not only did they refer to identifications, they also referenced sexual practices and desires. Gender identity, as a relatively fresh term, carried no such conceptual baggage. Moreover, theorizing gender in terms of identity had a specific utility for Stoller because it allowed him to focus on a person's self-image as a sexed being and leave aside issues pertaining to roles. The task of theorizing gender at the level of social expectations was one that Stoller left to social researchers. This made sense for a practicing psychoanalyst engaged in the business of trying to understand transsexualism.[13]

Money, meanwhile, attempted to restore a sense of unity to the concept of gender by introducing the term *gender identity/role*— abbreviated as G-I/R—in the early 1970s. Money remained adamant that these were two sides of the same coin, explaining their conceptual unity in tautological terms. Quite simply "gender identity is the private experience of gender role and gender role is the public expression of gender identity."[14] Money's attempt at recovering gender's conceptual unity did not succeed, for once the distinction had been made between identity and role it fell prey to the dichotomizing impulses of a binary logic. This was reflected in scholarship; before long, sociology reclaimed its mantle as the appropriate domain for theorizing gender roles,[15] although it conceded some of that authority to social psychology.[16]

By splitting identity from role in this way, Stoller offered the possibility that a person could have a gendered identity without necessarily being locked into social expectations of how that identity should be expressed or indeed experienced. It also allowed for temporal change in terms of social expectations, all the while holding gender identification constant. Thus on the surface at least, Stoller's intervention appeared significantly more productive (in the Foucauldian sense) than Money's response to it. Stoller brought gender's dynamism to the fore. At a time of great epistemological and ontological change brought about (in part) by a raft of political and social movements and cultural and economic change, Stoller imbued gender with a fluidity that ensured its survival. Yet at the same time, as will become clear, Stoller's interventions proved to be as constraining as they were enabling.

IDENTITY AS ESSENCE

Stoller's second intervention was to offer a term for the outcome of the second critical period of gender acquisition that occurred during the first 18 months of life. Money had already provided an *explanation* for the process vis-à-vis the acquisition of a native language. Stoller dubbed the *outcome* of that process one's "core gender identity," which he defined as that apparently unalterable sense that one is either a male or a female.[17] He described it in the following way:

By "the sense of maleness" I mean the awareness *I am a male*. This essentially unalterable core of gender identity is to be distinguished from the related but different belief, *I am manly* (or masculine). The latter attitude is a more subtle and complicated development. It emerges only after the child has learned how his parents expect him to express masculinity; that is, to behave as they feel males should.... [T]he knowledge that *I am a male*, with its biological rather than gender implication, starts developing much earlier than the sense that *I am masculine*.[18]

We can tease out the subtleties of that distinction by looking at its application to the statement "I am not a very masculine man." Here the speaker has a clear sense of his core identity *as* male and at the same time a recognition that the way he enacts his masculinity falls short of sociocultural expectations about what being a man is. Stoller's elaboration of Money's original concept of gender transformed it still further by giving it an enhanced discursive power at the level of subjectivity. It accommodated variation between individuals in terms of their investments in gender and at the same time highlighted the possibility of fluctuation within any given individual.[19] Like Money, Stoller was clear about what constituted appropriate characteristics and behaviors for men and women, girls and boys. While some of those views appear terribly outmoded today, just as many continue to have traction.[20]

The idea of a core gender identity that was overlaid by a growing sense of its meaning in terms of social expectation was crucial to Stoller's ideas about transsexualism. His analysis was conditional upon on this idea of a core that was the property of every individual and thus crucial to subjectivity. A male-to-female transsexual's core identity, Stoller believed, was corrupted by a noxious or pathological relationship with the mother—one that could be described in crude terms as a smothering type of relationship. It was Stoller's view that a mother who held her male baby too close (both literally and figuratively) for a prolonged period interfered with the child's ability to properly individuate.[21]

Stoller shared with Money the view that anatomy and parental interaction were central to the production of transsexuality. It is here that we get the strongest sense of Stoller the psychoanalyst. The contribution of "natural appearing" genitalia to identity development extended beyond signifying that the sex assignment at birth was a correct one. Genitalia also functioned at the level of sensation and thus contributed to "primitive body ego, sense of self and awareness of gender."[22] While these sensations derived primarily from external structures, in the case of female infants Stoller suggested they also derived from some "dim sensation" emanating from the vagina.[23] No evidence was offered to account for this dim sensation. Its assumed veracity can be read as indicative of Stoller's commitment to aspects of a psychoanalytic paradigm, in particular to Freud's distinction between so-called immature and mature—that is, clitoral versus vaginal—orgasm in adult female sexuality.

In terms of the infant-parent relationship, Stoller assumed a reciprocal exchange between parental expectations and a straightforward identification by the child with its same-sexed parent.[24] By this account, the constitution of each parent's respective gender identity was an important factor in the process of gender acquisition. Money held the same view. Other important factors were "libidinal gratifications and frustrations in the parental child relation, as were many other psychological aspects of pre-oedipal and oedipal development."[25] Against his psychoanalytic training, Stoller, like Money, disputed the privileging of castration anxiety and penis envy to the earliest manifestations of gender identity formation. While very careful not to discredit the explanatory power of such ideas and thus alienate his psychoanalytic colleagues, Stoller justified his critical position by arguing that the formative period of a gendered identity (i.e., Money's critical period) preceded the phallic stage of development as understood in classical psychoanalysis. The development of one's gendered identity was, by his account, an ongoing process of achievement that continued well into late adolescence, building on and overlaying the core identity established during the postnatal critical period. Stoller did not dispute that castration anxiety and penis envy had a role in gendered identity formation, but in his view they impacted on an already established core.

While Stoller was able to develop an account of the male-to-female transsexual, an account of female-to-male transsexuality was beyond his grasp. Stoller suggested that the development of a core gender identity in females was a nontraumatic learning process that preceded any awareness that there were people who were better off than she: that is, people designated male.[26] Against Freud, Stoller argued that a girl had no need to surmount her relationship with her mother to become feminine—assuming of course that daughters have straightforward relationships with their mothers. He also believed that the more feminine the mother, the easier it would be for a girl to create an "appropriate" gender identity:[27] This ease of identification explained, for Stoller, the comparative rarity of female-to-male transsexualism, since in general women were most likely to have primary responsibility for the care of babies and infants.[28] Arguably Stoller's radical departure from Freud with respect to female development compromised his ability to theorize female-to-male transsexualism. Nevertheless he attempted to explain the phenomenon by suggesting that in a few rare instances a family dynamic that consisted of a psychologically absent mother and an excessive physical and emotional closeness between the child and the father *might* be responsible. Perhaps, he suggested, "it may be a hint that too much father and too little mother masculinizes girls."[29] Given that Stoller's own clinical evidence did not support such a neat inversion of his theory, he was forced to concede the idea was entirely speculative. The existence of female-to-male transsexuals did, however, tempt Stoller to postulate that perhaps biological forces were in some way responsible for the formation of corrupted as well as normative gendered identities.

THE "FORCE" IS WITH(IN) YOU

As I suggested earlier, Stoller's separation of identity from role served to endow the concept of gender with enough flexibility to survive the radical epistemological transformations of the subsequent 40 years. The notion of a *core* identity also contributed to the ongoing vitality of gender, since the very term implies some form of essence. At first glance the invocation of biological forces (however mysterious) appears to have provided Stoller with a means to at least partially ground gender in the body. Money had long since achieved this by drawing on Stockard's theory of prenatal critical periods *and* by insisting that learning was a function of biology mediated through the central nervous system. It was arguably more difficult for Stoller to retain an explicit link with the corporeal since he had categorically bracketed "gender" off from "sex" and was far less concerned with any constraints imposed by Cartesian dualism than was Money. Yet despite his claims to the contrary, Stoller did in fact have an awful lot to say about the body and about biology. His attempts to escape the body were surely doomed, given that one's sense of self is always necessarily and inextricably tied to embodiment.

Was it really necessary, he asked, to draw on biology to explain his data? While acknowledging that he was unable to categorically answer in the affirmative, Stoller also acknowledged his own bias: "I cannot believe that biological substrates are as powerless as some learning theorists seem to believe."[30] Stoller's biological forces were amorphous; he described them as forms of energy that possibly emanated (in keeping with the dominant discourses of the day) from the endocrine and central nervous systems. Together they were said to influence the formation of a gendered identity and—in the regular course of events—appropriate gendered behaviors.

In this Stoller was in agreement with Freud's assertion that the role of biological forces was essential though immeasurable in personality development. After Freud, Stoller proposed that, while hidden from both conscious and unconscious awareness and thus not readily identifiable by either the individual patient or by clinicians, such forces nevertheless seemed to provide at least *some* of the "drive energy" for an individual's gender identification. Stoller remained optimistic that developments in neurological and medical research would one day shed light on the matter despite the fact that none had during the 60-odd intervening years. His colleague, endocrinologist Harry Benjamin, who was one of the collaborators on the Gender Identity Project, understood the body to be far more implicated in aberrant forms of identity than most clinicians working in the field at that time were ready to admit. Benjamin proposed that genetic and hormonal processes provided fertile ground for the development of such "disorders": "the soma...has to provide a 'fertile' soil on which the 'basic conflict' must grow in order to become the respective neurosis."[31] Benjamin was already an established expert on transsexualism and part of Stoller's team; thus his ideas would have wielded some considerable influence on Stoller and the other psychiatrists and psychologists at the Gender Identity Research Clinic. Again this points to the futility of Stoller's attempts to even hypothetically leave the body behind as if matter somehow didn't matter.

While transsexualism was the primary focus of Stoller's clinical work, the intersexed proved most useful to his theoretical endeavors. Those he regularly referred to as "experiments of nature" seemed to demonstrate with "unusual clarity" the influence of these forces, in his view.[32] Stoller believed quite sincerely that intersexed individuals provided the opportunity to examine the consequences of removing or manipulating morphological variables in order to determine "in what way [their] absence distorted the process [of normal development]."[33] The reference to clarity here is tenuous given that the examples he offered were individuals whose gendered identifications were not easily accounted for by either their genital anatomy or parental attitudes, as we shall see. With no material evidence to identify what forces might be involved in the process, Stoller consequently had no understanding of their mechanics.

IT'S CHEMICAL, OR PERHAPS IT'S GENETIC . . .

Stoller could do little more than speculate on the particularities of the forces he was invoking, since neither the endocrinological nor neurological research were able to provide any conclusive answers. While he drew on Money's concept of gender, Stoller did not engage with the idea of a neural template. Given the way that Money's template doubled Freudian explanations of gender acquisition, this would seem somewhat remiss, not least because it provided a model of the very thing that Stoller so desperately seemed to be seeking. The best he could do was suggest that one day such a force may be identified as "the algebraic sum of the activities of a number of neuro-anatomical centres and hierarchies of neuro-physiological functions. At present we cannot be so specific."[34] He proposed the following:

A sex-linked genetic biological tendency towards masculinity in males and femininity in females works silently but effectively from foetal existence on, being overlaid after birth by the effects of environment, the biological and environmental working more or less in harmony to produce a preponderance of masculinity in men and femininity in women. In some the biological is stronger and in others weaker.[35]

This is a reiteration, albeit a hesitant one, of Money's gendermap. But Stoller's apparent privileging of any of the physiological signifiers of sex as the ground for masculinity and femininity was an idea that Money refused to entertain. He believed unequivocally that hormones produced by the fetal gonads were responsible for the development of a cognitive schema that coded for both masculinity *and* femininity in any given individual. More importantly, Money steadfastly refused to accept that biological forces had the capacity to *override* the sex of assignment and rearing if the latter were executed "correctly"—that is, unambiguously. An ambivalent gendered identity was, in Money's view, always an effect of uncertainty or prevarication on the part of a child's parents or physicians about the child's gender identity; in other words a direct effect of experience, of environment.

Stoller remained unconvinced. Experimental research on lower mammals offered Stoller the strongest available evidence for his proposition, though he conceded its limitations. Extrapolating research findings from lower animals was, he believed, "exhilarating but dangerous [since] the higher the animal, the more difficult it is to trace the course of a piece of behavior from its biological origins to its ultimate action."[36] "Nature's experiments" were in some ways then a safer option and so became Stoller's privileged subjects through which to understand the process of gender identification. In this he was not alone; he was simply following a long tradition in the medical and sexological sciences, one taken by Freud before him and others contemporarily.

His interest was motivated by the belief that the intersexed offered the opportunity to study "in *purer culture* than is possible in the anatomically and endocrinologically *normal*, the variables responsible for this development."[37] It was so much harder to study the "relative importance of each of these factors in *normals*,"[38] he argued, because of the inherent difficulty in distinguishing the influence of any one factor from the others.[39] As noted in the preceding discussion, to conceive of such an investigation, the intersexed (in all their possible manifestations) had to be understood as the product of some form of defective development. In this too Stoller's work followed a long tradition of medical and scientific studies that have sought to demarcate the boundaries of normality by turning to those whose bodies and/or subjectivities betray some level of anomaly. Pointedly, sexual difference beyond the normative two is never indexed as anomalous or even nonconformist, always "abnormal," "defective," or "unfinished" and most recently, "disordered."

In what can only be described as a most curious turn, the medically trained Stoller invoked the mystical by suggesting that the (mysteriously wayward) variables of sex and gender in the intersexed were "manipulated by *fate*."[40] While Money had endeavored to discredit the somatic signifiers of sex as the ultimate determinants of gender, Stoller accorded biological forces the capacity to override the two most eminent variables in all the accounts of gender acquisition: genital appearance and parental influence.

Individuals who developed gendered identities that contravened their genital appearance and assigned sex offered, for Stoller, proof of the (mysterious) power of biology. In the "Contribution" article Stoller provided two case studies to support this claim. The first concerned a child named Mary, who had presented as an unremarkable female at birth[41] but at the age of 14 had been subject to a physical examination and a chromatin test that found a Y chromosome, a small erectile phallic structure, and hypospadias.[42] Stoller describes her as "active and forceful" in infancy and throughout childhood, completely "lacking in gentleness"—to the despair of her mother,[43] who was described in the text as a "graceful, feminine, neurotically masochistic 'perfect lady.' "[44] The mother reported Mary had always identified with male peers, taken "male roles" in play, and shunned all attempts by family members to make her behave in ways that were in keeping with the prevailing social expectations of a little girl.

Stoller's case notes indicate that there was much more than Mary's behavior at stake: the mother was reported to have invested an extraordinary amount of energy—using bribery, threats, and various other forms of manipulation—to get her to "dress, walk, sit, talk, *think, feel*, and otherwise act as a feminine girl," all to no avail.[45] Given that Stoller himself had opened the space between identity and role in gender—with the former indexed to self-image and the latter to behaviors—the slippage between acting, feeling, and thinking in this passage is rather curious to say the least. Hausman has suggested that it is indicative of an internal inconsistency in Stoller's taxonomic distinction and questions, as I do, how it is possible to "feel oneself to be a role."[46] Stoller offered no explanation for collapsing such crucial elements of identity into the panoply of behavioral variables in either of the texts in which this case study appeared. One might speculate that the slippage was a by-product of *his own* exhilaration at the apparent veracity of tracing an aspect of behavior "from its biological origins to its ultimate action," to borrow from his own ruminations.

Following the diagnosis, Stoller and colleagues decided that the child should be informed of its "proper" sex, not least because s/he appeared to the attending clinicians as "grotesque" in female attire.[47] Against the expectation that the child might have a strong affective response to the news, Stoller reported that it was received in a rather matter of fact way. This "poised and well integrated reaction" affirmed for the clinicians that they had made the correct decision.[48] Mary became Jack and was reported by Stoller to have subsequently gone on to make an easy transition, having known all along that s/he was *really* a boy in spite of all evidence to the contrary.

It is worth noting that Stoller's invocation of biology slipped from the presumption of causality at the level of hormones to land squarely on the Y chromosome without so much as a comment, let alone a rationale. One can only speculate as to why. Perhaps Stoller believed that either or both of these factors were responsible, yet this is never made clear at any point in his discussion. Rather, it seems to have been enough that chromosomes and hormones both register at the level of the internal body.

Evident too is a contradiction between an intersexed diagnosis and the idea that the child had a "proper" or "true" sex. Proper, that is, in the sense of a singular monosex: as male or female. Unlike Money (and many predecessors, peers, and successors), Stoller did recognize the possibility of a hermaphrodite subjectivity, yet he asserted that in this particular case, "pre-consciously, the 'girl' must always have known *his true* gender identity [as authentically male]."[49] This statement highlights a stubborn commitment to dimorphic sexual difference in the face of overwhelming evidence to the contrary. It could equally be argued that this child's identification with its male peers was a response to either (or both) the proscriptive expectations of what was appropriate behavior for girls in the mid-1960s and the mother's desperate attempts to manipulate the child's gender, by fair means or foul. Binarian concepts of sex and gender, as articulated through the semantics of "proper" and "true," better describe the ways in which sex differences were—and continue to be—thought about, rather than reflecting how things actually or necessarily are. Nowhere are the pitfalls of this commitment to binary logic more evident than in the second case study Stoller offered to support his theory of the power of biological forces in gender identity.

Agnes,[50] the subject of Stoller's second case in the "Contribution" article, was presumed by *all* attendant medical professionals to be intersexed. Agnes featured in Stoller's text as an exemplary case of the power of biological forces. She presented with what Stoller described as a very feminine-looking body and demeanor, along with a fully developed penis and scrotum. Having grown up as a boy, Agnes reported that she had spontaneously developed female secondary sex characteristics at puberty. Stoller called in a number of clinicians to assist with Agnes's diagnosis and they eventually settled on Testicular Feminization Syndrome (TFS). The name of this syndrome, which has its origins in endocrinology, has in more recent times been replaced by the term Androgen Insensitivity Syndrome (AIS).[51] The condition is specific to individuals with an XY karyotype and gonadal testes who appear at birth as unremarkably female because—as the contemporary diagnostic term suggests—their cell receptors are unable to respond to testosterone produced by the fetal gonads. The cells instead respond solely to the estrogenic substances produced by the testes.[52] As a result, such persons are born with unremarkable female external genitalia and later develop the secondary sex characteristics associated with female morphology—although they do not menstruate.

It is clear that morphologically Agnes did not and could not fit the criteria for such a diagnosis since s/he had both a fully formed penis and testicles, and the diagnosis is contingent upon female genitalia.[53] But once the diagnosis was made, Stoller and his colleagues demonstrated an unwavering commitment to it. This is evidenced by the fact that Agnes's case was described in the literature as "unique." The only other feasible explanation for Agnes's feminine appearance was that it had been induced by synthetic estrogen intake during adolescence. This explanation was ruled out because it was unthinkable to these clinicians that a child could self-medicate with the correct amounts of estrogen at exactly the right time. Agnes's apparent spontaneous change of sex from male to female (or was it from male to intersex) was less problematic for Stoller than the idea of a life-long feminine identity, which seemed inexplicable, despite the fact that transsexuality was his primary area of expertise. Having painted himself into a conceptual corner, Stoller had but one means of escape:

So we again fall back on the biological "force" to explain the fact that the core gender identity was female, despite the fact that the child was an apparently normal-appearing boy and was also genetically male.[54]

At the age of 20 Agnes was granted the surgery s/he desired: removal of the penis and testes and the creation of an artificial vagina. Post-operatively, the pathologist who examined Agnes's gonadal tissue concluded that her testes had been producing large amounts of estradiol (testicular estrogen) since puberty. Some years later, Agnes revealed to Stoller that s/he had been born male and had indeed self-medicated with his mother's estrogen tablets (stilbestrol) for a prolonged period during adolescence. Agnes's story of spontaneous change of sex at puberty had been a ruse to access surgery. By the late 1960s, sex reassignment surgery was fully legitimated as a means to inscribe a singular bodily sex on those born without one, but access to the same procedures by transsexuals remained constrained by doctors' codes of practice regarding the removal of or interference with healthy functioning organs.[55] And so it was that one of the cases Stoller relied most heavily upon to evidence the power of biological forces in gender identity was, in fact, fraudulent.[56] But rather than being forced to rethink his theory, Stoller simply found another way to use the material Agnes had provided: to support the development of his theory of transsexual "acquistion," a project to which much of his career was dedicated.

What is noteworthy in the case of Agnes is the way in which all of the medical experts interpreted the seemingly incontrovertible—albeit inexplicable—material evidence of Agnes in a way that ensured their assumptions and theoretical investments remained intact. Agnes's diagnosis (TFS) was clearly contraindicated by the presence of a fully formed penis and scrotum. Yet the diagnosis was upheld because of the clinician's disbelief that a child could possibly self-medicate "correctly." Once established, the diagnosis accorded to Agnes did not merely influence the pathologist's findings, it actually determined how he interpreted the fact that Agnes's gonadal tissue contained more than twice the amount of estradiol usually found in an adult male. In reality, Agnes's testes had never produced excessive amounts of estradiol, since the production of normally expected levels of the substance had in fact been supplemented exogenously.

Yet Stoller would not or could not abandon the idea that unknown biological forces were integral to gender identity development. He acknowledged the controversial nature of his proposition to a psychoanalytic audience. While his analyst colleagues might accept the idea that constitutional biological factors influenced sexuality and personality development, he doubted that many would accord such forces the power to override genital appearance and parental influence. Despite placing himself in what we might—tongue in cheek—call a conflicted position with respect to his own colleagues, Stoller believed that Freud had been correct to assert that "reproduction [was] the fundamental purpose behind all sexual behavior," even that with no apparent connection to the libidinal.[57] He also agreed with Freud that masculinity, femininity, and sexuality were all fundamentally organic.

In the case of [constitutional] bisexuality, we can see that the brain is not the *tabula rasa* some allege. While the newborn presents with a most malleable central nervous system upon which the environment writes, we cannot say that the central nervous system is neutral or neuter.[58]

Stoller's invocation of biology slipped all over (and through) the body: from hormones to chromosomes, to the central nervous system, neurons, and back. While readily admitting that he had no idea of what form such forces might take, Stoller steadfastly refused to relinquish a role for them in gender. This explains in part the slippage to which I refer, for it is surely difficult to attribute causality to a phenomenon for which you can find no definitive supporting evidence.

More importantly, two other reasons account for the slippage. The first of these was a consequence of Stoller's insistence on bracketing sex from gender in the Cartesian tradition. Conceptualizing the mind and body as distinct and separate spheres proved impossible for Stoller to sustain, not least because the dominant medico-psychiatric understanding of transsexualism—which was, after all, Stoller's primary theoretical project—proposes a dissonant relation between one's sense of self and one's embodied self. Equally important was Stoller's agreement with and commitment to Freud's belief that gender had a constitutional basis. This may explain why Stoller did not (or perhaps could not) take up Money's hypothesis of a neural template that coded for both masculinity and femininity *and* androgyny, since Money rejected the idea of gender being constitutional on the one hand, and he considered Frued's theory of identification to be a partial account of gender acquisition on the other.

On The Matter of Hermaphrodite Subjectivity

While Stoller was one of the few mid-twentieth-century clinicians to acknowledge the possibility of a hermaphroditic gender identity, he was reluctant to concede that the bearer of such an identity could be well adjusted—in other words, psychologically healthy. In a paper entitled "Gender-Role Change in Intersexed Patients," Stoller challenged a growing number of reports that claimed to refute Money's assertions that gender identity in hermaphrodite individuals was fixed early in life and that subsequent attempts at reassignment were fraught with danger for the individual.[59] The reports Stoller referred to represented case reports of intersex children and adults whose transition from one gender to the other following reassignment had seemed, on the face of it, unproblematic. What these reports suggested was that the first few months of a child's life were not quite as important for gendered identities as Money had claimed.

What Stoller found after reviewing the evidence was that each case was marked by a degree of uncertainty about the child's gender during its formative years. Little wonder then that such individuals could make a successful transition or that clinicians were able to report positive outcomes. Persons who unequivocally believed they were male or female would always consider themselves as such. But for persons who believed themselves to be both male and female—or neither—a successful transition from ambiguity to "one of the *two usual* genders" was entirely possible.[60] Stoller suggested that in such cases, "the capacity to shift gender role was as much an unalterable part of the [person's] identity as was the inability to shift [by] *normals*."[61] Such persons constituted, for Stoller, a third gender with a hermaphroditic identity.

The reference to male and female as the "usual genders" brings with it some acknowledgement of multiplicity—as one would expect in the context of a discussion about hermaphroditic identity. Yet there is an implicit refusal in Stoller's work that anyone would wish to—or indeed could—actually migrate from a masculine or feminine gender toward a hermaphroditic one. As is the case with transsexual reassignment, successful transition is framed in terms of a unidirectional movement between the two usual genders. Stoller's subsequent writings framed the issue of transition in terms of movement between "one of only two *possible* sexes."[62] The slippage between gender and sex in this statement is curious, since Stoller had clearly defined sex as a referent for the materiality of bodies. More important, however, is the obvious discordance between Stoller's expression of what was possible in sex and his knowledge of the multiplicity of sexual variation. Within the context of this discussion Stoller effectively rendered the intersexed outside of the species *homo sapiens* by stating that they were in "that peculiar position of agreeing with all the world that there are ... *only two* sexes, while [they] belong to neither."[63]

Stoller elaborated what he believed were the necessary conditions for a third-gender identity to manifest. Effectively his explanation was a clean inversion of Money's schema of the necessary conditions for the establishment of an *un*ambiguous gender identity. Ambiguous-appearing genitals lead to parental uncertainty regarding children's "proper" anatomical sex. As a result, parents treat such children ambiguously and socialize them accordingly. This in turn results in the defective processing of parental attitudes by the children, and so an incongruous gender identification results.[64] Little wonder Stoller considered it extremely unlikely for someone with such an identity to be psychologically well and healthy, for this explanation drips with failure. Money steadfastly refused even the possibility—let alone the legitimacy—of a hermaphroditic gender identity. That was because in his view the constructs of masculinity and femininity—while admittedly stereotyped and idealized—were ubiquitous, which meant that the only viable alternative to masculinity was femininity (and vice versa), *not* androgyny.[65]

Yet while a hermaphroditic subjectivity did fall within the realm of possibility for Stoller, he was barely able to accord such people their full humanity. They had, in his view, three options: they could wait for the day when they could be "fixed so that [they] could belong" or,

bow to [their] fate of *not really belonging to the human race*; or [make] the best of both worlds, as seems to occur in those rare hermaphrodites who appear to live comfortably in alternating genders.[66]

My reading of the options Stoller is offering here to those who fell into his third sex (supplemental) category is one of "conform or (likely) be damned." Conformity in this context was measurable by degree. Full conformity required that one be "fixed" or rather one's body be fixed, reconfigured to approximate maleness or femaleness by surgical and chemical means; fixed also in the sense of being stabilized.[67]

Stoller betrayed his commitment to the binarian framework of dimorphic sexual difference that renders two sexes and consequently two genders as mutually exclusive oppositional types. While alternating between these two types may render an individual human, to refuse both the first and third of the former options renders the refuser nonhuman: outside of the species human. Stoller did not indicate to what species they might instead belong, although one may assume it would be akin to the species "monster."

"PREPOSTEROUS DIGRESSIONS"

In order to talk about hermaphrodites at all requires some recognition of the material reality that humans come in more than two varieties. In light of that, to claim that there are only two *possible* sexes not only betrays a commitment to what *ought* to be, rather than what *is*, it belies the material evidence. The understanding that sexual differentiation produces an array of human types is constantly subsumed within a medical discourse that understands sex through a reproductive paradigm. This is how and why the idea that female *or* male are the only "natural" conditions of the human body is continually reinvented.[68] Trying to capture all bodies and subjectivities in these terms appears to be motivated, in Robyn Weigman's words, by the "violently ironic hope of returning [nondimorphic] bodies to 'nature.' "[69]

This begs the question posed by Foucault in the memoirs of Herculine Barbin: "Do we *truly* need a true sex," when surely all that really matters is "the reality of the body and the intensity of its pleasures."[70] Money and colleagues did go some way toward displacing the notion of a "true" single sex hidden by an ambiguous body when they offered the idea of a "best" sex. Yet the former continued—as it does to this day—to underpin medical and many cultural discourses on differently sexed bodies. The idea that every*body* is the bearer of a single sex has been with us for almost two centuries now.[71] And while I would suggest it is unlikely to hold up for another two centuries, what is likely is that Foucault's question will remain in the affirmative for as long as we continue to invest in the binary logic of dimorphic sexual difference and base sexual identities on the object of desire.

THE SEX/GENDER SPLIT

Now to Stoller's third and best-known intervention in gender theory: the conceptual splitting of gender from sex. The first two interventions he made—splitting gender identity from role, and coining the outcome of Money's postnatal critical period as "core" gender identity—can be seen as preparatory steps for the third. For Stoller the sex/gender split was the theoretical move that allowed him to focus more keenly on the role that postnatal environmental factors played in both normal and aberrant gender identifications. That he was unable to break the link between sex and gender is a point that seemed to escape many of those who appropriated the term from sexology (in spite of their own contributions to gender's dynamism).

Stoller, as we know, eschewed the term *sex* because of its biological connotations and as with *sexuality* because of the array of meanings it had accrued. Gender offered significantly more promise since it came without a raft of conceptual baggage. More importantly, Stoller was able to wrest it free from the messy realities of carnality and the flesh. Gender allowed Stoller to discuss, in isolation, psychological phenomena such as thoughts, behavior, and personality. As for sex, while he claimed to have little to say about it, sex was everywhere in his treatise on gender. For the purposes of his research, considering sex and gender as separate orders of data allowed Stoller to demonstrate that there was no necessary one-to-one relation between them. He wanted to show that in some instances the two functioned completely independently, despite appearing synonymous and despite their "inevitable entanglement."[72] So just as splitting gender identity out from gender role had a theoretical utility for Stoller, so did the splitting of gender from sex.

This third intervention into the theory of gender represented a definitive moment in the history of the concept, one that would have ramifications far exceeding what was imaginable at that time. Stoller's reformulation of gender and sex proved particularly useful to a burgeoning feminism—and to social theory more generally—because it established a dichotomous relation between the two terms that allowed for analyses of social and political inequalities between men and women that were free from the constraints (in theory at least) of biological determinism. Stoller's work had an added credibility because he rehabilitated from Freudian psychoanalysis a nonconflict-ual feminine identity during infant and early childhood development. While the terms of the debate have shifted considerably over the past 40 years, the sex/gender dichotomy has become as naturalized as gender itself in popular discourse, in school and university curricula all over the English-speaking world—and beyond. The efficacy of the split continues to be hotly debated in feminist, cultural, and sexuality studies yet remains, for the most part, assumed all the same.[73]

Before wrapping up this discussion I want to return to John Money, specifically his ongoing engagement with those who have found the term *gender* useful over the past 40 or so years. For Money, gender acquisition hinged on the idea that learning was a function of biology, since it involved neural pathways mediated by the central nervous system. He remained highly critical of the reductionism that rendered sex the property of nature and gender that of nurture (although with respect to Stoller he showed especially good grace—not a trait for which Money was well known when it came to those whose theo-retical commitments were different from his). As discussed, Money appropriated the concept of a critical period from embryology to bridge the gaping chasm that is the nature/nurture divide. While in many quarters it is a received wisdom that feminist analyses were first responsible for developing critiques of the sex/gender distinction, Money's ongoing engagement—from the outset—needs to be recog-nized irrespective of whether he was responded to, or even heard. Money lamented the sex/gender split and its effect but recognized at the same time that it was incredibly useful to a wide constituency. In his view it clearly "filled a linguistic void and satisfied a conceptual need of many people—not however, the same conceptual need for which I framed the definition . . . people adopted the term and gave it their own definition."[74]

While Money made clear that this was an entirely regrettable con-ceptual turn, one that effectively bastardized gender, the fact that it did undergo such a significant transformation is indicative of its power and its dynamism. Money originally deployed gender to replace the verbosity of phrases he was using in the absence of a singular term to reference social inscription as a sexed being. Gender was conceptual-ized as an umbrella term that incorporated the body and the erotic aspects of sexed subjectivity. Thus sex, gender, and sexuality were woven in a tight triadic relation. It was however a hierarchical rela-tion with gender clearly at the zenith (try thinking about sexuality without reference to gender). In addition, its relation to the body is equally hierarchical under these terms, since where there is a mismatch between identity and morphology the body must always give way to the psyche, to identity, to gender.

What was so regrettable for Money was the fact that relegating sexual practices to the category of sex, as Stoller had done, effectively reinstated

the metaphysical partitioning of body and mind. Sex was ceded to biology. Gender was ceded to psychology and social science. The ancient regime was restored.[75]

Money remained insistent that sex and gender were neither synonyms nor antonyms, even though they were often used as such. In defining sex as what you are born with (male or female), and gender as what you acquire, "gender becomes sex without the dirty and carnal part that belongs to the genitalia *of reproduction*."[76] Indeed, once sexuality was relegated to biology through sex, gender was no longer able to contain desire.

CONCLUSION

Robert Stoller's interventions had a direct effect on the way in which gender came to be used outside of sexology. While his conceptual turn opened up what could be done with gender theoretically (and indeed what *was* done with it), at the same time the sex/gender split constrained how to think about gender. Once stripped of all connotations to sex and the flesh, gender was ready to be harnessed for its political utility by the women's movement in the early 1970s. Stoller's work proved to be especially appealing to an emergent second-wave feminism. Its appeal was twofold: first it recovered a nonconflictual feminine identity from psychoanalytic precepts, and second, gender as a sphere separate *from* sex allowed physical differences between men and women to be set aside in the fight for equality. Theorizing gender as a purely social artifact was designed to avoid the pitfalls of the reductive biological analyses that had historically been invoked to justify Othering, whether through racism, homophobia, or the subordination of women.

When the category of sex became the point of departure, the sexed body was deemed to be somehow above (or beyond) critique. Subsequently one of the central concerns in feminist theory has been to try to chart a space between sex and gender. This has served to reinforce the idea that sex represents the raw material for gender to work upon while the latter represents the "more fully elaborated—and rigidly dichotomized—social production and reproduction of male and female identities and behaviors."[77] The gender identity paradigm ultimately locked feminist debates into a binary logic that theorists continue to try to wrest free of to this day.[78] At the same time, the (apparent) discovery of the problems inherent in the split served to energize an entire industry within feminist theorizing of the body and (dimorphic) sexual difference.

CHAPTER 3

FEMINIST ENCOUNTERS
WITH GENDER

INTRODUCTION

That gender is indispensable to feminist theorizing—both as an object
of analysis and an analytical tool—seems so self-evident that it surely
goes without saying. Yet it is precisely because gender has achieved
that status that its historical legacy is worth examining. It bears repeat-
ing that gender's history as an ontological category is very specific and
relatively recent in English, and it is intricately linked to technological developments and political projects. In this chapter I continue the
conceptual history of gender by exploring the various ways that feminist scholars engaged with the work of Money and of Stoller over
the course of the 1970s. At its heart this chapter considers second-
wave feminism's engagement with the intersexed via gender.[1] That
has determined my selection of material in the following pages. From
the moment that feminists turned to sexology for evidence and for
concepts with which to refute the sexism so inherent in the social theory of the day, that engagement has had particular effects for feminist
theorizing *and* for the material reality of the intersexed.

The contributions of feminists to the concept of gender are extensive and by now well documented. The institutionalization of gender
studies in the academy (through women's studies) is as much a testament to the efficacy of those interventions as it is to gender's import
as a conceptual device. Feminism's engagement with gender is one
important episode in a larger history of the concept. While it is one of
a number of episodes, over the past 25 years or so, gender has often
been attributed to feminism as though the term had no history outside

of that tradition. In fact it has become something of a received feminist wisdom that gender was the invention of feminism.[2] It seems that feminists began to embrace the concept of gender as their own contribution to discourse around the time that gender's earlier association with sexology began to fade into the background.[3]

While feminists offered strong critiques of the binary logic of the nature/culture dichotomy, the historical link between the category of sex and the category of nature failed to make the agenda of early second-wave analyses.[4] Understandings of the term "sex" consolidated around the idea that it was the biological basis upon which cultural gender overlaid.[5] In effect, sex—like nature—was rendered passive and oppositional to the active category of cultural gender. The inescapability of sex was assumed, as was the body's apparent immutability. As a result the essentialism inherent in the categories man and woman and male and female was left unexamined. Indeed, recourse to an essential woman-ness lay at the heart of the reification of the sign "Woman." The category "sex" remained, by and large, above (or beyond) critique for many years in feminist theorizing, for considerably longer than was the case with gender.

Stoller's *Sex and Gender* was widely received outside of psychoanalytic circles, most particularly by feminists in the social sciences. The sex/gender split provided a nascent women's liberation movement with a powerful intellectual basis upon which to repudiate biological determinism and assert demands for sexual equality."[6] Early feminist scholars who took up Stoller's concept of gender assumed a mind/body relation in the tradition of Cartesian dualism. Sex was grounded in and through the body, whereas gender was equated with the mind, the psyche, and the social. This analysis made it possible to argue that the liberation of women—and men—was achievable through the reorganization of social institutions and the reeducation of sexual subjects. Gender offered so much promise to feminism precisely because it was understood at one level to be malleable and thus amenable to change. The idea that gender was a culturally inscribed, learned attribute made possible the idea that what was learned might well be unlearned or in fact replaced by something altogether different.

This understanding of the sex/gender distinction as a distinction between the body and consciousness necessarily committed its proponents to a Cartesian dualist idealism.[7] John Money had argued strongly against such a position.[8] He had long championed the idea that sex was but one element of gender rather than its opposite.

Nevertheless, Money's research was useful to feminism because it offered empirical evidence that it was possible (for the intersexed) to be socialized into a gender. That idea was seized upon to demonstrate that women's subordinated sociocultural, political, and economic status was neither natural nor inevitable. Instead it was quite literally produced by culture—itself a production.

Some of the first feminists to use gender as a conceptual device during the 1970s produced texts that were foundational to the feminist canon. The conceptual work of Kate Millett and Germaine Greer, for example, influenced much of the theorizing—and politicizing—that followed in their collective wake. While most of the following discussion turns on the work of feminist scholars in the social sciences, I begin with the work of Millett and Greer, both literary scholars. Of particular interest to this chapter is the way that gender migrated across to academic feminism from sexology, and the various ways that the intersexed were invoked in feminist scholarship.

The focus is directed toward sociology, anthropology, and psychology since all share the same object of analysis—social relations. It is clear from the feminist literature that ideas from each of these fields informed and were informed by one another, as evidenced by the number of interdisciplinary feminist anthologies that appeared during the 1970s. It is also the case that sociology and anthropology share some methodological and theoretical frameworks while psychology for its part has a particular interest in "the masculine" and "the feminine," and in identity and personality formation. My choice of discipline was also influenced by the fact that Money was heavily informed by anthropology and sociology, and psychology was the discipline of his earliest training.[9] This triangulation of thought marked his work from the outset, so it seems fitting for a genealogy of gender to follow similar lines.

I am also interested in the precise ways in which gender was understood within feminism, since it is clear that the concept did not land easily or quietly in feminist thought. Gender was the subject of enormous debate for the best part of a decade, its meanings rigorously contested within and outside of feminist scholarship as was its purported use value to feminism. Little wonder that traces of conceptual confusion run through many of the feminist analyses of the period. Terms such as *sex role* and *sexual identity* continued to be widely used and maintained a strong currency well into the 1980s. Although *gender* began to appear in more and more titles of articles and book chapters throughout the 1970s, reference to the term in a title offered no guarantee that the concept would be used within the text.[10]

Notwithstanding the scholarship of those whose work features in the following pages, many influential feminist scholars did not use the term gender at all during the 1970s. Certainly as a concept gender has become integral to the way that English speakers understand themselves today—individually, socially, and politically. Yet gender's absence in the important early works of figures such as Sandra Bem, Betty Friedan, Sherry Ortner, and Adrienne Rich did nothing to diminish the potency of their respective analyses.[11] That scholarship, along with some of the radical feminist treatises,[12] relied instead upon older terms such as sex role and sexual identity to do the work that has since become gender's (almost) exclusive preserve.[13]

Those who first picked up gender from sexology through the work of Money and Stoller tended to do so without examining the assumptions underpinning many of their claims. As I demonstrate, while the intersexed served the antideterminist project of feminism well, the relation was not reciprocal. But by mid-decade a handful of feminist critiques of Money's theories and methodologies began to surface. Some took aim at Money's refusal to surrender the body *in* gender, accusing him of purveying a biological determinism dressed up in cultural clothing. Others took issue with Money's manipulation of language, still others with the way his ideas served to reinforce sex stereotypes. Just one took aim at Money's willingness to surrender the bodies of the intersexed to gender. Together they represent a second level of engagement with the work of Money. As will become clear, most of these critiques stopped short of a full engagement with the implications of ICM because the emphasis remained on the constructed nature of gender, be it through language, theory, or social roles. The literal construction of sex went unnoticed.

John Money consistently engaged with feminism for the best part of three decades in what became, over time, a one-way conversation. Indeed the index of one of his most popular early texts, *Man and Woman, Boy and Girl* (published in 1972), references more than 50 items as "quotable material" for Women's Liberation.[14] Was this an attempt on the part of Money to frame the terms of feminist debates? Perhaps, but ultimately his influence was limited because of his inability to stem the tide of popularity enjoyed by a gender decoupled from sex. Nonetheless particular ideas of Money that proved highly influential and have since become axiomatic have become so in part because of the enthusiasm with which feminism took them up.

As well as being interested in how precisely feminists engaged with the concept of gender, I was also interested in how they engaged with the intersexed—given the latter's status as evidence base. What is striking in the literature is a certain ambivalence on the part of feminist scholars toward the intersexed. This ambivalence manifests in all sorts of ways, but ultimately it serves to reinforce the abject status of the latter. There was very little ado about the way the intersexed were socialized into a gender nor the rigor with which they were "assisted" to do so.

GENDER MEETS FEMINISM

Among the very first feminists to use gender and draw directly from the sexual sciences were literary scholars Germaine Greer[15] and Kate Millett.[16] Australian born, UK based, agent-provocateur, and sex radical, Germaine Greer published *The Female Eunuch* in 1970. Like many of her feminist sisters, Greer was suspicious of the agenda of the medical and physical sciences and questioned whose interests were being served by the relentless exaggeration of differences between the sexes. For Greer,

the dogmatism of science expresses the status quo as the ineluctable result of law.... The new assumption behind the discussion of the body is that everything that we may observe *could be otherwise*.[17]

Greer urged women to question the most basic of assumptions about what constituted feminine "normality". This she believed was vital for the successful liberation of women and necessary for expanding the possibilities of different ways of knowing. Yet despite Greer's distrust of science, it was to Stoller she turned to support her argument that dimorphic sexual difference had no mandate in biology. It is noteworthy that the chapter entitled "Gender" in *The Female Eunuch* was almost exclusively devoted to a discussion of chromosomal variation, that is, variation beyond the XX and XY configurations that signify femaleness and maleness. In this way she foreshadowed the current context where genetic explanations are de rigueur in the sexual sciences.

Variation was invoked by Greer to challenge the apparent naturalness of sexual difference to the order of two. She sought to discredit the idea of dichotomous sex by highlighting sexual diversity across animal and plant species. With respect to human diversity, Greer's interpretive lens was considerably narrower. She referred to girls with well-developed clitorises and boys with genitals that were "underdeveloped...deformed or hidden."[18] Citing Stoller, Greer suggested that medical investigations could establish the correct sex of such individuals and cosmetic surgery would resolve "some of these difficulties."[19] So Greer unwittingly reinforced the very thing she was concerned to dismantle by not attending to the fact that those she referred to as girls and boys were being surgically shoehorned into a gender.[20] The inescapability of the binary framework undermined her capacity to dismantle the idea of dichotomous sex (as gender). What are we to make then of Greer's declaration that everything that could be observed about the body "could be otherwise"?

As part of her larger project, Greer sought to discredit the idea of male superiority by pointing to the vulnerability of the Y chromosome and the plethora of medical conditions associated with it, that is, medical conditions associated with having the condition of maleness:

Along with his maleness, the fetus then inherits a number of weaknesses which are called sex-linked, because they result from genes found only in the Y-chromosome [or from] mutant gene[s] in the X-chromosome which the Y-chromosome cannot suppress, . . . transmitted by females, but only effective in males.[21]

While her argument could not dismantle dichotomous sex, I would suggest that Greer was considerably more successful at "observing otherwise, the sexual hierarchy." By pinning her analysis on the fragility of the Y-chromosome, she offered a convincing account that there was no support for male superiority in nature.

Greer's distinction between sex and gender differed from that of most of her contemporaries (as will become clear), in that sex referred exclusively to erotic behavior and sexual practices. Gender—purged of its connection to the erotic—still retained a strong connection to the body.[22] For Greer, "whatever else we are or may pretend to be, we are certainly our bodies."[23]

Kate Millett's highly influential text, *Sexual Politics*, offered an analysis of the production of knowledge as a mechanism for justifying and maintaining women's subordination.[24] Her contribution to feminism (and to the social sciences more generally) was significant for the way that it explicitly promoted the development of social theory from the position of Other. Millett turned to the work of Money and Stoller to support her argument that gender was a cultural artifact and that social arrangements under patriarchy had their basis in cultural imperatives and so were not inevitable. Unlike Greer, Millett placed considerable faith in science. She considered that distinctions made between the sexes by the physical sciences were considerably more valid—and thus more credible—than those promoted by the social sciences. Science offered "clear, specific, measurable and neutral" theories, whereas those produced by the social sciences were "vague, amorphous [and] often quasi-religious" in her view.[25] So confident was Millett of the capacity of the physical and biological sciences to be objective that she declared,

Important new research not only suggests that the possibilities of innate temperamental differences seem more remote than ever but even raises questions as to the validity and permanence of psycho-sexual identity [and so] gives fairly concrete positive evidence of the overwhelmingly cultural character of gender, i.e. personality structure in terms of sexual category.[26]

Millett's faith in science was such that she offered her wholehearted endorsement of the idea that "gender role is determined by postnatal forces, regardless of the anatomy and physiology of the external genitalia" despite acknowledging the decided lack of clear-cut evidence.[27] A gendered identity was the most primary identity of every human being—the first, the most permanent and pervasive. As proof, Millett pointed to the sexological evidence that suggested it was easier to perform sex change surgery on intersexed people given an "erroneous" gender assignment than it was to undo a lifetime of socializing into a gender.

The idea that the bodies of the intersexed were more malleable than psychosocial identity pervaded early feminist notions of mind/body relations. Money's and Stoller's idea that the bodily morphology of hermaphrodites was more readily altered (through surgery) than was an established psychosocial identity was accepted at face value. At the same time biological sex—that is, the biological sex of everybody else—was understood as immutable. The resultant tension went unrecognized by the early feminist proponents of gender.

FEMINIST SOCIOLOGY

The following discussion traces gender's (uneasy) settlement into feminist sociology. A review of the sociological literature of the 1970s indicates that, as with other disciplines, gender did not integrate easily or rapidly into theory despite being used as early as 1970. While sociology has been credited with mainstreaming the concept, a specific sociology of gender did not begin to consolidate until the end of the 1970s.[28] It developed rather slowly from courses on sex roles that began to be taught in North American universities from the late 1960s onward.[29]. As sociology departments began to hire and promote increasing numbers of women academics during the late sixties and early seventies, there was an attendant growth in the number of "sex role" courses offered. This trend was evident across a variety of disciplines in the social sciences and humanities and reflected the continued hegemonic status of Parsonian thought in social theory.[30]

Because so little attention had been paid to women's issues historically, there was of course a huge gap in the sociological literature. That gap was filled for a time with material on sex differences from psychoanalysis, psychology, anthropology, and sexology. Course conveners also drew on the early manifestos, anthologies, and ethnographies of the women's movement. The widely cited Roszak and Roszak collection is one such example including as it does radical feminist material by the Redstockings, Robin Morgan, and Valerie Solanis.[31] Texts such as these are indicative of the reciprocal relation of the women's movement to the academy, informing as well as being informed by it.

Such divergent sources provided the mainstay of teaching material on North American campuses until the arrival of so-called bona fide sociology texts dealing specifically with sex and gender. When those texts arrived, they continued to include contributions from other disciplines. While it has been claimed that this was a specifically feminist tendency toward cooperative scholarship, that cooperation sat very well with the interdisciplinary traditions of the social sciences.

Parsonian role theory, as I discussed in Chapter 1, had dominated the social sciences since the mid-1950s; however, over the course of the 1960s alternative theories began to make some inroads, providing new directions for the field. Tracing sociology back through the twentieth century, feminist critics argued that the lack of attention paid to women in most sociological analyses was a direct result of masculinist commitments to the apparently important stuff of social life. Women's activities had historically been deemed unworthy of scientific enterprise, as Anne Oakley discovered when she first proposed undertaking a sociological analysis of housework.

Increasing numbers of feminists entering sociology resulted in a corresponding increase in qualitative research. Yet it was not until the mid-1970s that the impact of feminist analyses really began to show. While the subordination of women had long been on the agenda, it had generally been ignored by male sociologists. But things began to change. In practical terms, it became increasingly difficult for the editorial boards of journals to continue to dismiss or ignore articles on women's issues, and as a result, such issues began to gain some credibility within the academy, opening the work up to a wider academic constituency.[32]

The mid-1970s represents something of a watershed in sociological history as the development of a specifically feminist perspective offered an important contribution to the sociology of knowledge.[33] This led to a whole range of new research topics, including the distribution of economic and occupational opportunities, the impact of sexual stratification on quality of life, and the sexism that infused social theory and pedagogy. The focus on each of these areas was deemed necessary in determining the shape of a social inquiry that would truly reflect women's lived experiences.

We find one of the first references to gender in a sociological text in Harriet Holter's *Sex Roles and Social Structure*. Holter was an Oslo-based sociologist who drew heavily on the psychological and sociological literature from North America. Her empirical account of patterns of "sex role differentiation in Norwegian society" identified some of the processes she believed were intrinsic to it.[34] While Holter used the term gender liberally, there were no direct references to either Stoller or Money in her text. Holter framed corporeal sex in terms of "sex differentiation" and as distinct from "the relationships between men and women" (as gender).[35] Yet biology was no passive entity acted upon by culture in this account. Holter was keenly aware of biology's involvement in a much larger relation. For her the reason that biological traits were not sufficient in themselves to account for gender differences was because biology always operated "in interaction with social, economic and technological factors."[36] This is much the same argument that Money would put forth seven years later in *Sexual Signatures*.

Jessie Bernard's *Women and the Public Interest* was another of the very earliest sociological feminist analyses to deploy the term gender.[37] Well known for her later work on the institution of marriage, Bernard here offered an analysis of women's relation to public policy that highlighted inherent conflicts between women's interests and the public interest. For Bernard, gender relations were a cultural and therefore artificial phenomenon that could—and must— be revolutionized if they were to properly serve contemporary life. As she noted, "the kind of life we lead in this day and age [is] a life that demands all the talents the human species can muster from its genetic pool, whatever the sex of the body which harbours them."[38] Although, as we shall see, Bernard didn't quite have every*body* in mind.

Many feminists who turned to sexology used Money's hermaphrodite research—often read through Stoller's *Sex and Gender*—and that research provided the evidence base for Bernard to emphasize the truly social and *acquired* nature of gender. Her use of Stoller was somewhat more idiosyncratic. In a strange twist of *his* logic, Bernard drew on

Stoller's work to argue that while individuals with "errors of the body" served to highlight "some of the anomalies possible in the sphere of sexuality...there is no overlap between male and female populations. They are categorically different."[39]

Such an interpretation of Stoller's work illustrates the kind of ambivalent relation to the intersexed that I referred to earlier. The relative rarity of the intersexed demonstrated to Bernard on the one hand that biological factors in gender warranted no further consideration. On the other hand—and at the same time—their rarity meant that the intersexed were of no value as the subjects of sociological research:

> Although they teach us a great deal about the normal aspects of sex and gender, they cannot be invoked in sociological analyses. Further discussion would distort the picture by overemphasizing rare exceptions.[40]

I would beg to differ. Further engagement might have led Bernard to discover that sexual difference was not quite as clear-cut as she believed it to be. In fact, such a rigid model of dimorphic sexual difference— as utterly and mutually exclusive—would surely fail to hold. Not all her contemporaries were quite as uncompromising. Ann Oakley, educated at Oxford University, was another important feminist scholar to employ the term gender very early on. Oakley's work was widely cited by those North American feminists who picked up the term.[41] Parsonian functionalism had held sway over sociology for almost three decades by the time Oakley published. She and her contemporaries were certainly involved in bringing that era to a close, yet at the same time their ideas were inflected with Parson's role theory. Indeed, Oakley and other feminist sociologists are said to have given Parsonian functionalism a new lease on life.[42] This is hardly surprising, since one key focus of feminist analyses was the oppressive nature of social roles organized by sex. Meanwhile, gender identity slipped under the analytical radar so to speak, and as with sex it seemed for a time beyond critique.

Like many of her contemporaries, Oakley was concerned with developing and articulating theories of masculinity and femininity alternative to those that dominated the social sciences. She too resorted to concepts that circulated throughout the physical and biological sciences. Money's work was especially useful to Oakley; she cited it extensively and illustrations of fetal differentiation that featured in many of his texts appeared in hers. Indeed, she reproduced many of his ideas almost verbatim. Her *Sex, Gender and Society* would prove an important vehicle for the transmission of Money's research and theories of gender acquisition into feminism.[43]

Money's findings convinced Oakley that the role of biology in determining a "normal" individual's gendered identity was minimal, since any predisposition toward a male or a female identity could be "decisively and ineradicably" overridden by cultural learning. The evidence, she said, was provided by researchers "in the field of hermaphroditic disorders and problems of gender identity [who] seem very impressed by the power of culture to ignore biology altogether."[44] Unlike Bernard, Oakley had a different view of the usefulness of the intersexed to sociological research:

There are many points at which the study of intersexuals throws light on the nature-nurture controversy, and they are too valuable to be ignored. For example, intersexed patients reared as females have strong feminine fantasy lives and characteristically feminine erotic inclinations despite the virtually total absence of female hormones.[45]

The feminine fantasy lives and erotic inclinations, of which she wrote in this passage, were constituted by "romantic courtship, marriage and heterosexual erotic play."[46]

For Oakley, inequality between the sexes was a consequence of males and females being taught from birth onward to behave differently and expect different social behavior from one another. Yet at no point did she consider the implications of her analysis for her evidence base. Oakley's understandings of gender and the (female) body read as if they were those of Money. His work appeared to decouple gender from the body by demonstrating that gendered behaviors were not necessarily determined by one's bodily form. Oakley wrote:

Biological sex can be and often is reconstructed to allow the individual to play his or her gender role without confusion and risk of social ridicule. Here it is biology that is *plastic in the literal sense and altered to conform with identity: not identity that is shaped by biology.*[47]

So while gender identity was clearly plastic, sex was not. But Oakley was not referring to just anyone's sex, she was referring solely to the sex of the intersexed. Like many of her contemporaries she did not make a connection between the medical practices she referred to and the historical use of genital surgery such as clitoridectomy as a behavioral modification "tool" for unruly women and girls.

Studies of homosexuals and transsexuals also provided valuable sources of data for understanding gender acquisition, in Oakley's view. Again she reiterated Money, this time with reference to his understanding of same-sex desire as a cross-coding of gender. Careful to sidestep any confusion over what her terms were, Oakley defined intersex as a biological condition, and homosexuality and transsexuality as disorders of gender, that is "disorders in the social-cultural acquisition of gender role and gender identity."[48] Remember that Money's account of sexuality was always haunted by the specter of disorder because binary gender was the interpretive frame for a bipolar model of sexuality. This meant that desire for men was straightforwardly feminine whether experienced by men or by women, and desire for women was masculine no matter who the desirer was (the very possibilities of which complicated matters in themselves). Yet it was precisely this knotting of gender to (women's) sexuality that Oakley wanted to unravel.

Nonetheless, Money's work was clearly of great value to Oakley on a number of levels, as was Stoller's reconfigured gender—as a cultural artifact. For Oakley the distinction between it and sex was important since "the constancy of sex must be admitted, but so also must the variability of gender."[49] The same applied the distinction between "male" and "female" on the one hand and "masculine" and "feminine" on the other. The apparent contradiction in this seemingly straightforward inversion of immutable sex and variable gender with plastic sex and intractable gender was not, upon closer inspection, a contradiction at all. Sex was assumed to be constant in males and females, gender variable in men and women, girls and boys, but vice versa in the intersexed.

By disentangling gender from sex, Oakley believed she would be able to counter the dogmatism of the humanities "with insight and . . . separate value-judgements from statements of fact."[50] Yet by reiterating both Money's and Stoller's claims in an uncritical way, Oakley failed to address the inherent contradictions that resulted in her own. Ultimately her challenge to the existing dogma of the social sciences fell short because her ideas reinforced the equally dogmatic assertions of a different tradition. For Money, neither gender nor sex were inevitable on one level, since each could be manipulated by the scalpel and/or by acculturation. And yet both were saturated with inevitability at another level, since even at its most plastic, the body of which Oakley spoke was constrained by the either/or proposition that is sex, as understood by Money, his predecessors, and those who found his work useful to their own projects.

FEMINIST PSYCHOLOGY

Since psychology was the discipline in which Money originally trained, it is not unreasonable to expect that feminist psychologists would have been among the first to adopt the term gender. Yet this does not appear to be the case. The trend in psychology during the 1970s echoed that of sociology and anthropology as feminist scholars relied on Stoller's conceptual reformulation and Money's evidence base. In this section I turn to the work of Nancy Chodorow, Dorothy Dinnerstein, Dorothy Ullian, and Rhoda Unger.[51] Chodorow's academic background was sociology but her work is included here because she relied so heavily on a psychoanalytic framework and indeed had a dual career as a psychoanalyst and an academic.

While much of the feminist scholarship undertaken by sociologists and anthropologists concerned issues of social roles and structural dynamics, in psychology issues of identity formation and personality development were, unsurprisingly, prominent. Tensions were evident between two strong theoretical traditions in this branch of feminist scholarship from the outset, tensions that centered on the nature/nurture debates. Batting for the primacy of nature were models based on Freudian concepts that posited anatomical difference as the primary basis for differences in male and female personality, while on the other side of the divide those differences were framed in terms of environmental conditioning.

Some feminist psychologists attempted to reconcile the two traditions by offering models that incorporated elements of both biological and social learning theories. Dorothy Ullian,[52] for example, proposed an integrated model that recognized that environmental and biological influences were differentially important at various stages of a child's development. She argued that gender identifications were inherently unstable in children precisely because the process *was* developmental. In this regard Ullian's model nicely complemented the idea of critical periods that was so key to Money's model.

Rhoda Unger[53] turned her attention to the politics of research, sex research to be precise.[54] Of particular interest was research that focused on sex differences. Unger offered a strong critique of the legitimizing function of traditional scholarship because it defines what comes to be taken as knowledge in a way that implies institutional and personal interests play no part in its production. Within her broader critique of the inherent bias in research on sex differences, Unger offered a limited critique of the compulsory sexing of infants at birth, albeit one without an analysis of ICM.

At the time Unger's *Female and Male* was published, the sex/gender distinction had almost completely solidified in feminist scholarship. Nonetheless, Money's hermaphrodite research proved extremely useful to Unger, since she devoted almost 20 pages of discussion to hermaphrodite nomenclature, drawing extensively from Money and Ehrhardt's *Man and Woman, Boy and Girl.*[55] Unger had turned to Money's work because she was not confident (and rightly so, in my view) that comparative studies between species could offer convincing explanations of the human condition (although of course Money himself did rely on animal studies for some of the claims for which he had limited empirical support).

For Unger, Money's evidence was considerably less problematic than were some of his interpretations, another point on which I concur. After assessing Money's evidence and interpretations, Unger concluded that under his formulation, "the components of the female gender pattern—immaturity, decreased social and intellectual competence, decreased autonomy . . . and so on—are maladaptive for any individual in our society, regardless of his or her biological sex."[56] She went further:

> Biological sex appears to be a result of a sequence of choices, judgements about an organism's sex are almost always dichotomous [and] distinctions are based on the presence or absence of a functional penis . . . . *no one is ever labelled "sex ambiguous."*[57]

While it might be true that no one is *permanently* labelled "sex ambiguous," Unger's reading of Money's work should have alerted her to the fact that the intersexed are commonly burdened with such a label, however temporarily. As the above quotation indicates, Unger was highly critical of Money's early interpretations of "appropriate" demonstrations of female subjectivity.[58]

Like many of those who turned to Money's data, Unger made little attempt to preserve the humanity of those who provided her with an evidence base. Her discussion of individuals diagnosed with Turner Syndrome, for example, categorically stated that these were "*not* aberrant females [but] essentially neuter individuals whose external genitalia are similar to females.[59] They are defined as females because of the inadequacy of our dichotomous classification system for sex."[60] Unger's recognition that the classificatory system itself was inadequate is an acknowledgement that material reality can never be fully apprehended within the terms of a binary framework. The statement was made in the context of a discussion about the capacity of people with this diagnosis to conceptualize space-form relationships and comparative studies that suggested "normal females" suffered similar perceptual difficulties. While this would explain the emphasis Unger placed on distinguishing the real from the simulant, it had the effect of rendering the intersexed as outside the realm of the fully human. It is ironic, then, that Unger should articulate the hope that gender decoupled from sex would "provide a useful tool for our ultimate understanding of people—sex unspecified."[61]

Unger's work exemplifies how Stoller's reformulated gender had more conceptual currency for feminist scholarship than did Money's original. For Unger the term *sex* had merit only as a descriptor whereas explanatory power was precisely what made *gender* useful to her. Since gender did not have the same biological implications as sex it could be put to work to discuss characteristics and traits considered appropriately masculine or feminine. Using gender to discuss the nonphysiological aspects of sex allowed for a reduction in assumed parallels between biology and psychology. In other words, gender offered the means to counter biologically determinist accounts of social and relational phenomena.[62]

Dorothy Dinnerstein's widely cited *The Mermaid and the Minotaur* appeared in 1976.[63] Dinnerstein situated gender relations as the central coordinating matrix for all other social arrangements. Existing gender relations were, in her opinion, impossible to sustain in light of the rapid technological changes of recent history. Dinnerstein considered that women's responsibility for the care of the young lay at the heart of social, political, and personal neuroses that were endemic to contemporary life and, echoing Friedan, formed the basis of human malaise.

Prevailing gender relations were effectively obsolete, she argued, yet they persisted because of a nostalgic attachment to "a suicidal stance toward the realities on which our collective survival hing[ed]."[64] While her analysis was complex, Dinnerstein's solution for change was considerably less so: increasing men's involvement in childrearing and reducing women's involvement correspondingly would, she believed, revolutionize the social fabric. Simple solutions aside, what makes Dinnerstein's work important to the current discussion is that it offers an example of how, once gender began to settle into feminist scholarship, it became *the* signifier of the social by virtue of the sex/gender distinction. It is noteworthy that the definitional section in Dinnerstein's book did not include gender, despite its liberal use in the text. This would suggest that gender's meaning was already being fully assumed.

Nancy Chodorow was another to propose that basic differences in male and female personality resulted from the differential experience of social environments.[65] She too was unconvinced by biological determinist arguments and equally unconvinced by arguments that privileged patterns of socialization. The way out of the impasse, in her view, was to understand how particular behaviors were given meaning via interpersonal relationships. For Chodorow, feminine personality came to define itself relationally in connection with others because of women's responsibility for the rearing of children.[66] Masculine personality, on the other hand, was structured by individuation and by a certain tension between individuation and a residual dependency. Thus for Chodorow masculine personality development was considerably more problematic than its feminine counterpart. She argued that the tension of which she spoke resulted in men being "psychologically defensive and insecure [despite] guaranteeing to themselves, socio-cultural superiority over women."[67] In fact, for Chodorow male-female relations equated with the relations of colonialism, where existing gender roles served as the primary instruments of oppression.

Chodorow cited a range of post-Freudian clinical and theoretical writings that influenced her model of the ways that perceptions of gender difference are produced and reproduced.[68] Drawing on Money's and Stoller's notion of a core gender identity, Chodorow defined that aspect of identity as a person's cognitive sense of gendered self; in other words, the knowingness that one is a male or a female. Echoing Money, Chodorow stated that this core identity was established in the first two years of life and, while a person's sense of adequacy as a gender built on that core, such a sense would not and could not change that most "fundamental" of identities.[69]

It was Chodorow's argument that a core masculine identity was qualitatively different from a core feminine one, and that difference lay at the heart of personality differences between men and women. This insight provided for Chodorow the key to understanding

the extent to which psychological and value commitments to sex differences are so emotionally laden and tenaciously maintained [and] the way gender identity and expectations about sex roles and gender consistency are so deeply central to a person's consistent sense of self.[70]

Chodorow argued strongly against essentialist accounts of difference by contrasting her analysis with both the Lacanian school of thought advanced by French feminists such as Luce Irigaray and more orthodox Freudian approaches such as that of Juliet Mitchell. Chodorow questioned the merits for feminism of chasing the tail of gender difference as a central organizing concept, since such differences could never be "absolute, abstract, or irreducible."[71] She was adamant that because gender differences were created socially, experientially, and psychologically—in other words, relationally—they could not exist in and of themselves.

Chodorow maintained that male and female bodies had relevance for questions of gender difference since

> we live an embodied life: we live with those genital and reproductive organs and capacities, those hormones and chromosomes, that locate us physiologically as male or female.[72]

However, she was at pains to point out that perceptions about anatomical sex differences had to be shaped by factors other than biological ones. While it was impossible to know what children would make of their bodies in a genderless or "non-sexually organized world," Chodorow argued that "it was not obvious that major significance [would be attached] to biological sex differences, to gender differences, or to different sexualities."[73] While firmly grounded in psychoanalysis, Chodorow's perspective attempted to bridge the nature/nurture dichotomy through this relational model, otherwise known as Object Relations theory. Chodorow's analysis was, for the most part, sympathetic to Money's account of gender, not least because it invoked the notion of a core identity. It also recognized differential socialization of boys and girls as a major component of gender and accounted for what Money conceptualized as complementarity in gender through her emphasis on relationality. Moreover, Chodorow's model also retained gender's relation to the body, in a way that many other feminist analyses were unable to do, since most turned to the concept of gender as a way *not* to talk about the body.

FEMINIST ANTHROPOLOGY

Anthropology had long held an interest in the social relations between men and women across cultures. Texts such as Margaret Mead's *Sex and Temperament* and *Male and Female* had gained the status of anthropological classics, yet they represented an exception rather than a rule in their analyses of the relations between men and women.[74] For the most part, anthropologists—and Mead was no exception on this count—took their cues directly from biology, asserting the time-worn argument that the earliest sexual divisions of labor were a direct result of women's reproductive and nurturing capacities.[75] The hunter/gatherer theory of social relations was the received anthropological wisdom that explained male domination across cultures.

Gender's entry into anthropological feminism began in the mid-1970s with the publication of *Toward an Anthropology of Women*. The collection represented a rejoinder to traditional anthropological discourses about women. Editor Rayner Reiter explained:

> Looking for information about ourselves and about women in other societies, feminists have had to join Third World peoples, American Blacks, and Native Americans in expressing their distrust of the body of literature which mainstream anthropology has called objective.[76]

Despite the increasing problematization of women's status in the Western context since the 1960s, there was a dearth of anthropological material that specifically took women's perspectives into account. Those that did tended to be marginalized within mainstream anthropological research and teaching and consigned to what Reiter termed a feminist ghetto.[77] *Toward an Anthropology* might well have been headed for a similar fate had it not been for the inclusion of an essay written by a young graduate student whose name was Gayle Rubin.[78]

Rubin was the first feminist anthropologist to use gender in print as far as I can determine. Her work was foundational to many subsequent political and theoretical projects because she was among the first to use gender as an analytical *tool* with which to examine social life. While feminists like Oakley, Millett, and Greer were undoubtedly influential, Rubin's concept of the *sex-gender system* had a particular conceptual weight of its own. Rubin defined the object of her analysis as a "systematic social apparatus that takes females as a raw material and fashions domesticated women as products."[79] As the title of this important work, "The Traffic in Women," suggested, her analysis turned on the commodification of the female subject—across cultures. Rubin employed a hybrid of Marxist, structuralist, and psychoanalytic approaches in an attempt to get to the heart of the social conditions behind the oppression and subordination of women. For Rubin it was important to identify the root causes of women's oppression in order to determine exactly what was required to create a society free of hierarchical gender. She argued that kinship systems that relied on the exchange of women (as gifts) lay at the heart of the issue: it was these relations that facilitated the exchange of "sexual access, genealogical statuses, lineage names and ancestors, rights and people."[80]

Rubin's use of terminology was somewhat different than that of her contemporaries (Greer excepted). Rubin wrote of a sex/gender system, which she defined as "the set of arrangements by which a society transforms biological sexuality into products of human activity, and in which these transformed sexual needs are satisfied."[81] Rubin claimed (after Levi-Strauss) that the sexual division of labor functioned as a taboo against sameness. By exacerbating biological differences, males and females were rendered as two mutually exclusive categories. It was this, she suggested, that created gender. In her analysis gender was not merely a socially imposed division, it was also the product of "the social relations of sexuality."[82]

The suppression of similarities between men and women served the interests of heterosexuality, Rubin argued, and it was on this point that much of her analysis rested. She believed that gender entailed more than an identification with a single sex; it also necessarily required that sexual desire be directed toward the other (one). The sexual division of labor served as a taboo against sexual arrangements that did not include a man and a woman and in this way heterosexual marriage was imposed upon cultural members. In other words, gender necessarily demanded a heterosexual outcome. For Rubin, "at the most general level, the social organization of sex rests upon gender, obligatory heterosexuality, and the constraint of female sexuality."[83]

Rubin turned to Freud to explain the mechanisms by which children were transformed into a single sex and a single gender. For Rubin, Freud's analysis provided "a description of the mechanisms by which the sexes were divided and deformed, [and of the means by which] bisexual, androgynous infants are transformed into boys and girls."[84] The acculturation of children into a gender was an effect of the lability of the pre-Oedipal child's relatively unstructured sexuality, a structure that contained all the "sexual possibilities available to human expression."[85] In any particular society only some of these possibilities could be expressed because of prohibitions on those not deemed gender appropriate. By the end of the Oedipal phase a child's libido and its identity as a gender was thoroughly organized so as to conform to the rules of the domesticating culture.

By making explicit the link between gender and (hetero)sexuality, Rubin's analysis demonstrated that she was—at some level—drawing on Money's concept of gender, yet nowhere in "The Traffic in Women" is there an indication of whence she took the term.[86] This is unfortunate not least because erotic and libidinal practices were so central to Money's gender, and his embellishment of Freudian explanations of gender acquisition through the idea of complementation offered a fuller—however skewed—account of that process. By retaining the link between gender and the erotic, Rubin departed from most of her contemporaries (and many of her successors), whose use of Stoller's gender effectively banished desire from the frame.

By the time that Marilyn Strathern[87] offered her analysis of the process of stereotype *making*, Stoller's reformulated gender appears to have naturalized in anthropological writing. This is evident in the way that Strathern offered gender as a referent for cultural stereotypes and sex as the "physiological basis for discrimination."[88] Strathern argued that gender constructs not only drew upon sexual difference as a source of symbolism, they also operated as a mode of ordering social relations.[89] Gender, by her account, functioned as a language tool for making sense of things over and above any *actual* differences between men and women. In its operations, however, gender set up boundaries between males and females *and* provided the rules for communication between these two apparently mutually exclusive categories.

Strathern argued that the Western preoccupation with the nature/culture divide underpinned and motivated scientific research and, increasingly, a growing body of feminist theory. The relentless quest to understand the cultural and biological composition of maleness and femaleness always has difference at its heart. Yet it was not a difference that signified (let alone celebrated) diversity; rather it was of another order altogether. Difference was used to symbolize and reinforce a dichotomous relationship between males and females, and by extension between nature and culture.

CONTESTED MEANINGS, CONCEPTUAL CONFUSIONS

By the mid-1970s it was clear that Stoller's reformulated gender—as distinct from sex—had naturalized in anthropological and sociological feminist writing particularly. As debates continued about definitional terms, a number of scholars grappled with the conceptual difficulties of the sex/gender split. Articles appeared in feminist and more generalized academic journals and anthologies questioning the efficacy of using the terms *gender sex* and *sex role* interchangeably. The debates focused on three key areas: the erratic and inconsistent use of both sex and gender; the slippage between gender role and sex role; and the relation of the term *role* to the term *identity*. Everyone who engaged in the debates agreed on one thing: consistent terminology was important if a rigorous analysis of gender was to ever fully develop.

The work of sociologist Mary Chafetz offers a particularly lucid example of why some conceptual clarity was needed. In the introductory chapter to the first edition of *Masculine/Feminine or Human?* Chafetz debated the semantics of the terms *gender role* and *sex role*. She contrasted what she called "innate gender" with "learned sex" and concluded that "sex role is a different order of phenomenon than gender. The relevant terms are not 'male' and 'female,' which are gender terms, but 'masculine' and 'feminine.' "[90] By contrast, the same chapter of the second edition (entitled "Is Biology Destiny?") reads: "Gender role is a different order of phenomenon than sex. The relevant terms are not 'male' and 'female,' which are sex terms, but 'masculine' and 'feminine.'[91]

While the first edition had contained no references to either Money or Stoller, the second included three pages of discussion about the potential links between hormones, chromosomes, and behavior in which Money and Ehrhardt were cited. It was precisely this haphazard use of gender that fueled debates within feminism about appropriate terminology and inspired calls for conceptual clarity. This illustrates well the way in which gender as a concept took time to evolve toward a greater precision in the feminist literature. It continued to be used interchangeably with sex as a referent for social behaviors and expectations (i.e., social roles), and it continued to compete with sexual identity until the 1980s.[92]

Meredith Gould and Rochelle Kern-Daniels believed the terminological confusion in feminist theory stemmed from the fact that so many of the roles assigned to women (such as primary caregiver of children) derived from, or had some loose association with, their reproductive roles. Thus sex and gender seemed to blend together in apparently seamless ways. However, they warned of the dangers in not closely examining that apparent seamlessness: "Perpetuating this overlap implicitly sanctions a neo-Freudian argument for the role and utility of women in society, and hence some version of anatomy as social destiny."[93]

The authors advocated strongly for consistency in language use that would enable a sociology of sex and gender.[94] In their view and in keeping with Stoller's distinction, biological characteristics and social-cultural differences were not interchangeable and therefore neither were sex and gender. Gender's inherent sociality meant that it could be used to encompass all behaviors and attitudes that were "socially constructed, socially perpetuated and socially *alterable*."[95] After Stoller, they advocated using gender for everything recognized as masculine or feminine within a social context and sex as the signifier for everything outside of the social that could be relegated to biology. Today this is a given but it clearly hasn't always been so.

Others weighed in on the terminology debates by taking issue with the semantics of terms such as *role*. Sociologist Helena Lopata for example, articulated a preference for the term *sexual identity*— and later, *gender identity*—over *sex roles*. In her view, social roles better described social functions such as parenting, friendship, and the professions (such as those performed by doctors and teachers, for example). In an interesting turn, Lopata (with coauthor Barrie Thorne) argued that role was not altogether applicable to gender, since the latter described "learned behavior differentiated along the lines of biological sex."[96] In these terms it made no more sense to talk about sex roles or gender roles than it did to talk about "race roles." For Lopata, the only redeeming feature of the term *role* was its ability to evoke a sense of enculturation, but it came at a high price. The term *sex role* masked issues of power and inequality because it focused on individual socialization rather than on larger social structures. In the process, questions of economy, history, and politics were left aside. Her analysis can be read then as a critique of the Parsonian tradition that had for so long dominated the social sciences.

It was not Lopata's intention to deny the salience of maleness or femaleness in social interactions but to highlight that what was at stake was "a pervasive sexual identity" that underpinned almost all social roles.[97] For Lopata, gender referred to something fundamental (and so less changeable) that infused specific social roles engaged in by individuals. At the end of the day, "it seems being a woman is not a social role but a pervasive identity and a set of self-feelings which lead to the selection or the assignment by others of social roles."[98] By this account social roles organized by sex were more appropriately under-stood as sets of relations rather than sets of expectations. They were therefore subject to considerably more flux than one's sense of self as a sex—that is, one's gendered sense of self. So rather than simply draw a distinction between sex and gender, Lopata cleaved identity from role just as Stoller had done more than a decade before. Gender identity was given an immutability and intractability much like that given to biological sex within the context of the sex/gender distinction. The facticity of gender identity (like sex) was assumed and therefore placed beyond question. On the other hand, gender roles—being thoroughly cultural—*were* questionable. They were also malleable and so—while currently oppressive—needn't always be so.

Anthropologist Marilyn Strathern was another to question the way that gender was being used. While conceding that the manipulation of gender had enabled feminists to make rights claims, she was crit-ical of the way that some were deploying the concept. Attempts to undermine the legitimacy of patriarchy by showing that it had no mandate in biology rendered culture an instrument of oppression that could offer no real vehicle for reform. Reformist or revolutionary aims that challenged the very notion of social relations would be forever limited to social forms whose legitimacy depended on so-called immutable biological facts. In other words, these kinds of strategies could only lead back to the very essentialism that revolutionists and reformers sought to overthrow.

Nancy Chodorow had similar concerns about feminists using gender *differences* as a central organizing category of analysis. Her unease extended to the Western preoccupation with the nature/culture divide that she believed was increasingly providing the ground for a (then) growing body of feminist theory. The problem for feminism lay in the fact that in the relentless quest to understand the cultural and biological composition of maleness and femaleness, sex differences were invoked to both symbolize and to reinforce a dichotomous relationship between nature and culture. Chodorow was in essence then, offering a critique of the sex/gender distinction.

While some of these terminology debates focused on the sex/gender distinction and others on a distinction between role and identity, still others sought to distinguish gender roles (as learned behavior and expectations) from sex roles in the context of erotic activities. Many of these debates centered around a concern with semantics, but there were also important debates about the appropriateness for feminism of using gender as an organizing principle. The debates were themselves necessary to the process of establishing gender in the feminist lexicon, and the degree of contestation surely reflects the importance of gender to feminist discourse.

Chodorow excepted, early feminist writers who used Stoller's and Money's ideas—whether explicitly or implicitly—uncritically accepted medical explanations of the dichotomous nature of sex and in so doing reinforced and reproduced sex-gender as a binary proposition. Rubin's analysis, to take one example, explicitly positioned the body as the raw material upon which gender was put to work. By positioning biological sex in this way, the very attempts to undermine its centrality served to invoke it. Many feminists writing during the period under discussion accepted the existence of real biological phenomena that differentiated women and men and were used in essentially similar ways across cultures to generate distinctions between males and females and between men and women.[99] As a result, attempts to undermine biological determinist analyses led to the privileging of a cultural determinism that always referenced back to a kind of "biological foundationalism."[100] This conceptual move effectively provided tacit support for the ongoing co-option of the intersexed into the imaginary of dimorphic sexual difference. Despite second-wave feminists' familiarity with Money's clinical research, and despite strong critiques of the medicalization of women's bodies and a robust activism around a woman's right to control her body and sexuality, ICM was not subject to any rigorous feminist critique until 1975.

EARLY FEMINIST CRITIQUES OF ICM AND BINARY SEX-GENDER

While the intersexed were everywhere in the feminist literature of the 1970s, it was not until mid-decade that a handful of critiques began to appear that tackled Money's theories and methodologies. It is to those critiques that I turn now. Together they represent a small body of work that offered a specifically feminist analysis of various aspects of Money's project and found them wanting. Juxtaposed with the earlier material we can begin to see feminism's shifting relation to the intersexed over the past three and half decades. Yet a strong critique of Money's ideas still did not necessarily extend to a recuperation of the intersexed subject or to a critique of ICM.

The very first substantive feminist critique of hermaphrodite case management appeared, as I said, in 1975, and it was effectively the only one to retrieve the intersexed from pathology. Social psychologist David Tresemer (1975) offered an astute and sensitive reading of the prevailing treatment model that had for the most part been overlooked by feminists.[101] Tresemer, like many of his peers, attempted to dismantle the assumption that observed differences between the sexes were reflected in, and hence mandated by, biology. He recognized that an assumption of bipolarity demanded an exaggeration of perceived differences between the sexes. In a scorching critique, Tresemer suggested that in spite of influential social theorists such as Levi-Strauss and Piaget pointing to the primitive nature of binary concepts,

it is our more advanced civilization that treats the intersexual as an unclassifiable monster and tries, through surgical and/or behavioral engineering to fit the person into one role or the other. Thus bipolarity better describes what we think about sex differences rather than what they necessarily are.[102]

Tresemer aimed at the is/ought distinction that underpins the medical practices of ICM and drives so much of the work of the biomedical sciences. He said that the binary "nature" of gender had to be discussed, not assumed, precisely because such ideas denied legitimacy to those who were intersexed. Tresemer was effectively pinpointing the way that technology was used to reinforce ideology, co-opting the intersexed into the logic of binary sex through chemistry and surgery:

The dual-role system is affirmed in the case of biological hermaphrodites when physicians are enjoined to help the horrific "it" become at least a partially acceptable "him" or "her."[103]

Tresemer's analysis remains, to this day, exemplary for its critical engagement with the material reality of the intersexed. In the earlier discussion of Rhoda Unger's work I mentioned that she had offered a limited analysis of ICM within her broader exploration of sex difference research. Hers was also a critique of the is/ought distinction manifest in psychology and the biosciences. She asked, What were the implications of binary constructs of gender for the intersexed, at least in Western societies, where only two sexes were socially defined and so effectively only two "really" existed? It seemed that the birth of an intersexed infant inevitably required (or perhaps more correctly, compelled) the adults around the child to "engage in a kind of 'construct-a-sex' game."[104] In Unger's view little or no allowance was made for genital "ambiguity" because gender was always linked to genital appearance. Consequently those children whose anatomy fell outside the parameters of what was constituted "normal" faced the prospect of surgical mediation to give the appearance of either maleness or femaleness. Unger identified the conditions that made it possible to reinforce the ideology of binary sex through technology and critiqued Money's ideas about what were appropriate feminine and masculine behaviors. But her analysis fell short of engaging with the material production of sex and thus with the intersexed.

One of the first feminist social constructionist analyses was Kessler and McKenna's *Gender: An Ethnomethodological Approach*.[105] While social constructionism had been circulating in sociology for over a decade when Kessler and McKenna wrote the text, it was not then a favored methodology in feminism. Kessler and McKenna used it to show that "a world of two 'sexes' [was] the result of the socially shared, taken-for-granted methods which members use to construct reality."[106] This perspective located all social members, including researchers and theorists, firmly within the social interactions of everyday life.

A crucial part of Kessler and McKenna's argument hinged on the fact that gendering was never a one-off event at birth but functioned as a ritualistic process of daily life. The very first instance of gendering they called gender "assignment," in order to differentiate it from all subsequent occurrences. The idea of gendering as a process generated a set of research questions, which included the following: "How, in any interaction, is a sense of the reality of a world of two, and only two, genders constructed?"[107] And moreover,

What kinds of rules do we apply to what kinds of displays, such that in every concrete instance we produce a sense that there are only men and women, and that this is an objective fact, not dependent on a particular instance?[108]

In order to tackle those questions, Kessler and McKenna proposed the idea of gender attribution, defined as a complex interactive process. They noted that in most interactions, participants were simultaneously involved in both attributing gender and having gender attributed to them. And of course individuals self-attributed also. In order to examine how gender was constructed conceptually—and literally—by members of the scientific community, Kessler and McKenna turned to medical and biological research on the intersexed. Indeed a great deal of their text was dedicated to the subject. In order to highlight the constructedness of the ideas they were concerned to dismantle, Kessler and McKenna used the term gender even for those aspects of being a woman/girl or man/boy traditionally understood as biological, such as chromosomal or hormonal.

Theirs was a convincing account of the way that the *idea* of dichotomous sex—as mutually exclusive and oppositional categories— led those who worked with the intersexed to believe in the idea that they were *really* male or *really* female. That is, the intersexed could be conceptualized only as a blend or combination of the two existing categories, never in their own right (and so positioned in discourse as intersexed). Of course the concept of sexual ambiguity has meaning only within a conceptual framework constituted by two—and only two—legitimate categories. For Kessler and McKenna the facticity of the intersexed highlighted the process of gender attribution.

Kessler and McKenna's was an astute and highly critical analysis of the production of dichotomous sex within the sciences. Yet their methodological framework did not prevent them from relying on the very material of whose production they were so critical. Demonstrating the ambivalence that is everywhere in the feminist scholarship under question, Kessler and McKenna referred to people "born with various...biological *abnormalities*" linked to chromosomes, the internal organs associated with reproduction, the external genitalia, and hormones.[109] They too found Money's research and Stoller's ideas about gender useful for refuting the idea that a person's gender was determined by biology. What evidence did they draw upon? That offered by Money that the intersexed could grow up normatively gendered. Kessler and McKenna's discussion of chromosomal variance, for example, noted that "there [had] been no report of AIS affected individuals developing anything other than normal female gender identities."[110] Their analysis stopped short then of examining the normative terms upon which this account of an unproblematic gender acquisition relied. This meant that it also stopped short of scrutinizing the material practices of clinicians and their quite literal construction of sex. Thus it also stopped short of exploring the material reality of gender for the intersexed. Kessler and McKenna's work, like Unger's, highlights once more that the relation of feminist scholarship to those who fall outside the privileged endpoints of a binary structure is marked by an ambivalence that is both a stimulus for, and an effect of, a blind spot.

That same ambivalence is also evident in the work of medical ethicist Janice Raymond, who was another to offer a strong critique of Money's work. Raymond believed Money's work to be dangerous. Not only did it enjoy wide acceptance among feminists but it had become a "kind of bible on sex differences."[111] For Raymond, transsexual surgery (the key focus of her analysis) operated on a historical continuum of medical practices that legitimated surgical intervention as a form of behavior modification. She cited the nineteenth-century practice of clitoridectomy and its contemporary equivalent in North Africa, yet remained strangely silent about the place of clitoridectomy in contemporary ICM—despite being fully conversant with its centrality through her reading of Money. So too, her apparent acceptance of ICM surgeries on infants and adults would seem at odds with her position on transsexual sex reassignment.[112]

As part of her denunciation of transsexualism and the sex change "industry," Raymond argued that Money's interactionist approach was merely a ruse that masked an inherent biological determinism. In her view Money's claim that the nature/nurture debate was obsolete merely served to shift the terms of the debate from the idea that biology equaled destiny, to the idea that socialization equaled destiny. Moreover, Raymond was critical of the way that the idea that socialization mapped onto prenatal hormonal influences had taken on the force of a natural law. While conceding the power of socialization in constituting gendered identities, under Money's paradigm Raymond believed it became both absolute and static. Yet she did not extend that critique to a consideration of the oppressive nature of gender identity for the intersexed—as mandate for, and purported outcome of, surgical and chemical body modification.

Marilyn Strathern offered a similar critique of Money. His version of gender—as, presumably, any other—reflected less any concrete reality than a set (or sets) of ideas, in Strathern's view:

The sex differences that ideas about gender rest upon are both gross anatomical characteristics and variations in quality of behavior and mentality. . . . In most societies gender thus has the appearance of being a straightforward representation of natural sex characteristics.[113]

Indeed, while Money certainly did try to reconcile the nature/culture split, his reliance on other binary concepts and his compulsion to meta-theorize resulted in some of his ideas appearing as straightforward representations of highly complex phenomena. As Kay Deaux reminds us, this is actually the case with most concepts of masculinity and femininity.[114]

In a collection entitled *Women Look at Biology Looking at Women*, Barbara Fried used the work of Money to examine the way that language use shapes perceptions of reality and moreover shapes descriptions of reality—particularly the "reality" of sex and gender.[115] Fried turned to Money's theory of gender acquisition and his linking of gender to native language acquisition. She used that connection to demonstrate the means by which language not only "communicates the link between one's sex and one's gender identity [but actually] *constitutes* that link."[116] For Fried,

the fundamental problem with accepting *a priori* sexual duality as a primary construct of reality is that all of our discussions about sex and gender must then take place *within* this construct. All that the work on the relationship of sex to gender has done is move us from a consideration of human activity in two categories (male and female) to one in two pairs (male, masculine; female, feminine).[117]

Fried also made the point that, although the relationship between biology and environment is extremely complex and on many levels unfathomable, researchers like Money et al. framed those relationships in terms of simple and accessible dichotomies. In so doing, Money disregarded the internal mechanisms that influence how so-called facts come to be perceived, both by him and by us. Her close reading of the way Money interpreted the evidence before him demonstrated just how culture bound his scientific interpretations were.

Money's methodologies came under scrutiny in Fried's critique as well. How useful was it, she asked, to compare intersexed individuals with "controls" who, while sharing some characteristics (such as class, IQ, and "family situation"), did not share any of those associated with being intersexed? In Fried's view the presumption that behavioral differences between such groups could be attributed to biological differences was a fallacy that ignored human consciousness and, at the end of the day, implied more than it proved.

Not only did Fried tackle Money at a methodological level, her analysis also took aim at the tautological structure of the English language itself: a language differentiated according to sex by gender.[118] For Fried, gender was by definition a dualistic concept "since the word is merely the symbol for our belief in a dualistic world."[119] And it is that belief that has "played a role so fundamental in ordering human experience that, in general, the lives of women and men in this and every other known society are undeniably different."[120] That Fried should address the way that language shapes and constrains the very possibilities of what can be thought, in her discussion of Money, is not insignificant given how intricately gender was tied to the language in his account.[121] Yet Fried's critique of Money's work was not altogether unproblematic either. Her reading of Money suggested that if something wasn't sex then it must be gender and vice versa. This, I suggest, is an example of a misperception of Money's ideas that might well be read as an early precursor to the now common claim that for Money gender is all about "nurture."

Most of these critiques appeared toward the end of the 1970s and no doubt contributed to feminists disengaging from Money, just as his uncompromising stance on the sex/gender distinction did. The movement away from Money's work resulted in the intersexed slipping from feminist view. Where once hermaphrodite research formed a central part of the evidence base for Anglo-American feminism, by the 1980s the intersexed were almost nowhere to be found in the feminist literature, save for a few historical figures and the odd science fiction character.[122] While the relation of feminism to the intersexed had been in many ways problematic, the intersexed were nonetheless *present in the present* for the duration of feminism's engagement with sexological research. The subsequent disengagement had the effect of casting the intersexed out of the here and now in feminist discourse, out into the realms of the mythical, the historical, and for a time, the aspirational.

OH ANDROGYNE, SWEET ANDROGYNE

It is to the figure of the androgyne that I want to turn now, or more precisely its promotion as an ideal type within feminism. The androgyne's popularity is evident in feminist scholarship, and in feminist discourse more generally across the 1970s and well into the 1980s. As the following examples demonstrate, the lack of attention paid in most feminist accounts to the plight of the intersexed paralleled utopic visions of an androgynous, genderless (or gender-free) world. Once again ambivalence marks the relation between feminism and the intersexed.

For Gayle Rubin the whole point of a feminist revolution was to liberate all of humanity from the straitjacket of gender:

If the sexual division of labor were such that adults of both sexes cared for children equally, primary object choice would be bisexual. If heterosexuality were not obligatory, this early love would not have to be suppressed, and the penis would not be overvalued. If the sexual property system were reorganized in such a way that men did not have overriding rights in women (if there was no exchange of women) and if there were no gender, the entire oedipal drama would be a relic.[123]

For Rubin, androgyny represented a nostalgic yearning, since in her analysis it was the original, untainted, pure state of childhood, a state that preexisted the "division and deformity" of androgynous infants into boys and girls.[124] Philosopher Alison Jaggar appealed to a similar androgynous sensibility, calling for the creation of a culture that incorporated the most positive aspects of "both the present male and present female cultures."[125] While idealized in both these accounts, androgyny is never quite present, rather it lies somewhere in the past and in a more hopeful future.

Other accounts were less benign. Psychologist June Singer offered a model that privileged "feminine values" and would be a precursor to later cultural feminist conceptions of Woman—capital W. Androgyny, said Singer, was an extraordinary state of consciousness that could collectively deliver a world free from the constraints of differentiated genders. Hers was a vision of a world where values traditionally associated with women such as cooperation, the pursuit of collective goals, intuition, and an emphasis on relationships were preferable to competition, individualism, rationality, and power and violence, respectively.[126] In other words, androgynous individuals represented a kind of reified prototypical femininity. Androgyny was not—under the terms of this model—hermaphroditism, nor was it bisexuality, despite often being confused with either or both of them.

For Singer hermaphroditism was a *"physiological* abnormality in which sex characteristics of the opposite sex are found in an individual."[127] She noted that in literature and mythology "hermaphrodites are [either] weaklings or monsters; in any case, *anomalies.*"[128] Bisexuality, on the other hand, referred to a psychological condition that Singer believed resulted from confusion about one's masculinity or femininity and a lack of clarity with respect to one's gender identification. A pathologizing impulse is writ large here. Both states of being—one framed as physiological and the other as psychological—are pathologized in essentially the same way. This is surely the most extreme expression of what I call a monosexual bias to be found in any of the material under discussion. Singer situates the intersexed firmly outside the realms of humanity and bisexuals as already always disordered.

Androgyny was said to find its ultimate bodily expression through hetero-sex, or more precisely, "through coitus in a dissolution of gender identity."[129] Under these terms a clear and stable gender identity becomes the necessary precondition for its dissolution, and of course the necessary precondition for a stable gender identity is a singularly sexed body and a heterosexual orientation. While others who promoted androgyny as an ideal type did not fall prey to such a vigorous monosexism,[130] Singer's work demonstrates some of the excesses to which Money's ideas about gender and sexuality can, and have, been, deployed.[131] While Money did allow for the possibility of an androgynous identity, such an identity was not in his view a viable mode of being. Certainly in the intersexed, androgyny was a sign of maladaption.

Tresemer again was one of the few feminist scholars to recognize the ambivalent relation between a utopian androgyny and the intersexed. He historicized that link by noting that in spite of all the negative connotations associated with hermaphroditism as anomalous or freakish, there was an equally strong tradition of "reverence and awe for the biological hermaphrodite as a metaphor of psychological androgyny," for example in the work of Jung and in the historical record.

From 1979 onward, nothing more was said about the intersexed in feminist discourse, save for Anne Fausto-Sterling's *Myths of Gender*, which appeared in 1985. Of course the intersexed did retain a presence in medical and sexological discourse. But it would be another decade until feminism embarked on a strenuous reengagement with

ICM or the work of Money. That scholarship features in the following chapter.

SETTING THE TERMS, BITING THE HAND

Before concluding, I turn to Money's long engagement with feminism, an engagement that was for a time reciprocal, though often uncomfortable. Indeed, with the passing of time feminism's relation to the work of Money could well be described as biting the hand that fed it. Money had initially offered himself as an ally of the feminist project but over the years became increasingly critical of its direction and alienated from its foci. As the preceding discussion illustrates, in many ways that disenchantment had become mutual.

As mentioned earlier, the index of one of Money's most widely cited texts, *Man and Woman, Boy and Girl* contains the heading "Women's Liberation, quotable material."[132] Under this heading lie a raft of entries that direct readers to specific material in the text: material that Money clearly viewed as useful to a liberationist agenda. The index entries offer perhaps the most explicit example of how Money attempted to engage with feminist debates. Among the entries to which I refer is the rather provocatively titled "Priority of the Female in Differentiation."[133] Turning to the relevant page, the reader will find the following statement:

Stated in non-technical terms, the lesson of embryonic anatomy is that it is easier for nature to make a female than a male. The familiar embryonic and foetal rule is that something must be added to produce a male. Quite possibly, the same paradigm may apply also to gender-identity differentiation, though there is yet no conclusive proof of this hypothesis.[134]

This theory, recoined in the late 1980s by Money as the "Eve/Adam principle," gained considerable traction in medical and psychological circles over the course of the 1950s and 1960s before being promoted enthusiastically within feminism.[135] Citing an earlier work of Money's, Millett for example had stated decisively in *Sexual Politics*:

It is now believed that the human foetus is originally physically female until the operation of androgen at a certain stage of gestation causes those with Y-chromosomes to develop into males.[136]

Indeed this understanding of fetal development rapidly gained axiomatic status among feminists and remains to this day a given. The idea that all human embryos begin life as female (rather than, say, hermaphrodite) provided compelling evidence for feminists to repudiate biologically determinist claims that male superiority was natural. It also served the interests of those feminists who sought to invert the hierarchical relation of man/woman through the reification of values traditionally associated with "Woman-ness." Unfortunately there are a number of problems with appealing to theories such as this.

First, the concept of female as default is underpinned by the time-worn assumption that links activity to maleness (something happens to "make" a male), and passivity to femaleness (female bodies are the result of *nothing* happening, hence the "default sex").[137] Second, inverting a hierarchy does little to disrupt or challenge it in any significant way because the power relations inherent to it are maintained. Consequently, the hierarchy remains vulnerable to further reversals. Third, the appeal itself reinforces the binary opposition of male/female that not only obscures any similarities between the sexes at a physiological level—of which there are many—but obscures differences within the sexes and also serves to vanquish those that fall outside of the binary structure. This is another example of just how complicated and often contradictory the relation between feminist and medicoscientific understandings of bodies and subjectivities were, and in many ways, continue to be.

Money's initial support for the emancipatory project of women's liberation gave way over time to increasing frustration—and indeed vitriol—about the way that gender was put to work in feminist scholarship and activism. His frustration centered around the consolidation of the sex/gender split, which he had always contended to be a false dichotomy that failed to account for mechanisms of learning and the role of the central nervous system. What sealed it for Money was the fact that the sex/gender distinction severed sex in all its lusty carnal glory from gender and in doing so effectively neutered the latter. It was Money's view that gender in its neutered form fed into a sex-negative neo-Puritanism that underpinned North American culture.

The neutering of gender is part of a tidal wave of antisexualism that spreads its octopus tentacles into the politics of what could become a new and dictatorial era of antisexualism. America is, by reason of its historical roots in the antisexualism of Puritanism, vulnerable in this respect.[138]

Money had become increasingly dismayed with the radical feminist analysis of pornography as articulated by groups such as Women Against Pornography (WAP) and individuals such as Andrea Dworkin. An analysis of all pornography as violent and degrading to women was, in his view, particularly crude and itself demeaning to women. It was a crude analysis because it failed to recognize the specificity of different genres of pornography and the corresponding specificity of its audience. He believed the analysis degrading to women because it rendered all women as victims—or at least potential victims—of a rampant and inevitably violent male sexuality.

In one school of social dogma...pioneered by militant women against pornography, all erotic imagery, not only that of sadomasochistic violence or rape, is equated with pornography; all pornography is, by their own definition, equated with the subjugation of women as men's sex objects and the victims of their power and violence.[139]

Money's dismay—manifest as fury—led him to blame feminism, along with social constructionism, for enabling a sex-negative culture that positioned women as hapless victims. This ultimately served to undermine gender equality:

In radical feminism, rape was radically redefined, as if by fiat, as being not an act of sexual assault or coercion, but an act of male violence and aggression perpetrated against women.... The feminist movement had given its opponents...the first inch of the mile they would need to defend the continuance of the tradition that woman, the weaker sex, is dependent on man's power of protection. Woman's role was surreptitiously being reiterated as the role of martyrdom, and of being helpless victims of the men who sacrificed them, incompetent to fend for themselves.[140]

Money's fury made all feminists "scapegoats of America's sexual crisis."[141] Moreover, it blinded him to a raft of sex-positive feminist analyses that in many respects complemented his own.

CONCLUSION

Gender finally settled into the feminist lexicon during a historical period of great change in political and academic feminism.[142] What had begun as a predominantly white middle-class movement was increasingly faced with challenges from within, most particularly from women of color over the politics of representation under the reified sign of "Woman."[143] Those challenges occurred in tandem with a transition in political strategy: from a politics of equality toward one of difference. The 1980s also saw the beginning of a turn toward poststructuralism in feminist theory, a turn that was to have significant theoretical ramifications.[144]

The epistemological debates that ensued went to the very heart of what was being struggled over and indeed structured the terms of those debates with respect to how it was possible to "know" nature, to know sex, and indeed to know "the body." Feminist philosophers weighed in on the debates by arguing that it was not possible to know nature, a perspective that provided the thrust of many of the feminist critiques of the body during the 1980s and 1990s. The apparent naturalness of sex—a category once seemingly beyond question—was put under the spotlight, placing the sex/gender distinction itself under scrutiny. The distinction that had once been so fruitful for feminist analyses at one level came to be more and more constraining precisely because it was so thoroughly immersed in a dualistic logic.[145]

Yet at the same time those constraints proved to be highly productive, as manifest through the (apparent) discovery of the problems inherent in the sex/gender distinction. That discovery served to energize an entire industry within feminist theorizing of the body and of sexual difference. By the 1990s, a central concern of feminist scholarship was the "problematic space" created by the sex/gender distinction.[146] In a sense, by grappling with the very issue of access to reality (a thoroughly philosophical pursuit), and by seeking to manipulate the English language, these theorists were grappling with issues similar to those faced by Money in his quest to find a concept to account for identities with no straightforward relation to the body.

It was during that same period (at the end of the twentieth century) that a number of feminist scholars began to reengage with ICM and the plight of those who are intersexed. Academic feminists once again turned their gaze toward a mainstream medical practice that had for the most part escaped questioning. In the following chapter I turn to this body of work when I explore the way that gender is articulated by intersex individuals and advocacy groups and by the academics who serve as allies. As I demonstrate, gender is as highly charged and contested within that domain as it ever was in feminism.

The concern of this chapter has been to make visible the irregular and inconsistent use of the concept of gender in feminist scholarship throughout the 1970s and highlight the ambivalent relation of feminism to the intersexed in order to locate "feminist gender" as one episode in a much larger conceptual history. Although gender first entered feminist discourse at the beginning of the 1970s, calls for conceptual clarity and consistency were still being made as late as 1979. This provides compelling evidence that gender's settlement in feminism was far from unproblematic. Despite a number of early critiques of Money's theories and methodologies, and despite a certain unease articulated by some feminists very early on about relying on gender as a central organizing principle, the usefulness of the concept to the theoretical and political projects of feminism eventually outweighed any such concerns—at least for a time.

Gender as a concept is as dynamic as anyone's embodied experiences *as* a gender, subject to the vagaries of particular historical and political moments. Given how contested gender was within feminism over the course of the 1970s, its ascendence as the central organizing concept is nothing short of phenomenal. Within five years of becoming embedded in feminist thought, gender was being written about and talked about as if it had *always* existed, as if its meaning was universal, and as if gender had been the invention of feminism itself.

While feminism has been called upon to acknowledge and engage with how class, race, age, and context intersect with the sign of "Woman", until recently it did not have to directly confront or engage with the multiplicity of sex. Ironically, this was precisely what Money himself confronted and engaged with all along. What seems increasingly obvious is that feminism's ambivalent relation to the category of sex and its seeming reluctance to critically engage with the matter of matter meant the binary logic so central to sexological and medico-scientific understandings of gender, sex, and sexuality was reinforced. As Biddy Martin has noted,

gender has come to do the work of stabilizing and universalizing binary oppositions at other levels including male and female sexuality, the work once done by the assumption of biological sex difference.[147]

One of the consequences of an investment, unwitting or otherwise, in the binary logics of sex-gender is that the intersexed can only ever be in-between. It is but a short leap from there to the idea that they are unfinished. While that particular logic might make some sense within a clinical frame, I am not convinced of its usefulness in a sociocultural context. I am interested in how we might, after Greer, *think otherwise*. What kinds of interventions might disrupt the circular reasoning that continues to haunt contemporary debates around (dimorphic) sexual difference? How might an engagement with the material reality of differently sexed bodies impact on notions of sexual difference? These are some of the questions I explore in more depth in the final chapter. Why? Because these questions are becoming more pressing as the intersexed stake a place within culture, and more specifically a place in the here and now.

CHAPTER 4

OF "LOVEMAPS" AND LIMERENCE

INTRODUCTION

This chapter is concerned with the issue of desire and is organized around an analysis of the erotic component of Money's "gender". Many of the current axioms regarding both gender and sexuality can be traced directly to Money, and of course desire is, and always has been, central to his theorizing of gender. Recall that by Money's account, gender operates as an overarching term that includes, but is not limited to, the erotic:

> Used strictly and correctly, gender is conceptually more inclusive than sex. It is an umbrella under which are sheltered all the different components of sex difference, including the sex-genital, sex-erotic, and sex-procreative components.[1]

No wonder the disentanglement of sexuality from gender has proved such a difficult task. A genealogy of gender that did not consider the erotic would effectively neuter the concept—removing, as Money would say, any association with the "dirty carnalities of lust."[2] Such an omission would serve also to reinforce the sex/gender distinction, a distinction that I have attempted to both analyze and resist.

The previous two chapters have followed a temporal trajectory by focusing on various interventions made by others into the concept of gender after its introduction by Money in the mid-1950s. In Chapter 2 I examined the multiple interventions of psychoanalyst Robert Stoller, who in the mid-1960s made a distinction between gender identity and gender role but, more importantly, was the first to conceptually split sex from gender. The impact of the sex/gender distinction was enormous. Sex—itself once an umbrella term that incorporated the physiological, psychological, sexual, and cultural components of selfhood—became the referent for all things biological ("nature") and gender the referent for the sociocultural ("nurture") elements of subjectivity. While theoretically useful for Stoller, the sex/gender distinction would circumscribe the ways in which its proponents were able to address the sexual.

Chapter 3 traced the concept of gender after Stoller's interventions, as it was taken up by the women's movement from the late 1960s to the late 1970s. Gender provided feminists with a means of articulating a theoretical and political position regarding male-female relations. The concept of gender allowed feminism to repudiate biologically determinist explanations for women's inferior social, economic, and political status. Sex was seen as the raw biological material upon which gender did its work: the former was rendered passive, subservient even, to its sociocultural counterpart. Stripped of its connotations to sex and to the flesh, gender became a potent conceptual tool as well as a central object of analysis. Even though it took almost a decade for "gender" to settle into the feminist lexicon, it soon became indispensable to that project: so indispensable, in fact, that feminism began to claim gender as its own invention over the course of the 1980s and 1990s. With time the constraints of the sex/gender distinction for feminist theorizing began to show, constraints imposed by the logic of the binary. At the same time those constraints served to energize an entire field of scholarship that took as its object the problematic space *between* sex and gender.

In both of the preceding chapters it has been my intention to highlight the consequences of the sex/gender distinction for understandings of what it means to be human. Stoller effectively reinstated the Cartesian dualism of mind and body, a dualism that Money steadfastly refused to entertain in all of his theorizing for over 50 years. Feminism for its part reinforced and reinscribed that duality through its investment in the sex/gender distinction. By bracketing off the sexual as somehow outside the horizon of gender, neither Stoller nor the majority of feminist theorists throughout the 1970s and 1980s had a great deal to say about what actually *constituted* the sexual.[3] Such investments have had significant implications for the intersexed, since gender—in all its manifestations—has, to date, depended upon their relegation as less than fully human. At the same time the intersexed form one of the grounds from which the non-intersexed have been and continue to be rendered fully human.

While Chapter 1 looked at Money's very earliest theorizing, here the focus turns to the erotosexual component of Money's gender *after* he extrapolated his ideas to the wider population.[4] The first section situates the intersexed in relation to early sexological theories just as previous chapters have located them in relation to the wider concept of gender. The figure of the hermaphrodite has fulfilled a vital role in the development of theory and taxonomies in the sexual sciences, right from the very earliest application of the scientific method to erotosexual desire. The intersexed are everywhere implicated in gender and by extension sexuality, since historically they have provided the sexual sciences with an evidence base for the ubiquity of dimorphic sex—as paradoxical as that may seem.

In the second section I consider the various ways that desire—particularly same-sex and other forms of so-called aberrant desire—has historically been theorized in sexology. Money's ideas did not come to life in a vacuum; his theories can be situated within the broader context of the history of sexological thought. While early discourses on sexuality may seem "bizarre, outrageous, or even comically absurd" to contemporary eyes, they nonetheless reveal a continuity of governing assumptions that permeate contemporary sexological research.[5] A close reading of Money's work supports that claim.

I begin by examining some of the methodological hallmarks of the sexual sciences before turning to five enduring (and not unproblematic) principles that are woven through sexological theory. All of the methodologies and principles under discussion are the legacy of Karl Heinrich Ulrichs,[6] who began publishing his ideas in pamphlet form in the late 1860s. The work of Ulrichs prefigured the development of the sexual sciences, since he was the first to apply the scientific method to the study of the erotic, although he was not himself medically or scientifically trained.[7]

While Money's theories offered a range of new terminologies and invigorated systems of classification, the foundational principles that underpin those theories (and methodologies) were by no means new. In keeping with the tradition of the sexual sciences, Money devoted much of his career to mapping and naming all manner of desires[8] just as he attempted to provide an exhaustive nomenclature of hermaphroditism. Despite his efforts to recognize and legitimate desires previously categorized as "perverse," one of the outcomes of his commitment to a dimorphic frame is that desire for men is always already feminine and desire for women always already masculine. This means that desire for "the same" can never be quite right and indeed such desire represents, for Money, transposed desire. Consequently, his theories of sexual desire fall under the rubric of inversion theory. The idea that one's anatomy equates to one's psychology (except of course if you are intersexed), and the idea that an individual's erotic orientations have some kind of constitutional basis haunt Money's ideas, notwithstanding his refusal of the nature/nurture distinction and notwithstanding his reputed status as a nurturist. Little wonder he painted himself into a conceptual corner.

HERMAPHRODITES IN SEXOLOGICAL THOUGHT

The late nineteenth century was the period that marked the birth of the sexual sciences. Historians have credited sexologists with the invention of the homosexual subject, most notably Foucault (and many subsequent others from various fields).[9] Yet others have suggested that the historical record does not support such a claim in any straightforward manner. Rather, they suggest that medical and psychiatric discourses were appropriated from the narratives produced by their patients, along with those of the sexual reformers, and put to work within a clinical frame of reference.[10] By this account official medical and scientific discourses are actually more accurately described as a type of *counter*discourse to that produced by those who dared speak in their own name. Yet neither of these perspectives takes into account the prevalence and influence of those who simultaneously occupied the subject positions of reformer, sexual scientist, *and* same-sex desirer.

During the nineteenth century various representations of disorderly bodies converged with representations of nonnormative sexualities. The figure of the hermaphrodite provided an evidence base from which many early sexologists generated a plethora of classifications and theories of sex and desire.[11] The embryological literature of the mid- to late nineteenth century offered a useful analogy for their concepts. That analogy derived from the understanding that all human embryos begin life in sexually undifferentiated form and from the fact that the penis and the clitoris[12]—like the ovaries and testes—develop from homologous structures: in other words, from identical tissue. The idea of original underlying fetal bisexuality or bipotentiality was a popular one because it offered early sex researchers a means to comprehend (in binarian terms) how aberrant desires developed and where their origins lay.[13]

The embryological analogy also functioned at another level. Hermaphroditism was understood then—as it is today—as a mixture of features generally considered the exclusive property of males or of females. Comparisons between hermaphrodites and same-sex-desiring non-hermaphrodites seemed entirely appropriate, since sexual attraction to men was deemed to be an irrevocably feminine desire regardless of whether the desirer inhabited a male or a female body (and vice versa). This entanglement remains, of course, not least for those who are engaged in trying to disentangle gender from sexuality and from sex. Ulrichs was the first to attempt a scientific account of sexuality. He made explicit the link between hermaphroditism and same-sex desire by proposing that the latter constituted a hermaphroditism of the soul.[14] This enabled him to propose the existence of a "third sex" who, while equivalent to men and women, was qualitatively different from them.

The idea of a third sex has a long history reaching back to the work of Plato, albeit with diverse meanings in different historical contexts.[15] While the earliest references to a third sex marked deviant bodies, from the late nineteenth century on the term became increasingly used to signify deviant *sexualities*. Ulrichs called his third sex "Urnings," a term appropriated from Plato's *Symposium*. For Ulrichs the existence of hermaphrodites offered proof that Urnings or Uranians were a product of nature. His theories were not without controversy, however.[16]

Some of the controversy generated by Ulrichs's work arose from the fact that he was not medically trained. For many within the psychiatric and medical fraternity that was sufficient grounds for dismissing his ideas, but to add insult to injury he was also a self-declared Urning. This rendered him in the eyes of many critics someone who needed treatment, not an audience. Ulrichs's ideas were also attacked by the likes of Karl Maria Benkert, the earliest known proponent of the term *homosexual* (ca. 1869), because by Ulrichs's account the male Urning possessed a "feminine soul," During the period marking the unification of the Germanic states, a specifically masculinist culture had developed, whose proponents were particularly hostile to the feminization of male-to-male desire. From the outset a tension existed between concepts of same-sex desire that relied on a notion of transposition or crossing and those that promoted male-to-male desire as a pure and idealized form of male bonding.[17]

Magnus Hirschfeld is said to have been responsible for popularizing the term *third sex*. He offered a schema of nonnormative sexualities and subjectivities that relied heavily upon the figure of the hermaphrodite.[18] Indeed each of the types in Hirschfeld's model represents a type of hermaphroditism. The g*enital type* referred to genital ambiguity and correlates (along with the next type) with what we understand today as intersex—a condition of the body and only the body; the *somatic type* referenced ambiguity at the level of secondary sex characteristics (distribution of adipose tissue and body hair, vocal tone, etc.); the *psychic type* signified transsexed subjectivity; and the *psychosexual type* included those with same-sex desires.[19] Hirschfeld qualified his third-sex model thus:

Since in our use of language we usually describe the bearers of semen cells simply as men and the possessors of egg cells flatly as women, there are therefore women with manly and men with womanly characteristics and these mixed forms are the ones *that are understood* under the expression of sexual intermediaries. We can order them most clearly as the sexual difference themselves, according to the 4 categories.[20]

Another of the early sexologists to fuse nonnormative desires and subjectivities with hermaphroditism was Richard von Krafft-Ebing, author of *Psychopathia Sexualis*. His work differed markedly from many of the early sexologists and reformers because it was grounded within the clinical frame of psychiatric medicine.[21] That field's dominant paradigm at the end of the nineteenth century regarding sexual behaviors and subjectivities turned on notions of degeneration that were part and parcel of a larger colonial anxiety regarding progress and race.[22] It was in this climate that the locus of medicine shifted from the body to incorporate the self, even as the organic inherited body remained as the theoretical foundation upon which psychiatrists like Krafft-Ebing based their claims, as the following quotation makes evident:

Intermediary gradations between the pure type of man and woman [are] possible, quite in accordance with the original bisexual predispositions of the foetus. These grades may be due to some interference in the evolution of our present mono-sexuality (corresponding physical and psychical sexual characteristics) based upon degenerative, especially hereditary degeneration conditions.[23]

For Krafft-Ebing sexuality referred to so much more than desire, orientation, and sexual practices: it also explicitly incorporated character, thought, will, and feeling. His classificatory system involved a four-stage progressive schema. In other words, Krafft-Ebing's was a developmental model. Each stage was represented by a specific type that ranged from the predominantly homosexual individual who bore a trace of heterosexual inclination (the psychosexual hermaphrodite) through to the most extreme type whose fully fledged "abnormal sexual instinct" was paralleled by a physiological transformation.[24] Individuals who fell into that category were said not only to embody the character and emotions of "the other," but were believed to undergo a bodily transformation so that they came to resemble the "opposite sex anthropologically."[25] Said transformations related to body shape, adipose distribution, the pitch and timbre of the voice, and complexion among others and thus were analogous to Hirschfeld's somatic hermaphrodite.

The above quotation provides an exquisite example of the way in which the aspects of the erotic and what we now know as gender were conflated with notions of progress, purity, and taint. Recourse to fetal development offered something of a dilemma for many of the sexologists and sexual reformers of the late nineteenth century precisely because their theories were developed within the sociopolitical climate of colonialism. Sexual dimorphism was believed to be a mark of advanced racial development: the more sexually dimorphic a population, the more civilized that population was said to be. In other words, monosexuality at the level of the body and the psyche represented the height of civilization. This resulted in the emergence of an ambiguous image of same-sex desire represented on the one hand in terms of a degeneration away from an *original* heterosexuality, and on the other hand as an atavistic regression toward a polymorphous sexuality.[26]

Contradictory representations of the hermaphrodite figure had, since classical antiquity, alternated between a mythic idea representing the union of all that was good in the male and female sexes and hermaphrodites as teratological monsters of excess. Elizabeth Grosz has noted that throughout history all the major terata have tended to be monsters of excess: that is, people "with two or more heads, bodies, or limbs, or with duplicate sexual organs."[27] Foucault registered that excess at another level with his suggestion that, historically, those deemed terata represented a double violation of the natural order— half human and half animal—and so constituted at the same time both "the impossible and the forbidden."[28]

By the early twentieth century, advances in medical technologies had begun to complicate hegemonic understandings of bodily sex. As it became increasingly clear that a person's somatic sex could not be relied upon as an absolute, it became harder for clinicians to justify the sex assignment of hermaphrodites on physiological grounds alone. This is the context in which increasing emphasis began to be placed on psychosocial factors such as social identity and sexual orientation in assigning a sex.[29] By the mid-1940s, that emphasis had thoroughly consolidated, as the work of psychologist Albert Ellis makes clear:

[A] *heterosexual hermaphrodite* is one whose sexual desires are directed towards members of the other sex to which he or she has been *raised*. A *homosexual hermaphrodite* is one whose libidinous desires are directed toward members of the same sex in which he or she has been *raised*. A *bisexual hermaphrodite* is one, no matter how reared, whose sex desires are directed towards both males and females.[30]

Echoing Krafft-Ebing's dictum, Ellis was of the view that an individual's erotic inclinations and orientations were not only a consequence of upbringing but were also an inseparable part of a person's psychosocial masculinity or femininity. This led him to frame the intersexed as heterosexual, homosexual, and bisexual (or alternatively, "psychosexually immature").[31]

Clearly Ellis's understanding of psychosocial status was fully saturated in a binary logic, but that in itself was not as significant as his framing of the intersexed as hetero-, homo-, and bisexual. By apprehending hermaphrodites' erotosexual status within the logic of bipolar sexuality, Ellis effectively made redundant the figure of a third sex. In other words, this conceptual move resulted in the epistemological and ontological erasure of the hermaphrodite subject. The significance of Ellis's ideas for John Money's theorizing will become evident when the discussion turns to Money's work later in the chapter.[32]

METHODOLOGICAL CONSIDERATIONS IN SEXOLOGY

In addition to generating a set of enduring conceptual principles, the early sex researchers employed various methodologies that became deeply embedded in the sexological tradition. While the work of Ulrichs prefigured the development of sexology as a discipline, the historical record makes clear that the field remains indebted to him on many counts. Ulrichs gathered information in the form of case studies, developed and refined a comprehensive classification schema, made a distinction between acts and identities, and accumulated data in a way that was devoid of moral approbation.[33]

Case studies became a hallmark of sexological enquiry and continue to be so to this day. A specific form of documentation, case studies are often marked by extraordinary detail regarding the presentation of the individual subjects, their medical diagnoses, personal histories, and so on. A notable feature of case studies is the opportunity afforded

individual subjects to contribute their own autobiographical statements, many of which are presented verbatim in case notes. While in
some instances autobiographical statements can be found interspersed
with clinicians' commentary, it was not unusual for them also to be
presented in stand-alone form.[34]

The second methodological hallmark of the sexual sciences is the
ongoing development of comprehensive classifications of sexual types.
Proponents of the scientific method expect that its application can and
will reveal the mysteries of sex in all their glory, since one of the central demands of the scientific method is that its subject matter yield to
taxonomic classification and categorization. By developing and continually refining classification systems, sexologists have attempted to
capture, in their entirety, fully exhaustive categories of nonnormative desires and, in many instances, exhaustive categories of sexual
types or characters. While Ulrichs was scorned by many of his contemporaries, his schemas remain significant for both their detail and
complexity.

Demarcating acts from orientations is the third sexological hallmark. Such a distinction was articulated by Ulrichs as early as 1868.[35]
It is perhaps most evident in his discussion regarding men whose primary attractions were directed toward women but who sometimes had
sex with other men. "Uraniasters," as he called them, were altogether
different from Urnings because the former "is and remains a man.
His nature as a man is only temporarily driven into the background.
His male susceptibility to the love of women never ceases."[36] This distinction is evident also in the work of Krafft-Ebing, who stressed the
need for clinicians to make clear distinctions between "perversity" and
"perversion" in order to maintain the integrity of their diagnoses. He
insisted:

Perversion of the sexual instinct,... is not to be confounded with *perversity*
in the sexual act; since the latter may be induced by conditions other than
psycho-pathological. The concrete perverse act, monstrous as it may be, is
clinically not decisive. In order to differentiate between disease (*perversion*)
and vice (*perversity*), one must investigate the whole personality of the individual and the original motive leading to the perverse act. Therein will be
found the key to the diagnosis.[37]

The fourth legacy that Ulrichs provided the early sexual scientists was
the idea that there was no place for moral judgments in the collection
of data. Many sexologists—although clearly not Krafft-Ebing—took
seriously Ulrichs's view that as professionals they had a responsibility,

indeed an obligation, to document human sexuality in all of its manifestations without taint of moral judgment. Havelock Ellis and Magnus Hirschfeld, for example, were among those who devoted their careers to amassing considerable amounts of data on sexual "anomalies" (read nonprocreative sexual behaviors) without pathologizing the behaviors or their protagonists. Hirschfeld articulated his position on the matter in the following way:

> The first commandment is to represent in a truly factual manner without any emotional expression; to be as objective as possible, to weigh the facts as far as possible, and in every respect to be without prejudice.[38]

Despite the efforts of the likes of Ulrichs, Ellis, and Hirschfeld to resist pathologizing nonnormative desires, they had little control over how their work was used by others. Indeed their data was appropriated by psychiatrists and by physicians to supplement the existing range of diagnostic options available at that time. Nonetheless, successive generations of sex researchers have held firmly to this principle. Alfred Kinsey, for example, firmly believed that sex research should involve the "accumulation of scientific fact completely divorced from questions of moral value and social custom."[39] Money's approach was similar, most notably realized through his renaming (and reclassifying) of the nomenclature of perversion. Replacing the term *perversion* with *paraphilia* was a deliberate attempt to circumvent the moral overtones associated with the former.

SEXOLOGICAL AXIOMS

Five key axioms have persisted in sexological thought from its inception and remain even today, rarely if ever questioned by those working in the field. These axioms not only underpin understandings of sexuality, they also underpin the way that gender is understood in the sexual sciences. The first and arguably most fundamental of these is the idea that the reproduction of the species represents the ultimate aim of human existence. This idea was popularized in the early 1800s by Charles Darwin's grandfather Erasmus, who declared sexual difference and sexual reproduction "the chef-d'oeuvre, or capital work of nature."[40] In accordance with this principle, sexual practices are driven by a reproduction imperative rather than the pursuit of pleasure. This premise not only fails to account for forms of sexual expression that fall outside of a heterosexual matrix, it also fails to account for those nonpenetrative expressions that fall within it.

The ascension of Darwinism in the mid- to late nineteenth century, or more precisely its application to human social existence, had a profound effect on the way the corporeal body came to be understood in relation to the social body. Effectively the Darwinian revolution institutionalized a reproductive paradigm that remains to this day at the center of biological and social inquiry. Its "totalising effects" transformed dimorphic sexual difference into a binary principle considered stable across time and space.[41] This had a number of significant consequences, two of which are relevant to the current discussion. The first was that all nonprocreative (hetero)sexual behaviors were cast as preliminary to the main event, as the term *foreplay* attests. The effect, as Carol Vance so eloquently suggests, was that "reproductive sexuality (glossed as heterosexual intercourse) appears as the meat and potatoes in the sexual menu, with other forms, . . . arranged as appetizers, vegetables, and desserts."[42]

A second related effect was that all nonprocreative sexual behaviors became a set of symptoms located on a continuum between normality and pathology. With reproduction as the touchstone of normative sexuality, every subject was potentially vulnerable to the taint of perversion. As a result, the line between normality and deviance became increasingly blurred because so-called normal sexuality always contained within it elements of perverse desire.[43] As medical science became increasingly credited with the ability to provide insights into the "truth" of nature through its exclusive access to the "unassailable reality of bones and organs," such truths were upheld as the legitimate foundation of moral order.[44] Among those unassailable truths was the principle that there are two and only two human sexes, male and female.

The idea that sex in all its guises is binary or dimorphic is the second maxim that has lain at the heart of the sexological project from the outset. Here I refer to sex indexed to bodies in terms of discrete categories of maleness or femaleness and as indexed to erotic practices, desires, fantasies, and tastes. The assumption that all forms of life were grounded in sexual dimorphism saturated the early classification systems, since understandings of sexual desire were predicated on the notion that opposites attract.[45] Again Karl Ulrichs's nomenclature served as a prototype of subsequent classification schemas grounded in this principle. Ulrichs proposed that in the case of Urnings, the virile Mannlinge's attractions were always directed toward the effeminate Weiblinge, paralleling mens' "natural" attraction to women and vice versa. In other words, masculinity and femininity were deemed complementary through their oppositionality.

Over time this assumption proved increasingly problematic for Ulrichs's theorizing, but rather than abandon sexual dimorphism as his central principle, Ulrichs responded by creating "a dizzying array of categories" of sexual variance.[46] At the same time, his reading of the embryological literature ultimately convinced Ulrichs that far too much emphasis was placed upon differences between the sexes, male and female. The existence of rudimentary physical structures (specifically, the Mullerian and Wolffian ducts) of the other in males and females was proof for Ulrichs that an individual with the body of one sex could have the soul of the other. Despite such insights, sexual dimorphism retains its tenacious hold in contemporary sexology, even (or especially) among those whose clinical work brings them into contact with the intersexed. For generations now, sex researchers and theorists have tended to interpret their data to "fit" the principle of sexual dimorphism, however awkwardly, rather than question its reach and its relevance in the face of evidence that calls the idea into question.

The third tenet woven through the history of sexological thought is the idea that the desire (or orientation) toward one's "own sex" represents an inverted form of normative desire. Normative in this context constitutes desire for males as a necessarily feminine trait and therefore the rightful property of female persons and conversely, desire for females as a masculine trait that is the rightful property of male persons. Ulrichs's theories again provided a prototype of the inversion model, and while his neologisms failed to stand the test of time, traces of his ideas and methods remain.

While it was certainly not the only model used by the early sexual scientists, the inversion model came to dominate the field as evident in the work of Havelock Ellis and Edward Carpenter, among others. It is important to note at this point (as a number of historians and critics of the sexual sciences have), that the invert was not the equivalent of the contemporary homosexual. Rather, inversion functioned—like (Money's) gender—as an umbrella term. It incorporated a range of deviant sexualities, homosexuality being just one of many.[47] As I go on to demonstrate, the specter of inversion continues to underpin contemporary theories of human sexuality and gender.[48]

The fourth axiom evident throughout sexological thought is the idea that deviant (that is, nonnormative) desires have some sort of constitutional or inherent basis. This principle is generally articulated through the idea that sexuality—like gender—has its origins during the first three months of embryonic development. Recourse to prenatal development carries with it a potency not dissimilar to that offered by genetic explanations, since implicit in both is a sense of the immutable. Ulrichs was arguably the first to draw an analogy with the undifferentiated fetus. Differentiation in utero was, for him, a process that led to three possible outcomes: male, female, and Urning. Invoking the figure of the hermaphrodite allowed Ulrichs to argue that the Urning fetus developed a hermaphroditic soul.

Those who were labeled perverts were considered by many doctors and psychiatrists of the day to be suffering from a congenital condition. More progressive doctors asserted that certain deviant sexual practices—once regarded as the choices of sinners or criminals—were in fact the involuntary symptoms of an individual's entire personality. In other words, they were "born that way." By claiming that the treatment of perverts was a medical rather than a criminal issue, doctors were able to enlarge medicine's terrain.[49] Moreover, the emphasis on personality paved the way for the then-nascent field of psychoanalysis (and later psychology) to take on a significant role in the management of aberrant desire.

The fifth persistent maxim evident in the sexological literature is the idea that genital morphology determines the sex of one's feelings. The development of a biology of binary sexual difference seemed to offer the means through which differences between the sexes could be reliably represented.[50] Weaving genital anatomies into the fabric of psychologies meant that "feelings [came to be] thought of as female or male in exactly the same sense as [a] penis or clitoris: anatomy equalled psychology."[51] Herdt has suggested that the issue of anomalous individuals became a primary preoccupation of both the sexual scientists and the sexual reformers during the late Victorian period. Such preoccupations led to the proliferation of classificatory schemas designed to identify and account for those whose minds, behaviors, and/or bodies defied the principle of sexual dimorphism. Krafft-Ebing's work particularly is notable for its attempt to demonstrate a link between "morbid love" and anatomical anomaly.[52] Why such intense interest? Could it be because a binary model has such a limited reach? Does an inability to contain or explain sexual variance produce or stimulate the compulsion to explain? Thanks to Foucault, the idea that the late 1800s marks the birth of the homosexual as a subject has become widely accepted.[53] From that moment there was a subject to be worked on, to be discovered and uncovered. Equally importantly, the technologies required for that work—both medical and therapeutic—now existed. Applying a Foucauldian analysis of power to the late-nineteenth-century preoccupation with sexual deviance—where power does things and produces things—we can say that dimorphism itself produced anomaly and generated its proliferation.[54] This in turn stimulated entire industries of thought and clinical practice.

The legacy of conflating psychologies and anatomies is, of course, no less evident today; personality traits and characteristics continue to be promoted as specifically gendered in psychological theory and practice; in medical, sexological, and biological research; and throughout many disciplines within the humanities and social sciences (including a considerable amount of feminist theorizing). The media and populist literature also contribute—albeit in more simplistic forms—through television and film, print, and literature generated by the self-help industry, for example. The net effect of such widespread reinforcement and support from so many quarters has led to this idea taking on the guise of eternal verity. So how does the conflation of psychologies and anatomies play out in Money's theorizing of sex and desire?

MONEY ON SEX AND DESIRE

John Money's theories of sexuality—like those of gender—were indebted to the intersexed. Normative acculturation into a gender included acculturation into normative sexuality—that is, to heterosexuality. Instances of nonconformity to assigned sex could manifest in various ways for the intersexed but were most likely to do so through a person's sexual life. Sexual nonconformity became gender nonconformity through bisexual or homosexual desire.

Money remained insistent that *most* case-managed or "clinically habilitated" intersexed individuals who were raised as girls grew up to have a completely unambivalent *hetero*sexual status. Recall that in the early work of Money and the Hampsons a person's psychological health was measured in no small part on their expressed and/or actualized sexual orientation.[55] Those girls who expressed a desire for women must have been subjected, according to Money and colleagues, to some kind of masculinization process in utero. They identified the prenatal period—specifically the first critical period for gender—as the point at which it was possible that a stimulus was able to exert itself on the developing brain. Just how this process worked and what it involved, they could not say. As the architect of intersex case management protocols, Money had a vested interest in the capacity of those protocols to produce "heterosexual hermaphrodites" since, above all, a heterosexual status provided evidence of the veracity of his treatment model.[56] Not only were the intersexed expected to be or become exemplary males and females, they were also expected to become exemplary heterosexuals.

Just as Money insisted that gender was not the product of nature or of culture but rather a complex interaction of both, so too in his view was sexuality. And he insisted, after Albert Ellis and many of his sexological forebears, that sexuality was a component of gender rather than a separate element of subjectivity. Ever critical of social and biological determinist explanations, Money argued for the merits of a different form of determinism—a developmental determinism. For Money people's sexual status or orientation was an outcome of their developmental history, including their prenatal history. What mattered was not whether any particular determinant was innate or acquired but rather that it *was* a determinant. Why? Because he was equally convinced that sexual status and orientation became hardwired in the brain in the same way as gender. Any deviation from the "proper" developmental path requires, in fact demands, an account of how it happened or, more precisely, what went *wrong* and when.

Almost all of the fundamental tenets and methodologies developed by Ulrichs in the first instance almost a century and a half ago are writ large in Money's work. Traces of Ulrichs's ideas can be found all through Money's theories of sexuality just as they are evident in his theories of gender. Money proposed that every individual possessed a structure similar to the template that coded for gender. In fact this second structure was said to be overlaid by the gender template. In the mid-1980s, Money coined this second template a "lovemap." This represented the very first determinant of a person's future sexual styles and erotic preferences. Money defined it thus:

A personalised, developmental representation or template in the mind and in the brain that depicts the idealised lover and the idealised program of sexuo-erotic activity with that lover as projected in imagery and ideation, or actually engaged in with that lover."[57]

Here we have an example of the way in which the idea that one's sexuality had a constitutional basis played out in Money's theories. Not only did this lovemap develop in utero, it became hardwired into the brain after being acted upon by postnatal environmental stimuli. As with the map that coded for gender, once a person's lovemap became hardwired, it was apparently not amenable to change. Imprinting implied immutability, as did the idea of hardwiring. Remember that Money's theories of gender turned on the concept of critical periods, and so it is hardly surprising that his explanations of sexuality did as well. His developmental explanation of erotosexual status involved a series of stages or sequences that began in prenatal life. Sometime during prenatal development, a range of sexually dimorphic traits bedded down in the brain, predisposing a person toward a particular erotosexual orientation as heterosexual, homosexual, or bisexual. Sexual status was as much a component of gender identity, he insisted, as any other.

Citing experimental animal research and "people with a known history of abnormal hormone levels in prenatal development," as direct forms of evidence, Money once again extended his ideas from the intersexed to the general population to explain how everybody came to have a sexual orientation.[58] This is another example of how the "abnormal" to "normal" trajectory played out in Money's work. The prenatal phase was not, in Money's view, an exclusive determinant, nor was it the primary (read most important) stage in this process. Rather, the primary origins of one's sexual orientation were to be found in the same developmental period of late infancy and early childhood when gender identity differentiated as male or female. Once established, hormonal changes at puberty then brought that orientation into full expression.

Locking sexuality's origins into the earliest years of life stifled Money's attempts to adequately theorize sexuality. The demonstrable variance in sexual experiences and practices over the course of a life span could hardly be explained by constructs of stasis and fixedness. The time lag between the initial establishment (some of it prenatal) and the manifestation of an individual's sexual life was equally problematic, not least because, by his own admission, very little data existed about the qualitative dimensions of sex.

Yet Money tenaciously held to the view that a person's sexual status was defined on the basis of a partner's body morphology and genitalia (which were presumed to match, of course) as the following definition makes clear (note the framing of sexuality *as* gender):

The definitive characteristic of a homosexual or heterosexual gender identity is whether the sex of the body morphology and of the external genital anatomy of the partner with whom one is capable of falling in love is, respectively, the same as or different than one's own. For the bisexual, either may qualify.[59]

Because sexual partnerships of males with females were more prevalent than males with males or females with females, same-sex desire signified to Money that the coding for sex had somehow become crossed.[60]

Hog-tied by the binary he could not or would not relinquish, Money painted himself into a conceptual corner. It was not that he viewed homosexual or lesbian desire as sick or bad, since like all good sexual scientists he approached his work from a morally neutral position. It was just that his model could account for those who breached heteronorms (by accident or design) only in terms of something gone awry. At the same time Money was insistent that for gays, lesbians, and bisexuals, crossing referred to just one component of a person's gender coding—the erotosexual component, since:

There may be very little that is crosscoded in homophilia, which is indeed the case in gay men whose gender coding is all masculine, except for the sex of the partner with whom they fall in love [and vice-versa for lesbians].[61]

Here we see an attempt at the recuperation of homosexual and lesbian subjects. A person's sexual status was to be considered independent of any and all other components of gender (such as an occupation, recreational and/or intellectual interests, and domestic life). Yet ultimately *all* behaviors and interests that confound stereotypes are, in Money's schema, cross-coded or transposed phenonomena.

As was his wont, Money did not let a lack of conclusive evidence get in the way of postulating causal explanations. The weight Money ascribed to hormones—prenatal and pubertal—as determinants of sexual orientation exceeded the available evidence.[62] In saying this I am not trying to deny that hormones are implicated in either the quality or the rhythms of a person's sexuality. It is to point to the mismatch between the strength of Money's assertions and the lack of evidential support.[63] He concurred that endocrinological research into sexual orientation had failed to produce any conclusive evidence that hormone saturation at a particular stage of fetal development triggered either sexual dimorphism or the direction of one's desires. And so it was with postnatal environmental determinants.

Money acknowledged that the sexological knowledge of the day did not allow for any hypotheses to be made regarding the types of biographical conditions that might facilitate heterosexuality, homosexuality, or bisexuality in non-intersexed children. But that did not deter him from coming up with a range of conditions that he believed to be *likely* determinants: conditions that reiterated the equation of anatomies with psychologies, that is, that one's genitals determine one's gender. For the non-intersexed Money offered three scenarios, each with a necessary precondition. Societal prohibitions on juvenile sexual rehearsal play were at the top of the list, stigmatization by the peer group was ranked as the second precondition, and adversarial parental relations were the third.

According to Money, the period at which young children engaged in juvenile sexual rehearsal play was critical to their future sexual status and sexual health. In his view, a major feature of childrearing practices in Western societies was the mismanagement of this phase of a child's life through prohibition, censure, and punishment. When not mismanaged, juvenile sexual rehearsal play inevitably evolved into heterosexual rehearsal play in a seemingly unproblematic teleological fashion. Children reared in such environments were said to "fraternise heterosocially rather than homosocially at puberty and thus into their sexuality." The implication is that juvenile sexual rehearsal play works to augment gender identity through a (hetero)normative outcome. Of course, whether there was any direct causal relation between the suppression of such play and a cross-coding of sexual orientation, Money was unable to say with any certainty. The ethnographic record, however, led Money to believe there might well be one.[64] That would explain why:

In societies where boy-girl sexual rehearsal play is not punished or prevented, adult homosexuality is absent or rare. Boy-boy or girl-girl sexual rehearsal play, where it is by custom not illicit, does not lead to homosexuality in adulthood, although it may lead to bisexual adaptability.[65]

Yet the question must be asked, if the childrearing practices of Western societies contribute toward same-sex desire in the way Money suggests (that is, through mismanagement), why do they not produce considerably more people with homo- or bisexual orientations? Most children raised in such contexts are subject to the very prohibitions he identified.

As to the influence of peer groups in determining a child's future sexuality, recall the role of peers in the establishment of one's gender identity. Learning to be a gender involved learning what was appropriate to yours and what was not. This involved a process of identification *and* complementation, establishing self and other.

From this perspective something in the child's biography had to work upon a preexisting tendency toward homosexuality or heterosexuality. That something was, in all likelihood, the influence of a child's peers.

Money wrote of the positive and negative operations of peer influence; their setting of "fashions and standards of conformity, impos[ing] sanctions, and stigmatiz[ing] nonconformists."[66] For children with "anatomically normal" genitals, stigmatization about their nonconformity to normative gender roles and stereotypical behaviors served as a determinant of future development.[67] With respect to the intersexed, Money offered differential scenarios to account for cross-coding depending on whether a person was raised as a girl or a boy. For those reared as girls he identified prenatal masculinization of the brain as a necessary precondition, and for those reared as boys, stigmatization by peers was said to be responsible. Money made a direct correlation between the possession of differently formed genitalia and same-sex desire (referenced to the body morphology of one's partner). Variant genitals invited stigmatization and prohibited some individuals from being "*properly* a boy."[68] Effectively, by this account, the genesis of lesbian desire in the intersexed was to be found in the womb (a product of nature, even if it was nature gone awry), while gay desire was born of the playground; hers is "nature made" and his is made by culture. Corrective surgery was held up as a form of insurance against stigmatization by a child's peers in the first instance and therefore as insurance against the development of a crossed or transposed gender manifesting as bisexuality, or as homosexuality.

The idea that "correct" genitalia would assure a proper gender is in keeping with the nineteenth-century principle that sex physiology determined the sex of one's feelings. In most Western contexts (at least), girls are extended considerably more latitude with respect to gendered behaviors than are boys. As a result tomboyism is tolerated in girls in ways that its male equivalent, sissiness, is not in boys. Nonetheless, both are implicated in discourse as evidence of "queerness." The discourses to which I refer include, but are certainly not limited to, the discursive formations of the sexual scientists, since they are deployed in the narrative accounts of many gay men and lesbians, their parents and siblings, and the wider culture.

The third explanation offered by Money for the origins of crosscoding in young boys concerned the father's role in facilitating a protohomosexuality. A clinical consultation with the parents of a five-year-old boy who would today be considered as gender dysphoric inspired Money to develop a new hypothesis on how fathers contributed toward "the genesis of feminism [read feminization] in a son's G-I/R (gender-identity/role)."[69] Offering a psychoanalytic type of explanation with a twist, Money posited that an adversarial relationship between a young boy's parents set the stage for (and constituted a necessary environmental condition for) a father to court his son's allegiance, casting the child in the role of a "wife substitute—if not for the present—then for the future."[70] This particular hypothesis reveals

Money at his creative best and for that reason I quote at length his view on a little boy's response to marital disharmony:

The son, for his part, may solicit his father's allegiance as a formula for keeping him in the household, and for preventing a parental separation. If the father has already gone, or even if he had died, the son's gender transposition may serve to solicit his daddy's miraculous return. His life becomes a living fable of the boy who will become daddy's bride, for the evidence is plentiful that a daddy can be counted on to return to the home that his wife keeps ready for him. . . . The young son who becomes self-allocated to the role of *daughter* [as wife-in-waiting], and thereby becomes a bonding agent who keeps the family intact, is likely to keep that role of bonding agent intact in perpetuity [reaching] adulthood with a gender status that is homosexual or, maybe, in a rare minority of cases, transexual [*sic*] or transvestophile.[71]

Money went on to cite "new preliminary evidence, unpublished" that suggested that cross-coding of this sort could be rectified if the child was able to be relieved of the self-imposed responsibility of holding the family together. In other words, it was possible to redirect the child toward a heteronormative outcome. This rather florid hypothesis was devised on the basis of a single case, yet its implications are enormous in light of what can only be described as a growth industry in the United States of therapeutic interventions on children considered to be gender identity disordered (or dysphoric). These interventions are specifically designed to ensure that children do not grow up to be gay.[72]

RELATIVITY IN SEX

While cognizant of the dangers of cultural relativity, Money was convinced that his theories of sexuality, like those of gender, had universal application and were responsive to cross-cultural variation. How, precisely? His advice for dealing with cultural relativity was simply to tolerate it. Money pointed to relativity in genetics and the fact that femaleness was a straightforward matter of two Xs and maleness, of one X and one Y, despite the "undisputed evidence" of many other configurations (XXY, XYY, and XO being cases in point). Similarly, in human sexology the idea that men have penises and women vulvas was tolerated despite their relativity with respect to the intersexed. Yet the penis/vulva criterion remained for Money a "good enough approximation for stipulating that masculine is what males do and feminine is what females do,"[73] even though it was far from ideal. Sexuality tied to gender and gender roles, which are in turn tied to genital anatomy, represents a triangulation that seeks to stabilize. Jay Prosser articulates the process and its outcomes thus:

> Sex, gender, and desire are unified through the representation of hetero-sexuality as primary and foundational. Female, femininity, and woman appear as stable and conjoined terms through their opposition to male, masculin-ity, and man. Gender in other words, appears *as* identity. What stabilizes the association and keeps the two sets discrete and antithetical is the apparent naturalness of heterosexual desire.[74]

Money's assertion that relativity was tolerable lends weight to one of the strongest criticisms leveled at the application of the sci-entific method to human social existence; that complex unstable phenomena—as the sexual surely is—must be reduced and homog-enized in the interests of analytical convenience. Consequently, the "multiple meaning of all sexualities [get] dissolved into global identi-ties that [obscure] more than they reveal, beyond the social responses" they serve to legitimate.[75] Moreover, taxonomies by their very nature assume a degree of permanence or stability of their objects that render them somehow ahistorical. How ironic then that Money should cast broadsides at poststructuralism and feminism for their use of cultural relativity (as well as their anti-biologist tendencies). In the mid-1990s Money would refer to Foucault as the "high priest [of] politically correct scholarship."[76]

It is clear in his writing that Money was fully cognizant of the effects of the "cultural fixation" on sexual difference.[77] Indeed he argued that this fixation had "insidiously infected sexual science so as to ensure that its focus is on explaining sex difference, not sex similarity."[78] Despite that level of critical awareness, Money's own work has been hugely instrumental in reinforcing those very differences. This is an inevitable result of his unwavering commitment to the idea that there are only two human sexes. The idea that "if males do it, it is mascu-line and if females do it, it is feminine" is clearly based on ideological norms that reflect what people *ought* to do rather than reflecting accu-rately what people *actually* do.[79] Money recognized that ideological norms rely upon criteria that, while appearing to be based on "eternal verities . . . are actually culture-bound dogmas of history, authority, and the cultural heritage," all the while creating theories that augmented and reproduced those very same dogmas.[80]

Another long-standing sexological principle evident in Money's work is the distinction between acts and identities. Money devoted a considerable amount of his career to mapping out and accounting for sexuality in all its manifestations. His nomenclature of sexuality was multilayered and included a range of subcategories, one of which was designed to account for those whose sexual behaviors were out of step with their (inevitably hetero-) sexual identities: most obviously a heterosexually identified male who, in varying contexts, engaged in sexual behaviors with other men. Money, like many of his predecessors believed that

a sexual status (or orientation) is not the same as a sexual act. It is possible to participate in homosexual acts, and even to be cajoled or coerced into participation without becoming predestined to have a permanent homosexual status—and vice versa for heterosexuality.[81]

Money offered as examples people confined to sex-segregated institutions such as prisons or boarding schools who engaged in sexual acts with their cohorts during the period of their "confinement" and who, once outside of that context, resumed exclusively heterosexual (or homosexual) behaviors.

MONOSEXUALITY

During the course of developing his theories on sexuality Money found value in framing sexual status in terms of mono- versus ambisexuality. This allowed him to map heterosexuality and homosexuality in a relatively clear-cut manner. By Money's account "a strong prenatal proclivity" that was reinforced postnatally would increase the odds of a monosexual outcome be it homo- or hetero-sexual.[82] In the case of a heterosexual outcome, this process would occur "with or without a weak deflection towards homosexuality, and vice versa for homosexuality."[83] Since heterosexuality was normative—both statistically and ideologically—it warranted little more than a straightforward developmental explanation. Homosexuality, on the other hand, warranted more attention because it was nonnormative and therefore must, by Money's account, be more complicated.

Money suggested that a homosexual outcome required strong postnatal reinforcement or an endorsement of gender cross-coding. Money qualified that statement by stressing that endorsement could function at any number of levels and did not necessarily equate to children's engagement in genital same-sex practices, although of course it might, since "genital sex" was but one of the many components of Money's gender. Yet genital contact between boys and other males was not in itself sufficient to form the basis of a homosexual status in adult life, in Money's view: "Boys who in late childhood establish an explicitly sexual and genital relationship with an older, pedophilic male lover are not inevitably foreordained to have a homosexual status in adolescence and adulthood."[84] Yet this statement is at odds with his claim that in a homosexually oriented individual, cross-coding of the erotosexual component of gender had to be considered "alone and independently of all the other components."[85] The above quotation links directly to one of Money's more provocative and controversial assertions: namely that intergenerational sex in and of itself was not harmful to children. He believed that harm in such contexts was the result of coercion or force, not of sex.[86]

By contrast, it was entirely possible in Money's view that cross-coding might well be endorsed by a sensuous and/or affectionate (that is, a specifically nonsexual) relationship between a child and another male, particularly the father. By positioning a boy's affectional relations with his father in this way, Money accorded that relationship the power to produce same-sex desire in a way that early sexual experiences did not. It is noteworthy that since the late 1990s there has been increasing emphasis on the perils of the so-called crisis of masculinity. One of the most often cited strategies for circumventing or relieving such a crisis is the promotion of precisely this type of relation between fathers (or father figures) and their sons.[87] Applying Money's logic to the current context, one could propose that promoting these types of affectational relations between fathers and sons would lead to a higher prevalence of homosexual and/or bisexual men. There is, however, no evidence to support that.

AMBISEXUALITY

For Money bi- or ambisexuality had to be understood as a matter of degree and as a matter of temporality. He made those distinctions in part as a response to, and rebuttal of, the work of Kinsey, a point I take up further toward the end of this section. In Money's view, very few bisexuals were attracted in equal proportions to both men and women. While he thought it possible for a person to have a "prenatal proclivity" toward bisexuality, that proclivity would need to be worked upon by postnatal forces of similar proportions. This was, in his view, highly unlikely since the "gravitional pull, socially" was always in the direction of monosexuality, not least because children encountered very few role models of "a bisexual mode of existence."[88] In those very rare cases of equal attraction, Money suggested that the capacity for an erotic response (of equal measure) for both men and women "was designed into them."[89] The yardstick of a truly (50:50) bisexual orientation was in his view the capacity to fall in love equally both with men and with women. Yet Money did not stipulate what he meant by equally or how it might possibly be measured. Was it necessary to have an equal number of what he referred to as limerent experiences with men and with women over the life span? How might it be possible to determine equalness since, just as no two sexual experiences can be said to be exactly the same, neither can one's experiences of falling in love be said to be qualitatively the same experience.

It was more likely, he suggested, that people whose sexual status was ambisexual were disproportionately attracted to men or to women, respectively. Returning to his proclivity hypothesis, Money suggested that the necessary conditions for a predominantly heterosexual form of bisexuality would include "a strong prenatal proclivity towards heterosexuality and a strong postnatal defection towards homosexuality...and vice versa for a predominantly homosexual bisexuality."[90] He was also of the view that this, the most common form of sexuality, was marked by restriction since the person's capacity to fall in love would be limited to the dominant sex of attraction.

Taken to its logical conclusion this would suggest that such subjects are really, underneath it all, homosexual or heterosexual. In other words: monosexual. Here we see an example of the way that the modernist epistemology of sexuality perpetually banishes bisexuality from the here and now.[91] While our current model of sexuality is technically bipolar rather than binary, sexuality is intricately tied to binary gender and in fact is subordinate to it. As a result sexuality appears (or is made to appear) to mimic the dyadic character of gender, demanding that everything be apprehended in either/or terms. It seems that one of the few ways that bisexuality can be rendered intelligible is by co-option into one or the other of the two *legitimate* sexual categories such that bisexuals are "really gay," or "really straight." It remains rare for someone to be deemed "really bisexual."[92] As a result, bisexuality becomes an abstract theoretical concept that does not, and cannot, exist in the here and now.[93] Cast out of the present, an abstracted bisexuality reinforces the supposed naturalness of a monosexual order and its privileged categories.[94]

With respect to temporality, Money made a distinction between concurrent and sequential bisexuality. Concurrent bisexuality, as the name suggests, references sexual expression and/or desire toward males and females in a simultaneous fashion. While some might consider this form of bisexuality to offer "the best of both worlds," for Money it had a dark underbelly, with the specter of malignancy ever present.[95] That malignancy played, out in Money's view, through a vociferous homophobia. He went on to name examples of malignant bisexuals in the North American context and included in his list the likes of J. Edgar Hoover, Joseph McCarthy's legal counsel Ray Cohn, politicians whom he described as "fanatical homophobic ultraconservatives of the religious new right," and many conservative religious leaders.[96]

Others to qualify as malignant bisexuals were gaybashers, those ostensibly "straight" men who pick up gay men, engage in sexual acts with them (be they consensual or nonconsensual), and then, in Money's words, "exorcise their own homosexual guilt" by assaulting or murdering their victims.[97] Malignant bisexuals suffered from what Money called an *exorcist syndrome* where a person's internalized "homophobic war against their own homosexuality [became] externalised into a war against homosexuality in others."[98] Interestingly Money considered that society at large showed evidence of lesser degrees of this very same syndrome. Why else, he asked, would otherwise-decent people persecute or tolerate the persecution of gays and lesbians, rather than tolerating instead those who "are destined to have a different way of being human in love and sex."[99] Indeed, it was precisely this form of intolerance, he believed, that formed the breeding ground for generation after generation of malignant bisexuals, a point that is surely difficult to argue with.

Concurrent bisexuality's counterpart was its sequential form, which, compared to the former, was remarkably benign. Determining its prevalence was problematic according to Money, since its pervasiveness in "contemporary western cultures [was] masked behind the prevalence statistics of homosexuality."[100] In other words, it was masked by the rhetoric of sexual identity politics that renders people who come out after living as heterosexual or bisexual as "really gay" all along.

Sequential bisexuality was relatively benign in Money's view but not completely so. Despite Money's insistence that homoeroticism was neither pathological nor paraphilic in and of itself, the explanations he offered drip with failure and, in many instances, trauma. To give some examples, Money suggested that while the transition from one form of monosexuality to the other could occur autonomously, it might equally result from a broken home environment, the death of a parent, or "sexual apathy in the marriage."[101] The later expression of homosexuality (following a heterosexual phase) may even, he suggested, be "associated with the recovery from illness or debilitation (e.g., recovery from alcoholism) that had masked the homosexual potential."[102]

Transition in the other direction (that is, toward heterosexuality) was likely to be regarded (and recorded) as a successful outcome of therapeutic intervention precisely because it was a movement toward a norm. At the same time, same-sex desire was a condition that could not be cured even if it was to be averted in the young.

Money held particular contempt for those who claimed to have successfully cured homosexuality. He was adamant that claims of successful outcomes (posited by their interlocuters as cures) were fallacious, illusory in much the same way as claims of curing left-handedness. In both cases, the appearance of a successful reorientation to heterosexuality/right-handedness was indicative of an ever-present and underlying bisexuality/ambidexterity. In this sense any shift in one's sexual status was in reality a shift from ambi- to monosexuality.

Money took the opportunity in the context of this discussion to roundly criticize the work of Kinsey et al.[103] The unidimensionality of the Kinsey scale meant that it could provide no information on the number of same-sex encounters across a lifetime nor whether such encounters were sequential or concurrent with an individual's heterosexual encounters. Most problematic for Money was the fact that a person who had thousands of sexual partners over a lifetime could score the same (bisexual) ranking on the scale as someone who had had just two sexual partners—or in fact just two sexual experiences. Because of this he deemed Kinsey's scale to be a blunt instrument that revealed little about people's sexual status as homosexual, heterosexual, or bisexual. While Kinsey's work can certainly be critiqued for its reliance upon a unidimensional rather than a multidimensional continuum, it was precisely his point that sexual practices and behaviors did not constitute particular types (e.g., the homosexual, the heterosexual). Long before the *Sexual Behavior* volumes were published Kinsey had made a strong case that while there were individuals who were exclusively homosexual or exclusively heterosexual in their practices, "the picture is one of endless intergradations between every combination of homosexuality and heterosexuality."[104] For that reason Kinsey was adamant that the terms should never be used as substantive nouns, since one could really speak only of homosexual or heterosexual acts, fantasies, and/or erotic conduct.[105]

Since Money's theories of sexuality were grounded in a determinist frame, he was especially critical of the concept of object choice in sex.[106] Voluntarism of course represents the antithesis of determinism, in all its guises. For Money the notion of object choice represented the scientific fallacy that hetero- and homosexuality involved voluntary choice. The danger of recourse to voluntarism for Money was that sexuality was then explained by fiat and so "constitute[d] the fallacy of scientific nihilism."[107] He had this to say on the matter:

> Being homosexual (or bisexual or heterosexual) is not a preference or choice. It is a status... concordant or discordant with the reproductive status of the genitalia, or an androgynous combination of both possibilities. The ultimate criterion of homosexuality, bisexuality, or heterosexuality is not simply the sex of the partner with whom one's own sex organs are shared, but the sex of the partner toward whom one undergoes the experience of being love-smitten.[108]

Here we catch a glimpse of Money the romantic, as love ultimately determines one's sexuality. But importantly, his framing of genitals in this way again privileges reproduction as the raison d'être of human sexuality. While genitalia represent one of the anatomical sites of reproduction, it is not clear how genital "reproductive status" is relevant to sexuality for those whose sexual practices and capacity to fall in love lie with people whose bodies resemble their own "genitally." Nor is it clear for those whose favorite sexual practices have little to do with peno-vaginal encounters and/or the "spilling" of sperm.

PARAPHILIC DESIRE

Money reconfigured the century-old categories of perversion by organizing them into six metacategories that he called "grand paraphilic stratagems."[109] Within those six categories he distributed more than 50 distinct types.[110] While space does not permit an in-depth investigation of the multitude of paraphilias that Money categorized and classified, it would be remiss to examine his models of sexuality without reference to them, given the status they were accorded in relation to sexual orientation. It was Money's view that the past classification of same-sex desire as paraphilic was scientifically untenable since "paraphilia is an opportunistic trespasser into the lovemaps of either heterophilia or homophilia, or of those lovemaps that combine both, bisexuality."[111] Everyone was susceptible to paraphilic tendencies since they constituted an effect of a warped or "vandalised gendermap and/or lovemap."[112]

Just as there was no conclusive evidence for the precise role hormones played in determining a person's sexual orientation, no conclusive evidence existed regarding physiological factors involved in a paraphilic sexuality. Nonetheless Money suggested the best present hypothesis was that the "temporal lobe or limbic brain [was subject to] epileptic dysfunction" in the prenatal phase and was later acted upon by postnatal developmental factors.[113] Equally, it might result from biographical experiences such as humiliation and trauma resulting from being punished for engaging in sexual rehearsal play. Just as Krafft-Ebing had insisted on a distinction between perversion (as sexual instinct) and perversity (as sexual acts), so did Money.

Unusual sexual activities expressed as an *embellishment* of one's regular sexual activities were not paraphilic in Money's view. In order for such activities to be so, they needed to have an obsessive, compulsive, or addictive element to them that foreclosed the capacity for orgasm by other means. Obsessive paraphilia served as a ruse, he said, to separate corrupted forms of lust from virtuous forms of love in an individual. While paraphilias could be ameliorated, Money did not believe they could be cured per se.[114] Why not? Because under his terms, sexual tastes were generally established (hardwired) prior to adolescence and manifested later.

Money's ideas of the sexual—as a component of gender—fall prey to the logic of a binary framework, just as his understandings of "the body" do. In the following chapter I raise the idea of a specifically hermaphroditic eroticism in part to demonstrate the impossibility of such a thing within current conceptions of the sexual. But more than this, I do so because growing numbers of those who are intersexed are demanding that we expand our understandings of the sexual in order to create a space to think about and talk about forms of eroticism that cannot be apprehended—let alone comprehended (even as paraphilic)—within the epistemological frameworks we currently have at our disposal.

Exploring the Limits of Money's "Sex"

A number of contemporary theorists of sexuality have entered into a critical dialogue with Money's ideas as part of a broader engagement with the sexual sciences. All share a concern with the consequences of Money's commitment to the fundamental sexological principles identified in the first sections of this chapter. They also share a recognition of the extraordinary complexity of erotic desires, tastes, and styles and the vital importance of factoring in context and the meanings people give to their sexual experiences and relations. Tolman and Diamond argue strongly—as did Money—for the merits of an interactionist approach in sex research against the more usual bifurcation of nature versus nurture.[115] In theory interactionism offers a useful means of accounting for the ways in which physiological, sociocultural, and political factors work together to produce and shape subjective sexual desires, styles, and practices. Yet Money's work must surely serve as a caution that even when the interactions of the biological and the sociocultural are taken into account, there is no guarantee that such an approach will achieve the kind of work that Tolman and Diamond envisage.

In the contemporary sexual sciences, scant recognition is given to the existence of a plurality of homosexualities and even less to a plurality of heterosexualities. While Money's understandings of same-sex desire recognize a certain degree of plurality in sex, his ideas nonetheless fall prey to the homogenizing impulses of taxonomy that are part and parcel of the scientific method.[116] For William Simon one of the major obstacles to recognizing the plurality of sex has been the "naturalization of [the sexual] with its commitment to concepts of the sexual as a matter of organs, orifices, and phylogenetic legacies."[117] Indeed Money's work is saturated in all three. His account of a person's sexual status focuses on the body morphology of those with whom they are able to fall in love, but as Edward Stein argues, it is not clear that Money's focus on genital and body morphology can do the work he believes that it can. Stein asks pointedly, what exactly does Money mean by "same," and moreover, how similar do two bodies have to be to qualify as being of the same morphology?[118] For Money the answer to both those questions was straightforward, since he believed that all bodies can, and it seems should, be divided into two distinct classes. His account of sexual orientation is problematic for the very reason that people's tastes in terms of body morphology vary dramatically, but more importantly, they do so independent of sexual orientation(s). Thus there is a case to be made that bodily and genital morphology are but two factors in the melange of sexual tastes.

The concept of phylogenetic legacies[119] makes its appearance in Money's work to explain masculine and feminine roles including erotosexual and reproductive roles. His commitment to the idea of reciprocity between men and women in sex (and in gender) meant that same-sex relationships—like their heterosexual equivalents—figure in Money's work in terms of complementarity: one partner is cast in the role of the man and the other, in the role of the woman, irrespective of the "bodily sex" of either party. He was convinced that sexual compatibility was a function of complementarity, whatever one's proclivities or orientation. Appropriately matched lovemaps (of whatever flavor) were essential to the sexual health and well-being of individuals, and therefore to the well-being of the wider populous. That idea, however, was always—consciously or otherwise—filtered through Money's heteronormative lens.

As to the third concept, Money bemoaned a lack of reasonable theories of orifices in sex and indeed of scientific explanations regarding "oral sex, nipple sex ... clitoral sex and vaginal sex, penile sex, scrotal sex."[120] He believed such work important because of the relative differences between people with respect to which organs and orifices provided the greatest orgasmic satisfaction. Moreover, he considered this type of work necessary to determining, "how many different orgasmic spectrums there are, and how to fit each person on the right one with a matching partner."[121] Therein lay the future challenge of the sexual sciences in Money's view.

Money's reliance on a developmental framework revealed its limits through the framing of same-sex desire as a form of transposition or cross-coding, in Walter Bockting's view. Over 40 years of research has produced little evidence to support gender role complementarity in gay male relationships. This is not to deny that this may be one model in same-sex relations, but rather to suggest that it is certainly not the only model, nor is it necessarily the dominant one. Similarly, while heterosexual reproductive sex may lie at the heart of many individuals' sexual and gendered identities, it cannot be said to be true for all.[122]

Attending to how meaning is made by sexual "actors" may well create opportunities for the development of more sophisticated understandings of the erotic. Sexology has been roundly castigated in recent times not only for its failure to explore how people make such meaning, but also for its failure to attend to the issue of subjective experience. Both Deborah Tolman and Walter Bockting suggest that descriptive rather than developmental models offer a far more productive means to understanding the interrelatedness (or otherwise) between gender identity and sexual orientation(s). Descriptive models can also be put to work to develop richer and more fruitful understandings of how different forms of sexual desire are dependent upon different kinds of interactions between the physiological and the contextual. Examining the role of context and its interplay with bodily processes and temporal changes makes intuitive sense in thinking through the very messy and complex business that is the sexual.

Money's commitment to binary sex-gender and reciprocity, along with his fixation on prevalence and frequency, leads at best to a limited understanding of human sexuality. Together those commitments lead Money to oversimplify relations of infinite complexity, even though his explanations are far from simple, as I have demonstrated. Money's entangling of intrapsychic experience (as identity) with observable behavior (role) necessarily assumes a direct parallel between social reality and psychic reality, which allows him to "ignore the complexity of links between the sexual aspects of self and all other aspects of self and the ways in which gender roles reflect the linking of individual history with that of surrounding social life."[123]

Money's theorizing of the sexual is also compromised by the degree of faith he bestowed on the explanatory powers of neurophysiology and bodily chemistry—sans direct evidence. Despite being unable to offer any solid data to support his claims, Money never shied away from venturing into the realms of causality, even while warning of its dangers. He was at the same time highly critical—dismissive even— of psychological explanations of sexuality grounded in the concept of motivation.

In many of Money's texts, lengthy autobiographical accounts taken from case notes shed some light on the subjective quality and the meaning of sexuality for a number of his patients, yet most of his writing fails to explore those elements in any depth. He was more concerned that the data support the veracity of his theoretical position, rather than explore the ways in which it might complicate—both strengthen and weaken—normative understandings of sex-gender? As Edward Stein notes, Money's account does offer room for an alternative reading of sexual orientation, one that is not based on sex-gender as discrete (binary) categories.

By Stein's account Money's reference to mentality (identity) and behavior (role) appears to move him toward a focus on how the social overlays the body rather than on the body itself. Stein suggests that a straightforward one-dimensional view of sexual orientation that Money seeks to retain is undermined precisely because he links it to gender. As a result sexual orientation seems to fall into the study of culture rather than the study of anatomy and physiology where Money would prefer it to be.[124] That is because he locates the prenatal phase of development as the first but not the primary— or most important—determinant of sexual orientation. Yet the value of Money's understanding of gender acquisition lies precisely in his understanding that the body is always in inter*active* relation with the sociocultural environments it inhabits, rather than a passive recipient of cultural inscription as Stein's analysis suggests. I return to this point in subsequent chapters.

In keeping with the parallel trajectories of the book, I began this chapter by tracing the historical role of the hermaphrodite figure in sexual scientific thought. This allowed me to demonstrate the various ways that the intersexed have historically figured in sexological understandings of human subjectivity and their centrality within that body of knowledge. Some sexologists of the mid- to late nineteenth century drew on embryological understandings of fetal development and the phenomenon of hermaphroditism to develop expansive classification systems of nonnormative subjectivities. Others such as Albert Ellis during the mid-twentieth century provoked the conceptual and ontological closure of sexual difference and with it the redundancy of a "third sex." This effected the ontological erasure of hermaphrodite subjects for the remainder of the twentieth century. By the time Money began his research in the mid-1950s, the intersexed had become "human paradoxes," as the title of Money's doctoral thesis evidences.

The apprehension of hermaphrodites' erotosexual status within a normative (bipolar) framework of homo-, hetero-, and bisexual made possible their conceptualization *as* paradoxical. That same normative framework—underpinned as it is by the axioms of dimorphic sexual difference and reproductive imperatives—also enabled an apparently unproblematic understanding of the intersexed as partial or unfinished males or females. It is to the implications of these factors that I turn in the following chapter, where I introduce an altogether different form of expertise on gender. The next chapter turns to the intersexed to explore how gender is theorized by those from whom the concept derived.

CHAPTER 5

DANGEROUS DESIRES: INTERSEX
AS SUBJECTIVITY

*We've been led to believe that ... somehow we exist outside of
nature. Its like we've been told that the Emperor is wearing
clothes and we really believe he's not naked and we don't
believe our own two eyes. But we were born that way (Jesse).*

INTRODUCTION

In previous chapters I have examined the ideas of a range of gender
theorists, sexological, medical, and feminist. Now I turn to a different
form of expertise altogether, that of contemporary intersexed people.
So far I have demonstrated how John Money's original gender theories were derived from these people's historical equivalent. Some of
the people whose voices feature in the following pages were among
the first and second generations to be subject to the then-new case
management protocols devised by Money more than 50 years ago.

As a growing body of knowledge, intersex discourse cannot be
read without reference to medical understandings of sexual variation
(in medical terms, sex ambiguity or more recently disorders of sexual
development), since medical science has a privileged status to tell us
the "truth" of hermaphroditism. Since the late nineteenth century a
wealth of material has been produced in the medical and sexological
literature, some of which has been discussed in the preceding chapters. That literature demonstrates an unwavering commitment on the
part of clinicians involved in ICM to the idea that the human species

(along with most other species)[1] is sexually dimorphic. It is a commitment grounded not in any biological reality but in concepts that are deeply embedded in the social imaginary. Interpreting the intersexed through a dimorphic lens reinscribes and reproduces the terms of a binary logic even in those models that are potentially expansive, as Money's own work demonstrates.

The very idea of ambiguous sex is paradoxical because it involves the morphological characteristics of two norms (female and male) in such a way as to transcend the norms themselves.[2] Embryologists have long known that before seven weeks, fetuses are not differentiated as male or female but exist in what can be described as a hermaphroditic state. Can we thus think of the undifferentiated fetus as an entity of *multi-* rather than *bi*potentiality? From that perspective we can begin to envisage the intersexed as the norm from which typical male and typical female forms derive.[3] From about seven weeks onward, most of us began to differentiate into male or female form while some of us continued to develop as hermaphrodite.

Yet this is not the way that embryological development is understood in the medical and biological sciences, nor by extension within the broader social domain. Since the mid-twentieth century the female form has been paradoxically understood as the default sex, an entity born of inactivity and absence. As noted in the previous chapter, this idea derived from Alfred Jost's embryological research on rabbits.[4] Jost identified prenatal androgenic surges as a critical factor in male differentiation and development, whereas the development of the female fetus appeared to have no such dramatic equivalent—it seemed to just *happen*—and hence became known in embryological theory as the default sex.[5] Jost initially cautioned that more subtle processes were likely to be involved in female development, though he did not explore the issue further in his own research.[6] Ascribing passivity to the female fetus reproduces the hierarchical dominant/subordinate relation of binary sex. More importantly, for the purposes of the current discussion, the default sex hypothesis situates femaleness as the ground of "humanness" rather than as one deviation from the norm I have invoked here.

Despite the historical persistence of hermaphrodites and intersexed people across time, place, and cultures, there is very little material on the historical record that addresses the experience of hermaphrodite subjects *living as* hermaphrodite or intersex subjects *living as* intersex subjects.[7] There is even less that allows for the possibility that they could or would be anything other than pathological. This is a direct effect of four interconnected ideas that are as persistent, it seems, as hermaphrodites themselves. They include first, the idea that what is at issue is purely physical or physiological and second, the idea that each body should or must contain just a singular sex. The one-sex-per-body model links in turn to the third idea—that there are two and only two social sexes (or genders). From there it is but a short leap to the fourth idea, and that is that there are *really* only two sexualities whose reference points are, of course, the two social sexes—and around it goes. An ontological status as intersexed or hermaphrodite is rendered impossible under the terms of this tautological frame. Talk about gender trouble! To take Beauvoir's epigram "one is not born a woman…"[8] and (following Prosser) give it a new spin, let us say that one is not born a woman or a man but *must* become one—and just one.[9]

The existence of the intersexed highlights the fiction that the binary categories man/woman, male/female and the categories of sexuality, heterosexual and homosexual, are in any sense natural.[10] This is especially the case with respect to those who are actively engaged in making sense of their embodied experiences of physical forms that exceed cultural intelligibility (although clearly not medical intelligibility).[11] They are part of a broad-based political movement known as intersex activism, a movement generated by medical practices and protocols unique to the late twentieth century. One of the movement's key concerns has been to bring to account those very practices and the theories that underpin them.

Intersex politics is informed by various bodies of knowledge that themselves continuously shape—and are shaped by—the multitude of ways that gender is constituted. While the influence of medical and sexological discourses is clearly evident in the discourses of intersex activism, so too is the influence of feminist, gay and lesbian, and queer theories of gender and sexuality, along with feminist critiques of the medicalization of women's bodies.[12] Drawing upon these political, analytical, and discursive technologies, intersex activists have challenged—to greater or lesser degrees—the epistemological and ontological boundaries of sex-gender.

Given that this is a genealogy of gender, the types of ideas that circulate in this discursive realm and the various ways in which gender is understood by the intersexed are of particular interest. Some of the questions that underpin the following discussion include: To what extent does gender matter within this body of knowledge? What are the various ways that intersexed adults make sense of the intricate relation between their (differently) embodied experiences and who they are in the world? I draw on a range of different materials in this chapter, including official organizational texts produced and distributed by advocacy groups via the Internet, data from interviews,[13] and the writings of individuals who have made public their stories on Web sites and in academic journals and monographs.[14] In all these different texts we can see a range of medical, theoretical, and political discourses on gender converging.

The chapter is made up of four sections. The first provides an overview of the historical conditions in which a broad-based intersex politics began in North America in the early 1990s, spearheaded by the Intersex Society of North America (ISNA). ISNA's ideas gained traction over a relatively short period of time, aided in no small part by the extended reach of the Internet, and they represent what was for a time the dominant voice of this political movement, especially in locations where English was the first language.[15] That status was achieved in part through the reproduction of ISNA's ideas and ideals by other advocacy groups, academic allies, LGBT organizations, and print and television media.

The second section discusses the various types of knowledge that inform how gender is understood in intersex discourses, and the specific ways in which they do so. While traces of medical knowledge can be found everywhere in this domain, so too can the discursive tools of feminism, gay and lesbian theory, and the more recent project of queer. From the resultant mix of (competing) interests and ideas a series of tensions are produced. Some are a consequence of putting medical knowledge to work for political purposes. I am interested in what is enabled by such a strategy and at the same time what is constrained. What effects do the normalizing tendencies that lay at the heart of the medical model bring to bear on such an alliance? What are some of the practical effects of the alliance for future generations of the intersexed?

During the course of preparing the manuscript for this book there have been significant and dramatic changes to the medical nomenclature for intersex that have polarized activists *and* medics alike, around the globe. The ensuing debates are highly charged for reasons that will become clear in the following pages. This terminology change is part of a larger project to institute a revised model of care. The answers to the above questions are no longer hypothetical; the future is now. There is an increasingly clear sense of the benefits and risks of engaging on medicine's terms, many of which are writ large within the context of the new nomenclature.

Intersex politics has been wrestling with the idea of gender now for almost two decades as a consequence of being the most recent domain to be theoretically concerned with the concept.[16] Because historically the intersexed have had their genders managed and/or regulated by others (including the judiciary and medical science), self-determination has always been a central concern within this political domain. Intersex activism, like any social movement, is marked by fractures, but the one point on which there is consensus is the need to bring an end to routine cosmetic procedures on infants and young children. This includes the removal or reduction of phallic tissue and surgical construction of vaginas. According to the Consortium on the Management of Disorders of Sex Development and to the latest face of mainstream activism—Accord Alliance—this is precisely what the new terminology is designed to enable, along with better patient care.[17]

Much of the lobbying to date has focused on the rights of children and infants. This emphasis has had the effect of rendering the needs of adult intersexed people beyond the terms of the debates. But what of their fate? The overwhelming emphasis on safeguarding the needs of future generations of infants and children, and safeguarding their right to bodily integrity, means that there has been little space to talk about or even conceptualize an adult selfhood *as* hermaphrodite or *as* intersex outside the trauma narrative.[18] One of the pressing issues for the people I interviewed was the project of making sense of themselves as *sexual* subjects. That task is rendered all the more challenging since the only available framework with which to do so—sexuality referenced to sexual object—is unable to contain, let alone explain, an erotosexual status *as* hermaphrodite/intersex. Hence the third section of the chapter returns to the issue of desire, an important issue in the process of "making sense" of oneself.

Building on the analysis of Chapter 4 I examine the notion of a specifically hermaphroditic or intersex eroticism. It is important to stress that I am not referring here to the objectification of the intersexed as some kind of fetish object. Rather I want to explore the ways in which the very idea of such an eroticism confounds current conceptions of sexuality and, by extension, gender. Such forms of eroticism exceed unidimensional constructs that rely upon maleness and femaleness as their reference points and upon homosexuality and heterosexuality as their endpoints. The historical persistence of hermaphrodites (and more recently, the intersexed) and the demand by some for recognition *as* hermaphrodite/intersexed subjects, along with the legal recognition of that subjectivity in some jurisdictions, suggests that it is time to seriously consider how to extend the ways we currently know the body, gender, and sexuality.

In the final section I turn to the issue of bodily integrity and draw on Elizabeth Grosz's reading of Merleau-Ponty's corporeal phenomenology. Grosz's analysis provides a way to think through some of the issues in ways that refuse a separation between one's body, the degree of intactness of that body, and one's being in the world. It is by situating the body—in all its messy glory—as the primary instrument or medium through which we experience the world that we can begin to create possibilities for thinking differently about what constitutes sex-gender and sexuality. Therein we may just find spaces to account for those who are most marginalized by such regimes.[19]

Three arguments are woven through this chapter. The first is that Cartesian dualism plays out, not just on medical understandings and practices relating to intersexed bodies, but also in the way that advocacy groups and some intersex individuals understand themselves as subjects. The second related argument concerns the extraordinary resilience of the sex/gender distinction. That is, even for the most liminal of sexual subjects, sex remains the signifier of a "natural" body against a socially and culturally constructed gender. The third point is that binary gender categories are complicated by those who exceed them: challenged by some and actively reinforced by others—with varied consequences.

ISNA's History: From Small Beginnings

During the late 1950s, an infant assigned male and given the name Charlie had his sex reassigned at age 18 months. He was renamed Cheryl and suddenly *his* small penis became, in the eyes of the attendant physicians, *her* enlarged—and thus unacceptably sized—clitoris. At the age of 21, Cheryl Chase[20] accessed some of her medical records[21] in order to find out why she had been clitoridectomized.[22] It would be another decade and a half before she began dealing with the information contained within those case notes, information that included a clinical diagnosis of "true hermaphrodite." The term disturbed Chase greatly with its connotations of monstrosity and freakishness. Her discovery of a medical article written in the late 1950s that claimed just 12 cases of true hermaphroditism had ever been recorded only served to reinforce her distress. It is hardly surprising, then, that Chase wondered if there might be anyone else in the world like her, or indeed anyone whose experiences might be similar to her own.

But find others, she did. Chase told her story to friends and acquaintances, and within the space of a year had established contact with half a dozen others, two-thirds of whom had been surgically mediated—in her words, "genitally mutilated."[23] And so it was that the Intersex Society of North America came into being.[24] Initially the organization was set up as a peer support group to provide a sense of connection, if not community, for those rendered all but invisible by the treatment model designed to *fix* them. In 1993, Chase wrote to the editor of *The Sciences* announcing ISNA's formation in response to an article by Anne Fausto-Sterling, which had asserted that the imposition of genital surgery on intersex infants was misguided.[25] That letter resulted in other intersexed people contacting Chase, each recounting stories of isolation and shame—stories that resonated with her own.[26] Before long, ISNA extended its focus from peer support to advocacy in a tactical response to the seemingly entrenched attitudes of clinicians convinced of the rightfulness of their clinical practices and motivations.

Over the course of the subsequent decade and a half ISNA's political energies focused on bringing an end to what they referred to as "unwanted genital surgeries," although not to the exclusion of peer support.[27] The organization's position on genital surgery was that cosmetic procedures should be left until an individual was in a position to weigh up the risks and benefits and thus make a fully informed decision. In other words, surgery should be an option. Yet in order for a shift of that magnitude to occur in the patient's relation to surgery, an equally sizeable shift was needed in the attitudes of clinicians who supported and rationalized the surgical interventions in the first place.

ISNA understood that if it were to effect any change in medical practice, it was vital to build strategic alliances and open the lines of communication with the medical community. Thus ISNA's primary source of engagement in the past few years has been with medical science. ISNA positioned itself against current clinical practice in a number of ways, most obviously by developing an alternate model of care that it referred to as a "patient centered" model. This was pitched against what ISNA dubbed a "concealment centered model."[28]

Medical practitioners, for the most part, shunned invitations to engage in dialogue with ISNA throughout the 1990s. One of the ways that some professional medical bodies and individual clinicians responded to ISNA's challenge to their practices was to flatly refuse to recognize either the legitimacy of the organization or its claims. Early on, Chase had spurned the idea of picketing. She was of the view that doctors were more likely to listen to reasoned debate and respond to first-person accounts than to demonstrating activists. However, ISNA took to the picket lines after learning that the U.S. Congress had passed legislation that banned the practice of clitoridectomy for cultural or religious purposes in the United States, but exempted intersex children from protection by this law.[29] Intersex activists and supporters picketed the annual meeting of the American Academy of Pediatricians (AAP) in Boston on October 25, 1996.[30] ISNA had sent a letter to AAP officials prior to the convention, inviting clinicians to talk before, during, or after the convention, but the AAP did not respond. Instead, a public relations representative of the convention distributed a press release stating that the optimal time for intersex surgery was six weeks to 15 months of age and, while officials would meet privately with the press, they would not be meeting with "any Hermaphrodites with Attitude."[31]

From that point on, ISNA engaged in dialogue whenever it was possible, and when their claims fell on deaf ears, members of the organization demonstrated. A decade after the first demonstration the organization could rightly claim to have "gone from [the] picket lines to having a seat at the table in medical conferences."[32] In 2003 ISNA formed its own Medical Advisory Board made up of pediatric endocrinologists, medical ethicists, geneticists, psychiatrists, and other medical professionals sympathetic to ISNA's aims. As the organization forged ever-closer alliances with the medical profession, a marked shift became evident in the organizational rhetoric. No longer was ISNA interested in trying to destabilize, let alone challenge, the normative (read binary) concepts of sex and gender. Nor was it interested any longer in challenging the hegemonic status of medical understandings about intersex; now the emphasis was on engaging with medicine on its terms. Gender was no longer on ISNA's agenda.[33]

Early on, ISNA conceptualized intersexuality in the following way: "intersexed people are not 'both sexes in one' but are a biological uniqueness of their own form."[34] The intersexed were positioned as one of at least three types of humans within a discrete model of difference, a model comparable with that used to classify blood groups, for example, where there is no obvious sense of ordering, even though each type falls along a single axis.[35] This was a serial rather than a supplemental concept. By late 2002, a decentering of gender from ISNA's official discourse was evident. Intersex was no longer to be considered outside a strictly binary frame; rather it had fully been co-opted into it. By the following year, ISNA's mission statement had been amended on its home page to read, "intersexuality is a problem of stigma and trauma, not gender," and later amended further to read, "intersexuality is *primarily* a problem of stigma and trauma, not gender." Now gender appeared to be an unproblematic category composed of two classes: men/boys on the one hand and women/girls on the other. Nowhere was this disavowal of gender as an intersex issue more obvious than in the organization's informational material for parents and the recommendations on how best to raise an intersexed child.

The FAQ section of the organization's Web site and a downloadable brochure entitled *Tips For Parents* provide guidelines on how to gender an intersexed child. Both documents were designed to lay to rest a range of "misconceptions" about intersex and to clarify the organization's position on existent medical practices and acceptable terminology. The content of the *Tips* document was later incorporated (with minor changes) into a 130-page document entitled *Handbook for Parents* published in 2006 by ISNA under the authorship of The Consortium (this would be the last initiative on the part of ISNA before it "shut up shop," so to speak, in 2008). The *Handbook for Parents* provides a contemporary window into both clinicians' and mainstream advocacy groups' understandings of gender, and provides the most current example of the intersection of medical and (some) activist understandings of intersex. The *Handbook* can be seen in part as a product of the merging of (some) activist and medical interests. The *Handbook* and the *Clinical Guidelines* codify a set of clinical practices and a model of care that represents the first substantive overhaul of ICM protocols since Money developed his over half a century ago. As with Money's protocols, the new ones aim to support intersexed individuals into a proper gendered identity.

The advice offered in the *Handbook* on rearing an intersexed child demonstrates a strong disavowal that gender is an intersex issue. Yet at the same time the revised ICM protocols are from a clinical perspective as much about gender as they ever were. The *Handbook* is designed to provide caregivers with information and advice, including a set of questions (with accompanying notes) to put to doctors. The questions are designed in turn to ensure parents and caregivers are equipped to make informed decisions on behalf of their offspring. One of those questions is of particular relevance to the current discussion. Question seven advises parents to ask the attendant clinicians: "Which gender assignment (boy or girl) do you think my child should be given? Which gender do you think my child is most likely to feel as my child grows up? What are your reasons?"[36] Doctors, according to the *Handbook*, are able to use current knowledge about "various DSD's to help you figure out if your child is likely to *feel* like a girl or a boy in the long run."[37] The target readership is also advised that doctors should take into account the extent to which "your child's brain was exposed to androgens before birth [because] evidence suggests that children exposed to higher levels of androgens are more likely to grow up to feel masculine. But no one can predict for certain what gender a child will ultimately grow up to feel (even without a DSD)."[38] Last but not least, the item strongly advises parents *not* to take seriously any suggestion that delaying surgery is akin to raising the child as a third gender. Why? Because "choosing a gender—boy or girl—for your child is *like choosing a gender for any child*; you use what is known to make an informed choice."[39] Should the child grow up and behave in gender atypical ways, parents are not to blame themselves or think the child is diseased or wrongly assigned, "it just means your child is a little different from the statistical average" and no less in need of love and support for being who they are.[40]

A number of issues are raised by the above advice. First, it reiterates the idea that gender is a strictly either/or proposition. Gender is referenced to boys and girls twice in the accompanying text and so is reduced to a discrete category of two classes: men/boys and women/girls. The slippage between gender role and identity, between the idea of "feeling like" a boy or a girl (sense of self) and acting in gender "atypical" ways (behaviors and presentation of self) is also noteworthy. The statement implicitly accepts that certain behaviors are the property of males and others the property of females. Furthermore it implies an inverse relation between the two. Gender as strictly binary is thus reinscribed tautologically, and it is but a short step from there to the idea that males/men and females/women constitute *opposite* sexes. This effectively means that there is no place in gender for an intersexed child and neither is there any place for adult intersexed persons in gender—in their own right. Here we can see the way that binary gender intersects with the sex/gender distinction and indeed relies upon it. However, the way the sex/gender distinction is used in the *Handbook* differs somewhat from its more usual conceptualization where sex signifies the biological and gender the sociocultural. This is not to deny that the more common usage underpins many of the ideas promoted by ISNA but rather that the usefulness of the distinction lies elsewhere.

The sex/gender distinction allows for the conceptualization of gender as a completely different order than that of sex, since the former is framed as binary and the latter as bipolar. While the end points of a continuum are privileged (hence bipolar), there are no clear or obvious points of demarcation as there are in a binary model. Thus the sex/gender distinction serves as the ground upon which to make such parallel constructions. This reduces hermaphroditism once again to the level of the body and *only* the body. John Money argued as much.

Second, the advice to parents with respect to prenatal androgen exposure (that is, surges of testosterone in utero effect a masculinization of the brain) draws upon Milton Diamond's theory of gender and other researchers involved in searching for the locus of brain sex.[41] Against Money, Diamond has argued for some time that gender acquisition occurs in utero as an effect of prenatal androgenic surges. In other words, gender by this account is really all about nature supplemented by nurture.[42] This understanding relies upon the testes-centric notion that male differentiation and sexual differentiation are one and the same thing. It equates maleness to presence (androgens) and femaleness to absence (no androgens) and upholds the idea that femaleness equates to passivity (default sex). This is not to suggest that ISNA wittingly promoted the presence/absence model, since the organization was consistently strident in condemning the fact that a high percentage of intersexed infants were assigned female because their phalluses failed to measure up, quite literally, to what clinicians deem to be an appropriately sized penis. ISNA long recognized this as the product of an intrinsic sexism in clinical practice. Chase explicitly condemned the presence/absence model in her earliest published writing in ways that make clear the influence of feminism on her personal perspective:

If I label my post-surgical anatomy female, I ascribe to surgeons the power to create a *woman* by *removing* body parts; I accede to their agenda of "woman as lack," I collaborate in the prohibition of my intersexual identity.[43]

In this statement, gender clearly matters. But for almost a decade now, ISNA and some of its affiliate organizations (such as IPDX) have stated in no uncertain terms that those they represent do not have issues with gender, but rather with the trauma and shame that result from medical practices codified under ICM.[44] These include clitoridectomies, repeated genital examinations (often in the presence of multiple witnesses), medical photography, and the practice of nondisclosure regarding diagnoses and/or medical records. ISNA's own recommendations for case management support freedom of choice in terms of treatment options for adult intersexed persons (including the option of no intervention):

Medically unnecessary surgeries should not be done without the patient's consent; the child with an intersex condition may later want genitals (either the ones they were born with or surgically constructed anatomy) different from what the doctors would have chosen. Surgically constructed genitals are extremely difficult if not impossible to "undo", and children altered at birth or in infancy are largely stuck with what doctors give them.[45]

Elective surgery offers the potential for self-determination, one realized through consumer choice.[46] Yet a caution is warranted. It should not be forgotten that medicine's quest to make the body conform to the parameters of binary sex is haunted by its continual failure to achieve that aim, despite claims by clinicians that their surgical techniques have become more refined over time.[47] That situation is unlikely to change by merely shifting the status of genital surgery from mandatory to elective. Yet choice remains highly circumscribed in this context. It is something of a Hobson's choice, since if you are not happy being one gender, the only legitimate option is to become the other. Under the terms of the current gender regime an individual's gender must be stabilized at all costs (nowhere more clearly evidenced than by the practices of ICM). Effectively any movement from one gender to the other has to be unidirectional and a singular event. The surgical technologies themselves remain unproblematized, as does medical mediation; being intersexed remains a "condition" in need of therapeutic management. I am not trying to suggest here that there is no place for medical intervention, since clearly there are specific health risks associated with *some* diagnostic categories, just as there are specific health risks associated with being male and being female. There can be no denying the need to stabilize, for example, compromised electrolyte levels or renal function. Rather, what I am questioning is the idea that being differently sexed is a medical condition in itself, since sexual variation is not life-threatening. Being intersexed ultimately violates *cultural* conventions about the apparent naturalness of dimorphic sex, binary gender, and normative (read mono-) sexuality.[48]

The third issue raised by the *Handbook*'s advice to parents concerns the inordinate amount of faith accorded to the predictive power of clinicians: that is, their ability to predict what gender the child will become as they grow up. Clinicians have of course been doing this over the past half century by following (most of) Money's ICM protocols, since gender assignments are made on the basis of a predictive "best sex." This advice vests in doctors the capacity of soothsayer. But more than this it reinforces the authority of the medical profession (along with psychologists and psychiatrists) as *the* experts of gender. By being emphatic that intersex is not about gender, ISNA ceded to medicine the authority to produce gender. The organization was unable ultimately to challenge the fact that ICM is done for gender, in the interests of an appropriate gender.

Despite ISNA's awareness that the violation posed by the intersexed is a cultural one, the organizational discourse nowhere indicates the dual problems perpetuated by the poisoned chalice of a binary gender supported (some would say, upheld) by medical technologies. By framing intersex as a medical issue, three of the central mechanisms that work to sustain medicine's power base can be seen in ISNA's model of care. First, gender assignment functions as a form of preventative care (against stigma and teasing); second, intersex continues to be framed under the jurisdiction of medical science; and so the issue remains, not whether to deal with it medically but rather, *how* and *when*.[49] In effect this model leaves intact the idea that being otherly sexed warrants medicalization in order to properly habilitate to one of two genders. With binary gender assumed, the body remains the key site of knowledge for the "problem" of intersex and, by extension, the key site for its amelioration.

The Terminology Debates

Language serves a range of functions. It is the most fundamental vehicle through which relations of power are constituted and reproduced, since legitimation is essential to the exercise of power.[50] We've looked at the way language operates in sexology and in ICM; now I want to look at how it operates in intersex discourse. As ISNA began to make inroads in its lobbying and advocacy work, it became increasingly concerned with the way that intersex was being written about and discussed by non-intersexed people. Among its initiatives was a set of guidelines that it developed for researchers and writers—outside of medical circles. The guidelines offered examples of "acceptable" ways to talk about and write about the intersexed in seemingly unproblematic ways. Yet these are not, by any stretch of the imagination, unproblematic issues. Warnings were issued against "us[ing] intersex people merely to illustrate the social construction of binary sexes" because "intersex people are no more responsible for dismantling gender roles or compulsory heterosexuality than anyone else."[51] The point is a fair one; it is clearly directed at those poststructuralist/queer scholars seeking to embrace intersex as the next cause célèbre. It is also fair by virtue of the fact that not everybody who is intersexed has a problem with their assigned gender or with the idea of sexual difference to the order of two.

The guidelines also cautioned non-intersexed people to avoid reducing intersex people to their physical conditions, to depict them instead "as multi-dimensional human beings with interests and concerns beyond intersex issues."[52] Yet paradoxically, the organization itself reduced intersexuality to little more than its physical manifestation(s). It did so in the first instance by using terms like "disorders of sexual differentiation . . ."[53] and "atypical reproductive anatomies."[54] Second, it defined intersex as a physiological variation of male and female sexual anatomy, as potentially meaningless as variation of eye or hair color.

Julia Epstein has suggested that the ability of physicians to manipulate anatomical sex renders intersex (problematically) akin "to a harelip or supernumerary toe. [That is,] something to be fixed and then forgotten."[55] As mainstream intersex activism increasingly consolidated around a politics of sameness, it is possible to see the progressive reduction of difference—to the point of inconsequential variation. Since 2001 ISNA asserted that intersexuality was nothing more than "an anatomical variation from the 'standard' male and female types; just as skin and hair color varies along a wide spectrum, so does sexual anatomy."[56] By appealing to the liberal tradition of fair treatment for all, the particular difference of being "differently sexed" was rendered benign. People who are intersexed, then, are just like "the people next door," just like the metaphorical (albeit unmarked) "you and me."[57] The repudiation of difference is politically useful; its utility lies in the fact that an appeal to sameness is considerably less threatening to the wider culture than that posed by an irreducibly different form of subjectivity. Of course there were consequences.

Situating male and female as the standard had a number of effects, the most obvious of which was the reinscription of the apparent naturalness of sexual dimorphism. As a result it is only those bodies that are differently sexed that ever require explanation; "standard" male or female types remain "unquestionably natural."[58] As David Valentine and Riki Anne Wilchins remind us, that very requirement warrants investigating because the naturalized status of the binary division obscures the processes by which *all* bodies—normative and otherwise—come to be understood through highly complex systems of meaning.[59]

Diagnostic categories are of huge significance to some intersexed people and deeply tied to their social identities. There are those who use chromosomal status, for example, as a key marker of identity. Mel identified as "an XXY" at various points during our conversation and at others as "an epicene."[60] Others hold their diagnostic category at arm's length, reluctant to use it as an identity marker: "I physically... as an intersex person... was born with a condition *known in the medical literature as* Kallman's syndrome."[61] Still others thoroughly disassociate themselves from diagnostic categories.

Some of the people I interviewed had strong opinions about using diagnostic categories in this way. They forcefully articulated the folly of basing one's identity on medical categories of disease and disorder. For example, Kelly was adamant that,

if I have this condition and you have that condition, well all it does is further separate us from ourselves.... It denies the possibility that there is anything other than male or female because once you medicalize this you are saying *and* you are accepting, that really you are a pathology... a flawed male or a flawed female.

The reasoning behind this refusal points to a number of key issues. Diagnostic categories inherently pathologize, so their usefulness as a way to overcome stigma and shame remains questionable; the reliance on such categories ensures the continued inscription of intersexed bodies as diseased, as disordered. Those same categories serve to obscure points of commonality by maintaining the idea that being intersexed is a problem "suffered" by individuals. This has the effect of depoliticizing the sociocultural imperatives that drive ICM and that are in turn upheld by those same practices. In other words, recourse to diagnostic categories reinforces the idea that the intersexed suffer from a physiological condition, rather than from the normalizing demands imposed by their sociocultural environments. This last point has parallels with the notion of disablism, where disability is the effect of attitudes and the material conditions of one's lived environments.[62]

Yet the compulsion to rely on diagnostic categories remains incredibly powerful for many, since almost everything we understand about intersex either comes from or is informed by, the medical literature. In light of the above quotation from Kelly, what are we to make of recourse to pathology? It might well be the case that different diagnoses and/or medical experiences result in differing degrees of trauma and shame and are therefore as significant to identity formation as they are to the shape of intersex politics.[63] There are anecdotal accounts of nonmedicalized intersexed people feeling unsure of where they fit within intersex politics and, worse, feeling guilty that others have been subject to greater harm than they. At a more productive level, recourse to diagnostic categories has seen the proliferation of niche-targeted support services tailored to particular "conditions".

This does not however diminish the potency of the point made about the fracturing effects of "if you have this and I have that." The pathologizing impulses imbedded in diagnostic categories remain, as does the potential for divisiveness, and as noted above, when the "problem" is individualized it becomes depoliticized. Clinicians had expressed concerns a number of years ago about the dangers of an overpoliticizing of intersex. From their perspective, the advances made by intersex activism seemed to be leading to the "over de-pathologizing" of intersex. Something had to be done.

At the same time that ISNA was distancing itself from gender, disavowing it as a problem in ICM, it was also distancing itself from the idea of intersex as an ontological status. Behind the claim that intersex was not a feasible ontological option lay the following rationale: "Intersex is not, and will never be, a discrete biological category any more than male or female is."[64] This reasoning gives pause for thought. Reversing the terms of the argument, it would seem that the feasibility of an identity as male or female could equally be called into question, since they too "are not and never will be" discrete biological categories. But of course the widespread recognition that they are not discrete biological categories has done little to diminish the discursive force of sexual difference to the order of two.

The refusal of an intersex or hermaphrodite subjectivity is made possible by refusing intersex as anything other than a physical state. Such a position brings into play another is/ought distinction and unwittingly provides evidence to support Money's theory of gender acquisition. By arguing against the idea of gender as a continuum, this discourse bears remarkable similarity to Money's understanding of gender as binary. By exploring the investments that advocacy groups have in a binary understanding of gender we can begin to see the political, epistemological, and ontological consequences of those ideas for all intersexed persons.

At the level of the body, by this account, females and males occupy the endpoints on the morphological continuum and the intersexed occupy points along the space between. The obvious appeal of a bipolar model lies in its ability to account for variation in ways that binary models preclude, since the latter can only account for n to the order of two. While bipolarity may seem to offer a way to account for sexual variation, it too is fraught with problems. The task of plotting the space between gives one pause for thought, for it quickly becomes clear that a single axis can never account for, or contain, all the possible variants at a physiological level. Developments in medical technologies have allowed for increasing access to the innermost workings of the body, but at the same time they have created more rather than less uncertainty with respect to sex. Why? Because there is no single marker of sex at a corporeal level, but rather a range of markers that may or may not align. Since a unidimensional model can deal with only one variable at a time, the question then becomes, which of those markers should be used to interpret sex? As will become apparent, the interpretive status of any single bodily signifier is historically contingent. Today, for example, it is neuroscientific and genetic explanations that hold sway. Although the multiple signifiers of sex have long been recognized, we are still some way, it seems, from developing multidimensional frameworks that can recognize and accommodate the interrelatedness of clusters of categories, some discrete and others continuous.[65]

THE TERMINOLOGY DEBATES—II

Making sense of oneself as differently sexed and/or otherly gendered is not without challenges in a climate where intersex is conceptualized solely as a condition of the body. Added to this are the constraints of language, since language is one of the most fundamental tools that people have available to make sense of themselves. The English language is not merely gendered, it is binarily gendered, and this places enormous limitations on the capacity to think and talk about being hermaphrodite or intersex in ontological terms. While existing bodies of knowledge constrain what can be thought, so too do the grammatical constraints embedded in English, evident in pronouns for instance. Yet it is worth recalling that gender was itself a product of the constraints of language. Because English is a living language, neologisms—be they new words or extended applications of existing terms—enable it to maintain its life breath. Since a growing number of intersexed people are not content to know that aspect of themselves in purely physical terms, it is worth considering what could be put to work from the existing lexicon that would allow for an understanding of the intersexed in ways that extend beyond the physical body. I return to this task in the following chapter.

For a long time the terminology debates in intersex politics revolved around the relative merits of the terms *hermaphrodite* and *intersex*. Debates were heated and passions ran high. It is to those debates that I want to turn for a moment in order to provide context for the most recent shift in terms of language. The oldest of all the terms under discussion is *hermaphrodite*. It has a history that long precedes its medicalization, eclipsing post-Enlightenment medical science by centuries. Hermaphrodite derives from the Greek cosmology, an entity borne of the fusing of the nymph Salmacis with Hermaphroditus, who was the son of the gods Hermes and Aphrodite. This association to the mythical was problematic for some people, but the most overwhelming objection to the term *hermaphrodite* related to the way it had been traditionally deployed in medical discourses for the past 100 years coupled with the medically designated qualifiers "true" and "pseudo." There is widespread agreement among intersex activists—of all persuasions—that the modifiers are offensive because they imply a form of authenticity and/or lack thereof. Moreover, they represent outmoded remnants of a Victorian nomenclature that preceded twentieth-century understandings of the body as offered by the fields of genetics, endocrinology, and embryology.[66] For these reasons *hermaphrodite* was condemned as stigmatizing and misleading. It was deemed to be misleading because the term implied for some the existence of two "complete" sets of genitalia: a physical impossibility if one is referring to the simultaneous possession of a penis *and* a (separate) clitoris for example, or similarly a vulva *and* scrotum.[67] One of the strongest critics of the use of the term *hermaphrodite*, Emi Koyama of IPDX, considered it "misleading, mythical and stigmatizing" because in biology *hermaphrodite* specifically refers to an organism with

both "male" and "female" sets of reproductive organs (like snails and earthworms). In humans there are no actual "hermaphrodites" in this sense . . . Can we use the word intersex instead when we are talking about humans? Snails are the hermaphrodites; humans are not.[68]

As a signifier *hermaphrodite* did not sit well with others because of its historic relation to the logic of teratology and its evocation of an exotic sexuality. For Lee Brown "people who were, and are, born with hermaphroditic conditions remain trapped within a discourse of exotic freaks and monsters."[69] Yet for some people *hermaphrodite* has considerable appeal. Those enamored of the term articulated a number of reasons for their preference. They suggested that *hermaphrodite* conveys a sense of the substantive rather than a sense of partiality and incompleteness. Just as significant was the sense of ambiguity invoked by the word: a referent to both sexes or perhaps indeed to neither. For these people any mythical connotations associated with the term *hermaphrodite* were actually implicated in its appeal.

The term *intersex* was embraced by many as an alternative to the term *hermaphrodite*—not least because it appeared to be free of any connotation of the mythical and had no accompanying qualifiers.

During the height of these debates, distinctions were made between inter*sexual* as the signifier of an identity experienced privately and promoted publicly (in other words, a gender) and inter*sexed* as a medical diagnosis.[70] A little background information on these terms is warranted. "Intersex", "intersexual," and "intersexed" were all introduced into the diagnostic lexicon in 1917 by the German geneticist Richard Goldschmidt, an early proponent of the idea that hermaphrodites were actually incomplete males or females. In his view all mammalian hermaphrodites were actually intersexes who had undergone an embryonic "sex reversal" in the womb.[71] Thus intersex is a specifically medical designation with no history (until recently) outside of medicine. "Inter" literally means between: thus to be intersexed is to fall *between* the two legitimate sex categories. Within such a framework the intersexed are always unfinished, partial males or partial females, in need of fixing. This idea underpins the rationale for medical interventions that include genital surgery and the removal of any and all tissue deemed surplus to the sex of assignment. Ultimately these measures are taken to neutralize any potential threat to a person's gender identity. So in this sense the history of the term *intersex* is part of a broader medical history of mythologizing dimorphic sexual difference.

Despite the popularity of *intersex* it certainly did not have universal currency among all those who may lay claim to it. For example, Lee had this to say about it:

I hate the term intersexed, it doesn't...doesn't put us anywhere. It puts us in between again and it still doesn't give us anything that we can *be*.[72] I see it [the mythical connotations] as *more* of a reason for taking back the word [hermaphrodite], for reclaiming it to say, well we're still here we're not hidden. We've been hidden for quite a while but hey, *hello*, we're here.

One of the effects of medicine's privileged status as "managers" of intersexuality has been that the surgical and chemical technologies of the late twentieth century have served to render the intersexed invisible for all intents and purposes. That, in turn, has reinforced the idea that hermaphrodites are nothing more than creatures of myth, existing beyond the realms of human. There is implicit in the previous statement, "doesn't put us anywhere...doesn't give us anything that we can *be*," a recognition of the limits of a continuum that privileges its endpoints. Those who might fall at other positions on the axis don't appear to count—at least not until they are *made* (as in reconstructed) to physically resemble those who occupy the (variously) privileged sites at either pole of dimorphic sexual difference.

As we reach the end of the first decade of the twenty-first century, these debates are now part of an already distant past. Since 2005 the stakes have shifted considerably. Now the issue is one of intersex *versus* disorder, as in "disorders of sex development". The debates have never been more heated—or more personal.

While ISNA was for a long time the most pervasive voice in this shifting terrain, today that is no longer the case. ISNA took a particular position in discourse in order to engage with the medical establishment—on medicine's terms. Certainly the effectiveness of that move can be evidenced by the inroads ISNA made over the past decade and a half. It generated conversations about the efficacy of (aspects of) the now 50-year-old treatment model among medics, made a place for itself at the clinical conference table, and motivated latitudinal and surgical outcome studies after a long period where their absence was bemoaned by activists and clinicians alike.[73]

As with any political strategy, embracing medical discourse brings with it a range of unintended consequences that can never, as Judith Butler would say, be predicted in advance. With the passing of time, some of those effects have become evident. Arguably ISNA's choice of medical doctors and other health professionals as coalitional partner(s) was always going to compromise the organization's representational capacity.[74] By that I mean ISNA's capacity to represent the (multiple) interests of its constituents. In recent years other voices have emerged offering an explicitly counterdiscourse to the hegemony of ISNA's ideas, especially the idea that intersex was not about gender.[75]

In order to move forward with its coalitional partners, ISNA made a choice to depoliticize the issue of intersex. ISNA was far too political for many doctors and off-putting for many parents because of the organization's history of activism. While the term *intersex* had a historical connection to pathology, it had nonetheless facilitated a politics that brought a whole raft of issues about sex-gender, medical assumptions and clinical practices, and bioethics to the fore. ISNA quite literally put ICM under the spotlight and firmly on the agenda as a *sociocultural* issue. More recently ISNA has spearheaded the promotion of the term *"disorders of sex development"* and the new nomenclature for intersex; a language with as much political valance as gender's third term, neuter. DSD is in fact, deliberately anti-identitarian and deliberately antipolitical. *Disorders of sexual development* are simply medical conditions in need of treatments. The language of DSD returns the "problem" of intersex to the individual and so evacuates it politically.

In the latter part of 2002, a group of intersex activists from around the world (including some former ISNA members and affiliates) set up an organization whose aims extended beyond the needs of infants and children. The Organization Intersex International (OII) wanted to provide a forum for people outside of the North American context.[76] Intersexuality is framed as a human rights issue that affects everybody, whether intersex or not, since OII views binary categories as damaging to all people. For that reason, OII uses the United Nations Universal Declaration of Human Rights as guiding principles. The organization is committed to building strategic alliances and, while it works alongside genetic researchers and social researchers, it has stopped short of building alliances with ICM clinicians.

OII's aim is to promote the exchange of ideas and create a space for a wide range of perspectives about intersex issues, from a variety of sources and geographical sites. It seeks to represent alternative perspectives on intersex issues, including the perspectives of adults and young people for whom being intersexed is *all* about gender. Against ISNA's disavowal of gender, OII argues strongly that reducing the importance of gender to the intersexed reduces the latter to its physical constitution and ensures that intersexed people remain the perpetual object of medicine. Just as importantly, diminishing the importance of gender obscures the fact that ICM is all about securing the establishment of a stable gendered identity—as a girl/woman or a boy/man. Clinicians, after all, have never suggested that ICM is not about gender.

Since 2005 OII has gained a strong voice through its opposition to the new nomenclature for intersex and the language of disorder. When it became apparent that ISNA had driven the terminology change, all hell broke loose. The battle lines were firmly drawn. And implicitly or explicitly, gender was once again the battleground on which the debates played out. While proponents of the new terminology said that it is designed to take the emphasis off genitals with the aim of reducing the incidence of genital surgeries, critics responded by saying that since genitals are used to read the sex of non-intersexed infants, this de-emphasis is unlikely to have the desired effect.[77] The belief that the nomenclature change will allow for more accurate diagnoses and an overall improved health care response is challenged by questions about the integrity of the DSD terminology. Not only is it inaccurate, say critics, it actually violates the principles and diagnostic nomenclature of cytogenetics. As to the offensiveness of the term *disorder*, proponents say "get over it"; just use the acronym rather than the term. The only way to effectively communicate with clinicians is to use a language they understand and so, in other words, the ends justify the means.[78] Pathologizing language is pathologizing language, say critics, and it demeans, dehumanizes, and stigmatizes.

One of OII's strongest critiques of the language of DSD highlights the political and economically driven nature of genetic research and the power relations inherent in the production of biomedical knowledge. Western medicine has now fully entered the "Age of Chromosomes" following the Human Genome project, and this is reflected in the new nomenclature. All of the various categories and classes that make up the DSD schema are prefaced by the chromosomal modifiers, X and Y. Yet sex chromosomes as portrayed by the nomenclature do not actually determine one's sex. It is genes rather than chromosomes that determine sex and most them reside on the automsomes, not the X and Y chromosomes. The DSD schema applies the modifiers to diagnostic categories for which there is no genetic origin. In other words this means that the DSD terminology breaches the principles of accepted diagnostic nomenclature used by clinical and molecular cytogeneticists. In effect, say Italiano and Hinkle, what has been instituted is ambiguous medicine that cannot in fact provide any greater diagnostic precision than its predessor.[79] Rather than clarity, the new nomenclature is likely to lead to greater confusion and increase the risk that medical conditions that appear at odds with the diagnostic classification will be overlooked. Then there is the issue of confusion for those faced with the diagnoses. As one respondent to the consensus document noted, "today, every patient is aware of the significance of 46,XX or 46,XY and [so], the name of the condition may not be adequate to the sex of rearing [or the social reality] of a specific patient."[80] Concerns have also been raised elsewhere that the language of disorder together with the privileging of a genetic paradigm will lead to a eugenic dystopia where sex diversity is screened out of the population.[81]

*   *   *

OII's agenda resonates in many ways with that of ISNA's earliest and with the early gay rights movement in challenging binary categories of sex-gender. However, that may well represent the comparative limit because intersex politics cannot be said to be an identity movement as historically understood. OII has no interest in establishing "another 'fixed' identity category [but rather] promoting the right to self identification whether as men, as women, or as intersexed."[82] For that reason OII's Canadian spokesperson Joëlle-Circé Laramée cautioned against the assimilation of intersex into GLBT groups in a 2005 press release:[83]

The history of intersex has been [one of] constant erasure and assimilation. [Thus] in order to speak clearly about intersex issues from many different perspectives, it is necessary to establish bridges with the whole human community and avoid becoming one more invizible minority within another minority.[84]

This represents a different order of coalitional politics, one that refuses to situate intersex within a rubric of identity politics, the hallmark of sexual minority politics throughout the late 1970s and 1980s. It is precisely because intersexed people's sexualities exceed simple classification as gay, lesbian, or bisexual that OII take the stand they do. Intersex persons span the gamut of sexualities and, in some cases, exceed them by queering erotic categories in ways that make absolutely no sense within the existing nomenclature of sexuality. It is to the issue of desire that I turn next.

HERMAPHRODISIAS

A "normal sex life" in medical terms constitutes the capacity to engage in penile-vaginal intercourse and is inevitably linked to reproductive imperatives, even in those instances where infertility directly results from medical intervention(s). While this premise has laid ICM professionals open to charges of enforcing heteronormativity, as I have argued, all sexual identities are invested in binary gender: gays, lesbians, and heterosexuals need to be able to distinguish the boys from the girls. Bipolar constructs of gender underpin and motivate the current treatment model because heteronorms (and their "others") depend upon gender to the power of two.

The people I interviewed talked of how challenging it was to discuss their erotic desires and desirability in ways that accounted for intersex as an indelible part of their selfhood. While the project of queer calls into question the whole notion of identity,[85] intersex activism is making rights claims on behalf of a specific (albeit diffuse and diverse) segment of the population. These particular claims operate at the level of a freedom *from* mandatory medicalization and the freedom to *be* different, indeed to be a thoroughly different kind of different. Yet as with gender, the rejection of sexual identity categories does not diminish the pressure to locate oneself sexually—be it as gay, straight, bi, or indeed, queer—since others have a vested interest in knowing *who* one is sexually and what forms one's desires take. That is because *most* erotic desires remain, by and large, linked to bodily specificities. Self-designation as hermaphrodite or intersex has significant implications for one's sexual self and for those with whom you share affectational connections. While such a move is undoubtedly disruptive to normative understandings of sexuality, it leaves the claimant in something of a netherworld, as Chase's rationale for using the term *lesbian* evinces:

> I claim a lesbian identity because women who feel desire for me experience that desire as lesbian, because I feel most female when being sexual, and because I feel desire for women as I do not for men. Many intersexuals share my sense of queer identity, even those who do not share this homosexual identity.[86]

Like Chase, Lee spoke of what might well be described as sexuality by proxy. Recognizing that others' need to define hir[87] relationships was incredibly strong, perhaps even compulsive, Lee assents to those relationships being defined by the sexuality of a lover. Yet the following statement betrays a sense of the paradoxical with respect to "fit," as well as an understanding that the model's intactness takes primacy over those that exceed it. As Lee told me,

> Other people are always going to define me and define my relationships depending on who I'm with and I just have to let go of that and let them do that . . . its not worth the hassle to argue with them about that. If my lover identifies as a certain thing then maybe to a certain degree then I have to identify as that as well, to fit within the framework.

Canadian activist and academic Morgan Holmes, on the other hand, defiantly queers her relationship with her male partner by refusing to be just another "happy het." Rather she insists that people know that her marriage "is that between a man and an intersexual."[88] In drawing a comparison between these two narratives, I do not mean to suggest that Lee has no awareness of the queering effects that being a herm has for hir own sense of self and desires, nor its implications for the wider population. The following comments indicate precisely just how keen Lee's awareness was:

> But if I take on the label "hermaphrodite" I can't have a [sexual] identity because there are no words for me. . . . What does it mean? Well it means

you can't be lesbian and you can't be gay and you can't be straight can you? There's got to be another label, you can't really be bisexual...you can play with *yourself* and be bisexual [laughs]. What am I when I have sex with a woman [or] with a man, am I you know, when I'm having sex with a man am I being gay? When I have sex with a woman am I being lesbian? When am I being straight? I've never been heterosexual...its impossible for me to be heterosexual.

These questions form the backdrop to the constant process of negotiation between Lee's sexual self and overall sense of self. In the context of a monosexual culture, the constancy of that process is an everyday effect of reductive normative idea(1)s about sexuality and selfhood that are so deeply embedded as to seem inescapable—in the current climate at least.

Because ISNA came to refuse the idea of intersex as a form of personhood—in its own right—it had little to say about the issue of desire (though it did of course have a lot to say about the effects of ICM on sexual *capacity*). Because it came to invest in binary gender, considerations of an intersex or hermaphroditic eroticism or even its possibility were foreclosed. Nowhere is that more evident than on one of the FAQ pages of ISNA's Web site where various intersex conditions are listed and explained. Under the category of "Progestin Induced Virilization" the following statement appears:

> After the onset of puberty the child may want to explore the option, hopefully with the aid of loving parents and peer counselling, of having surgery to allow expression of *either female or male sexuality*.[89]

This statement begs the question of just what is meant by "a male or a female sexuality." No further information is offered, so one can only speculate that it refers to heterosexual couplings and perhaps also to lesbian or gay male sexuality, in any case to monosexuality. However interpreted there is no place in this rhetoric for the types of eroticism referred to in the preceding paragraphs. Despite this refusal, I was assured that such desires do indeed exist. Said Kelly,

> We were talking earlier about a hermaphroditic eroticism.... So it's very important that the medical doctors understand that a hermaphrodite with our own body can both receive pleasure and give pleasure in and of itself. And that there is a certain desire.... We need to enlarge our idea of what is a healthy sex life. That is why it is important to me that we as hermaphrodites talk about eroticism from a hermaphroditic point of view.

Angela Moreno, a North American–based activist and partici-
pant in the ISNA-produced video *Hermaphrodites Speak*, was
clitoridectomized at 12 years of age. She had already discovered the
delights of her "enlarged" intact clitoris and so had something with
which to compare her postsurgical sexual response. Moreno frames
her presurgical sexuality in terms of something "other," something
uniquely hermaphrodite. While loath to say she has lost the intensity of her presurgical genital sensation lest it be interpreted to mean
she is unable to have "great sex," Moreno does describe her sexual
responsiveness as compromised, as "not-so-reliable." In her view:

> What has been taken is a very specific eroticism, a hermaphroditic eroti-
> cism. That must really scare people and really cause a great deal of
> anxiety.... [T]hat special part, our sexuality, that sacred sexuality, has been
> ripped from us...that very special form of sexuality, arousal, and all of that
> that was uniquely hermaphroditic was taken.[90]

Remembering Bodies

The rationale for cosmetic genital surgery is that it provides the
individual with "normal looking" genitals and the opportunity for a
"normal" social life and a normal sex life (read penile-vaginal intercourse), yet medics and critics alike know full well that surgery fails
to achieve that aim. As an increasing number of intersexed people's narratives circulate in the public domain, reports of severely
compromised erotic sensation and function resulting from clitoridectomy and vaginal surgeries have become commonplace, indicating
that these procedures leave more than physical scarring.[91] As Lee
explained to me,

> Not knowing what I was actually meant to look like, what my body was meant
> to look like...presurgery is that...you know if I'd had my way I would never
> have had surgery—never! The hard part is I've got no idea of what I was
> meant to...look like because I'm scarred. And...so the grief around that is
> phenomenal.

Elizabeth Grosz's discussion of the phantom limb offers a way of situating the above narrative.[92] The phantom limb, or indeed any body
part that has been removed surgically, represents for Grosz (after
Schilder) "an expression of nostalgia" for bodily integrity or unity.
It represents a psychic, as well as a physical, wound.[93] It is certainly
the case that many narrative accounts of the intersexed are haunted
by such nostalgia. As Holmes so poignantly states, "all the things

my body might have grown to do, all the possibilities, went down the hall with my amputated clitoris to the pathology department. The rest of me went to the recovery room—I'm still recovering."[94] Until recently, clinicians failed to consider the impact of their interventions (in reorganizing and/or removing bodily organs and other structures).[95]

As discussed in Chapter 2, even Money, with his acute awareness of the interaction between cells and experience, failed to take the interventions themselves into account. But any lack of medical documentation regarding the deleterious effects of surgery does not mean that there are none. Katrina Roen argues convincingly that surgical and psychotherapeutic interventions carried out during the earliest stages of a child's life are never simply forgotten, since "even when carried out on newborns, the body remembers...the experience of treatment is not erased."[96] This claim is supported by many of the stories that those who have been subject to such treatments have to tell.

The idea that the mind is somehow separate from the body indicates the tenacity of Cartesian dualism that continues to haunt medical approaches to ICM. However, it is an idea that is increasingly being challenged by some activists. Against the mind/body split, there is a strong case to be made, as Grosz does, for the

radical inseparability of biological from psychical elements, the mutual dependence of the psychical and the biological, and...the intimate connection between the question of sexual specificity (biological sexual differences) and psychical identity.[97]

While for Grosz, from whom I take this quotation, sexual specificity and sexual difference refer to differences between men and women, her argument is equally applicable when considering sexual difference beyond the order of two. Grosz's point makes perfect sense in considering the sexual specificity of males and females, and it makes just as much sense with respect to the intersexed. As Jesse reminds us:

You can do anything that you want with my genitals its not going to change things. I'll be an intersexual that's had surgery. My perspective is still going to be influenced by [being intersex].

Morgan Holmes makes the same point by drawing comparisons with others whose bodily integrity is compromised by the removal (forcible or otherwise) of body parts:

Having my genitals mutilated has made me no less intersexual; it has merely made me a mutilated intersexual—just as a woman who has her genitals mutilated is still a woman, as a person who loses a limb is still a human being.[98]

Insisting that intersexuality is something that cannot be removed or cured by chemical, surgical, or any other means makes it possible to begin to conceptualize a nonpathologized hermaphrodite/intersex subjectivity. This does, of course, require a shift in perspective that extends beyond the physical and into the realms of the psyche. To highlight the stark contrast between embodying a pathologized and stigmatized physicality and embodying intersexuality as an element of subjectivity expressive of the richness of human experience, I turn again to Jesse:

I had always thought of myself as a malformed male so I was a deformity. . . . and that my being intersex was merely a physical manifestation of that deformity. I didn't think it had anything to do with the way I perceived things . . . the way I looked at things. I didn't think it had any impact on my life except that it made me lesser than other human beings.

At the time the interview took place, Jesse's sense of self could not have been further from that of a malformed anything:

What does it mean to be an intersexual, an intersex man instead of a male man? I'm not a *deformed* anything. Actually genetically I'm female. Well that kind of put the intersex thing into really serious perspective. . . . That was an explosion that also came out of discovering different parts of my anatomy that I didn't even know I had. Because I used to look at myself as a deformed male that had a micropenis. That's a man minus something. When you discover you have a vagina [as well], that's a man plus something.

That shift in perspective, from deformity to integrity, was marked by a realization of the interconnectedness of the psychic, sensorial, and physical elements of self: "I thought that all of my gender nonconformities had to do with sexual orientation, the typical gay boy sissy stuff. It didn't occur to me that they could also be manifestations of being intersex and that I could be *more* than one gender." Even as it pushes the limits of what constitutes *a man* and indeed who can be a man, Jesse's statement "[I'm] an intersex man instead of a male man" serves to highlight just what a blunt instrument the English language is. It is somewhat paradoxical that our understandings of what it is to be male or to be female come from Money's (and other's) research on hermaphrodites. Yet our capacity to speak about being hermaphrodite/intersex—even at the most fundamental level of the body—has to be channeled through a binary (man/woman, female/male) logic to even begin to make sense. This demonstrates, how a dimorphic understanding of sexual difference quite literally neuters everything that falls outside of itself.

Drawing on Merleau-Ponty's corporeal phenomenology, Grosz offers a reading of the body as "one's being in the world," that is, as the primary instrument though which we receive information and knowledge and subsequently generate meaning.[99] In other words, our bodies are the medium through which we experience the world.[100] From this perspective the component parts of the self—physiological, psychological, and sensorial—are so inextricably connected that to speak of intersex as a purely physiological condition makes no sense.

Yet as I have discussed, ICM is premised upon the idea that removing the markers from an intersex body removes the condition of being intersex. Atypical genitalia are ambiguously male or ambiguously female and thus are considered amenable to "correction". As a consequence the intersexed have effectively ceased to exist outside of medical texts. Critics say that ICM functions similar to Klebs's nomenclature of "true" and "pseudo": it serves to erase the figure of the hermaphrodite, just as it reinforces gender boundaries.[101] But the very idea that intersexuality is a condition or state that can be cured is, in the words of Kelly,

A dangerous myth [and] a mutilating myth. And this is why people think we don't exist. But I'm here to say, well I do exist and I'm healthy. The fact that I *might* have a problem with osteoporosis is a condition in and of itself. But I resent...going from the osteoporosis to "well the fact is, you're a hermaphrodite and we really need to fix you up so you'll be a man or a woman"—NO!

Against medical science's refusal of the possibility of a hermaphrodite subjectivity, narratives such as the above are motivated by a refusal to be a mere condition in need of fixing. Such people are staking a place at the table as persons—in their own right. That means being accorded the same rights (and responsibilities) accorded to male and female persons. Invoking a signifying moment for civil rights in North America,[102] Kelly put it this way:

I feel like my sex should be recognized legally anywhere in the world and I should have equal human rights anywhere in the world as a hermaphrodite.... Talk about the back seat of the bus, we're not even on the bus. But I tell you what, I'm standing there waiting and I'm expecting to get on it.

A landmark case in Western Australia in 2003 saw legal recognition granted to an intersexed person *as* intersex. Alex MacFarlane, after years of lobbying to have his passport accurately reflect his sex, was awarded a passport that recognized his sex status as intersex. "X" literally marked the spot. Alex had previously succeeded in obtaining a birth certificate from his home state of Victoria stating he was "indeterminate."[103] In 2006 the Australian Bureau of Statistics announced that intersexed people would have the option to enter their own sex on the national census data forms for that year (although that data was not collected by the software used to sort the returns).[104] It is hoped that next time the information will be tabulated. These small shifts, accommodations if you will, are likely to have a ripple effect, however localized. Part and parcel of legal recognition is recognition that the right to personhood includes the right to bodily integrity. The near-universal demand among activists for an end to mandatory genital surgery is at heart a demand for just that. Why is this so important? For the very simple reason that keeping the genitals of babes intact is some insurance that they will get to enjoy the pleasures of their bodies as adults.

CONCLUSION

This chapter has been concerned with both the pervasiveness and the fragility of some of the central organizing principles of social, sexual, and political life. Specifically I refer to the dimorphic model of sexual difference, the binary model of gender, and a model of sexuality that is, depending on where you perceive the fences to be, variously bipolar or binary. By examining the narratives of the most recent political domain to be concerned with the concept "gender," I have demonstrated that binary concepts are both reinforced and complicated by those who exceed them. They are reinforced through recourse to Cartesian dualist notions of mind and body and of sex and gender, both of which have shown an extraordinary resilience to all kinds of social and political interventions. At the same time, these notions are complicated by the very fact that there exist people who fall outside their bounds: people who cannot be "apprehended by hegemonic discourses of sexual difference" to the order of two and who, in recent times, have begun to agitate for a place in the world—as intersex or hermaphrodite subjects.[105]

My intention in working through the implications of binary constructs for hermaphrodite subjectivities has been to locate spaces from which we can begin to think differently about what it means to be human and indeed, who counts as human. In the chapter that follows I make a case for the importance of thinking differently about some of the issues raised in the preceding pages, issues that have implications that extend well beyond intersex populations—to us all.

Chapter 6

By Way of Conclusion

The preceding chapters have traced the movement of the concept of gender into and across various bodies of knowledge. The point has been to demonstrate that gender's conceptual history consists of a series of episodes within a larger narrative. Following gender's entry into the English lexicon in the mid-1950s when John Money offered it as a new conceptual realm of sex, gender has come to serve as *the* overarching framework through which masculinities, femininities—and sexualities—are understood within English-speaking liberal democracies. Conceptually gender has become thoroughly indispensable to a significant number of theoretical and political projects generated from sexology, the social sciences, and feminism, to say nothing of its currency in popular discourse. At the same time it is clear that from the outset, gender's history has been fraught and often embroiled in controversy. It is, to be sure, a contested terrain, and that may well reflect gender's standing as the great conceptual device of the late twentieth century.

The research that informs this book emerged through a consideration of the work of Money, feminist genealogies of the concept of gender, and recent cultural critiques of intersex case management practices. Competing discourses about gender that have emerged at particular historical moments during the late twentieth and early twenty-first centuries have had significant effects at an epistemic level and at an individual level that is seldom recognized. My aim has been to demonstrate that each episode in the history of the concept has had significant material consequences for those who were and remain at the center of the idea of gender.

The central relation that the intersexed have historically had to gender is woven everywhere through this text. That is because even as they appear to stand outside of binary gender categories, it is the intersexed who have provided the ground for understandings of what gender is, how it is acquired, and of course what is considered to be "normal" in bodies. Paradoxically, those same ideas have rendered the intersexed marginal at best and at worst not fully human, at least not until they are "fixed" to ensure their genders become, *and* remain, fixed.

Today, after almost two decades of activism aimed at changing the material practices of ICM and thus the material reality of intersexed people, the political landscape looks quite different than it did in the early 1990s. Significant gains have been made during that period: there is now a greater community awareness of the intersexed and their medical (mis)adventures; new surgical outcome studies exist and latitudinal studies are under way; *some* clinicians are rethinking their practices and the merits of early surgery; there is now a substantial and growing body of scholarship addressing the ethical, legal, and sociocultural dimensions of ICM; and at least one legal jurisdiction recognizes the intersexed *as* intersex. Yet herein lies the first of two ironies: we have a legal decision that grants personhood to the intersexed yet at the same time, under medicojuridical conditions, the intersexed fail to qualify for personhood *because* they are intersexed.

Regardless of any legal precedent around personhood, genital surgery continues to be promoted and performed on infants. The quest by activists and advocates to stop these surgeries is some way from fulfillment, it seems, as is the hope that such surgeries will one day become elective. Again ironically, while genital surgery is not optional in ICM, over the same period that advocates have been calling for it to be so, genital surgery has become available as an elective for the general (predominantly female) population. Cosmetic genital surgery has joined the ranks of consumables and is said to represent the biggest growth area in so-called appearance medicine today.[1]

Meanwhile, members of the 2005 Chicago Consensus Group responsible for recodifying intersex authored a consensus statement on treatments for people diagnosed as CAH just three years earlier.[2] That document recommended genital surgery be performed on infants between two and six months of age on the grounds of "technical ease." Of the three stated surgical goals, the first was "genital appearance compatible with *gender*."[3] The consensus documents are of transnational authorship and published in major medical journals, and so have enormous reach. Not surprisingly they have proved highly influential to medical researchers and clinicians alike, as a search of the subsequent literature on ICM will attest.

When clinicians had earlier expressed concern about the "over de-pathologizing [of] sex anomalies,"[4] ISNA responded by taking a leading role in driving the nomenclature changes that repathologize sex diversity and at the same time depoliticize it. The organization's role in and reasoning for this initiative have been explained by Alice Dreger as follows:

> But it is inaccurate to suggest that we in ISNA followed the pediatric endocrinologists in using the term DSD. If anything, it was the other way around. On the surface, it might seem to make sense that the pediatric endocrinologists, with whom we in ISNA long struggled, coined the medicalized term—and ISNA just decided to reluctantly go along. After all, why would a shift to a medicalized term like "disorders of sex development" be primarily initiated by our side, when we had been arguing for de-medicalization of intersex? And yet, as I have explained elsewhere, so far as I can tell, most of the impetus came from us.... [We] became convinced that the term "intersex" was getting in the way of reforming the medical treatment of children born with intersex. We could not seem to move towards a consensus of treatment reform under the umbrella of that term. And treatment reform was the goal.... Bo, our clinical allies, and I knew enough about medical "consensus" conferences to know what Chomsky had shown: consensus is manufactured. We wanted to make sure "consensus" got manufactured in Chicago in the shape we believed was right for children with sex anomalies. So, in advance of the Chicago "consensus" conference (a strictly controlled, invitation-only affair), those affiliated with ISNA who would be attending the conference discussed specifically what to push.[5]

While there is no doubt that these aims are laudable, the means of achieving them seem incredibly risky. Is this the kind of political obsolescence that some advocates dreamt of in the late 1990s? Rhetorical questions aside, while the interests of children were at the forefront of this maneuver, the need to locate conceptual spaces that allow for the dignity and integrity of *all* intersexed people—in the present— remains. The language of disorder banishes intersex from the here and now in the same way that the disavowal of true hermaphrodites did in the late nineteenth and early twentieth centuries. Where does this leave adults, particularly those who insist their embodied experience of being intersex is as fundamental to their ontological reality as female embodiment and male embodiment is to others? Critical sexologist William Simon once wrote that the so-called first world has increasingly been faced with "a crisis of paradigms" concerning the sexual.[6] Could there be any more powerful evidence of such a crisis than the way that the very matter of intersex is approached and "dealt with" by medical science?

This crisis of paradigms cannot be said to simply reflect the failures or inadequacies of sexology since it is as much a product of the field's successes as of its shortcomings. The groundbreaking work undertaken by sexological researchers (both living and dead) has served to increase awareness about what Simon refers to as "the distribution of the experiences of the sexual and of its different meanings."[7] By Simon's reckoning the reason many of the older concepts have outlived their usefulness is because peoples' sexual realities continue to undergo change just as sexual meanings do.[8] Precisely the same can be said about people's gendered realities. For Simon this suggests that new concepts are called for and, while I take his point, I wonder if it is in fact necessary to reinvent the wheel. Where might opportunities lie to expand our understanding of sexual difference, beyond two? What preexisting concepts might help to make the kind of conceptual leap I am proposing?

Eve Kosofsky Sedgwick and Adam Frank have suggested that the limits of a lot of contemporary social theory stem from a tendency toward antibiologism, especially (though not exclusively) theory inflected by poststructuralism with its emphasis on the discursive.[9] The danger in this tendency, they say, is the loss of "conceptual access to an entire thought-realm" that offers opportunities to develop a "vision of difference [capable of resisting] binary homogenisation."[10] Since one of my objectives is to find ways to prise open spaces that would allow us to think differently about sexed embodiment, where better to turn than to the thought realm of sexology?[11]

There is no denying that historically the sexual sciences have contributed to and been instrumental in pathologizing sexual diversity in its many guises. Nor can it be denied that modern sexology has concerned itself with defining what it means to be a masculine man or a feminine woman and with enhancing their compatibility, as some of Money's ideas clearly demonstrate.[12] Yet sexological theory is capable of so much more than this. The field constitutes what Gayle Rubin once described as a rich vein of material for developing alternative conceptualizations of sexed subjectivity.[13] My explorations into the field leave me in no doubt of the wisdom of Rubin's claim.

What I want to propose is that we look to the potential in gender. If gender's conceptual clout is an effect of its capacity to survive transformation, how else might it be transformed? Could gender be used in the interests of those who have historically been most marginalized by it? Where do the limits of gender's capacities lie? These questions have import for all manner of theoretical and political endeavors because the persistent and seemingly unrelenting "desire for gender" is a desire shared by those intent on queering gender and by those who prefer to "play it straight."[14]

Earlier I flagged the merits of Money's conceptualization of gender over more recent interpretations that assume the sex/gender distinction. The strength of Money's theories lie in his refusal of that distinction; in his cognizance of the intricate relation between cells, environment, and experience; and in the capacity of his framework to readily accommodate temporal and sociocultural change. This is not to suggest that Money's ideas are unproblematic; indeed, at many points throughout the book I have been concerned to highlight precisely how problematic they are—and why. Nor is it my intention to elide the very real consequences of the application of Money's ideas to date on the lives of the intersexed. For too long the intersexed have paid the highest of prices for the unrelenting biomedical and cultural commitment to the narrowest possible view of sexual difference: that is, sexual difference to the order of two and only two.

In the biomedical context the commitment to dimorphic sexual difference can be attributed to biology's keen interest in sex *as* reproductive and to the fatalist impulses of functionalism. As indicated in Chapter 5, the epistemic legacy of Erasmus Darwin's infamous declaration that sexual reproduction and bodily sex difference represented nature's magnum opus continues to cast its shadow in biological, biomedical, and cultural discourse. A reproductive paradigm is not without its uses, of course, but its limits as an explanatory framework are all too apparent, not least because—and here I venture, nay, plunge down the slippery slope of generalization—most sexual encounters for most people, most of the time, are concerned less with procreation than they are with pleasure. And as Robert Padgug reminds us, biological sexuality (be it organs, orifices, chemicals etc.) is a necessary precondition for human sexuality but it is *only* a precondition, "a set of potentialities."[15] While intricately involved in *conditioning* human behavior, biology does not cause it.

*   *   *

To return to my earlier question of where in gender there might be a place for the intersexed, I want to propose that we first revisit the central mechanism through which gender is acquired in Money's account: the neural scaffold he called a gendermap. Under the terms of his acquisition model we are each born with a neural template that codes for both masculine and feminine behaviors. The template is both receptive and responsive to postnatal stimuli. It is through their interaction that subjects come to recognize which behaviors are appropriate to males and/or females, and (most) come to embody those that align with their assigned sex.[16] As with bilingualism, exposure to both sets of stimuli (or what Money called "bi-genderism") is a necessary condition of gender acquisition.[17] The first order of this framework then is concerned with human behaviors—organized by sex.[18]

Money's gendermap equates to a kind of neural scaffolding that codes for a rich and complex array of characteristics and behaviors. Perhaps we can understand it as a kind of database, a living repository of knowledge that shapes and is shaped by behaviors, affective responses, and embodied experiences. That we learn to differentiate which behaviors are masculine—and feminine—appropriate suggests that gender is as much a process of learning what is required to be a gender in any given sociocultural and temporal context as it is a process of "becoming."[19] As I indicated in the introductory chapter, suspending the notion of becoming invites a shift of attention toward the mechanisms involved in *learning to be* a gender. With that shift it becomes clear that the body is not some passive entity upon which culture etches; bodies are active participants in this process.

The application of recent discoveries in the fields of neurology and genetics to Money's account of gender acquisition complicates his ideas in highly productive ways. In neuroscience, for example, the concept of neural plasticity has rendered the hardwiring thesis for the most part redundant. Money relied on the idea that responses were imprinted and became hardwired in the brain as a way to argue for gender's immutability. Today it is understood that it is not responses per se that become hardwired, but rather one's capacity to respond. Evidence suggests that neural pathways continue to be plastic—that is, they continue to proliferate and transform—until the seventh decade, on average.[20]

The recent discovery that many if not most of the genes that code for sex-determination are located elsewhere than on the X and the Y chromosomes also has implications for our understandings of what sex is at a genetic level.[21] These findings disrupt the idea that genetic sex is a straightforward matter of Xs and Ys, just as they disrupt our previous understandings of what "sex-chromosomes" are and do. Evidence continues to mount that the facticity of the body far exceeds a dimorphic understanding of sexual difference. Together these discoveries create, or at the very least contribute to, the necessary conditions for new ways of understanding sex-gender and sexuality and for a reconsideration of who counts as human.

*   *   *

Another means of reinvigorating Money's theories may well lie in magnifying or amplifying his understanding of the interplay between the physiological, the sensorial, and the social. That is because Money's account posits gender acquisition as a thoroughly embodied process. One of the ways to do this would be to take seriously the complex interactions between what Margaret Lock refers to as local biologies,[22] and local systems of knowledge. In other words, this is also a call to focus on the agency of biologies rather than assuming that culture simply maps onto a raw (read passive) biological substrate. Local cultural systems are systems of knowledge that, when stripped of artifice and theory, function as common sense in any given cultural and temporal context.[23] The idea that there are only two sexes and two genders constitutes one such commonsense idea. But more than this it reflects the pervasive belief that this is "just how things are."[24]

Because binary concepts of gender and sexuality have become so deeply embedded in the local cultural knowledges of Western liberal democracies, each and every one of us is implicated in the invisibility of those who are differently sexed. That embeddedness is made manifest in countless ways, including the constant monitoring or policing of the behaviors of both self and others. It is also made manifest by the fact that sorting by sex-gender is something we are so well socialised into that it seems, "not just second—but first-nature."[25]

As I suggested in Chapter 5, attending to how meaning is made by sexual subjects offers opportunities to develop increasingly sophisticated understandings of just how complex individuals' erotic desires, tastes, and styles—and thus their subjective experiences—are. While Money's concepts are incredibly complex on many levels, they remain comprised by two factors: first, an overreliance on a closed system of sexual dimorphism, and second, their reliance upon a developmental paradigm. The failure to fully adapt to one's gender indicated, by Money's account, that something had gone wrong during one of two critical phases. That is because in developmental terms any phenomenon that deviates from what the model deems normal can be explained only as some earlier disruption to a normative process.

Tolman and Diamond suggest that descriptive models provide opportunities to explore how different forms of eroticism depend upon differing interactions between physiology and context through-out the life span in ways that are foreclosed or at the very least severely compromised by developmental models.[26] As with gender, our under-standings of what constitutes the sexual need to be unharnessed from the tyranny of sexual dimorphism if they are to ever reflect lived expe-rience. By decoupling Money's theories of sexuality and gender from a binary logic, we can begin to expand our ways of knowing to make spaces for forms of eroticism that seem incomprehensible within the epistemological frameworks we currently have available. This is pre-cisely what those who seek recognition for an ontological status *as* hermaphrodite or *as* intersex are demanding.

It should be clear by this point that, in advocating for the recog-nition of intersex persons *as* intersex in their own right, I am not suggesting that everybody who is intersexed *should* claim status as such or that they *should* be out there being good "gender warriors." While much of my focus has been on intersexed adults I am certainly not disinterested in the needs of the children. It would seem that to date the focus on children has been at the expense of the needs of adults. Yet must that be the case? I remain optimistic that the differ-ential needs of both adults and children can be addressed in ways that don't require one to be at the expense of the other. Morgan Holmes offers a compelling proposal in this respect. She argues for a serious rethink of what we understand the very concept of treatment to mean. Rather than limiting our view, as we currently do, to a "set of clinically grounded options," she suggests that we need to expand our vision of treatment to include a "set of behaviours and attitudes that we can take toward a child."[27] For Holmes the need to move away from the current clinical treatment model stems from the fact that the treat-ments offered (some would say imposed) serve to "undermine the (formerly) intersexed adult's sense of authenticity as persons, and as gendered subjects."[28] In other words, surgical and other ICM proce-dures don't just impact negatively on bodily integrity, they impact on the integrity of the whole person. Ultimately Holmes rests her case on a very simple but profound observation regarding the everydayness of social relations:

We must take as obvious the personhood of the intersexed child rather than take as obvious that the personhood of the intersexed child is somehow obscured by the state of the genitals. After all, it is worth remembering that any passer-by who sees the child will apprehend a person, not an "it."[29]

*   *   *

In the first chapter I noted Money's insistence that the appropriate sex of an intersexed individual must be determined on the basis of multidimensional factors rather than a single criterion. At the same time he was confident that this was not the case for those subjects that might be referred to as unremarkable males or females. Money believed that it was entirely feasible to assume that sex was univariate in character for most people, since each of the physiological signifiers of sex would line up with one another. By this account an individual possessing a penis would also be sperm producing, testes bearing, testosterone driven, and possessed of one X and one Y chromosome. People with a clitoris would carry ova, possess a uterus, be estrogen driven, and have two X chromosomes. Chromatin testing has yet to become routine, so the chromosomal status of *most* people remains unknown. While that is likely to change with the ascension of genetics as the new orthodoxy of medical science, at the present time the idea of alignment remains speculative.

A multispectral approach to sexed embodiment and subjectivity would not allow for a "feasible to assume" stance such as Money's because it would explicitly reject the idea that anyone's sex *can* be univariate or that it will remain stable over time. An example of such an approach was developed a century ago by one of Money's sexological forebears, Magnus Hirschfeld. I am referring to the doctrine of sexual intermediaries that he elaborated in print in 1910.[30] Hirschfeld's was not a theory per se but rather a metaframework—in his terms a "princical of division" that he designed to succeed closed systems of sexual distribution (a binary model being the most obvious example).[31]

For Hirschfeld, the idea of pure types of men or pure types of women was not just an ideological fantasy, it was an impossibility. Why? Because every person is constituted of differing proportions of masculinity and femininity, across multiple spectra. To complicate matters, a number of those dimensions involve temporal fluctuation (cyclic and/or sporadic) across a person's life span. Like many of his contemporaries and successors, Hirschfeld took his cues from the embryological evidence that all humans begin life in an undifferentiated form. What he did with it was something altogether different. For Hirschfeld, the retention of vestigal structures of the so-called other sex added weight to his proposal that differentiation led not to maleness or femaleness per se, but to a unique complexity. In other words, all of us are sexual intermediaries. He explained his proposal thus: "In every living thing that is produced by the union of the two sexes, we find beside the signs of the one sex, the one of the other, often far beyond the rudimentary and in very different gradations."[32] Lest the reader interpret this statement solely in terms of the somatic dimensions of sex, the sociocultural or relational dimensions of sexed subjectivity were equally implicated in Hirschfeld's proposal.[33]

Medical science, as we know, remains committed to the idea that there can and should be only two sexes, even though it has long understood that fetal life produces a spectacular array of bodily forms. Not so the medically trained Hirschfeld; the embryological evidence provided him with proof of the *impossibility* of discrete sex categories. He had this to say about the idea of the "univariate woman" and the "univariate man":

These kinds of representatives of their sex are, however, first of all only abstractions, invented extremes; in reality they have not as yet been observed.... In appearance as well as in essence there is such an extraordinary number of deviations and nuances that each individual appears as somewhat distinct.[34]

This meant that the figure of the supplemental third sex was also fictional under Hirschfeld's terms.[35] He went further; the very idea that sexual intermediacy was a pathological condition was "an indefensible standpoint for biologists of the Darwinian school."[36] But ultimately whatever understanding of sexual diversity (pathologizing or otherwise) one ascribed to was far less important in Hirshfeld's view than the need "to treat the sexual intermediaries, as a *widespread and important natural phenomenon*."[37] As he well knew, in framing normality as an ideological fiction the very idea of abnormality was rendered taxonomically meaningless.[38]

Hirschfeld's multidimensional framework was made up of four interactive elements, each composed of a further four subcategories that could in turn be broken down further.[39] In tabular form, Hirshfeld's schema looked something like Table 6.1.[40]

These dimensions are ranked from primary to fourth order with the sex organs—in the very broadest sense of the term—standing as the primary dimension. Drawing on the medicoscientific knowledge of the day, Hirschfeld cited germ cells (sperm and ova), ovi and spermatic ducts, sexual protuberance (penis-clitoris), and the sexual grooves (developing in female form as vulva and in male form as the urethral groove). At a somatic level the secondary characteristics of interest were hair distribution, larynx, chest, and pelvis. The third cluster referenced one's sexual life in terms of orientation, approach, disposition, and manner or activity. Finally, the fourth cluster represents what today we understand as gender, and here Hirschfeld grouped together emotional life, occupation, manner of thought, and

Table 6.1 Reproduction of Hirschfeld's 3^{16} schema.

Group A—Genital Primary sexual features	Group B—Somatic Secondary sexual features
1. Germ cell (sperm/ova)	1. Hair
2. Ovi/spermatic ducts	2. Larynx
3. Sexual protruberance (penis-clitoris)	3. Chest
4. Sexual groove	4. Pelvis
Group C [Sexuality] Tertiary sexual features	**Group D [Gender]** Fourth-order sexual features
1. Orientation	1. Emotional life
2. Approach	2. Manner of thought
3. Disposition	3. Occupation
4. Manner of activity	4. Clothing

dress. What makes this schema so dynamic is that variation is not just accepted but is in fact expected. Thus it assumes and so takes into account fluctuations within and between spectra as much as it does fluctuations between individuals.

Mapping Hirschfeld's concept of sexual difference across Money's seven signifiers of sex[41] allows for the recognition that no one's sex-gender is or can be constituted, embodied, or invested in, vis-à-vis our sexual selves, in quite the same way. Hirschfeld relied upon masculinity and femininity (today, gender) as his reference points, but because his system is open-ended it presupposes multiple dynamic subjectivities. Each is composed of a constellation of behaviors, characteristics, and capacities. Sexual difference then extends far beyond $n = 2$ and begins to look like something altogether different.

It is time that we put to one side questions about the quantitative aspects of gender (how many genders are there or can there be?), along with questions of motivation that focus on *why* people are the kinds of gendered and sexual subjects they are. A much more fruitful approach would surely be to focus attention on the means people use to negotiate and make sense of this particular mode of social and personal organization. This would offer productive opportunities to develop conceptual frameworks that are responsive to the theoretical qualifier known in the psychological sciences as individual differences. At worst we might learn that there really is no such thing as "normal." At most, a revitalized gender might just—after all these years—provide ways to recover the dignity, integrity, and humanity of those most marginalized by binary concepts of sexual difference.

Notes

Introduction

1. John Money and Anke Ehrhardt, *Man and Woman Boy and Girl: The Differentiation and Dimorphism of Gender Identity from Conception to Maturity* (Baltimore: Johns Hopkins University Press, 1972), 9.
2. Rosie Braidotti, *Nomadic Subjects: Embodiment and Sexual Difference in Contemporary Feminist Theory* (New York: Columbia University Press, 1994); Georges Canguilhem, *On the Normal and the Pathological*, trans. Carolyn Fawcett (Dordrecht: Reidel Publishing, 1978).
3. I refer here to the late David Reimer, whom Money recommended be reassigned and reared as a girl following the loss of his penis after a botched circumcision when he was an infant. See Bernice Hausman, "Do Boys Have to Be Boys? Gender, Narrativity, and the John/Joan Case," *NWSA Journal* 12, no. 3 (2000): 114–138.
4. Perhaps the most public of those attacks was that of *Rolling Stone* journalist John Colapinto. See John Colapinto, *As Nature Made Him: The Boy Who Was Raised as a Girl* (Sydney: Harper Collins, 2000).
5. Refer to "Notes on terminology and definitions" for an explanation of this hyphenation.
6. Money on the other hand has acknowledged—however disapprovingly—the ways in which feminism impacted on his theories of gender.
7. This is not to suggest that gender ceased to be a language tool but rather that its conceptual load increased exponentially when it became the signifier of characters, behaviors, and identities as masculine or feminine.
8. Natural gender, according to the *Oxford English Dictionary*, is a feature of modern English where "nouns are masculine, feminine or neuter according as the objects they denote are male, female, or of neither sex; and the gender of a noun has no other syntactical effect than that of determining the pronoun that must be used in referring to it" http://dictionary.oed.com/cgi/entry/50093521?query_type=word& queryword=gender, s.v. GENDER n. 2.
9. Hausman's exacting reading of the early work of Money serves as a foundation for some of the key arguments made in Chapters 1 and 3

(Bernice Hausman, *Changing Sex: Transsexualism, Technology and the Idea of Gender* [Durham, NC: Duke University Press, 1995], 72–109).

10. Ann Curthoys, ed., *Gender in the Social Sciences in Australia* (Canberra: Australian Publishing Service, 1998), 41; Gayle Rubin and Judith Butler, "Sexual Traffic," in *Coming out of Feminism?* ed. Mandy Merk, Naomi Segal, and Elizabeth Wright (Oxford: Blackwell, 1998), 36–73.

11. Donna Haraway correctly attributes the introduction of the term "gender *identity*" to Stoller (ca.1963) but incorrectly situates Money's project as successive to Stoller's. See Donna Haraway, *Simians, Cyborgs, and Women: The Reinvention of Nature* (New York and London: Routledge, 1991).

12. Rosie Braidotti, "Signs of Wonder and Traces of Doubt: On Teratology and Embodied Differences," in *Between Monsters, Goddesses and Cyborgs: Feminist Confrontations with Science, Medicine and Cyberspace*, ed. Ninna Lykke and Rosie Braidotti (London: Zed Books, 1996), 135–152.

13. See especially, Mary Hawkesworth, "Confounding Gender," *Signs: Journal of Women in Culture and Society* 22, no. 3 (1997): 649–685; Joan Scott, "Gender as a Useful Category of Historical Analysis," in *Culture, Society and Sexuality: A Reader*, ed. Richard Parker and Peter Aggleton (London and Philadelphia: UCL Press, 1999), 57–75; Steven Seidman and Linda Nicholson, eds., Introduction to *Social Postmodernism: Beyond Identity Politics* (Cambridge: Cambridge University Press, 1995), 1–35.

14. While many of these cultural critiques of intersex case management (ICM) assume the sex/gender distinction, there are those who draw attention to the theoretical dangers of doing so (see Anne Fausto-Sterling, *Sexing the Body: Gender Politics and the Construction of Sexuality* [New York: Basic Books, 2000]; Hausman, *Changing Sex*). In short, when sex is relegated to nature as "real" and gender to culture as "constructed," the material construction of "sex" realized through the reconfiguration and/or removal of body parts becomes obscured.

15. Sharon Crasnow, "Models and Reality: When Science Tackles Sex," *Hypatia* 16, no. 3 (2001): 138–148; Alice Domurat Dreger, "Ethical Problems in Intersex Treatment," *Medical Humanities Report* 19, no. 1 (1997); Dreger, " 'Ambiguous Sex'—or Ambivalent Medicine?" *Hastings Center Report* 28, no. 3 (1998): 24–35; Dreger, *Hermaphrodites and the Medical Invention of Sex* (Cambridge, MA: Harvard University Press, 1998); Dreger, "When Medicine Goes Too Far in the Pursuit of Normality," *New York Times*, July 28, 1998, 4; Dreger, ed., *Intersex in the Age of Ethics* (Hagerstown, MD: University Publishing Group, 2000); Anne Fausto-Sterling, "The Five Sexes: Why Male and Female Are Not Enough," *The Sciences*, March/April (1993): 20–25; Fausto-Sterling, *Sexing the Body*; Fausto-Sterling, "The

Five Sexes, Revisited," *The Sciences* 40, no. 4 (2000): 18; Fausto-Sterling, "How Sexually Dimorphic Are We? Review and Synthesis," *American Journal of Human Biology* 12 (2000): 151–166; Deborah Findlay, "Discovering Sex: Medical Science, Feminism and Intersexuality," *Canadian Review of Sociology and Anthropology* 32, no. 1 (1995): 25; Joel Frader, Dena Davis, Arthur Frank, and Paul Miller, "Health Care Professionals and Intersex Conditions," *Archives of Pediatrics & Adolescent Medicine* 158 (2004): 426–429; Myra Hird, "A Typical Gender Identity Conference? Some Disturbing Reports from the Therapeutic Front Lines," *Femininsm & Psychology* 13, no. 2 (2003): 181–199; Morgan Holmes, "Queer Cut Bodies: Intersexuality and Homophobia in Medical Practice" http://www.usc.edu/isd/archives/queerfrontiers/queer/papers/holmes.long.html; Holmes, "In(to) Visibility: Intersexuality in the Field of Queer," in *Looking Queer: Body Image and Identity in Lesbian, Bisexual, Gay and Transgender Communities*, ed. Dawn Atkins (New York: Harrington Park Press, 1998), 221–226; Holmes, "Rethinking the Meaning and Management of Intersexuality," *Sexualities* 5, no. 2 (2002): 159–180; Katrina Karkazis, *Fixing Sex: Intersex, Medical Authority and Lived Experience* (Durham, NC: Duke University Press, 2008); Suzanne Kessler, "The Medical Construction of Gender: Case Management of Intersexed Infants," *Signs* 16, no. 1 (1990): 3–26; Kessler, *Lessons from the Intersexed* (New Brunswick, NJ: Rutgers University Press, 1998); Iain Morland, "The Glans Opens Like a Book: Writing and Reading the Intersexed Body," *Continuum: Journal of Media & Culture Studies* 19, no. 3 (2005): 335–348, Morland, "Narrating Intersex: On the Ethical Critique of the Medical Management of Intersexuality, 1985–2005," PhD diss., University of London, 2005; Sharon Preves, "Negotiating the Constraints of Gender Binarism: Intersexuals' Challenge to Gender Categorization," *Current Sociology* 48, no. 3 (2000): 27–50; Preves, "Sexing the Intersexed: An Analysis of Sociocultural Responses to Intersexuality," *Signs* 27, no. 2 (2002): 523–557; Katrina Roen, "Editorial. Intersex Embodiment: When Health Care Means Maintaining Binary Sexes," *Sexual Health* 1 (2004): 127–130; Roen, " 'But We Have to Do Something': Surgical 'Correction' of Atypical Genitalia," *Body and Society* 14, no. 1 (2008): 47–66; Stephanie Turner, "Intersex Identities: Locating New Intersections of Sex and Gender," *Gender & Society* 13, no. 4 (1999): 457–479; Georgia Warnke, "Intersexuality and the Construction of Sex," *Hypatia* 16, no. 3 (2001): 126–137.

16. Julia Epstein, "Either/Or – Neither/Both: Sexual Ambiguity and the Ideology of Gender," *Genders* 7 (1990): 128–129.

17. See Dreger, *Hermaphrodites and the Medical Invention of Sex*, 33–35. Teratology emerged as a field in the early nineteenth century and was a precursor to the field of embryology. Teratology's concern was the study of "monstrosities."

18. Eighteenth-century physician James Parsons included a review of historical, cultural, and religious responses to the "otherly" sexed in his treatise on hermaphroditism, many of which involved ritual sacrifice (James Parsons, *A Mechanical and Critical Enquiry into the Nature of Hermaphrodites* [London: Printed for J. Walthoe, 1741]).

19. Epstein, "Either/Or," 116.

20. Here I am referring to L/G/B/T organizations and Web sites and queer studies, in particular.

21. See for example, Roger Adkins, "Where 'Sex' is Born(e): Intersexed Births and the Social Urgency of Heterosexuality," *Journal of Medical Humanities* 20, no. 2 (1999): 117–133; Dreger, *Hermaphrodites and the Medical Invention of Sex*; Preves, "Negotiating the Constraints"; Preves, "Sexing the Intersexed."

22. Findlay, "Discovering Sex."

23. Hausman, *Changing Sex*, 179.

24. See for example, Epstein, "Either/Or"; Kessler, "Medical Construction"; Kessler, *Lessons*.

25. Hausman, *Changing Sex*, 74–76.

26. Judith Butler, *Gender Trouble: Feminism and the Subversion of Identity* (New York: Routledge, 1990); Butler, *Bodies That Matter: On the Discursive Limits Of "Sex"* (New York: Routledge, 1993).

27. Dreger, "Hermaphrodites in Love"; Dreger, "Ethical Problems"; Dreger, "When Medicine Goes Too Far"; Dreger, "Ambiguous Sex"; Dreger, *Hermaphrodites and the Medical Invention of Sex*; Findlay, "Discovering Sex"; Hausman, *Changing Sex*; Holmes, "Queer Cut Bodies"; Kessler, "Medical Construction"; Kessler, *Lessons*; Preves, "Sexing the Intersexed"; Turner, "Intersex Identities."

28. Elizabeth Wilson, "Biologically Inspired Feminism: Response to Helen Keane and Marsha Rosengarten, 'On the Biology of Sexed Subjects'," *Australian Feminist Studies* 17, no. 39 (2002): 285.

29. Dreger, *Hermaphrodites and the Medical Invention of Sex*, 9.

30. Jennifer Germon, "Kinsey and the Politics of Bisexual Authenticity," *Journal of Bisexuality* 8, no. 3/4 (2008): 245–260.

31. Epstein, "Either/Or"; Epstein, *Altered Conditions: Disease, Medicine and Storytelling* (New York: Routledge, 1995); Fausto-Sterling, "The Five Sexes," 23.

32. Epstein, "Either/Or," 130.

33. Of course there are many intersexed adults who are quite happy being the gender they were assigned and having an unambiguous sexuality as heterosexual, gay, or lesbian.

34. The intersexed are everywhere visible in the medical literature thanks to medical photography. For a semiotic reading of how those images function see Hausman, *Changing Sex*, 84–90.

35. Epstein, "Either/Or," 130.

36. It might also be useful to think about how gender and ICM have served to extend the ways in which it is possible—in theory if not in

practice—to be or become a rational unified subject through being singularly sexed.

37. Cited in Kessler, *Lessons*, 90. Kessler proposes that is a more radical position than any call for the ontological status as hermaphrodite or as intersex can be. In an earlier work, Kessler claimed that those so-called true hermaphrodites—who possess an ovary *and* a testis either separately or combined as an ovotestis—are extremely rare in the first instance and in the second, that most people with "ambigenitals" are not really intersexed at all ("The Medical Construction of Gender," 5). This claim, in its own way surely constitutes another form of erasure.

38. Kessler, *Lessons*, 90.

39. I take up this issue in detail in Chapter 5 with respect to the recent and highly controversial shift in terminology from intersex to DSD or "disorders of sex development".

40. Morland, "The Glans Opens," 337.

41. Epstein, "Either/Or," 130.

42. Parsons, *A Mechanical Enquiry*, 6–7.

43. Warnke, "Intersexuality," 120.

44. There is also a substantive literature from the biological sciences that uses gender as an interpretive framework for understanding the behavior of animals, birds, and reptiles, a practice known as anthropomorphization. For some relatively recent examples, see Bruce Bagemihl, *Biological Exuberance: Animal Homosexuality and Natural Diversity* (New York: St. Martin's, 1999); Joan Roughgarden, *Evolution's Rainbow: Diversity, Gender, and Sexuality in Nature and People* (Berkeley: University of California Press, 2004).

45. Canguilhem, *On the Normal*.

46. See for example, Money, *Gay, Straight, and In-Between: The Sexology of Erotic Orientation* (New York: Continuum, 1988), 51–52, 76–77.

47. Canguilhem, *On the Normal*, 149.

48. Epstein, *Altered Conditions*, 11.

49. The scientific study and classification of monstrosities was coined *teratology* during the early nineteenth century; however, it should be noted that hermaphrodites had been classified as monsters in some contexts for centuries prior.

50. Elizabeth Grosz, "Intolerable Ambiguity: Freaks as/at the Limit," in *Freakery: Cultural Spectacles of the Extraordinary Body*, ed. Rosemary Garland Thomson (New York: New York University Press, 1996), 64.

51. Rosie Braidotti, "Signs of Wonder," 141.

52. Rosemarie Garland Thomson, *Extraordinary Bodies: Figuring Physical Disability in American Culture and Literature* (New York: Columbia University Press, 1997), 20.

53. Fausto-Sterling, "How To Build A Man," in *The Gender Sexuality Reader: Culture, History, Political Economy*, edited by R. N. Lancaster and M. di Leonardo, 244–48.; Fausto-Sterling, *Sexing the Body*.

54. Garland Thomson, *Extraordinary Bodies*, 12.

55. Ibid., 11.

56. Janet Price and Margrit Shildrick, "Uncertain Thoughts on the Dis/Abled Body," in *Vital Signs: Feminist Reconfigurations of the Bio/Logical Body*, ed. Margaret Shildrick and Janet Price (Edinburgh: Edinburgh University Press, 1998), 232.

57. In almost all of the medical literature written prior to the late 1990s, the debates centered around what form interventions should take, never whether interventions should be made. It is only in the past five or six years that the issue of nonintervention has entered into the discussion.

58. Jacqueline Urla and Jennifer Terry, "Introduction: Mapping Embodied Deviance," in *Deviant Bodies: Critical Perspectives on Difference in Science and Popular Culture*, ed. Jennifer Terry and Jacqueline Urla (Bloomington: Indiana University Press, 1995), 3.

59. Local cultural knowledge refers to everyday understandings that are specific to time, place and cultures.

60. Erving Goffman, "The Arrangement between the Sexes," *Theory and Society* 4 (1977): 301–331. Nancy Chodorow is also renowned for her relational model of gender. See Chodorow, "Being and Doing: A Cross-Cultural Examination of the Socialization of Males and Females," in *Woman in Sexist Society: Studies in Power and Powerlessness*, ed. Vivian Gornick and Barbara Moran (New York/London: Basic Books, 1971), 173–197; Chodorow, *The Reproduction of Mothering: Psychoanalysis and the Sociology of Gender* (Berkeley: University of California Press, 1978); Chodorow, "Feminism and Difference: Gender, Relation, and Difference in Psychoanalytic Perspective," *Socialist Review* 46 (1979): 42–69.

61. Goffman is recognized as one of the major contributors to symbolic interactionism, although this is not where he understood his own project to lie. Symbolic interactionism is concerned with the ways that people construct and present a sense of self and how meanings are created through interaction; thus it resonates with aspects of poststructuralism. For an analysis of some of the parallels between the two perspectives, see Robert Dunn, "Self, Identity, and Difference: Mead and the Poststructuralists," *Sociological Quarterly* 38, no. 4 (1997): 687–705.

62. Both Money and Goffman offered accounts of the ways that sex differences come to be elaborated personally and socially, but of course they each did so for very different ends.

63. Goffman's analysis of gender preempted poststructuralist critiques making similar claims. Since 1990, Judith Butler has become known as the proponent of the idea that gender is performative; however, Goffman's analysis preceded Butler's by a decade and a half.

64. Goffman, "The Arrangement," 315.

65. Ibid., 305.
66. As I demonstrate in Chapters 4 and 5, these are not the only sites in which this notion is reproduced.
67. Howard Becker, *Tricks of the Trade: How to Think About Your Research While You're Doing It* (Chicago: University of Chicago Press, 1998), 59.
68. See Rubin, "The Traffic in Women," 204.
69. At other points during the text I frame this same interaction as one between cells, environment, and experience.
70. See Money, *The Psychologic Study of Man* (Springfield, IL.: Charles C. Thomas, 1957).
71. Hubert Dreyfus and Paul Rabinow, *Michel Foucault: Beyond Structuralism and Hermeneutics*, 2nd ed. (Chicago: University of Chicago Press, 1983), 118.
72. Hausman, *Changing Sex*, 75.
73. See Richard Goldschmidt, *The Mechanism and Physiology of Sex Determination*, trans. William J Dakin (London: Methuen, 1923).
74. See for example, Jenny Morris, "Impairment and Disability: Constructing an Ethic of Care That Promotes Human Rights," *Hypatia* 16, no. 4 (2001): 1–16; Michael Oliver, *The Politics of Disablement: A Sociological Approach* (New York: St. Martin's, 1990); Tom Shakespeare, *The Disability Reader: Social Science Perspectives* (London: Cassell, 1998); Tom Shakespeare and Mairian Corker, *Disability/Postmodernity: Embodying Disability Theory* (London: Continuum, 2002).
75. I acknowledge the critique in recent years about the tendency for a hard version of the social model to (ironically) evacuate the body from disability by setting up a dualistic relation between impairment and disability (see Carol Thomas, *Sociology of Disability and Illness: Contested Ideas in Disability Studies and Medical Sociology* [New York: Palgrave, 2007]). I also acknowledge the fact that infants and children have limited to no social agency in clinical contexts when they are identified as being in need of treatment.
76. Stoller left the sociocultural components of sexed subjectivity to the social sciences.
77. That process was aided in no small part by feminism's adoption of the distinction.
78. John Money, "The Conceptual Neutering of Gender and the Criminalization of Sex," *Archives of Sexual Behaviour* 14, no. 3 (1985): 279–291; Money, *Gendermaps: Social Constructionism, Feminism and Sexosophical History* (New York: Continuum, 1995), 12.
79. The feminist literature of the 1980s and 1990s is not included in the analysis of this chapter except to evidence the curious though not uncommon claim that gender was a feminist "invention."
80. Money, *Gay, Straight*.

Chapter 1

1. Hereafter called *The Bulletin*.
2. Here I am thinking of the rather ambitious efforts of Marx, Freud, Parsons, and others to narrate and analyze complex social phenomena across time and across space by using singular comprehensive principles.
3. At that time, psychology was a program within the Philosophy Department of Victoria University, Wellington.
4. Anke Ehrhardt, "John Money, Ph.D. (Biography)," *The Journal of Sex Research* 44, no. 3 (2007), 223.
5. John Money, *Venuses Penuses: Sexology Sexosophy, and Exigency Theory* (Buffalo, NY: Prometheus Books, 1986), 5. Beaglehole had worked with Margaret Mead, Ruth Benedict, and other founders of psychological anthropology while on a Commonwealth Fellowship at Yale University during the 1930s. James Ritchie and Jane Ritchie, "Beaglehole, Ernest 1906–1965," in *Dictionary of New Zealand Biography Volume Five (1941–1960)* (Wellington: Ministry for Culture and Heritage, 2000), 42–43. Money has often drawn on anthropological data (his own and the work of others) to support his theories of gender and of sexuality. See, for example, John Money, et al., "Sex Training and Traditions in Arnhem Land," *British Journal of Medical Psychology* 47 (1970): 383–399.
6. John Money, Venuses Penuses.
7. John Money, *Lovemaps: Clinical Concepts of Sexual/Erotic Health and Pathology, Paraphhilia, and Gender Transposition in Childhood, Adolesence, and Maturity* (New York: Irvington, 1986), 6.
8. Unpublished. This information is taken from the prologue of John Money, *Venuses Penuses*, 5–18.
9. This turn of phrase would suggest some recognition of the possibility of a selfhood as intersex. However, as will be discussed in this and other chapters, medical and sexological discourses render the very idea so intolerable as to seem impossible.
10. John Money, "Hermaphroditism: An Inquiry into the Nature of a Human Paradox" (Ph D diss., Harvard University, 1952), 5.
11. Ibid., 2–3.
12. Anne Fausto-Sterling, *Sexing the Body: Gender Politics and the Construction of Sexuality* (New York: Basic Books, 2000), 38. See also Alice Domurat Dreger, "Doubtful Sex: The Fate of the Hermaphrodite in Victorian Medicine." *Victorian Studies* 38, no. 3 (1995): 335–370; Dreger, "Hermaphrodites in Love: The Truth of the Gonads," in *Science and Homosexualities*, ed. V. A. Rosario (New York: Routledge, 1997), 46–66. Kenneth Zucker, "Intersexuality and Gender Identity Differentiation," *Annual Review of Sex Research* 10 (1999), 5.

13. Bernice Hausman, *Changing Sex: Transsexualism, Technology and the Idea of Gender* (Durham: Duke University Press, 1995).

14. *Dorland's Medical Dictionary* (W. B. Saunders 2000), http://www.merckmedicus.com/pp/us/hcp/thcp_dorlands_content.jsp?pg=/ppdocs/us/common/dorlands/dorland/dmd-c-027.htm#951550

15. Dreger, *Hermaphrodites and the Medical Invention of Sex* (Cambridge: Harvard University Press, 1998), 149.

16. Franz von Neugebauer, "Hermaphrodism in the Daily Practice of Medicine Being Information Upon Hermaphrodism Indispensable to the Practitioner," *British Gynaecological Journal* 19 (1903): 226–263. Yet as one of Neugeberger's British contemporaries, David Berry Hart, noted, if there were no such thing as a "true hermaphrodite," the category "pseudo hermaphrodite" was a logical impossibility, being derived from a now nonexistent category. Thus he advocated in 1914 that hermaphrodite should be abolished completely from the medical lexicon (Dreger, *Hermaphrodites and the Medical Invention of Sex*, 156).

17. See, for example, J. R. Batanian et al., "Two Unbalanced Translocations Involving a Common 6p25 Region in Two Xy Female Patients," *Clinical Genetics* 59, no. 1 (2001): 52–57; M. Fernandez-Cancio et al., "Compound Heterozygous Mutations in the Srd5a2 Gene Exon 4 in a Male Pseudohermaphrodite Patient of Chinese Origin," *Journal of Andrology* 25, no. 3 (2004): 412–416.

18. John Money, Joan Hampson, and John Hampson, "Sexual Incongruities and Psychopathology: The Evidence of Human Hermaphroditism," *Bulletin of the Johns Hopkins Hospital* 98, no. 1 (1956): 44. Money eventually dropped the prefix *pseudo-* in an attempt to lay to rest the idea that the gonads *would* or *could* reveal the truth of a person's sex and because in his view, it failed to account for those individuals whose gonadal tissue was undifferentiated. A similar rationale of expediency in the interests of dialogue is offered today by those mainstream North American advocacy groups who have adopted the acronym DSD—or disorders of sex development—in place of "intersex."

19. Money, "Hermaphroditism: An Inquiry," 3.

20. Ibid., 4.

21. John Money, *The Lovemap Guidebook: A Definitive Statement* (New York: Continuum, 1999), 4.

22. Money, "Hermaphroditism: An Inquiry," 4.

23. Ibid., 6.

24. Alfred Kinsey, Wardell Pomeroy, and Clyde Martin, *Sexual Behavior in the Human Male* (Philadelphia: Saunders, 1948); Kinsey, Pomeroy, Martin, and Paul Gebhard, *Sexual Behavior in the Human Female* (Philadelphia: Saunders, 1953).

25. Evelyn Hooker, "A Preliminary Analysis of Group Behavior of Homosexuals," *Journal of Psychology* 42 (1956): 217–225; Hooker, "The Adjustment of the Male Overt Homosexual," *Journal of Projective Techniques* 21 (1957): 18–31; Hooker, "Male Homosexuality in the Rorschach," *Journal of Projective Techniques* 23 (1958): 278–281.

26. William Masters and Virginia E Johnson, *Human Sexual Response* (Boston: Little, Brown 1966). Although not published until the mid-1960s, Masters and Johnson began their research during the period under discussion.

27. William Simon, *Postmodern Sexualities* (London: Routledge, 1996), 23.

28. Money, *Venuses Penuses*, 8; Money, *The Adam Principle. Genes, Genitals, Hormones and Gender: Selected Readings in Sexology* (Buffalo, NY: Prometheus Books, 1993), 94–95.

29. These included journals such as the *AMA Archives of Neurology and Psychiatry*, *Journal of Clinical Endocrinology*, and *Psychosomatic Medicine*.

30. Lawson Wilkins et al., "Hermaphroditism: Classification, Diagnosis, Selection of Sex and Treatment," *Pediatrics* 16, no. 3 (1955): 287–302.

31. I use the word *indeterminate* tentatively. The dominant discourses on hermaphroditism have, for centuries now, framed hermaphroditism in terms of ambiguity, unfinished-ness, lack, or excess.

32. The use of the term sexual identity as a referent of erotic orientation as homo-, hetero-, or bisexual (understood today as *sexuality*) does not appear to have entered the English lexicon until much later.

33. Money, *Gay, Straight and In-Between: The Sexology of Erotic Orientation* (New York: Continuum, 1988), 53.

34. Ibid.

35. Money, "Hermaphroditism, Gender and Precocity in Hyper-Adrenocorticism: Psychologic Findings," *Bulletin of the Johns Hopkins Hospital* 96, no. 3 (1955): 258.

36. Ibid., 254.

37. Jerzy Szacki, *History of Sociological Thought* (London: Aldwych, 1979), 503.

38. Talcott Parsons and Robert Freed Bales, *Family: Socialization and Interaction Process* (Glencoe, IL: Free Press, 1955), 16. The stabilization of adult personality was another key role Parsons attributed to the family unit.

39. Dreger, *Hermaphrodites in Love*.

40. This section of the analysis is indebted to Bernice Hausman's account of twentieth-century medical responses to hermaphroditism. See Hausman, *Changing Sex*, 72–109.

41. Ibid.

42. Ibid., 77–79.

43. Privileging the psychosocial did not go uncontested at the time, nor does it today.

44. Albert Ellis, "The Sexual Psychology of Human Hermaphrodites," *Psychosomatic Medicine* 7 (1945), 109.

45. Ibid., 199

46. Hausman, *Changing Sex*, 79.

47. Jennifer Germon, "Degrees of Freedom: Inscribing Gender on the Intersexed Body" (MA diss., University of Auckland, 1998).

48. These are the diagnostic terms accorded by the American Psychological Association to people whose identity as male or female is at odds with their morphological status. Until 1973, homosexuals, lesbians, and bisexuals were deemed dysphoric with respect to their gender along with transsexuals, transvestites, and individuals with unusual sexual proclivities (or "paraphilias"). For an example of contemporary debates in psychiatric circles about whether GID constitutes a mental illness see Ken Hausman, "Controversy Continues to Grow over DSM's GID Diagnosis," *Psychiatric News* 38, no. 14 (2003): 25–26.

49. This concept had also been central to Lorenz's theory of imprinting.

50. Patrick Bateson and Paul Martin, *Design for a Life: How Behavior Develops*. (London: Vintage, 2000).

51. It is important to note that this reference to fetal hormones is in fact a reference to the androgenic substance testosterone. A surge of testosterone has historically been understood to "masculinize" the foetal brain. See Fausto-Sterling, *Sexing the Body*, 170–194.

52. John Money, *Gendermaps: Social Constructionism, Feminism and Sexosophical History* (New York: Continuum, 1995), 95.

53. John Money, "Propaedeutics of Deicious G-I/R: Theoretical Foundations for Understanding Dimorphic Gender-Identity/Role," in *Masculinity/Femininity. Basic Perpectives*, ed. June Reinisch, et al. (New York: Oxford University Press, 1987), 14. See also Money *Gendermaps*, 95–108.

54. Money and Patricia Tucker, *Sexual Signatures: On Being a Man or a Woman* (London: Sphere Books, 1977), 91.

55. It is not my intention to refute the idea that learning is a function of biology per se. However I do take issue with the immutability aspect of Money's claim with respect to gender. Gendering is an aspect of subjectivity that is continually reinforced and reiterated over the entire life course. For analyses of the self-fulfilling effects of the gendering process see, for example, Judith Butler, *Gender Trouble: Feminism and the Subversion of Identity* (New York: Routledge, 1990); Erving Goffman, "The Arrangement between the Sexes," *Theory and Society* 4 (1977): 301–331; Candace West and Don Zimmerman, "Doing Gender," in *The Gender and Psychology Reader*, ed. Blyth McVicker Clinchy and Julie Norem (New York: New York University Press, 1998), 104–124.

56. In the non-intersexed, incomplete coding was said to manifest in transsexualism (John Money and Anke Ehrhardt, *Man and Woman Boy and Girl: The Differentiation and Dimorphism of Gender Identity from Conception to Maturity* [Baltimore: Johns Hopkins University Press, 1972], 20).

57. This is not to suggest the process is either straightforward or painless.

58. Money and Ehrhardt, *Man and Woman*, 163.

59. Money and Ehrhardt, *Man and Woman*; Money and Tucker, *Sexual Signatures*; Money, "Gender: History, Theory and Usage of the Term in Sexology and Its Relationship to Nature/Nurture," *Journal of Sex and Marital Therapy* 11, no. 2 (1985): 71–79; Money, *Gendermaps*.

60. Money, *Gendermaps*, 112.

61. The hardwiring thesis has become increasingly undermined over the past decade as research by developmental neuroscientists has shown that neural pathways continue to respond to new stimuli over the entire life course. For an overview of some of the theoretical shifts in neuroscience since the late 1950s, see Guy McKhann, "Neurology: Then, Now, and in the Future," *Archives of Neurology* 59, no. 9 (2002): 1369–1373.

62. Money and Ehrhardt, *Man and Woman*, 19.

63. Their sample size was continually growing so that by the following year the number had risen to 94. Money, Hampson, and Hampson, "Sexual Incongruities," 43.

64. Money, "Hermaphroditism, Gender and Precocity," 254.

65. For an excellent discussion of the "misplacement" of the so-called male and female sex hormones, see Fausto-Sterling, *Sexing the Body*, 170–194.

66. Testosterone, for example, is produced by the ovaries and by the adrenal glands in women while estrogen is essential to masculine fertility and spermatogenesis. Moreover, in order for testosterone to be utilized by the body it must first undergo a process of conversion from testosterone to cholesterol in the first instance and then from cholesterol to *estra*diol in the second.

67. Money, *Gendermaps*, 254.

68. Agenesis is the medical term for the failure of a body part to develop. In the context of this discussion, ovaries are the body part in question (Peter Walker, ed. *Chambers Science and Technology Dictionary* [Edinburgh: Chambers, 1991], 17). It is with a certain amount of tongue in cheek that I want to point out that large numbers of people with a Y chromosome could be said to be gonadally agenesic for having failed to develop ovaries.

69. Morgan Holmes, "Mind the Gaps: Intersex and (Re-Productive) Spaces in Disability Studies and Bioethics," *Bioethical Inquiry* 5, no. 2–3 (2008): 169–181; Vernon Rosario, "From Hermaphrodites to Sox9: The Molecular Deconstruction of Sex," Paper presented at

the *Presentations in the History of Medicine* Series, Royal Australasian College of Physicians, Sydney, August 1, 2005; Rosario, "This History of Aphallia and the Intersexual Challenge to Sex/Gender," in *A Companion to Lesbian, Gay, Bisexual, Transgender, and Queer Studies* (Oxford: Blackwell, 2007) 262–281; Eric Vilain, "Genetics of Sexual Development," *Annual Review of Sex Research* 11 (2000): 1–24.

70. The disagreement of Money et al. with Krafft-Ebing also turned on the latter's understanding of male *or* female centers, one the property of males and the other the property of females, as the following discussion makes evident.

71. Money, Hampson, and Hampson, "An Examination of Some Basic Sexual Concepts: The Evidence of Human Hermaphroditism," *Bulletin of the Johns Hopkins Hospital* 97, no. 4 (1955): 308–309.

72. Ibid., 309.

73. Today there is an increasing emphasis on the role of chromosomes and the influence of genetics in sexual development. In the United States geneticists are at the forefront of the development of new treatment models and recent shifts in terminology as discussed in Chapters 5 and 6.

74. Money, Hampson, and Hampson, "Hermaphroditism: Recommendations," 288.

75. Ibid., 285.

76. It is worthy of note that Money fully embraced the sexual revolution just a few years later, and this was to have a significant effect on his ideas about female sexuality.

77. Money, Hampson, and Hampson, "Hermaphroditism: Recommendations Concerning Assignment of Sex, Change of Sex, and Psychologic Management," *Bulletin of the Johns Hopkins Hospital* 97, no. 4 (1955): 285.

78. When faced with cases that challenged the weight Money et al. gave to assigned sex, these two elements were often found to be wanting. See Robert Stoller, *Sex and Gender: On the Development of Masculinity and Femininity.* (London: Karnac Books, 1968).

79. Hampson, "Hermaphroditic Genital Appearance," 265.

80. Money, Hampson, and Hampson, "An Examination," 307. Note that this was the primary finding of Money's doctoral research.

81. Money, Hampson, and Hampson, "Hermaphroditism: Recommendations," 288.

82. Read homosexual, lesbian, or bisexual.

83. Money, Hampson, and Hampson, "Hermaphroditism: Recommendations," 292, emphasis added.

84. Parsons attempted to synthesize a general science of society with a set of universal categories that effectively transcended both space and time, leaving him open to charges of ahistoricism. For one of the most rigorous critiques of Parsons's theoretical project see

C. Wright Mills, *The Sociological Imagination* (London: Oxford University Press, 1959).

85. This statement begs the question of what role Hampson's knowledge and experience of her own body played in this understanding of female orgasm.

86. Money, Hampson, and Hampson, "Hermaphroditism: Recommendations," 295.

87. Money and Tucker, *Sexual Signatures*, 47.

88. Money, Hampson, and Hampson, "Hermaphroditism: Recommendations," 295. Here the authors are referring to people diagnosed as hyperadrenocortical females.

89. Until recently very little was known—though much was assumed—about the actual structure of the clitoris. Urological surgeon Helen O'Connell's groundbreaking research using MRI technology has changed all that. See Helen O'Connell and John O DeLancey, "Clitoral Anatomy in Nulliparous, Healthy, Premenopausal Volunteers Using Unenhanced Magnetic Resonance Imaging," *Journal of Urology* 173 (2005): 2060–2063.

90. Money, Hampson, and Hampson, "Hermaphroditism: Recommendations," 297.

91. Nonetheless, the paucity of evidence has not deterred generations of clinicians from following this recommendation.

92. It is important to note that this element of Money's protocols was not incorporated into ICM practices, at least not until very recently. This is one of the central factors that provided the impetus for a political movement known as Intersex activism. Refer to Chapter 6.

93. Money, Hampson, and Hampson, "Hermaphroditism: Recommendations," 295.

94. Ibid.

95. Jillian Lloyd et al., "Female Genital Appearance: 'Normality' Unfolds," *British Journal of Obstetrics and Gynaecology* 112 (2005): 643–646.

96. Iain Morland, "The Glans Opens Like a Book: Writing and Reading the Intersexed Body," *Continuum: Journal of Media & Culture Studies* 19, no. 3 (2005): 345.

97. Money, Hampson, and Hampson, "Hermphroditism: Recommendations," 293–294.

98. Hampson, "Hermaphroditic Genital Appearance," 267, emphasis added.

99. Money, Hampson, and Hampson, "Hermaphroditism: Recommendations," 295.

100. See Erving Goffman, *Stigma: Notes on the Management of Spoiled Identity* (Harmondsworth, England: Penguin, 1968). See also, Money's critiques of antisexualism in the North American context (John Money, "Sexual Reformation and Counter-Reformation in Law and Medicine," *Medicine and Law* 4 [1985]: 479–488; Money, "The

Conceptual Neutering of Gender and the Criminalisation of Sex." *Archives of Sexual Behaviour* 14, no. 3 [1985]: 279–291).

101. Money, Hampson, and Hampson, "Hermaphroditism: Recommendations," 295, emphasis added.

102. A 2002 study found that assigned males had an average of 5.8 genital surgeries and assigned females an average of 2.1 (Claude Migeon et al., "Ambiguous Genitalia with Perineoscrotal Hypospadias in 46,Xy Individuals: Long-Term Medical, Surgical, and Psychosexual Outcome," *Pediatrics*, no. 3 [September 2002]), http://www.pediatrics.org/cgi/content/full/110/3/e31).

103. Hampson, "Hermaphroditic Genital Appearance," 272.

104. Money, Hampson, and Hampson, "Hermaphroditism: Recommendations," 289.

105. Lewis M. Terman and Catherine C. Miles, *Sex and Personality: Studies in Masculinity and Femininity* (New York: Russell and Russell, 1936/1968), 6.

106. Hampson, "Hermaphroditic Genital Appearance," 266.

107. Ironically, their analysis did not extend to the presence of hermaphrodites/intersexed people. If every "fact" has a function how might we analyze the function of the historical persistence of hermaphrodites?

108. Barbara Fried, "Boys Will Be Boys Will Be Boys: The Language of Sex and Gender," in *Women Look at Biology Looking at Women: A Collection of Feminist Critiques*, ed. Ruth Hubbard, Mary Sue Henifin, and Barbara Fried (Boston: G. K. Hall, 1979), 37–59; Jerzy Szacki, *History of Sociological Thought*.

109. Kay Deaux, "Psychological Constructions of Masculinity and Femininity," in *Masculinity/Femininity. Basic Perspectives*, ed. June Reinisch, Leonard Rosenblum, and Stephanie Sanders (New York: Oxford University Press, 1987), 301.

110. Joan Hampson, "Hermaphroditic Genital Appearance," 266.

111. John Money, "Gender: History, Theory and Usage of the Term in Sexology and Its Relationship to Nature/Nurture," *Journal of Sex and Marital Therapy* 11, no. 2 (1985): 71–79.

112. Recent findings in genetic research indicate that chromosomal variation is in fact much greater in the general population than has historically been assumed. See Janine Cohen, "The Gender Puzzle," *Four Corners*: Australian Broadcasting Corporation, 2005; Pheobe Dewing et al., "Sexually Dimorphic Gene Expression in Mouse Brain Precedes Gonadal Differentiation," *Molecular Brain Research* 118, no. 1–2 (2003): 82–90; Rosario, "From Hermaphrodites to Sox9."

113. Money, "Hermaphroditism, Gender and Precocity," 258.

114. The examples he offered were the impact of rickets and cretinism on bone development prior to maturation (Money, Hampson, and

Hampson, "Imprinting and the Establishment of Gender Role," *AMA Archives of Neurology and Psychiatry 77* [1957]: 335).

115. Konrad Lorenz, *King Solomon's Ring: New Light on Animal Ways* (London: Methuen, 1961). It is worth noting that Lorenz did not have the same success with any other bird species on which he attempted the same experiment.

116. Money and Tucker, *Sexual Signatures*, 88.

117. Ibid., emphasis added.

118. Money, *Love and Love Sickness: The Science of Sex, Gender Difference, and Pair-Bonding* (Baltimore: Johns Hopkins University Press, 1980), 137.

119. Money, *Gendermaps*, 52. Prior to 1980 Money wrote of sex-irreducible versus "optional" (Money and Ehrhardt, *Man and Woman*, 19) or "arbitrary sex distinctions" (Money and Ehrhardt, *Man and Woman*, 19; Money and Tucker, *Sexual Signatures*, 33). It was not until 1980 that he codified four distinct dimensions in print (see Money, *Love and Love Sickness*, 137–144).

120. John Money, "Gender: History, Theory and Usage of the Term in Sexology and Its Relationship to Nature/Nurture," *Journal of Sex and Marital Therapy* 11, no. 2 (1985), 75–6.

121. Money, *Love and Love Sickness*, 138–139; Money, *Gendermaps*, 54. A huge emphasis is placed on urinary posture in ICM when phallic potential is being assessed, since being able to urinate from a standing position is deemed essential for boys and men. For a critique of the ethnocentrism inherent in this idea see psychobiologist Frank Beach (Beach, "Alternative Interpretations of the Development of G-I/R," in *Masculinity/Femininity. Basic Perspectives*, 29–34.

122. Money, *Gendermaps*, 57–58.

123. Ibid., 61.

124. Within the context of that discussion, Money was referring not to erotic roles in the sense of active/passive or dominant/subordinate but rather to male and female reproductive capacities.

125. Money and Tucker, *Sexual Signatures*, 147.

126. Money, *Love and Lovesickness*, 144.

127. Money, "Propaedeutics of Deicious G-I/R: Theoretical Foundations for Understanding Dimorphic Gender-Identity/Role," in *Masculinity/Femininity. Basic Perpectives*, 14.

128. See, for example, Milton Diamond and Keith Sigmundson, "Sex Reassignment at Birth: Long-Term Review and Clinical Implications," *Achives of Paediatrics and Adolescent Medicine* 15 (1997): 298–304. See also Fausto-Sterling, *Sexing the Body*.

129. Money, *Gendermaps*, 95.

130. Money, *Gay, Straight*, 68.

131. For an analysis of Money's reports that reads hypermasculinity and hyperfemininity as maladaptive, see Alexander Kaplan, "Human Sex Hormone Abnormalities," in *The Psychobiology of Sex Differences and*

Sex Roles, ed Jacquelynne Parsons (Washington: Hemisphere, 1980), 85. Kaplan discusses the implications of Money reporting that women diagnosed with Turner's syndrome (women with a single X chromosome) outdid control groups of non-intersexed women in their conformity to feminine stereotypes. See also Sandra Bem, "Gender Schema Theory: A Cognitive Account of Sex Typing," *Psychological Review* 88, no. 4 (1981): 354–364; Fried, "Boys Will Be Boys."

132. Money and Ehrhardt, *Man and Woman*, 111.
133. Ibid., 112, emphasis added.

CHAPTER 2

1. Robert Stoller, "A Contribution to the Study of Gender Identity," *International Journal of Psychoanalysis* 45 (1964): 220–226. A modified version of this paper later appeared as a chapter in Stoller's 1968 text, *Sex and Gender: On the Development of Masculinity and Femininity* (London: Karnac Books).

2. See Rosie Braidotti, *Nomadic Subjects: Embodiment and Sexual Difference in Contemporary Feminist Theory* (New York: Columbia University Press, 1994); Georges Canguilhem, *On the Normal and the Pathological*, trans. Carolyn Fawcett (Dordrecht: Reidel Publishing, 1978); and Julia Epstein, *Altered Conditions: Disease, Medicine and Storytelling* (New York: Routledge, 1995) for critiques of this tendency.

3. See, for example, Ann Curthoys, ed., *Gender in the Social Sciences in Australia* (Canberra: Australian Publishing Service, 1998); Moira Gatens, *Imaginary Bodies: Ethics, Power and Corporeality* (London: Routledge, 1996); Rachel Hare-Mustin and Jeanne Marbeck, "The Meaning of Difference: Gender Theory, Postmodernism and Psychology," in *The Gender and Psychology Reader*, ed. Blyth McVicker Clinchy and Julie Norem (New York: New York University Press, 1998), 125–143; Lynne Segal, *Slow Motion: Changing Masculinities, Changing Men* (London: Virago, 1990); Rhoda Unger, "Toward a Redefinition of Sex and Gender," *American Psychologist* 34 (1979): 1085–1094.

4. After graduating with an MA from Stanford University in California, Stoller gained a degree in medicine at the University of California (Berkeley and San Francisco), specializing in psychiatry. Before completing his residency at the University of Southern California, he served as a psychiatrist with the United States Air Force Medical Corps. OAC, "Stoller (Robert J.) Biography," http://www. oac.cdlib.org/findaid/ark:/13030/tf5s2006mg/bioghist/639277564; Louis West, Richard Green, and Peter Loewenberg, "Robert J. Stoller, Psychiatry and Biobehavioral Sciences: Los Angeles 1924–1991 Professor of Psychiatry," University of California, http:// dynaweb.oac.cdlib.org:8088/dynaweb/uchist/public/ inmemoriam/ inmemoriam1993/3502.

5. West et al., "Robert J Stoller"; Donna Haraway, *Simians, Cyborgs, and Women: The Reinvention of Nature* (New York and London: Routledge, 1991), 133.

6. Benjamin was the only endocrinologist involved in the project, at a time when endocrinology remained a significant force in explanations of sex diversity. That said, it must be noted that the "Age of Hormones" was by that stage waning.

7. Joanne Meyerowitz, *How Sex Changed: A History of Transsexuality in the United States* (Cambridge, MA: Harvard University Press, 2002).

8. The institute at Johns Hopkins from which John Money worked had by that stage been operational for the best part of a decade.

9. Money recounts that he first became aware of the term *gender identity* in correspondence with Evelyn Hooker, one of Stoller's colleagues at the University of California (UCLA). According to Money, he learned from Stoller that the members of a Los Angeles – based psychoanalytic group that met regularly from the late 1950s on were responsible for splitting gender identity from gender role (John Money, *Gendermaps: Social Constructionism, Feminism and Sexosophical History* [New York: Continuum, 1995], 23).

10. Stoller, "A Contribution," 220.

11. David Haig, "The Inexorable Rise of Gender and the Decline of Sex: Social Change in Academic Titles 1945–2001," *Archives of Sexual Behavior* 33, no. 2 (2004): 87–96.

12. Stoller, *Sex and Gender*, ix.

13. Bernice Hausman, *Changing Sex: Transsexualism, Technology and the Idea of Gender* (Durham, NC: Duke University Press, 1995), 103.

14. John Money and Anke Ehrhardt, *Man and Woman Boy and Girl: The Differentiation and Dimorphism of Gender Identity from Conception to Maturity* (Baltimore: Johns Hopkins University Press, 1972), 284.

15. See, for example, Harold Garfinkel, *Studies in Ethnomethodology* (Englewood Cliffs, NJ: Prentice-Hall, 1967); Ann Oakley, *Sex, Gender and Society* (New York: Harper Colophon, 1972).

16. See John Archer and Barbara Lloyd, *Sex and Gender* (Cambridge: Cambridge University Press, 1982); Nancy Chodorow, *The Reproduction of Mothering: Psychoanalysis and the Sociology of Gender* (Berkeley: University of California Press, 1978); Chodorow, "Feminism and Difference: Gender, Relation, and Difference in Psychoanalytic Perspective," *Socialist Review* 46 (1979): 42–69; Betty Roszak and Theodore Roszak, *Masculine/Feminine: Readings in Sexual Mythology and the Liberation of Women* (New York: Harper and Row, 1969); Julia Sherman, *On the Psychology of Women: A Survey of Empirical Studies* (Springfield, IL: Charles C Thomas, 1971).

17. Stoller, "A Contribution," 223.

18. Stoller, *Sex and Gender*, 40.

19. Hausman, *Changing Sex.*
20. An example of such intractable ideas is evident in Stoller's discussion of a young child (initially reared as a girl) who was reassigned as a boy (this child's "case" is discussed later in this chapter). Upon reassignment, the child came to be "among the first in his class in mathematics, a subject in which he did very poorly when he thought he was a girl" ("A Contribution," 222). The idea that boys have a *natural* aptitude for mathematics and thus girls a natural *inaptitude* has been thoroughly disavowed by a significant body of research but more importantly by the test results of school-age children. Yet the idea continues to hold sway as a cultural and social "fact."
21. Stoller, *Sex and Gender*, 97–103.
22. Stoller, "A Contribution," 223.
23. Ibid.
24. This brings to mind Money's assertion that gendered development relies upon both identification *and* complementation. and it appears to be a more sophisticated understanding of infant-parent relationships than a psychoanalytic model allows.
25. Stoller, "A Contribution," 223.
26. Stoller, *Sex and Gender*, 50, 52. Here Stoller's position aligns with that of object relations theory as exemplified by Nancy Chodorow.
27. Ibid., 263.
28. In recent times, the ratio of MtF and FtM transpeople has become somewhat less marked as increasing numbers of (apparently) born-women seek recourse to hormonal therapies and surgical procedures. See Holly Devor, *FtM: Female-to-Male Transsexuals in Society* (Bloomington: Indiana University Press, 1997); Morty Diamond, *From the Inside Out: Radical Gender Transformation, FtM and Beyond* (San Francisco: Manic D Press, 2004); Judith Halberstam, *Female Masculinity* (Durham, NC: Duke University Press, 1998); Halberstam, *In a Queer Time and Place: Transgender Bodies, Subcultural Lives* (New York: New York University Press, 2005); Jay Prosser, "Transsexuals and the Transsexologists: Inversion and the Emergence of Transsexual Subjectivity," in *Sexology in Culture: Labelling Bodies and Desires*, ed. Lucy Bland and Laura Doan (Cambridge: Polity, 1998), 116–131.
29. Stoller, *Sex and Gender*, 204–205.
30. Stoller, *Sex and Gender*, 83.
31. Benjamin in Hausman, *Changing Sex*, 122.
32. Stoller, "A Contribution," 220.
33. Ibid. Here we see a clear example of the normal/pathological relation at work and an illustration of how normality cannot be apprehended on its own terms.
34. Stoller, "A Contribution," 224.
35. Ibid., 225.

36. Stoller, *Sex and Gender*, 8.
37. Ibid., 220, emphasis added.
38. *Normals* was a term that Stoller used liberally in his writings for many years. Finally in the mid-1980s he acknowledged how value laden it was and abandoned it. See Stoller, *Presentations of Gender* (New Haven: Yale University Press, 1985).
39. Stoller, *Sex and Gender*, 40.
40. Ibid., ix.
41. Stoller made an extremely poignant comment in his discussion about Mary, when he suggested that "there was not even the appearance of an enlarged clitoris, *a common enough normal variation in females*" ("Contribution," 221, emphasis added). This begs a number of questions, including, What might this mean for the practice of clitoridectomizing XX infants? And, at what point does a clitoris actually exceed the range of normal variation?
42. Hypospadias is the name given to the relatively common condition where the urethral meatus (urinary outlet) is located elsewhere than at the tip of the penis.
43. Stoller, *Sex and Gender*, 221.
44. Ibid., 67.
45. Stoller, "A Contribution", 221–222, emphasis added.
46. Hausman, *Changing Sex*, 109.
47. Stoller, "A Contribution," 222.
48. Stoller, *Sex and Gender*, 70.
49. Ibid., 71, emphasis added.
50. Harold Garfinkel bestowed the pseudonym "Agnes" upon this individual. A great deal of Garfinkel's well-known text *Studies in Ethnomethodology* is based on Agnes's story.
51. This "condition" falls within the broader category of "male pseudohermaphroditism" due to the presence of testes rather than ovaries. In Money's earliest hermaphrodite typology the term *simulant female* was applied to individuals diagnosed thus.
52. Despite the naming of testosterone as male sex hormone and estrogen as female sex hormone in the early 1900s, it has long been understood in biology that such classifications are a (double) misnomer, since both substances are produced in varying quantities in both males and in females. Furthermore, both substances are necessary for protein synthesis, bone structure, and neural functioning regardless of sex.
53. There are parallels here with the case study Money offered to evidence his theory that *any* child could be reared successfully with an assigned sex: that of John/Joan (David Reimer, now deceased). As has become clear in recent years the John/Joan "experiment" was not the success that Money had claimed during the 1970s. These examples serve to remind us of the extent to which researchers can be blinded by an overzealous commitment to the theories they are promoting—often with very real and damning consequences.

54. Stoller, "A Contribution," 225.
55. Bernice Hausman cites a passage from David O. Caldwell's 1949 article "Psychopathia Transexualis" in which he argued that removing healthy breast and ovarian tissue from a female-to-male transsexual was "criminal" (*Changing Sex*, 119). Hausman recounts in an accompanying footnote, a conversation she had with a retired pathologist who spoke of his team's distress whenever healthy genital organs arrived at their laboratory for examination (Ibid., 225–226, fn 43).
56. Stoller noted that his "chagrin" at learning that he had been duped was tempered somewhat by his amusement at how skillfully Agnes had managed to fool him and his colleagues (*Sex and Gender*, 136).
57. Ibid., 6.
58. Robert Stoller, "The 'Bedrock' of Masculinity and Femininity: Bisexuality," *Archives of General Psychiatry* 26 (1972): 210.
59. Robert Stoller, "Gender-Role Change in Intersexed Patients," *Journal of the American Medical Association* 188, no. 7 (1964): 164–165.
60. Ibid., 165.
61. Ibid., emphasis added. Note the slippage between role and identity in this discussion, indicative again of the internal inconsistency of Stoller's taxonomy.
62. Stoller, *Sex and Gender*, 34, emphasis added.
63. Ibid., emphasis added.
64. Ibid., 23.
65. Money, *Gay, Straight and in-Between: The Sexology of Erotic Orientation* (New York: Continuum, 1988), 41, 81.
66. Stoller, *Sex and Gender*, 35, emphasis added.
67. For a particularly elegant analysis of the double nature of the meaning of "fixed" for the intersexed, see Katrina Karkazis, *Fixing Sex: Intersex, Medical Authority and Lived Experience* (Durham, NC: Duke University Press, 2008).
68. The use of the present tense here is deliberate since this attitude prevails in contemporary medical discourse.
69. Robyn Weigman, "Object Lessons: Men, Masculinity and the Sign Women," *Signs* 26, no. 2 (2001): 364.
70. Michel Foucault, *Herculine Barbin: Being the Recently Discovered Memoirs of a 19th Century French Hermaphrodite* (New York: Pantheon, 1980), vii.
71. See Thomas Laqueur, *Making Sex: Body and Gender from the Greeks to Freud* (Cambridge, MA: Harvard University Press, 1990); Londa Schiebinger, *The Mind Has No Sex? Women in the Origins of Modern Science* (Cambridge, MA: Harvard University Press, 1988); Bonnie Spanier, " 'Lessons' From 'Nature': Gender Ideology and Sexual Ambiguity in Biology," in *Body Guards: The Cultural Politics of Gender Ambiguity*, ed. Katrina Straub and Julia Epstein (New York: Routledge, 1991), 329–350; Bryan Turner, *Medical Power and Social Knowledge* (London: Sage, 1987).

72. Stoller, *Sex and Gender*, ix.
73. See Judith Butler, *Gender Trouble: Feminism and the Subversion of Identity* (New York: Routledge, 1990); Butler, *Bodies That Matter: On the Discursive Limits Of "Sex."* (New York: Routledge, 1993); Anne Edwards, "Discussion: The Sex/Gender Distinction: Has It Outlived Its Usefulness?" *Australian Feminist Studies* 10, Summer (1989): 1–12; and Moira Gatens, *Imaginary Bodies: Ethics, Power and Corporeality* (London: Routledge, 1996) for examples of such assumptions.
74. Money, "The Conceptual Neutering of Gender and the Criminalisation of Sex," *Archives of Sexual Behaviour* 14, no. 3 (1985): 282.
75. Ibid.
76. John Money, *Gay, Straight*, 52, emphasis added. Note Money's collapsing of genitalia with reproduction here. This seems an odd turn given that so much of the (considerable) work he produced between the 1950s and the publication of this text concerned sexual practices motivated purely by pleasure.
77. Eve Kosofsky Sedgwick, *Epistemology of the Closet* (Berkeley: University of California Press, 1990), 27.
78. See for example, the discussion of Sedgwick et al, on the merits of using analog as opposed to digital technologies as a metaphor for thinking through and beyond the binary logic of sex and gender (*Shame and Its Sisters: A Silvan Tomkins Reader* [Durham, NC: Duke University Press, 1995]).

CHAPTER 3

1. I make no attempt to offer a history of feminist gender, for that is another project altogether—and a substantial one at that. My exploration of gender through feminism is guided by the appearance and disappearance of the intersexed in that domain.
2. For examples, see Mary Crawford, "A Reappraisal of Gender: An Ethnomethodological Approach," *Feminism and Psychology* 10, no. 1 (2000): 7–10; Teresa de Lauretis, *Technologies of Gender: Essays on Theory, Film, and Fiction* (Bloomington: Indiana University Press, 1987); Mary Hawkesworth, "Confounding Gender," *Signs: Journal of Women in Culture and Society* 22, no. 3 (1997): 649–685; Donna Haraway, *Simians, Cyborgs, and Women: The Reinvention of Nature* (New York and London: Routledge, 1991); Linda Nicholson, "Interpreting Gender," *Signs: Journal of Women in Culture and Society* 20 (1994): 79–105.
3. David Haig, "The Inexorable Rise of Gender and the Decline of Sex: Social Change in Academic Titles 1945–2001," *Archives of Sexual Behavior* 33, no. 2 (2004): 94. Take for example Mary Hawkesworth's claim that "although originally a linguistic category

denoting a system of subdivision within a grammatical class, feminist scholars adopted the concept of gender to distinguish culturally specific characteristics associated with masculinity and femininity from biological features" ("Confounding Gender," 651). Because sexology is elided here, the statement implies that the term was adopted directly from linguistics.

4. An exception was the analysis offered by Marilyn Strathern, "An Anthropological Perspective," in *Exploring Sex Differences*, ed. Barbara B. Lloyd and John Archer (London and New York: Academic Press, 1976), 49–70.

5. My use of the term *sex* in this and the following discussion does not refer—unless otherwise indicated—to erotic or libidinal practices. Rather it refers to the category set up as gender's "other."

6. Ann Curthoys, ed., *Gender in the Social Sciences in Australia* (Canberra: Australian Publishing Service, 1998), 180; Curthoys, "Gender Studies in Australia: A History," *Australian Feminist Studies* 15, no. 31 (2000): 21.

7. Moira Gatens, "A Critique of the Sex/Gender Distinction," in *Beyond Marxism? Interventions after Marx*, ed. Paul Patton and Judith Allen (Leichhardt, NSW: Intervention, 1983), 143–160.

8. In his first published monograph Money offered a strong critique of the Cartesian dualism of body and mind and of nature and culture. Yet ironically his work relied upon binary concepts on many other levels. I would argue that this is indicative of the tension in his work between what is and what ought to be. See John Money, *The Psychologic Study of Man* (Springfield, IL: Charles C. Thomas, 1957).

9. Money had immersed himself in the social anthropology of Margaret Mead before leaving New Zealand and was later taught by sociologist Talcott Parsons at Harvard. His ideas were, of course, also informed by embryology, endocrinology, and a broad range of animal studies. However in the context of the current discussion I am concerned with the relation of Money to the social sciences, since that is where the greatest concentrations of feminist scholars were found.

10. See for example, Ruth Bader Ginsberg, "Equal Opportunity, Free from Gender-Based Discrimination," in *Sex Equality*, ed. Jane English (Englewood Cliffs, NJ: Prentice-Hall, 1977), 188–195.

11. Sandra Bem, "The Theory and Measurement of Androgyny," *Journal of Personality and Social Psychology* 37 (1971): 1047–1054; Betty Friedan, *The Feminine Mystique* (London: Gollancz, 1963); Sherry Ortner, "Is Female to Male as Nature to Culture?" in *Woman, Culture, and Society*, ed. Michelle Rosaldo and Louise Lamphere (Stanford, CA: Stanford University Press, 1974), 67–87; Adrienne Rich, *Of Woman Born: Motherhood as Experience and Institution* (Toronto and New York: Bantam Books, 1977).

12. See for example, Shulamith Firestone, *The Dialectic of Sex: The Case for Feminist Revolution* (New York: Morrow, 1970); Rich, *Of Woman Born*.

13. Bernice Hausman, *Changing Sex: Transsexualism, Technology and the Idea of Gender* (Durham, NC: Duke University Press, 1995).

14. Money and Anke Ehrhardt, *Man and Woman, Boy and Girl: The Differentiation and Dimorphism of Gender Identity from Conception to Maturity.* (Baltimore: Johns Hopkins University Press, 1972), 310.

15. Greer had won a Commonwealth Scholarship for her MA thesis (*USyd*), which she used to fund doctoral studies at Newnham College, Cambridge University. Graduating in 1968 with a PhD in English literature on Shakespeare's early comedies, Greer went on to teach at Warwick University (1967–1973). The publication of *The Female Eunuch* in 1970 made Greer a public figurehead for the women's liberation movement in Britain (Christine Wallace, *Greer, Untamed Shrew* [Sydney: Macmillan Pan, 1997]).Greer was also, during that period, the founding European editor of the anarchist sex magazine *Suck* (John Heidenry, *What Wild Ecstasy: The Rise and Fall of the Sexual Revolution* [Kew: William Heinemann, 1997]).

16. Sculptor, visual artist, and writer Kate Millett was the first American woman to be awarded an MA (1st class) from St. Hilda's College, Oxford University, in 1958. She was awarded a doctorate in comparative literature from Columbia University in 1970 and published her dissertation as *Sexual Politics* the same year.

17. Germaine Greer, *The Female Eunuch* (London: MacGibbon and Kee, 1970), 14, emphasis in original.

18. Ibid., 28.

19. Ibid., 29.

20. Anne Fausto-Sterling, "The Five Sexes:Why Male and Female Are Not Enough," *The Sciences*, no. March/April (1993): 24.

21. Greer, *The Female Eunuch*, 26.

22. The chapters "Gender" and "Sex" both appeared in the first section of the text under the heading "Body." Sex in Greer's account related solely to erotic behavior and sexual practices.

23. Ibid., 29.

24. Kate Millett, *Sexual Politics* (London: Granada, 1971).

25. Ibid., 28.

26. Ibid., 29.

27. Ibid., 30.

28. Curthoys, "Gender Studies in Australia," 25.

29. See Helen Hughes, *The Status of Women in Sociology 1968–1972: Report to the American Sociological Association of the Ad Hoc Committee on the Status of Women in the Profession* (Washington, DC: American Sociological Association, 1973).

30. Ann Curthoys, *Gender in the Social Sciences*; Arlene Kaplan Daniels, "Feminist Perspectives in Sociological Research," in *Another Voice*, ed. Marcia Millman and Rosabeth Moss Kanter (New York: Anchor Press, 1975), 340–380; Meredith Gould and Rochelle Kern-Daniels, "Towards a Sociological Theory of Gender and Sex," *The American Sociologist* 12 (1977): 182–189; Barbara Laslett and Barrie Thorne, ed., *Feminist Sociology: Life Histories of a Movement* (New Brunswick, NJ: Rutgers University Press, 1997).

31. Betty Roszak and Theodore Roszak, ed. *Masculine/Feminine: Readings in Sexual Mythology and the Liberation of Women* (New York: Harper and Row, 1969); Ella Lasky, ed. *Humanness: An Exploration into the Mythologies About Women and Men* (New York: MSS Information Corp., 1975).

32. Daniels, "Feminist Perspectives." While Daniels is not well known outside of the U.S. academy today, during the 1970s she was editor of the journal *Social Problems*, president of *Sociologists for Women in Society* and professor of sociology at Northwestern University (Chicago), and so in a good position to assess the impact of feminist scholarship on the field.

33. The development of a specifically feminist mode of inquiry across the academy more broadly led to the establishment of women's studies departments. By 1974 there were over 80 tertiary institutions in the United States offering women's studies programs with majors, while almost 1,000 more offered various women's studies courses ("The Feminist Chronicles." The Feminist Majority Foundation, http://www.feminist.org/research/chronicles/fc1974.html).

34. Harriet Holter, *Sex Roles and Social Structure* (Oslo: Universitetsforlaget, 1970), 52.

35. Ibid., 17.

36. Ibid., 18.

37. Jessie Bernard, *Women and the Public Interest: An Essay on Policy and Protest* (Chicago: Aldine-Atherton, 1971). At the time of publication, Bernard was Research Scholar, Honoris Causa, at the Pennsylvania State University. Bernard received her doctorate in sociology from Washington University in 1935.

38. Ibid., 277.

39. Ibid., 14–15.

40. Ibid., 19–20.

41. For examples, see Jane English, ed., *Sex Equality* (Englewood Cliffs, NJ: Prentice-Hall, 1977); Gould and Kern-Daniels, "Towards a Sociological Theory"; Ruth Hubbard, Mary Sue Henifin, and Barbara Fried, ed., *Women Look at Biology Looking at Women: A Collection of Feminist Critiques* (Boston: G. K. Hall, 1979); Millman and Moss Kanter, ed. *Another Voice*; Rayna Reiter, ed. *Toward an Anthropology of Women* (New York: Monthly Review Press, 1975).

42. Curthoys, *Gender in the Social Sciences.*
43. Ann Oakley, *Sex, Gender and Society* (New York: Harper Colophon, 1972).
44. Ibid., 170.
45. Ibid., 165.
46. Ibid.
47. Ibid., emphasis added.
48. Ibid.,167.
49. Ibid, 16.
50. Ibid, 17.
51. Nancy Chodorow, "Family Structure and Feminine Personality," in *Woman, Culture, and Society,* ed. Michelle Zimbalist Rosaldo, Louise Lamphere, and Joan Bamberger (Stanford, CA: Stanford University Press, 1974) 43–66; Chodorow, *The Reproduction of Mothering: Psychoanalysis and the Sociology of Gender* (Berkeley: University of California Press, 1978); Dorothy Dinnerstein, *The Mermaid and the Minotaur: Sexual Arrangements and Human Malaise* (New York: Harper & Row, 1976); Dorothy Ullian, "The Development of Conceptions of Masculinity and Femininity: Development of Gender Concepts," in *Exploring Sex Differences,* ed. Barbara B. Lloyd and John Archer (London and New York: Academic Press, 1976), 25–47; Rhoda Unger, *Female and Male: Psychological Perspectives* (New York: Harper & Row, 1979); Unger, "Toward a Redefinition of Sex and Gender," *American Psychologist* 34 (1979): 1085–1094.
52. Dorothy Ullian, "The Development of Conceptions of Masculinity and Femininity." 25–47. Dorothy Ullian developed this model while a faculty member of the Psychology Department at Wheelock College, Boston, Massachusetts (Lloyd and Archer, eds., *Exploring Sex Differences,* v).
53. Rhoda Unger gained her PhD in experimental psychology from Harvard University in 1966 and has had a long and distinguished career as professor of psychology and women's studies at Montclair and Brandeis Universities (Brandeis University, 2003).
54. Unger, *Female and Male.*
55. Accompanying the descriptions of each of the (then recognized) hermaphroditic diagnostic categories were six photographs, also taken from Money's *Man and Woman.* The photographs, taken in a clinical context, show individuals in awkward poses standing naked in front of a measuring grid. Each image is marked by a black circle that obscures the subject's face, no doubt to protect their identity. The circles have another effect: they serve to objectify the bodies of those being represented. Another of the images is a composition consisting of four frames, each offering close-up shots of the genitalia of infants diagnosed with androgenital syndrome. What is striking about these images is the adult fingers manipulating the surrounding flesh

to ensure maximum exposure of the genitalia for the camera (in one instance, the infant's clitoral hood is stretched back to expose the head of the genital tubercle or clitoral head). See Hausman, *Changing Sex*, 84–93, for an astute semiotic reading of these types of images.

56. Unger, *Female and Male*, 145.
57. Ibid., emphasis added.
58. I say earliest because there is evidence of a shift in Money's perspective over the course of the 1970s. Cf. Money and Ehrhardt, *Man and Woman*; Money and Patricia Tucker, *Sexual Signatures: On Being a Man or a Woman*. (London: Sphere Books, 1977).
59. Turner Syndrome refers to people with a single X chromosome (signified as XO).
60. Unger, *Female and* Male, 112, emphasis in original.
61. Unger, "Toward a Redefinition," 1093.
62. Ibid., 1086.
63. Dinnerstein was, at the time of writing *The Mermaid*, a practicing Gestalt therapist. The book, she said, had been a long time in the making and contained ideas that she had tested on her undergraduate students while teaching psychology at Rutgers University from 1966 to 1974 (Dinnerstein, *The Mermaid*, vii–xv).
64. Ibid., 231.
65. Chodorow, "Family Structure"; Chodorow, *The Reproduction of Mothering*.
66. Note that for Chodorow, women's responsibility for childrearing was not problematic as it was for Dinnerstein. Indeed, Chodorow saw its effects—women's relationality—as a positive outcome of social relations.
67. Chodorow, "Family Structure," 66.
68. Chodorow, "Feminism and Difference: Gender, Relation, and Difference in Psychoanalytic Perspective," in *The Gender and Psychology Reader*, ed. Blyth McVicker Clinchy and Julie Norem (New York: New York University Press, 1998), 390.
69. Ibid., 390–391.
70. Chodorow, "Family Structure," 43.
71. Chodorow, "Feminism and Difference," 384.
72. Cited in Jeffrey Weeks, *Sexuality* (London and New York: Routledge, 2003), 61.
73. Chodorow, "Feminism and Difference," 395, fn. 18.
74. Margaret Mead, *Sex and Temperament in Three Primitive Societies* (New York: Morrow, 1935/1963); Mead, *Male and Female: A Study of the Sexes in a Changing World* (Harmondsworth: Penguin, 1962).
75. Mead's methodologies have been heavily criticized since the 1980s, as has her unwavering belief in the positive value and neutrality of science. Yet as Rayna Rapp has noted, Mead's "insistence on the

plasticity of the life cycle and the cultural context within which sexuality, marriage and reproduction are structured and in turn, structure individual and group experiences" provided the ground for a feminist anthropology (Rayna Rapp, "Margaret Mead's Legacy: Continuing Conversations," The Scholar and Feminist Online, http://www.barnard.edu/sfonline/mead/rapp.htm). For a fascinating feminist recuperation of Mead that offers a strong critique of the new-Right agenda said to underpin the first and arguably most vitriolic detraction of Mead, see Micaela di Leonardo, "Margaret Mead Vs. Tony Soprano," The Nation, http://www. thenation.com/doc.mhtml?i=20010521&s=dileonardo, (2001).

76. Reiter, Toward an Anthropology of Women, 13.

77. The insight that feminist research risked being ghettoized was of concern to theorists across disciplines. See for example, Gould and Kern-Daniels, "Towards a Sociological Theory"; Unger, Female and Male; Unger, "Toward a Redefinition."

78. At the time she wrote "The Traffic in Women," Rubin was working toward a doctorate in anthropology at the University of Michigan and teaching in the Women's Studies program there. "The Traffic" was at one level a response to the limits of Marxist analyses of the oppression of women. Rubin cites a course taught by Marshall Sahlins at the Univerity of Michigan on tribal economics as the "immediate precipitating factor" for the paper (Gayle Rubin and Judith Butler, "Sexual Traffic," in Coming Out of Feminism? ed. Mandy Merk, Naomi Segal, and Elizabeth Wright [Oxford: Blackwell, 1998]: 38).

79. Gayle Rubin, "The Traffic in Women: Notes on the 'Political Economy' of Sex,"r in Toward an Anthropology of Women, ed. Rayna R. Reiter (New York: Monthly Review Press, 1975), 158.

80. Ibid., 177.

81. Ibid., 159.

82. Ibid., 179.

83. Ibid. I would suggest that the obligatory heterosexuality of which Rubin spoke also rested upon gender, as does female sexuality, indeed most sexualities.

84. Ibid., 185.

85. Ibid., 189.

86. The collection in which Rubin's article appeared contains a single collective bibliography that included Money and Ehrhardt's 1972 Man and Woman text. Although Rubin was the only author in the collection to use the term gender, the reference did not belong with her article but rather linked to the introductory chapter by the editor, Rayna Reiter.

87. Strathern was a British anthropologist who was awarded a PhD in anthropology from Girton College, Cambridge University. The article under discussion was written while Strathern was based at the University of Papua New Guinea.

88. Marilyn Strathern, "An Anthropological Perspective," 49.

89. For a similar analysis, see the earlier discussion of Erving Goffman's "The Arrangement Between the Sexes," *Theory and Society* 4 (1977): 301–331.

90. Mary Chafetz, *Masculine/Feminine or Human? An Overview of the Sociology of Sex Roles*, 1st ed. (Itasca, IL: F. E. Peacock, 1974), 3.

91. Mary Chafetz, *Masculine/Feminine or Human? An Overview of the Sociology of Sex Roles*, 2nd ed. (Itasca, IL: F. E. Peacock, 1978), 3.

92. Once gender had consolidated as the "correct" term in feminist theorizing, the term *sexual identity* was freed up for conceptualizing identities based on erotic and libidinal inclinations.

93. Gould and Kern-Daniels, "Towards a Sociological Theory," 184.

94. As it turned out, a "sociology of sex" did not eventuate, perhaps in part for the reason offered by Money: that *sex* was a dirty three-letter word, whereas *gender* was clean, having been stripped of any connection to carnality. A sociology of gender, however, did develop and is now a common subbranch of sociology.

95. Gould and Kern-Daniels, "Towards a Sociological Theory," 184, emphasis added.

96. Helena Lopata and Barrie Thorne, "Letters/Comments. On the Term 'Sex Roles,' " *Signs* 3 (1978): 719.

97. Ibid.; Helena Lopata, "Review Essay: Sociology," *Signs: Journal of Women in Culture and Society* 2, no. 1 (1976): 172.

98. Lopata and Thorne, "Letters/Comments," 721.

99. Linda Nicholson, "Interpreting Gender," *Signs: Journal of Women in Culture and Society* 20 (1994): 80.

100. Ibid., 82.

101. Tresemer received his doctorate from Harvard University and when he wrote this piece was practicing as a therapist and consultant in the state of Vermont. He wrote at a time when there was such a thing as the male feminist subject. It appears that extinction of this subject position paralleled the shift from a rights-based politic toward an epistemology of sexual difference.

102. David Tresemer, "Assumptions Made About Gender Roles," in *Another Voice*, 314–315.

103. Ibid., 326.

104. Unger, *Male and Female*, 12.

105. Suzanne Kessler and Wendy McKenna, *Gender: An Ethnomethodological Approach* (New York: John Wiley, 1978). Kessler and McKenna began writing this book while both were graduate students in the Social-Personality doctoral program at the City University of New York. They received their earliest training in social psychology under the guidance of Stanley Milgram, whom they credit with teaching them to study phenomenon for its own sake rather than wedding themselves to particular theories (Wendy McKenna

and Suzanne Kessler, "Afterword: Retropective Response," *Feminism and Psychology* 10, no. 1 [2000], 66). When *Gender* was published in 1978, McKenna was teaching at Sarah Lawrence College (and promptly lost her job because of it), while Kessler was a faculty member at the more progressive Purchase College, State University of New York (Ibid., 66–67).

106. Kessler and McKenna, *Gender*, vii.
107. Ibid., 45.
108. Ibid., 5–6.
109. Ibid., 47, emphasis added.
110. Ibid., 50.
111. Janice Raymond, "Transsexualism: An Issue of Sex-Role Stereotyping," in *Pitfalls in Research on Sex and Gender*, ed. Ruth Hubbard and Marian Lowe (New York: Gordian Press, 1979), 132. Raymond is best known for her excoriating attack on transsexualism and transsexuals in *The Transsexual Empire: The Making of the She-Male* (New York: Teachers College Press, 1994).
112. As Sylvia Baynes asks of Raymond, "why should it be considered right to operate on persons of physical ambiguity, but wrong to operate on those who feel a mental ambiguity?" (Baynes, "Trans-Sex or Cross-Gender? A Critique of Janice Raymond's *The Transsexual Empire*," *Women's Studies Journal* 7–8 [1991]: 59).
113. Strathern, "An Anthropological Perspective," 50.
114. Kay Deaux, "Psychological Constructions of Masculinity and Femininity," in *Masculinity/Femininity: Basic Perspectives*, ed. June Reinisch, Leonard Rosenblum, and Stephanie Sanders (New York: Oxford University Press, 1987), 301.
115. Barbara Fried, "Boys Will Be Boys Will Be Boys: The Language of Sex and Gender," in *Women Look at Biology Looking at Women: A Collection of Feminist Critiques*, ed. Ruth Hubbard, Mary Sue Henifin, and Barbara Fried (Boston: G. K. Hall, 1979), 37–59. Fried was a doctoral candidate in English literature at Harvard when she wrote this piece. Active in the women's movement, she was also an established freelance editor, writer, and organizer of various feminist "cultural events." (Fried, "Boys Will Be Boys," 59).
116. Ibid., 59, emphasis in original.
117. Ibid., 52.
118. Indeed, it is that tautology and the duality underpinning the English language that presents one of the greatest challenges to writing a history of the concept gender and to a critique of the sex/gender distinction.
119. Fried, "Boys Will Be Boys," 55. Philosopher Alison Jaggar offered a similar analysis of how we know the body and how we know nature. Arguing for a radical restructuring of language by adopting gender neutral pronouns and proper nouns, Jaggar adopted a form of

generic pronoun derived from plural forms: namely, tey, tem, and ter(s) (Alison Jaggar, "On Sexual Equality," in *Sex Equality*, ed. Jane English [Englewood Cliffs, NJ: Prentice-Hall, 1977], 95).

120. Fried, "Boys Will Be Boys," 55.

121. Recall that Money had taken gender from philology in the first instance, and linked gender acquisition to language acquisition in the second.

122. Anne Fausto-Sterling is the exception here. See her *Myths of Gender*, which represents the beginning of a long engagement with the intersexed and with Money's work that now spans more than two decades.

123. Rubin, "The Traffic," 199–200.

124. Ibid., 185.

125. Jaggar, "On Sexual Equality," 105.

126. June Singer, *Androgyny: Toward a New Theory of Sexuality* (New York: Anchor, 1976), 29. This would become a familiar refrain with the radical/cultural feminist turn.

127. Ibid., 30, emphasis in original.

128. Ibid., emphasis in original.

129. Ibid., 37.

130. Perhaps the best-known feminist psychologist to promote a positive model of androgyny was Sandra Bem. Her work has not been included in this discussion since she did not use the term *gender* until the 1980s, despite developing a tool to measure masculinity, femininity, and androgyny in the early 1970s.

131. I suggest that Money would balk at such a deployment.

132. Money and Ehrhardt, *Man and Woman*, 310.

133. This entry is cross-referenced to the equally provocative "Psychosexual Frailty of the Male."

134. Money and Ehrhardt, *Man and Woman*, 147.

135. The "female as default" theory came from embryological research (on rabbits), and was first proposed by Alfred Jost. Jost went on to become a collaborator of Lawson Wilkins, who as readers may recall was an early patron of John Money. For an astute critique of this particular received wisdom, see Anne Fausto-Sterling, *Sexing the Body: Gender Politics and the Construction of Sexuality* (New York: Basic Books, 2000), 197–205.

136. Millett, *Sexual Politics*, 30. See also Mary Jane Sherfey, *The Nature and Evolution of Female Sexuality* (New York: Random House, 1972).

137. Fausto-Sterling, *Sexing the Body*, 197–205.

138. Money, "The Conceptual Neutering of Gender and the Criminalisation of Sex," *Archives of Sexual Behaviour* 14, no. 3 (1985): 287.

139. Ibid.

140. Money, *Gendermaps: Social Constructionism, Feminism and Sexosophical History.* (New York: Continuum, 1995), 74–75.

141. Walter Bockting, "Ken from Mars, Barbie from Venus: What on Earth Has Happened with Sex?" *Journal of Sex Research* 34, no. 4 (1997): 413.

142. This very distinction is itself arbitrary.

143. Henrietta Moore, *A Passion for Difference: Essays in Anthropology and Gender* (Cambridge: Polity, 1994). For a range of critiques on the politics of race see, Patricia Hill Collins, *Black Feminist Thought: Knowledge, Consciousness, and the Politics of Empowerment* (New York and London: Routledge, 2001); Angela Davis, *Women, Race, & Class*, 1st ed. (New York: Random House, 1981); Bell Hooks, *Feminist Theory from Margin to Center* (Boston, MA: South End Press, 1984); Hooks, *Talking Back: Thinking Feminist, Thinking Black* (Boston, MA: South End Press, 1989).

144. Arguably an upsurge of interest in psychoanalysis (in the Lacanian tradition) paralleled an interest in the implications of a Foucauldian analysis for feminism.

145. An awareness of the constraints imposed by a binary logic with respect to debates about the body, sex, and gender has not, I suggest, prevented those debates from collapsing into one or another form of circularity or reversal.

146. Judith Butler, *Gender Trouble: Feminism and the Subversion of Identity* (New York: Routledge, 1990); Moira Gatens, "A Critique of the Sex/Gender Distinction," in *Beyond Marxism? Interventions after Marx*, ed. Paul Patton and Judith Allen (Leichhardt, NSW: Intervention, 1983), 143–160; Gatens, *Imaginary Bodies: Ethics, Power and Corporeality* (London: Routledge, 1996); Linda Nicholson, "Interpreting Gender," *Signs: Journal of Women in Culture and Society* 20 (1994): 79–105; Eve Kosofsky Sedgwick, "Gender Criticism," in *Redrawing the Boundaries: The Transformation of English and American Literary Studies*, ed. S. Greenblatt and G. Gunn (New York: MLA, 1991), 271–302. Gaten's early critique was exceptional in that it represents a precursor to the later analyses.

147. Biddy Martin, "Extraordinary Homosexuals and the Fear of Being Ordinary," *Differences* 6, no. 2 (1994): 104.

CHAPTER 4

1. John Money, *Gay, Straight, and In-Between: The Sexology of Erotic Orientation* (New York: Continuum, 1988), 52–53.

2. Ibid., 52. See also Money, *Gendermaps: Social Constructionism, Feminism and Sexosophical History* (New York: Continuum, 1995), 12.

3. I'm certainly not trying to suggest that there were no feminist scholars who addressed this issue, as the work of Gayle Rubin attests. However, Rubin's work falls under the rubric of gay and lesbian studies as much as under feminism. Indeed, she made a strong case that gay and

lesbian studies was the more appropriate domain for sexual theory than was feminism (Gayle Rubin, "Thinking Sex: Notes for a Radical Theory of the Politics of Sexuality," in *The Lesbian and Gay Studies Reader*, ed. Henry Abelove, Michele A. Barale, and David Halperin [New York: Routledge, 1993], 3–44).

4. The analysis in this chapter centers primarily on Money's 1988 text, *Gay, Straight and In-Between*, since it provides an account of his more fully elaborated theories of gender with respect to desire.

5. Catherine Gallagher and Thomas Laqueur, eds. *The Making of the Modern Body: Sexuality and Society in the Nineteenth Century* (Berkeley and London: University of California Press, 1987), xv.

6. Ulrichs was by trade a Hanoverian legal official who conducted a life-long campaign to decriminalize same-sex desire. Much of his work was written during the period of unification of the Germanic states and was a direct appeal against the adoption of section 143 of the Prussian legal code, which criminalized same-sex practices throughout Germany. The section was passed into law in 1871 as paragraph 175 of the German Imperial legal code (Vernon Bullough, *Sexual Variance in Society and History* [Chicago and London: University of Chicago Press, 1976]; Bullough, *Science in the Bedroom: A History of Sex Research* [New York: Basic Books], 1994).

7. Hubert Kennedy, "The Riddle of 'Man-Manly' Love: The Pioneering Work on Male Homosexuality," *Journal of Homosexuality* 33, no. 2 (1997): 125; Kennedy, "Karl Heinrich Ulrichs, First Theorist of Homosexuality," in *Science and Homosexualities*, ed. Vernon Rosario (New York and London: Routledge, 1997), 26–45.

8. Money was responsible for the development and renaming of a revised nomenclature of nonnormative desires. Previously known as the perversions, today—thanks to Money—they are known as the "paraphilias."

9. Michel Foucault, *The History of Sexuality, Volume 1. An Introduction*, trans. Robert Hurley (London: Penguin, 1990).

10. Joseph Bristow, *Sexuality* (London: Routledge, 1997), 179. See also Stephen Garton, *Histories of Sexuality: Antiquity to Sexual Revolution* (London: Equinox, 2004); David Greenburg, "Transformations of Homosexuality-Based Classifications," in *The Gender Sexuality Reader: Culture, History, Political Economy*, ed. Roger Lancaster and Micaela di Leonardo (New York: Routledge, 1997), 179–193.

11. It was not just the sexual scientists who turned to the figure of the hermaphrodite. Sigmund Freud, who wrote against much sexological theory, also made reference to the bisexual potential of the fetus and the physiological "residua of the 'other' " that remained in the body following differentiation. See Freud, "Three Essays on the Theory of Sexuality," in *Standard Edition of the Complete Psychological Works of Sigmund Freud* (London: Hogarth, 1953), 7.

12. The reproductive paradigm of sexuality promotes the complementarity of the penis and vagina as if they were natural homologues.

13. Katharina Rowold suggests that the theory of original bisexuality was arguably the most important principle of sexological theories of congenital sexuality (Rowold, "A Male Mind in a Female Body: Sexology, Homosexuality, and the Woman Question in Germany, 1869–1914," in *From Physico-Theology to Bio-Technology: Essays in the Social and Cultural History of Biosciences: A Festschrift for Mikulas Teich*, ed. Kurt Bayertz and Roy Porter [Amsterdam and Atlanta: Rodopi, 1998], 158). See also Vernon Bullough, "Introduction." in *The Homosexuality of Men and Women* (New York: Prometheus Books, 2000), 11–17; Gert Hekma, " 'A Female Soul in a Male Body': Sexual Inversion as Gender Inversion in Nineteenth-Century Sexology," in *Third Sex, Third Gender: Beyond Sexual Dimorphism in Culture and History*, ed. Gilbert Herdt (New York: Zone Books, 1994), 213–239; Gilbert Herdt, "Introduction: Third Sexes and Third Genders," in *Third Sex, Third Gender*, 21–81; Matt Reed, "Historicizing Inversion: Or, How to Make a Homosexual," *History of the Human Sciences* 14, no. 4 (2001): 1–29.

14. Ulrichs's biographer, Hubert Kennedy, suggests that during the nineteenth century it was commonly understood that a person's sexual instinct was located in the soul.

15. This tradition was refused by Money for reasons that will become apparent in the discussion that follows.

16. Uranian is said to be the English equivalent of the original German term, Urning.

17. Bullough, "Introduction"; Hekma, "A Female Soul."

18. Hirschfeld's model represents an amended version of his theory of sexual intermediaries, which I discuss in detail in the final chapter. Today it is the third-sex model for which he is best known. Not so well known is the fact that Hirschfeld offered it as a provisional and politically expedient version of his original schema in order to address the needs of those who were criminalized by the state and pathologized by psychiatry. For Hirschfeld the third sex was merely a fiction that served to bolster or supplement the apparent naturalness of the two privileged (and similarly fictional) categories of male and female.

19. J. Edgar Bauer, "Gender and the Nemesis of Nature: On Magnus Hirschfeld's Deconstruction of the Sexual Binary and the Concept of Sexual Human Rights," in *Two Is Not Enough for Gender (E)Quality*, eds. A. Hodzic and J. Postic (Zagreb: CESI and Zenska soba, 2006), 153–171; James Steakley, "*Per Scientiam and Justitiam*: Magnus Hirschfeld and the Sexual Politics of Innate Homosexuality," in *Science and Homosexualities*, 133–154.

20. Magnus Hirschfeld, *The Transvestites: The Erotic Drive to Cross Dress*, trans. Michael Lombardi-Nash (Buffalo, NY: Prometheus Books, 1991), 97, emphasis added.

21. James Jones has reported that Krafft-Ebing did however become enamored of Hirschfeld's ideas, particularly those concerned with homosexuality. Shortly before his death, Krafft-Ebing rescinded his view that homosexuality was a psychopathological condition, deciding instead it was a "natural occurrence" (Jones, *"We of the Third Sex": Literary Representations of Homosexuality in Wilhelmine Germany* [New York: Peter Lang, 1990], 63).

22. For further analyses of the intersection of race and sexuality in nineteenth-century sexological discourse, see Rudi Bleys, *The Geography of Perversion: Male-to-Male Sexual Behaviour Outside the West and the Ethnographic Imagination 1750–1918* (New York: New York University Press, 1995); David Halperin, *One Hundred Years of Homosexuality: And Other Essays on Greek Love* (London: Routledge, 1990); Reed, "Historicizing Inversion"; Siobhan Somerville, "Scientific Racism and the Invention of the Homosexual Body," in *Sexology in Culture: Labelling Bodies and Desires*, ed. Lucy Bland and Laura Doan (Cambridge: Polity, 1998), 60–76.

23. Richard Krafft-Ebing, *Psychopathia Sexualis: With Especial Reference to the Anti-Pathic Sexual Instinct. A Medico-Forensic Study*, trans. Franklin Klaf (New York: Arcade, 1998), 30.

24. Ibid., 258.

25. Ibid.

26. Bleys, *Geography of Perversion*. Today little trace of that contradiction remains. Rather, throughout the twentieth century medical and sexological discourses presuppose the "monstrous" rather than the "mythic" and through their practices attempt to liberate the subject from the stigma of physical ambiguity. Ironically it is contemporary medical practices that relegate human hermaphroditism to the realms of myth in their attempts to transform and contain unruly bodies.

27. Elizabeth Grosz, "Intolerable Ambiguity: Freaks as/at the Limit," in *Freakery: Cultural Spectacles of the Extraordinary Body*, ed. Rosemary Garland Thomson (New York: New York University Press, 1996), 46.

28. Michel Foucault, "The Abnormals," in *Ethics, Subjectivity and Truth: The Essential Works of Foucault 1954–1984*, ed. Paul Rabinow (New York: The New Press, 1997), 51.

29. Bernice Hausman, *Changing Sex: Transsexualism, Technology and the Idea of Gender.* (Durham, NC: Duke University Press, 1995), 77–84.

30. Albert Ellis, "The Sexual Psychology of Human Hermaphrodites," *Psychosomatic Medicine* 7 (1945): 109, emphasis in original.

31. Ibid., 109.

32. A note handwritten by Money, attached to a draft manuscript in the Money Collection at the Kinsey Institute, confirms that signficance: "I had completely forgotten that I wrote the review of Albert Ellis's paper. In fact, many years ago when I found a bibliographic reference to the Ellis paper, I did not recall ever having seen it, and was

vexed that I had not used it as a reference in my 1955 hermaphroditic papers!" (Money, n.d., John Money Collection, The Kinsey Institute for Research in Sex, Gender, and Reproduction).

33. Bristow, *Sexuality*; Bullough, *Sexual Variance*.
34. See for example Case 129 in Krafft-Ebing, *Psychopathia Sexualis*, 200. For examples in John Money's work, see John Money and Patricia Tucker, *Sexual Signatures: On Being a Man or a Woman* (London: Sphere Books, 1977), 156–158; Money et al., "Hermaphroditism: Recommendations Concerning Assignment of Sex, Change of Sex, and Psychologic Management," *Bulletin of the Johns Hopkins Hospital* 97, no. 4 (1955), 296–298; Money et al., "An Examination of Some Basic Sexual Concepts: The Evidence of Human Hermaphroditism," *Bulletin of the Johns Hopkins Hospital* 97, no. 4 (1955), 310–317.
35. This distinction continues to be made in social as well as sexological research. HIV/AIDS researchers for example have found that making clear distinctions between gay men and "men who have sex with men" offers a particularly fruitful strategy for safe sex research and educational campaigns.
36. Cited in Hirschfeld, *The Homosexuality of Men and Women*, trans. Michael Lombardi-Nash (New York: Promethus Books, 2000), 40.
37. Krafft-Ebing, *Psychopathia Sexualis*, 53.
38. Hirschfeld, *Homosexuality*, 27.
39. Alfred Kinsey, Wardell Pomeroy, and Clyde Martin, *Sexual Behavior in the Human Male* (Philadelphia: Saunders, 1948), 3.
40. Erasmus Darwin, *The Temple of Nature* (London: J. Johnson, 1803), 35–36.
41. Herdt, "Introduction," 32.
42. Carol Vance, "Anthropology Rediscovers Sexuality: A Theoretical Comment," in *Culture, Society and Sexuality: A Reader*, ed. Richard Parker and Peter Aggleton (London and Philadelphia: UCL Press, 1999), 44.
43. Robert Padgug, "Sexual Matters: On Conceptualising Sexuality in History," in *Culture, Society and Sexuality*, 15–28.
44. Thomas Laqueur, *Making Sex: Body and Gender from the Greeks to Freud* (Cambridge: Harvard University Press, 1990), 239.
45. Bristow, *Sexuality*; Herdt, "Introduction;" Kennedy, "Karl Heinrich Ulrichs."
46. Kennedy, "Karl Heinrich Ulrichs," 33.
47. Bleys, *Geography of Perversion*; Jay Prosser, "Transsexuals and the Transsexologists: Inversion and the Emergence of Transsexual Subjectivity," in *Sexology in Culture*, 116–131; Merl Storr, "Transformations: Subjects, Categories and Cures in Krafft-Ebing's Sexology," in *Sexology in Culture*, 11–26.
48. It is important to remember that the term *gender* was not available to the early sexual scientists, which explains its absence in sexual theory as either a descriptive or a conceptual device prior to the 1950s.

49. Jonathan Katz, *The Invention of Heterosexuality* (New York: Dutton, 1995), 92.

50. For analyses of the historical shift that led to such interpretations of maleness and femaleness in scientific thought see for example, Londa Schiebinger, *Nature's Body: Gender in the Making of Modern Science* (Boston: Beacon Press, 1993); Bonnie Spanier, " 'Lessons' From 'Nature': Gender Ideology and Sexual Ambiguity in Biology," in *Body Guards: The Cultural Politics of Gender Ambiguity*, ed. Kristina Straub and Julia Epstein (New York: Routledge, 1991), 329–350.

51. Katz, *The Invention of Heterosexuality*, 51–52.

52. Angus McLaren, *Twentieth-Century Sexuality: A History* (Oxford: Blackwell, 1999), 91.

53. Foucault, *The History of Sexuality*.

54. Foucault, *Discipline and Punish: The Birth of the Prison* (New York: Pantheon, 1977).

55. The scare quotes here are deliberate, for it is only by interpreting hermaphrodites' erotic orientations and practices through a lens of dimorphism that they actually make sense.

56. See Hausman, *Changing Sex*, 97–98; Hausman, "Do Boys Have to Be Boys? Gender, Narrativity, and the John/Joan Case," *NWSA Journal* 12, no. 3 (2000): 114–138.

57. Money, *Gay, Straight*, 127.

58. Ibid., 123.

59. Ibid., 32.

60. Ibid., 103.

61. Ibid.

62. Ibid., 114. Of course Money is not alone on this count; Magnus Hirschfeld did precisely the same thing at the turn of the twentieth century when he asserted that internal secretions were responsible for the force of libido. Hirschfeld went so far as to offer names for two key substances almost a decade before the so-called sex hormones were isolated. As his biographer, Charlotte Wolff, noted, Hirschfeld "tapped at the door of modern science but could not get it to open." It has since done so and a number of his ideas have been verified, one of which I take up in the final chapter (Charlotte Wolff, *Magnus Hirschfeld: A Portrait of a Pioneer in Sexology* [London; New York: Quartet Books, 1986], 15).

63. See William Simon, *Postmodern Sexualities* (London: Routledge, 1996) for a similar critique.

64. The ethnographic record to which he referred included his own explorations into anthropological fieldwork conducted among the indigenous people of Arnhem Land in the Northern Territory of Australia during the late 1960s. See Money et al., "Sex Training and Traditions in Arnhem Land," *British Journal of Medical Psychology* 47 (1970): 383–399.

65. Money, *Gay, Straight*, 124.
66. Ibid., 72.
67. Ibid., 73.
68. Ibid., 72, emphasis added.
69. Ibid., 82.
70. Ibid.
71. Ibid., 82–83. Recall Robert Stoller's etiology of transsexualism that cast the mother, or more specifically the mother/son relationship, as a causative agent. Money believed that his hypothesis upended Freudian Oedipal orthodoxy, by replacing the seduction of the mother with that of the father.
72. See Phyllis Burke, *Gender Shock: Exploding the Myths of Male and Female* (New York: Anchor Books, 1996); Eve Kosofsky Sedgwick, *Tendencies* (Durham, NC: Duke University Press, 1993).
73. Money, *Gay, Straight*, 80.
74. Prosser, *Second Skins*, 30–31.
75. Simon, *Postmodern Sexualities*, 21.
76. Money, *Gendermaps*, 27–30.
77. John Money, *Sin, Science, and the Sex Police: Essays on Sexology and Sexosophy* (New York: Prometheus Books, 1998), 52.
78. Ibid., 52.
79. Money, *Gay, Straight*, 80.
80. Ibid., 52.
81. Ibid., 12.
82. Ibid., 81.
83. Ibid.
84. Ibid.
85. Ibid., 103
86. Ibid., 135.
87. See for example, Steve Biddulph, *Raising Boys: Why Boys Are Different—and How to Help Them Become Happy and Well-Balanced Men* (Berkeley: Ten Speed Press, 1998); Celia Lashlie, *He'll Be Ok: Growing Gorgeous Boys into Good Men* (Auckland: HarperCollins, 2005); Celia Lashlie and Katherine Pivac, "It's About Boys: The Good Man Project" (Nelson, N. Z.: Nelson College, 2004).
88. Money, *Gay, Straight*, 81.
89. Ibid., 107.
90. Ibid., 81.
91. Steven Angelides, *A History of Bisexuality* (Chicago: University of Chicago Press, 2001).
92. Amber Ault, "Ambiguous Identity in an Unambiguous Sex/Gender Structure: The Case of Bisexual Women," *Sociological Quarterly* 37, no. 3 (1996): 449–463; Jo Eadie, "Activating Bisexuality: Towards a Bi/Sexual Politics," in *Activating Theory: Lesbian, Gay, Bisexual Politics*, ed. Joseph Bristow and Angelia R. Wilson (London: Lawrence & Wishart, 1993), 139–170; Kristin Esterberg, "The Bisexual Menace

Revisited: Or, Shaking up Social Categories Is Hard to Do," in *Introducing the New Sexuality Studies: Original Essays and Interviews*, ed. Steven Seidman, Nancy Fischer, and Chet Meeks (London: Routledge, 2007), 157–163; Clare Hemmings, "Resituating the Bisexual Body: From Identity to Difference," in *Activating Theory*, 118–138; Hemmings, *Bisexual Spaces: A Geography of Sexuality and Gender* (New York: Routledge, 2002).

93. Angelides, *A History of Bisexuality*; Hemmings, "What's in a Name? Bisexuality, Transnational Sexuality Studies and Western Colonial Legacies," *International Journal of Human Rights* 11, no. 1–2 (2007): 13–32.

94. There are parallels here with the epistemic and material banishment of the intersexed from the present. Cast out of the here and now, the intersexed bear the brunt of biomedicine's impulse to reinforce monosexuality at the level of the body such that each one (body) ought to have *just* one (sex). For a comparative analysis of the banishment of bisexuality and intersex, see Jennifer Germon, "Kinsey and the Politics of Bisexual Authenticity," *Journal of Bisexuality* 8, no. 3/4 (2008): 245–260.

95. Money, *Gay, Straight*, 108.

96. Ibid., 109–110.

97. Ibid., 110.

98. Ibid., 109.

99. Ibid., 110.

100. Ibid., 107. See also Money, "Bisexual, Homosexual, and Heterosexual: Society, Law, and Medicine," *Journal of Homosexuality* 2, no. 3 (1977): 229–231.

101. Money, *Gay, Straight*, 108.

102. Ibid.

103. Kinsey et al., *Sexual Behavior in the Human Male*; Kinsey et al., *Sexual Behavior in the Human Female* (Philadelphia: Saunders, 1953).

104. Alfred Kinsey, "Homosexuality: Criteria for a Hormonal Explanation of the Homosexual," *Journal of Clinical Endocrinology* 1, no. 5 (1941): 424–428.

105. Kinsey et al., *SBHM*, 617.

106. While today determinism is most usually associated with either the biological or the cultural, Money's determinism incorporated both.

107. Money, *Gay, Straight*, 85.

108. Money, *Sin, Science*, 70.

109. Money, *Reinterpreting the Unspeakable. Human Sexuality 2000: The Complete Interviewer and Clinical Biographer, Exigency Theory, and Sexology for the Third Millenium* (New York: Continuum, 1994), 205–207. These stratagems included the following: sacrificial/expiatory, marauding/predatory, mercantile/venal, fetishistic/talismanic, stigmatic/eligibilic, and solicitational/allurative.

110. More recently it has been suggested by Anil Aggrawal that the total number of paraphilias is in excess of 500 specific types. Yet a cursory glance at the types of sexual practices and desires that constitute this number indicates that almost any form of sexual activity or fantasy would in fact qualify. The inclusion of homosexuality and lesbianism is justified by the author on the grounds that they continue to be stigmatized in many cultural contexts. Sexual harassment and the (now) rather quaintly named wife swapping are also included. Tellingly, in the introductory chapter Aggrawal acknowledges that no clear definition of what constitutes normalcy in sex exists (Anil Aggrawal, *Forensic and Medico-Legal Aspects of Sex Crimes and Unusual Sexual Practices* [Boca Raton, FL: CRC Press, 2009]).

111. Money, *Gay, Straight*, 131.

112. Ibid., 134. See also Money and Lamacz, *Vandalized Lovemaps: Paraphilic Outcome of Seven Cases in Pediatric Sexology* (Buffalo, NY: Prometheus Books, 1989).

113. Money, *Gay, Straight*, 133.

114. Ibid., 172.

115. Deborah Tolman and Lisa M. Diamond, "Desegregating Sexuality Research: Cultural and Biological Perspectives on Gender and Desire," *Annual Review of Sex Research* 12 (2001): 33–74.

116. Plurality is most evident in Money's theorizing of bisexuality and the paraphilias.

117. Simon, *Postmodern Sexualities*, 27.

118. Edward Stein, *The Mismeasure of Desire: The Science, Theory, and Ethics of Sexual Orientation* (New York: Oxford University Press, 1999).

119. "That which is phylogenetic is given to each member of our species and is shared by everyone as part of our species' history" (Money, *Gendermaps*, 36). In other words, it refers to that which is genealogically shared by all members of a species.

120. Money, *Gay, Straight*, 104.

121. Ibid.

122. Walter Bockting, "Ken from Mars, Barbie from Venus 411–422.

123. Simon, *Postmodern Sexualities*, 25.

124. Stein, *Mismeasure*, 63.

CHAPTER 5

1. I base the parenthetical claim on the widespread use of animal research to evidence medical and sexological theories of human development and behavior, particularly sexual behavior. For a recent example of this in relation to the intersexed see Phoebe Dewing et al., "Sexually Dimorphic Gene Expression in Mouse Brain Precedes Gonadal Differentiation," *Molecular Brain Research* 118, no. 1–2 (2003): 82–90.

2. Julia Epstein, *Altered Conditions: Disease, Medicine and Storytelling* (New York: Routledge, 1995), 104.

3. This is the case made by Epstein in her substantive account of the ways in which disease and disorder (including the "dis-order" of intersexuality) come to be framed in medical accounts: "it is the true hermaphrodite who should be the norm from which all unambiguous females and males are seen to deviate" (Ibid.). See also Ashley Tauchert, "Fuzzy Gender: Between Female-Embodiment and Intersex," *Journal of Gender Studies* 11, no. 1 (2002): 29–38. Tauchert proposes a model derived from mathematics (known as "fuzzy logic") that situates the intersexed in similar terms; that is, ambiguity is not a problem that needs resolving but constitutes the standard from which those at the privileged endpoints of a binary economy deviate. Both of these perspectives account for those who are excluded under the terms of Aristotelian logic (A cannot equal not-A), in ways that *do not* pathologize or teratologize (that is, make monstrous).

4. Alfred Jost, "Problems of Fetal Endocrinology," In *Recent Progress in Hormone Research*, ed. Gregory Pincus (New York: Academic Press, 1953), 379–419. For an astute contextual reading of the effects of Jost's ideas on medical research see Anne Fausto-Sterling, *Sexing the Body: Gender Politics and the Construction of Sexuality* (New York: Basic Books, 2000), 199–203.

5. Money promoted this idea in much of his published work, referring to the principle as "Eve first, then Adam." See for example John Money, *Gay, Straight, and In-Between: The Sexology of Erotic Orientation* (New York: Continuum, 1988), 13–14, 18–20.

6. Female development remains, to this day, an area seriously underresearched precisely because the default hypothesis renders it already fully accounted for, even as it explains so little.

7. The best-known memoir is that of Herculine Barbin. See Michel Foucault, *Herculine Barbin: Being the Recently Discovered Memoirs of a 19th Century French Hermaphrodite* (New York: Pantheon, 1980).

8. Simone de Beauvoir

9. Jay Prosser, *Second Skins: The Body Narratives of Transsexuality* (New York and Chichester: Columbia University Press, 1998), 32–33. For Prosser, Beauvoir's epigram lends itself to being reread as a specific narrative of transsexuals' "struggle toward sexed embodiment. One is not born a woman but *nevertheless* may become one–given substantial medical intervention, personal tenacity, economic security, social support, and so on."

10. Roger Adkins, "Where 'Sex' Is Born(e): Intersexed Births and the Social Urgency of Heterosexuality," *Journal of Medical Humanities* 20, no. 2 (1999): 117–133; Carl Elliot, "Why Can't We Go on as Three? (Intersexuality as a Third-Sex Category)," *Hastings Centre Report* 28, no. 3 (1998): 36–39: Fausto-Sterling, *Sexing the Body*; Felicity Haynes and Tarquam McKenna, eds., *Unseen Genders: Beyond*

the Binaries (New York: Peter Lang, 2001); Peter Hegarty and Cheryl Chase, "Intersex Activism, Feminism and Psychology: Opening a Dialogue on Theory, Research and Clinical Practice," *Feminism and Psychology* 10, no. 1 (2000): 117–132; Curtis Hinkle, "Resisting Sexism from All Sides," www.intersexualite.org.; Suzanne Kessler, "The Medical Construction of Gender: Case Management of Intersexed Infants," *Signs* 16, no. 1 (1990): 3–26; Sharon Preves, "Negotiating the Constraints of Gender Binarism: Intersexuals' Challenge to Gender Categorization," *Current Sociology* 48, no. 3 (2000): 27–50; Katrina Roen, "Queerly Sexed Bodies in Clinical Contexts: Problematising Conceptual Foundations of Genital Surgery with Intersex Infants," in *Sex and the Body*, ed. Annie Potts, Nicola Gavey, and Ann Weatherall (Palmerston North: Dunmore Press, 2004), 89–106; Roen, " 'But We Have to *Do Something*': Surgical 'Correction' of Atypical Genitalia," *Body and Society* 14, no. 1 (2008): 47–66; Riki Wilchins, "A Certain Kind of Freedom: Power and the Truth of Bodies—Four Essays on Gender," in *Genderqueer: Voices from Beyond the Sexual Binary*, ed. Joan Nestle, Riki Anne Wilchins, and Clare Howell (Los Angeles: Alyson Books, 2002), 21–63.

11. Importantly, not all people diagnosed as intersexed are unhappy with the medical treatments received, nor indeed with their gender assignments. But because so many are reported in the medical literature as "lost to follow-up," there is no way of accurately assessing the number of successful outcomes or "satisfied customers." Clearly those lobbying for changes to ICM implementation *do* have a problem with those practices. This includes individuals who, for one reason or another, were never subjected to medical interventions themselves. It is also important to stress that intersexed critics of ICM may or may not have an issue with their gender assignment or with the *idea* of gender as a binary. Additionally, there is no way of estimating how many people remain unaware that they were ever diagnosed as intersexed. That lack of knowledge cannot be simply taken to mean such people are fully habilitated into the gender they were reared.

12. Cheryl Chase, founder of ISNA, sees many parallels between the struggles of gay activists and those of intersexuals, particularly their respective pathologization and subjection to medical practices motivated by social intolerance. See Hegarty and Chase, "Intersex Activism."

13. The ethnographic component of this chapter consisted of a series of face-to-face interviews conducted between December 2001 and February 2002, with self-identified intersex and hermaphrodite individuals residing in various locations in North America, Australasia, and India. The interview data were supplemented by follow-up discussions by email, telephone, and in person. As stated in the introductory chapter, no claims are made to representation. My intention

is to highlight ruptures in what, until recently, *appeared* to be a unified narrative among intersex communities and groups.

14. For example, see Dawn Atkins, ed., *Looking Queer: Body Image and Identity in Lesbian, Bisexual, Gay and Transgender Communities* (New York: Haworth Press, 1996/1998); Alice Domurat Dreger, ed., *Intersex in the Age of Ethics* (Hagerstown, MD: University Publishing Group, 2000); Catherine Harper, *Intersex* (Oxford: Berg, 2007); Morgan Holmes, "I'm Still Intersexual," *Hermaphrodites with Attitudes*, Winter 1994, 5–6; Holmes, "Queer Cut Bodies: Intersexuality and Homophobia in Medical Practice," http://www.usc.edu/isd/archives/queerfrontiers/queer/papers/holmes.long.html; Suzanne Kessler, *Lessons from the Intersexed* (New Brunswick, NJ: Rutgers University Press, 1998).

15. In making this claim I am cognizant of Stephanie Turner's point that despite its name, the World Wide Web is not global in its reach and is thus limited to those with the economic means to access technology. This raises questions regarding the representativeness of those who do use the Internet. See Turner, "Intersex Identities: Locating New Intersections of Sex and Gender," *Gender & Society* 13, no. 4 (1999): 463.

16. There are strong parallels here with the way feminism wrestled with the concept of gender for the best part of a decade before any widespread agreement could be reached among feminists as to its conceptual *and* political utility.

17. This group (hereafter called The Consortium) was formed following a meeting of international ICM clinicians in Chicago in October 2005 at which new treatment guidelines and a new nomenclature were endorsed. The Consortium is made up of clinicians involved in ICM, people who are intersexed, and parents of intersexed children and adults. In 2006 The Consortium published two important and influential documents: a set of clinical guidelines and a handbook for parents of intersexed children.

18. See Curtis Hinkle, "People without Faces," Intersex Pride, http://intersexpride.blogspot.com.

19. This is precisely how Money conceptualized gender, although as I have demonstrated, he did so for very different ends.

20. Chase has recently disclosed that this is, in fact, a pen name (See http://www.accordalliance.org/our-people.html).

21. As many others have reported, Chase had difficulty accessing her full medical records. Many physicians have been reluctant to release full details of people's medical histories because they believe the information is too confronting for an individual to bear despite the centrality of disclosure in the original model.

22. Chase recounts that at the age of ten, her parents disclosed some of her medical history to her, telling her that she had been sick as a baby

and had had to go to the hospital to have her clitoris removed because it was too large, and advised that she never share this information with anyone else (Chase, "Affronting Reason," 211).

23. Ibid., 213. See also, Hegarty and Chase, "Intersex Activism."

24. The formation of ISNA in 1993 has been well documented elsewhere by Chase and others. For some examples see, Chase, "Affronting Reason"; Hegarty and Chase, "Intersex Activism"; Fausto-Sterling, *Sexing the Body*.

25. Anne Fausto-Sterling, "The Five Sexes." In the British context an informal peer support group for parents of children diagnosed with AIS began in 1998. Initially it functioned as a one-woman telephone support service but later expanded and formalized itself as the AIS Support Group (AISSG) in 1993. This organization now has many branches across the United Kingdom, Europe, Canada, North and South America, Australia, New Zealand, India, and South Africa. AISSG is one of a range of diagnostic-specific peer support/advocacy groups that provide targeted information, resources, and peer support to affected individuals, parents, and families.

26. As I have discussed in Chapter 2, over the past half century little consideration has been given to the impact on children (or adults for that matter) of repeated genital examinations, often conducted by teams of doctors, or by individual clinicians in the presence of groups of medical students. Yet intersexed people report that being subject to a collective medical gaze is both traumatic and a source of deep shame. For a broad analysis of the impact of others' unfettered access to one's body—particularly by those in positions of authority—and on the issue of stigma, see Erving Goffman, *Stigma: Notes on the Management of Spoiled Identity* (Harmondsworth, England: Penguin, 1968).

27. http://www.isna.org/

28. Dreger, n.d. www.isna.org/compare; www.isna.org/faq/patient-centered. Concealment is used to refer to the case management model devised by Money and so named because of the widespread practice by physicians of withholding information from patients, including adults seeking information on their medical histories (as in the case of Chase). As should be clear from the discussion in Chapter 2, this practice clearly breached Money's recommendations and so cannot be said to be intrinsic to the original model. There is a sense in which Money's protocols can be said to be concealment-centered since genital modification for the purposes of refashioning the soma to resemble femaleness or maleness inherently works to conceal from culture, human sexual variation and thus sexual diversity. From this perspective any and all models that employ such practices would qualify as concealment centered, including the latest clinical guidelines introduced in 2006 by The Consortium, for reasons that will become clear in the

following discussion (see Consortium on the Management of Disorders of Sex Development, *Clinical Guidelines for the Management of Disorders of Development in Childhood* [Rohnert Park, CA: Intersex Society of North America, 2006]).

29. Hegarty and Chase, "Intersex Activism," 11.

30. www.isna.org/books/chrysalis/beck.

31. *Hermaphrodites with Attitude* was the original title of ISNA's newsletter (changed to *ISNA News* in 2001). The phrase was the motto of early intersex activism in North America, employed in the same defiant sense in which Queer Nation used the now infamous slogan "we're here, we're queer, get used to it!"

32. www.isna.org/faq/history.

33. During the 1990s, gender was a key issue for many ISNA members including Chase, as evident in the organization's newsletters and in much of the published material in which intersex advocates recounted their stories. Stephanie Turner documented the centrality of gendered analyses to intersex discourse in an article published in the journal *Gender and Society* in 1999 that explored the tensions inherent in seeking recourse to a politics of identity (Turner, "Intersex Identities").

34. www.isna.org/faq (1996).

35. Edward Stein, *The Mismeasure of Desire: The Science, Theory, and Ethics of Sexual Orientation* (New York: Oxford University Press, 1999).

36. Consortium on the Management of Disorders of Sex Development, *Handbook for Parents* (Rohnert Park, CA: Intersex Society of North America, 2006), 49. This question was originally framed in the *Tips* document as "which gender *identity* (boy or girl) should this child be given—that is which gender is my child most likely to feel as she or he grows up?" (*Tips*, 2004, emphasis added).

37. Ibid., emphasis added.

38. Ibid.

39. Ibid., emphasis added. The claim that choosing a boy gender or a girl gender for the child is the same as choosing the gender for any child is rather specious to say the least. For it is surely nonsense to suggest that parents are able to exercise choice in determining the gender assignment of their newborn. Genital appearance serves as the primary signifier of sex and thus of gender for most children. For parents to choose, for example, a female gender for an infant sexed as male—that is, a child with an "appropriately sized" penis—would surely call into question their fitness as parents.

40. Ibid.

41. Diamond is a long-time rival of Money who has achieved notoriety in recent years for whistle-blowing the so-called John/Joan case. Today he works as an ally of IS advocacy groups and has devised

an alternate model of ICM that argues for (a) minimal intervention and (b) gender assignments based on chromosomes and gonads. See Milton Diamond and Keith Sigmundsen, "Management of Intersexuality: Guidelines for Dealing with Persons with Ambiguous Genitalia," *Arch Pediatr Adolesc Med* 151 (1997): 1046–1050. See also Jill Becker, Karen Berkley, Nori Geary, Elizabeth Hampson, James Herman, and Elizabeth Young, eds., *Sex Differences in the Brain: From Genes to Behavior* (New York: Oxford University Press, 2007).

42. Recall that for Money, gender was all about nature working in concert with nurture, which I argue is a considerably more sophisticated analysis than those offered by the timeworn nature/nurture debates.

43. Chase, "Affronting Reason," 214, emphasis in original.

44. After alerting ISNA to my research mid-2001, I received an email from Koyama in her capacity as communications officer at ISNA informing me that "most intersexed people *do not* have gender issues" (Koyama, personal communication September 9, 2001).

45. www.isna.org/faq/gender_assignment.

46. Elective surgeries fulfill the Western liberal democratic ideal of the individual quest toward self-actualization; fulfill the requirements of capital by generating income; and fulfill the requirements of consumerism, as a commodity.

47. For clinicians' assessments of such failures see, for example, Sarah Creighton, "Long-Term Outcome of Feminization Surgery: The London Experience," *British Journal of Urology International* 93, Supplement 3 (2004): 44–46: Sarah Creighton and Catherine Minto, "Managing Intersex: Most Vaginal Surgery Should Be Deferred," *British Medical Journal,* 323, no. 7324 (2001): 1264–1265; J. Daaboul and Joel Frader, "Ethics and the Management of the Patient with Intersex," *Journal of Pediatric Endocrinology & Metabolism* 14, no. 9 (2001): 1575–1583; Catherine Minto et al., "Management of Intersex—Specialists Reply," *Lancet* (North American edition) 358, no. 9298 (2001): 2085–2086.

48. Julia Epstein, "Either/or—Neither/Both: Sexual Ambiguity and the Ideology of Gender," *Genders* 7 (1990): 99–142.

49. Irving Zola, "Medicine as an Institution of Social Control," *Sociological Review* 20 (1972): 487–504.

50. Michel Foucault, *Discipline and Punish: The Birth of the Prison* (New York: Pantheon, 1977); Foucault, *The Politics of Truth*, eds. Sylvere Lotringer and Lysa Hochroth (New York: Semiotext(e), 1997); David Swartz, *Culture & Power: The Sociology of Pierre Bourdieu* (Chicago: University of Chicago Press, 1997).

51. *ISNA Guide to Writers and Researchers.* These guidelines are now located on the Web site of Intersex Initiative (IPDX), a site produced and maintained by ISNA's former communications officer, Emi Koyama. See Emi Koyama, "Suggested Guidelines for Non-Intersex Individuals Writing About Intersexuality

and Intersex People," (http://www.ipdx.org/articles/writing-guidelines.html).

52. Ibid. (retrieved November 17, 2001).
53. www.isna.org/faq/conditions.
54. www.isna.org/articles/tips_for_parents.
55. Epstein, *Altered Conditions*, 116.
56. ISNA, *ISNA News* (2001). This represents a repudiation of a politics of difference, one of the cornerstones of identity politics that has, in the past, proved politically useful to rights-claiming groups.
57. Turner, "Intersex Identities."
58. David Valentine, "'I Went to Bed with My Own Kind Once': The Erasure of Desire in the Name of Identity," *Language & Communication* 23, no. 2 (2003): 220.
59. Ibid., 221.
60. Epicene is defined in the *Oxford English Dictionary* as "partaking of the characteristics of both sexes" (http://dictionary.com).
61. Drew, emphasis added.
62. For examples of the social model of disability from which this idea comes, see for example, Michael Oliver, *Understanding Disability: From Theory to Practice* (Houndmills, Basingstoke: Macmillan, 1996); John Swain, Sally French, and Colin Cameron, *Controversial Issues in a Disabling Society* (Philadelphia, PA: Open University Press, 2003). See also Tom Shakespeare, ed., *The Disability Reader: Social Science Perspectives* (London: Cassell, 1998); Tom Shakespeare and Mairian Corker, *Disability/Postmodernity: Embodying Disability Theory* (London: Continuum, 2002); Carol Thomas, *Sociology of Disability and Ilness: Contested Ideas in Disability Studies and Medical Sociology* (New York: Palgrave, 2007).
63. Vernon Rosario, personal communication, August 1, 2005.
64. www.isna.org/faq/gender_assignment (2006).
65. Stein, *Mismeasure*, 39–70.
66. Dreger, "Top Ten Myths About Intersex," *ISNA News* (2001): 3, 5–6; www.isna.org/faq/language; Money and Anke Ehrhardt, *Man and Woman, Boy and Girl: The Differentiation and Dimorphism of Gender Identity from Conception to Maturity* (Baltimore: Johns Hopkins University Press, 1972).
67. It is, of course, possible to have both a penis and a vaginal opening or pouch. The point that appears to be being made (one rarely stated explicitly) is that human hermaphrodites are not self-fertilizing or parthenogenic entities.
68. Emi Koyama, "So, You Wanna Know About 'Hermaphrodites'?" Intersex Initiative, www.ipdx.org/articles/hermaphrodites.html.
69. Lee Anderson Brown, "Sites of Gen(D)Eration" (paper presented at the *Representing Sexualities Conference*, University of Sydney, NSW Australia, 1995), 1.

70. Kessler, *Lessons*, 84–85.

71. Richard Goldschmidt, *The Mechanism and Physiology of Sex Determination*, trans. William J. Dakin (London: Methuen, 1923). It is worth noting that today the term *sex-reversed* is used in the medical literature to describe individuals whose chromosomal makeup does not match their morphological appearance as male or as female.

72. For a recent analysis of the implications of mainstream IS politics' refusal of an ontological hermaphroditism/intersex, see Hinkle (2006).

73. See Sarah Creighton, "Surgery for Intersex," *Journal of the Royal Society of Medicine* 94, no. 5 (2001): 218–220; Creighton, "Long-Term Outcome"; Creighton and Minto, "Managing Intersex"; Creighton, Minto, and Stuart Steele, "Objective Cosmetic and Anatomical Outcomes at Adolescence for Ambiguous Genitalia Done in Childhood," *Lancet*, no. 358 (2001): 124–125.

74. In an open letter posted on ISNA's Web site in 2008 announcing the disbanding of the organization, ISNA claims it was haunted by its own more radical historical stance. The letter says that history compromised the organization's credibility with the medical community and thus its capacity to bring about change to medical practices. This is why ISNA was disbanded in favor of the new organization, Accord Alliance (http://www.ISNA.org/home).

75. I am not suggesting that ISNA was the only intersex advocacy group in existence in North America by any means. Other groups such as Bodies Like Ours had long encouraged discussion and debate on Web-based forums, as have the diagnostically specific support groups. My point is that ISNA produced a *dominant* discourse that seemed to echo everywhere, due in no small part to the organization's media savvy.

76. As its name indicates, OII is concerned with working across national boundaries. In keeping with the transnational focus, the organization offers its Web-based material in nine languages with representation in a range of countries including Canada, the Americas, France, Australia, Germany, Portugal, Sweden, and most recently China.

77. Dreger, "Changing the Nomenclature/Taxonomy for Intersex: A Scientific and Clinical Rationale," *Journal of Pediatric Endocrinology and Metabolism* 18, no. 8 (2005): 729–733. Dreger, "Why 'Disorders of Sex Development'? (on Language and Life)," http://www.alicedreger.com/dsd.html, 2007; Dreger, "Footnote to a Footnote"; Katrina Karkazis, *Fixing Sex: Intersex, Medical Authority and Lived Experience* (Durham, NC: Duke University Press, 2008).

78. Dreger, "Why 'Disorders'?"; Dreger, "Footnote to a Footnote."

79. For a detailed analysis of the DSD nomenclature from a cytogeneticist perspective see, M. Italiano and Curtis Hinkle, "Ambiguous Medicine and Sexist Genetics: A Critique of the DSD Nomenclature," (2008), http://www.intersexualite.org/sexist_genetics.html.

80. Durval Damiani, "Ambiguous Terms Still Persist in the Consensus," *British Medical Journal* (2006), http://adc.bmj.com/cgi/eletters/91/7/554.

81. Morgan Holmes, "Mind the Gaps: Intersex and (Re-Productive) Spaces in Disability Studies and Bioethics," *Bioethical Inquiry* 5, no. 2–3 (2008): 169–81.

82. www.intersexualite.org/home.

83. It is increasingly common for the letter *I* to be tagged onto the acronym GLBTQ (as GLBTIQ) as if intersexuality was itself a mode of sexuality. It is to this issue that Laramée's point is directed.

84. Joelle-Circe Laramee, "Rejecting Assimilation within the GLBT Identity Movements." OII, www.intersexualite.org/English-Index.html#anchor_526.

85. Judith Halberstam, *In a Queer Time and Place: Transgender Bodies, Subcultural Lives, Sexual Cultures* (New York: New York University Press, 2005); Eve Kosofsky Sedgwick, *Epistemology of the Closet* (Berkeley: University of California Press, 1990); Steven Seidman, *Difference Troubles: Queering Social Theory and Sexual Politics* (Cambridge: Cambridge University Press, 1997); Seidman, ed., *Queer Theory/Sociology* (Cambridge and Oxford: Blackwell, 1996); William Simon, *Postmodern Sexualities* (London: Routledge, 1996); Arlene Stein and Ken Plummer, "'I Can't Even Think Straight': 'Queer' Theory and the Missing Sexual Revolution in Sociology," in *Queer Theory/ Sociology*, ed. Steven Seidman (Cambridge and Oxford: Blackwell, 1996), 129–144; Riki Wilchins, "A Certain Kind of Freedom: Power and the Truth of Bodies—Four Essays on Gender," in *Genderqueer: Voices from Beyond the Sexual Binary*, ed. Joan Nestle, Riki Wilchins, and Clare Howell (Los Angeles: Alyson Books, 2002), 21–63.

86. Chase, "Affronting Reason," 216.

87. "Hir" is used as a non-gendered pronoun, and is often used in conjunction with another, "ze." See for example their sustained use in Kate Bornstein's, *My Gender Workbook: How to Become a Real Man, a Real Woman, the Real You, or Something Else Entirely* (New York: Routledge, 1998).

88. Holmes, "In(to) Visibility: Intersexuality in the Field of Queer," in *Looking Queer: Body Image and Identity in Lesbian, Bisexual, Gay and Transgender Communities*, ed. Dawn Atkins (New York: Harrington Park Press, 1998), 225.

89. www.isna.org/faq/conditions/progestin, emphasis added.

90. Moreno in Chase, *Hermaphrodites Speak!* (San Francisco: Intersex Society of North America, 1997).

91. In making this point, I certainly do not wish to minimize or trivialize the effect of physical scarring on either bodily integrity or erotic sensation.

92. Grosz's analysis is concerned with psychoanalytic understanding of female sexuality as already castrated and the implications that has for silences around both clitoridectomy and hysterectomy. Since her primary concern is with the abject status of the female body, my use of her analysis takes a rather different turn from hers.

93. Elizabeth Grosz, *Volatile Bodies: Towards a Corporeal Feminism* (Bloomington: Indiana University Press, 1994), 73.

94. Holmes, "I'm Still Intersexual," 6.

95. Again I point to the recent research of Creighton, Minto, and colleagues that focuses specifically on long-term surgical outcomes.

96. Roen, "Queerly Sexed Bodies," 102.

97. Grosz, *Volatile Bodies*, 85.

98. Holmes, "In(to) Visibility," 225.

99. Grosz, Volatile Bodies, 86–87.

100. This way of understanding corporeality is in many ways similar to Money's understanding of the role of the central nervous system in mediating experience and learning, although he was unable to acknowledge the rupture of bodily integrity caused by genital surgery.

101. Brown, "Fractured Masks—Voices from the Shards of Language," *Polare* 61 (2005): 12–15; Dreger, "When Medicine Goes Too Far in the Pursuit of Normality," *New York Times*, July 28 1998, 4; Fausto-Sterling, *Sexing the Body*; Kessler, *Lessons*.

102. Rosa Parks became the face of defiance for the North American civil rights movement after refusing to give up her seat to a white passenger and move to the back of the bus as was expected of African Americans in the Southern states until the late 1960s.

103. Julie Butler, "X Marks the Spot for Intersex Alex," *West Australian*, November 1, 2003.

104. According to the ABS's Director of Population Census Development and Field Organization, Dave Nauenburg, because the census forms had already been printed, people who identified as other than male or female would have the option of handwriting their descriptor of choice in that year's census. Nauenburg went on to state that ABS would not collate any resulting data but rather a computer program would randomly allocate a male or female sex status to those who did not tick the requisite boxes. Australian IS activists hailed this as a significant step toward official and legal recognition ("Census to Recognize Intersex Australians," Fairfax Digital, http://www.theage.com.au/news/national/census-to-recognize-intersex-australians/2006/03/01/1141095787949.html).

105. Iain Morland, "The Glans Opens Like a Book: Writing and Reading the Intersexed Body," *Continuum: Journal of Media & Culture Studies* 19, no. 3 (2005): 335.

CHAPTER 6

1. Virginia Braun, "In Search of (Better) Sexual Pleasure: Female Genital 'Cosmetic' Surgery," *Sexualities* 8 (2005): 407–424.

2. CAH is the acronym given to the diagnostic condition, Congenital Adrenal Hyperplasia. Said to have chromosomal origins, the condition compromises steroid production resulting in too little cortisol and aldosterone and too much androgen. Participants in the 2005 Consensus group included Cheryl Chase and other ISNA representatives.

3. Joint LWPES/ESPE CAH Working Group, "Consensus Statement on 21-Hydroxylase Deficiency from the Lawson Wilkins Pediatric Endocrine Society and the European Society for Paediatric Endocrinology," *Journal of Clinical Endocrinology & Metabolism* 87, no. 9 (2002): 4050. As I noted in the previous chapter, clinicians have never been in any doubt that their practices are *all about* securing gender.

4. This quote is taken from an entry posted by Alice Dreger on her blog on November 17, 2007 (http://www.alicedreger.com/dsd.html) entitled "Why 'Disorders of Sex Development'? (On Language and Life)." The full quotation reads, "Part of the reasonable fear among medical professionals is over-de-pathologizing sex anomalies. (If a girl is born with a big clitoris, you don't just say "gee, that's just one of nature's variations," you say "there's nothing wrong with a big clitoris but we do need to find out if this baby has congenital adrenal hyperplasia or some other underlying metabolic problem that might risk her health, fertility, or life." Sometimes a big clit is just a big clit, and sometimes—albeit rarely—it's a sign a girl is going to die in a few days if you don't get her a good endocrinologist)." To date there remains little sign that clitoral surgery is on the wane, even though the "over de-pathologization" issue has been addressed.

5. Dreger, "Footnote to a Footnote on Roving Medicine," http://www.thehastingscenter.org/Bioethicsforum/Post.aspx?id=2484. The Bo referred to in this quotation is Bo Laurent (formerly Cheryl Chase).

6. William Simon, *Postmodern Sexualities* (London: Routledge, 1996), 26.

7. Ibid.

8. Ibid., 27.

9. Antibiologism emerged in feminist theorizing in response to the way that biological determinism had historically been used (and in some quarters, continues to be used) to justify the subordination of women.

10. Sedgwick, et al., *Shame and Its Sisters: A Silvan Tomkins Reader.* (Durham, NC: Duke University Press, 1995), 15.

11. Since the late 1990s, a new body of work has emerged within feminist scholarship that engages with scientific material in exciting and productive ways (known as the new science studies or new materialism). This work does not take material from the biological sciences

merely as its object of analysis but rather as a source of concepts and methodologies. I offer this text as a small contribution to that field. See, for example, Anne Fausto-Sterling, "The Bare Bones of Sex: Part 1–Sex and Gender," *Signs: Journal of Women in Culture and Society* 30, no. 2 (2005): 1491–1527; Elizabeth Grosz, *The Nick of Time: Politics, Evolution and the Untimely* (Crows Nest, NSW: Allen & Unwin, 2004); Helen Keane and Marsha Rosengarten, "On the Biology of Sexed Subjects," *Australian Feminist Studies* 17, no. 39 (2002): 261–285; Margaret Lock, "Anomalous Ageing: Managing the Postmenopausal Body," *Body and Society* 4, no. 1 (1998): 35–61; Elspeth Probyn, *Blush: Faces of Shame* (Minneapolis: University of Minnesota Press, 2004); Elizabeth Wilson, *Neural Geographies: Feminism and the Microstructure of Cognition* (New York: Routledge, 1998); Wilson, "Gut Feminism," *Differences: A Journal of Feminist Cultural Studies* 15, no. 3 (2004): 66–94; Wilson, *Psychosomatic: Feminism and the Neurological Body* (Durham, NC: Duke University Press, 2004).

12. Janice Irvine, *Disorders of Desire: Sex and Gender in Modern American Sexology* (Philadelphia: Temple University Press, 1990), 11.

13. Gayle Rubin, "Thinking Sex: Notes for a Radical Theory of the Politics of Sexuality," *The Lesbian and Gay Studies Reader*, eds, Henry Abelove, Michele A. Barale, and David Halperin (New York: Routledge, 1984/1993), 3–44.

14. Robyn Weigman, "The Desire for Gender," in *A Companion to Lesbian, Gay, Bisexual, Transgender, and Queer Studies*, eds, George Haggerty and Molly McGarry (Oxford: Blackwell, 2007), 217–236. Weigman's piece is a meditation on the place gender has come to occupy within the realm of Queer, or more precisely the way that gender transitivity (particularly as made manifest through female masculinities) has come to stand *for* queer.

15. Robert Padgug, "Sexual Matters: On Conceptualizing Sexuality in History," in *Culture, Society and Sexuality: A Reader*, ed. Richard Parker and Peter Aggleton (London and Philadelphia: UCL Press, 1999), 21.

16. I use the qualifier "most" to acknowledge that not everybody's embodied gender easily or consistently aligns with their assigned sex.

17. John Money and Anke Ehrhardt, *Man and Woman, Boy and Girl: The Differentiation and Dimorphism of Gender Identity from Conception to Maturity* (Baltimore: Johns Hopkins University Press, 1972), 163.

18. This point should not be confused with a humanist perspective that privileges a rational, atomized, individualized male fantasy figure.

19. Sandra Bem uses the concept of "gender natives" to signify this process of learning (or ingesting) the requirements of gender. See Sandra Lipsetz Bem, *The Lenses of Gender: Transforming the Debate on Sexual Inequality* (New Haven, CT: Yale University Press, 1993).

20. Carl Elliot, "Why Can't We Go on as Three? (Intersexuality as a Third-Sex Category)," *Hastings Centre Report* 28, no. 3 (1998): 36–39; Fausto-Sterling, *Sexing The Body: Gender Politics and the Construction of Sexuality* (New York: Basic Books, 2000), 238–242, 370–371.

21. Annemiek Beverdam and Peter Koopman, "Expression Profiling of Purified Mouse Gonadal Somatic Cells During the Critical Time Window of Sex Determination Reveals Novel Candidate Genes for Human Sexual Dysgenesis Syndromes," *Human Molecular Genetics* 15, no. 3 (2006): 417–431; Koopman, "The Genetics and Biology of Vertebrate Sex Determination," *Cell* 105 (2001): 843–847; Vernon Rosario, "From Hermaphrodites to Sox9: The Molecular Deconstruction of Sex," Paper presented at the Presentations in the History of Medicine Series, Royal Australasian College of Physicians, Sydney, (August 1, 2005); Rosario, "This History of Aphallia and the Intersexual Challenge to Sex/Gender," in *A Companion to Lesbian, Gay, Bisexual, Transgender, and Queer Studies*, ed. George Haggerty and Molly McGarry (Oxford: Blackwell, 2007), 262–281; Eric Vilain, "Genetics of Sexual Development," *Annual Review of Sex Research* 11 (2000): 1–24.

22. Margaret Lock, "Anomalous Ageing: Managing the Postmenopausal Body," *Body and Society* 4, no. 1 (1998): 35–61.

23. Elliot, "Why Can't We?"

24. Clifford Geertz cited in Elliot, "Why Can't We," 37.

25. Roger Adkins, "Where 'Sex' Is Born(e): Intersexed Births and the Social Urgency of Heterosexuality," *Journal of Medical Humanities* 20, no. 2 (1999): 119.

26. Deborah Tolman and Lisa M. Diamond, "Desegregating Sexuality Research: Cultural and Biological Perspectives on Gender and Desire," *Annual Review of Sex Research* 12 (2001): 33–74.

27. Morgan Holmes, "Mind the Gaps: Intersex and (Re-Productive) Spaces in Disability Studies and Bioethics," *Bioethical Inquiry* 5, no. 2–3 (2008): 175.

28. Ibid.

29. Ibid.

30. Magnus Hirschfeld, *The Transvestites: The Erotic Drive to Cross Dress*, trans. Michael Lombardi-Nash (Buffalo, NY: Prometheus Books, 1910/1991). Today Hirschfeld is commonly credited with being an early proponent of a supplemental third-sex model (that is, an additional category that serves to bolster the privileged status of male and female and their hierarchical relation to one another). Yet as J. Edgar Bauer has demonstrated, Hirschfeld's third-sex model represents a politically expedient reworking of the original. It was designed to address the immediate needs of sexual minorities subject to Paragraph 175 of the German Imperial Code that outlawed sex between men (Bauer, "Gender and the Nemesis of Nature: On Magnus Hirschfeld's

Deconstruction of the Sexual Binary and the Concept of Sexual Human Rights," in *Two Is Not Enough for Gender (E)Quality*, ed. A. Hodzic and J. Postic [Zagreb: CESI and Zenska soba, 2006], 153–171). I am indebted to Bauer for his systematic study of the ways in which Hirshfeld's work operates to undermine the ideology of sexual difference to the order of two. See also Bauer, "Magnus Hirschfeld's Doctrine of Sexual Intermediaries and the Transgender Politics of (No-) Identity" (paper presented at the *Past and Present of Radical Sexual Politics* conference, Amsterdam, Holland, October 1–4, 2007).

31. Hirschfeld, *The Transvestites*, 225.

32. Ibid., 231.

33. Bauer, "Gender and the Nemesis"; Bauer, "Magnus Hirschfeld's Doctrine."

34. Hirschfeld, *The Transvestites*, 227.

35. This seemed to be the most difficult element of Hirschfeld's concept for his peers to actually grasp. In the other frameworks in circulation at the time, third sexes represented entities in their own right but only so far as they performed a supplemental function to the other two sexes. Hirschfeld was motivated to comment on the misreadings of his concepts after encountering the expression "intermediaries theory" referenced to his name on three occasions in then-recent sexological texts. "They did not fully understand my concept," he lamented, "and I was inspired to write this all-inclusive description" (*The Transvestites*, 228).

36. Ibid.

37. Ibid.

38. In this sense Hirschfeld's concepts can be said to have foreshadowed the aspirations of the project of queer (as proliferation) by the best part of a century.

39. One of the examples Hirschfeld offered to illustrate this point was to take hair distribution and further subdivide it: head hair, facial hair, and body hair.

40. Hirschfeld, *The Transvestites*, 226, emphasis added.

41. With the exception of chromosomes, Hirschfeld had accounted for each of these elements at some level in his work.

BIBLIOGRAPHY

Aartsen, E., R. Snethlage, A. Van Geel, and M. Gallee. "Squamous Cell Carcinoma of the Vagina in a Male Pseudohermaphrodite with 5alpha-Reductase Deficiency," *International Journal of Gynecological Cancer* 4, no. 4 (1994): 283–287.

Abelove, H. "Some Speculations on the History of 'Sexual Intercourse' During the 'Long Eighteenth Century' in England." In *Nationalisms and Sexualities*, edited by A. Parker, M. Russo, D. Sommer, and P. Yaeger, 335–342. New York: Routledge, 1992.

Abelove, H. "Freud, Male Homosexuality, and the Americans." In *The Lesbian and Gay Studies Reader*, edited by H. Abelove, M. A. Barale, and D. Halperin, 381–393. New York: Routledge, 1993.

Acton, William. *The Functions and Disorders of the Reproductive Organs in Childhood, Youth, Adult Age, and Advanced Age, Considered in Their Physiological, Social, and Moral Relations.* Philadelphia: Presley Blakiston, 1875.

Adams, J. M., T. M. Adams, K. A. Dunn, and S. M. O'Hara. "An Uncommon Finding: Ovotestes in a True Hermaphrodite." *Journal of Diagnostic Medical Sonography* 19, no. 1 (2003): 51–54.

Adkins, Roger. "Where 'Sex' Is Born(e): Intersexed Births and the Social Urgency of Heterosexuality." *Journal of Medical Humanities* 20, no. 2 (1999): 117–133.

Aggrawal, Anil. *Forensic and Medico-Legal Aspects of Sex Crimes and Unusual Sexual Practices.* Boca Raton, FL: CRC Press, 2009.

Al-Attia, Haider M. "Gender Identity and Role in a Pedigree of Arabs with Intersex Due to 5 Alpha Reductase-2 Deficiency." *Psychoneuroendocrinology* 21, no. 8 (1996): 651–657.

Alderson, Julie, Anna Madill, and Adam Balen. "Fear of Devaluation: Understanding the Experience of Intersexed Women with Androgen Insensitivity Syndrome." *British Journal of Health Psychology* 9, no. 1 (2004): 81–100.

Alexander, Tamara. "The Medical Management of Intersexed Children: An Analogue for Childhood Sexual Abuse." (1997), http://www.isna.org/articles/analog.

ALGLG. *Outlaw: A Legal Guide for Lesbians and Gay Men in New Zealand.* Auckland: Auckland Lesbian and Gay Lawyers Group Inc, 1994.

Alsop, R., A. Fitzsimons, and K. Lennon. *Theorizing Gender.* Cambridge: Polity, 2002.

Andermahr, Sonya, Carol Wolkowitz, and Terry Lovell. *A Glossary of Feminist Theory*. London: Arnold, 1997.

Angelides, Steven. *A History of Bisexuality*. Chicago: University of Chicago Press, 2001.

Angier, Natalie. *Woman: An Intimate Geography*. London: Virago Press, 1999.

Anonymous. "Book Review. Early Modern Hermaphrodites: Sex and Other Stories." *Contemporary Review* 281, no. 1640 (2002): 191.

Anonymous. "A Mother's Story." AISSG Australia, http://home.vicnet. net.au/~aissg/a_mother's_story.htm.

Archer, John, and Barbara Lloyd. *Sex and Gender*. Cambridge: Cambridge University Press, 1982.

Aronson, Josh. *Sound and Fury*. Loganholme, Qld.: Marcom Projects, 2000.

Assorted Letters. (2006), http://adc.bmj.com/cgi/eletters/91/7/554.

Atkins, Dawn, ed. *Looking Queer: Body Image and Identity in Lesbian, Bisexual, Gay and Transgender Communities*. New York: Harrington Park Press, 1998.

"Attorney General's Commission on Pornography. Final Report." Washington, DC: U. S. Department of Justice, 1986.

Ault, Amber. "Ambiguous Identity in an Unambiguous Sex/Gender Structure: The Case of Bisexual Women." *Sociological Quarterly* 37, no. 3 (1996): 449–463.

Bagemihl, Bruce. *Biological Exuberance: Animal Homosexuality and Natural Diversity*. New York: St. Martin's, 1999.

Bailey, M. "Foucauldian Feminism Contesting Bodies, Sexuality and Identity." In *Up against Foucault*, edited by C. Ramazanoglu. 99–122. London: Routledge, 1993.

Bancroft, John. *Deviant Sexual Behaviour: Modification and Assessment*. Oxford: Clarendon Press, 1974.

Bannister, Robert C. *Jessie Bernard: The Making of a Feminist*. New Brunswick, NJ: Rutgers University Press, 1991.

Batanian, J. R., D. K. Grange, R. Fleming, B. Gadre, and J. Wetzel. "Two Unbalanced Translocations Involving a Common 6p25 Region in Two XY Female Patients." *Clinical Genetics* 59, no. 1 (2001): 52–57.

Bateson, Patrick, and Paul Martin. *Design for a Life: How Behaviour Develops*. London: Vintage, 2000.

Bauer, J. Edgar. "On the Nameless Love and Infinite Sexualities: John Henry Mackay, Magnus Hirschfeld and the Origins of the Sexual Emancipation Movement." *Journal of Homosexuality* 50, no. 1 (2005): 1–26.

Bauer, J. Edgar. "Gender and the Nemesis of Nature: On Magnus Hirschfeld's Deconstruction of the Sexual Binary and the Concept of Sexual Human Rights." In *Two Is Not Enough for Gender (E)Quality*, edited by A. Hodzic and J. Postic, 153–171. Zagreb: CESI and Zenska soba, 2006.

Bauer, J. Edgar. "Magnus Hirschfeld: Panhumanism and the Sexual Cultures of Asia." *Intersections: Gender History and Culture in the Asian Context*, no. 14 (2006), http://intersections.anu.edu.au/issue14/bauer.htmi#t96.

Bauer, J. Edgar. "Magnus Hirschfeld's Doctrine of Sexual Intermediaries and the Transgender Politics of (No-) Identity." Paper presented at the *Past and Present of Radical Sexual Politics Conference*. Amsterdam, 2007.

Bayertz, Kurt, and Roy Porter, eds. *From Physico-Theology to Bio-Technology: Essays in the Social and Cultural History of Biosciences: A Festschrift for Mikulas Teich.* The Wellcome Institute Series in the History of Medicine. Amsterdam and Atlanta: Rodopi, 1998.

Baynes, Sylvia. "Trans-Sex or Cross-Gender? A Critique of Janice Raymond's *The Transsexual Empire.*" *Women's Studies Journal* 7–8 (1991): 53–65.

Beach, Frank. "Alternative Interpretations of the Development of G-I/R." In *Masculinity/Femininity: Basic Perspectives*, edited by June Reinisch, Leonard Rosenblum, and Stephanie Sanders, 29–34. New York: Oxford University Press, 1987.

Beardsley, Elizabeth Lane. "Referential Genderization." *Philosophical Forum* 5 (1973): 285–293.

Becker, Howard. *Tricks of the Trade: How to Think About Your Research While You're Doing It.* Chicago: University of Chicago Press, 1998.

Bedell, Madelon. "Supermom!" In *Sex Equality*, edited by Jane English, 239–247. Englewood Cliffs, NJ: Prentice-Hall, 1977.

Beiber, Irving. *Homosexuality: A Psychoanalytic Study.* New York: Basic Books, 1962.

Bejin, A. "Sexual Behavior: Sociological Perspectives." *International Encyclopedia of the Social & Behavioral Sciences*, edited by Neil Smelser and Paul Baites, 13977–13981. Amsterdam: Elsevier, 2004.

Bellinger, M. "Subtotal De-Epithelialization and Partial Concealment of the Glans Clitoris: A Modification to Improve the Cosmetic Results of Feminising Genitoplasty." *Journal of Urology* 150 (1993): 651–653.

Bem, Sandra Lipsetz. "The Theory and Measurement of Androgyny." *Journal of Personality and Social Psychology* 37 (1971): 1047–1054.

Bem, Sandra Lipsetz. "Gender Schema Theory: A Cognitive Account of Sex Typing." *Psychological Review* 88, no. 4 (1981): 354–364.

Bem, Sandra Lipsetz. "Masculinity and Femininity Exist Only in the Mind of the Perceiver." In *Masculinity/Femininity: Basic Perspectives*, edited by June Reinisch, Leonard Rosenblum, and Stephanie Sanders, 304–311. New York: Oxford University Press, 1987.

Bem, Sandra Lipsetz. *The Lenses of Gender: Transforming the Debate on Sexual Inequality.* New Haven, CT: Yale University Press, 1993.

Bem, Sandra Lipsetz. "Dismantling Gender Polarization and Compulsory Heterosexuality: Should We Turn the Volume Down or Up?" *Journal of Sex Research* 32, no. 4 (1995): 329–334.

Benjamin, Harold. "The Transsexual Phenomenon." IJT Electronic Books. Symposium Publishing, http://www.symposion.com/ijt/benjamin/chap_01.htm.

Benjamin, Harold. *The Transsexual Phenomenon.* New York: Warner Books, 1966.

Berger, Peter L., and Thomas Luckmann. *The Social Construction of Reality: A Treatise in the Sociology of Knowledge*. London: Allen Lane, 1967.

Bergler, Edmund. *Counterfeit Sex: Homosexuality, Impotence, Frigidity*. New York: Grune and Stratton, 1951.

Bergler, Edmund. *Homosexuality: Disease or a Way of Life?* New York: Hill and Wang, 1956.

Bergler, Edmund, and William S. Kroger. *Kinsey's Myth of Female Sexuality: The Medical Facts*. New York: Grune and Stratton, 1954.

Bernard, Jessie Shirley. *Women and the Public Interest: An Essay on Policy and Protest*, Aldine Treatises in Social Psychology. Chicago: Aldine-Atherton, 1971.

Bershady, H. J. *Ideology and Social Knowledge*. Oxford: Basil Blackwell, 1973.

Best, Shaun. *Understanding Social Divisions*. London: Sage, 2005.

Beverdam, Annemiek, and Peter Koopman. "Expression Profiling of Purified Mouse Gonadal Somatic Cells During the Critical Time Window of Sex Determination Reveals Novel Candidate Genes for Human Sexual Dysgenesis Syndromes." *Human Molecular Genetics* 15, no. 3 (2006): 417–431.

Biddulph, Steve. *Raising Boys: Why Boys Are Different—and How to Help Them Become Happy and Well-Balanced Men*. Berkeley: Ten Speed Press, 1998.

Blackless, Melanie, Anthony Charuvastra, and Amanda Derryck. "How Sexually Dimorphic Are We? Review and Synthesis." *American Journal of Human Biology* [H. W. Wilson—GS] 12, no. 2 (2000): 151.

Bland, Lucy, and Laura Doan, eds. *Sexology in Culture: Labelling Bodies and Desires*. Cambridge: Polity, 1998.

Bleys, Rudi. *The Geography of Perversion: Male-to-Male Sexual Behaviour Outside the West and the Ethnographic Imagination 1750–1918*. New York: New York University Press, 1995.

Blizzard, R. M. "Intersex Issues: A Series of Continuing Conundrums." *Pediatrics* 110, no. 3 (2002): 616–621.

Bockting, Walter. "Ken from Mars, Barbie from Venus: What on Earth Has Happened with Sex?" *Journal of Sex Research* 34, no. 4 (1997): 411–422.

Bodeker, Heike. "Portrait of the Artist as a Young Herm." http://www.qis.net/~triea/hieke.html.

Bordo, Susan. *Unbearable Weight: Feminism, Western Culture, and the Body*. Berkeley: University of California Press, 1993.

Bornstein, Kate. *Gender Outlaw: On Men, Women and the Rest of Us*. London: Routledge, 1994.

Boukari, Kahine, Maria Luisa Ciampi, Anne Guiochon-Mantel, Jacques Young, Marc Lombes, and Geri Meduri. "Human Fetal Testis: Source of Estrogen and Target of Estrogen Action." *Human Reproduction* 22, no. 7 (2007): 1885–1892.

Bornstein, Kate. *My Gender Workbook: How to Become a Real Man, a Real Woman, the Real You, or Something Else Entirely*. New York: Routledge, 1998.

Bradley, S. J., G. D. Oliver, A. B. Chernick, and K. J. Zucker. "Experiment of Nurture: Ablatio Penis at 2 Months, Sex Reassignment at 7 Months, and a Psychosexual Follow-up in Young Adulthood." *Pediatrics* [NLM—MEDLINE] 102, no. 1 (1998): e9.

Braidotti, Rosie. *Nomadic Subjects: Embodiment and Sexual Difference in Contemporary Feminist Theory*. New York: Columbia University Press, 1994.

Braidotti, Rosie. "Signs of Wonder and Traces of Doubt: On Teratology and Embodied Differences." In *Between Monsters, Goddesses and Cyborgs: Feminist Confrontations with Science, Medicine and Cyberspace*, edited by Nina Lykke and Rosie Braidotti, 135–152. London: Zed Books, 1996.

Brandeis_University. "Women's Studies Research Center Scholars Program—Rhoda Unger." Brandeis University, http://www.brandeis.edu/centers/wsrc/scholars/Scholars/R_Unger.html.

Braun, Virginia. "In Search of (Better) Sexual Pleasure: Female Genital 'Cosmetic' Surgery." *Sexualities* 8 (2005): 407–424.

Bray, Alan. *Homosexuality in Renaissance England*. London: Gay Man's Press, 1988.

Bray, Abigail, and Claire Colebrook. "The Haunted Flesh: Corporeal Feminism and the Politics of (Dis)Embodiment." *Signs: Journal of Women in Culture and Society* 24, no. 1 (1998): 35–67.

Briffa, Tony, Geoffrey Blundell, and Lisa Stephens. "Beyond He, She, and It." *New Scientist* [H. W. Wilson—GS] 170, no. 2293 (2001): 54.

Bristow, Joseph. *Sexuality*. London: Routledge, 1997.

Bristow, Joseph. "Symonds's History, Ellis's Heredity: Sexual Inversion." In *Sexology in Culture: Labelling Bodies and Desires*, edited by Lucy Bland and Laura Doan, 79–99. Cambridge: Polity, 1998.

Brown, Lee Anderson. "Sites of Gen(D)Eration." www.angelfire.com/realm2/isnetwork.

Brown, Lee Anderson. "Fractured Masks—Voices from the Shards of Language." *Polare* 61 (2005): 12–15.

Brown, Tara. "He's the Man." *Sixty Minutes*. Produced by L. Howse and C. Talberg, Channel Nine Network, Australia, Sunday September 4, 2005.

Brown, T. M. "Descartes, Dualism, and Psychosomatic Medicine." In *The Anatomy of Madness, Essays in the History of Psychiatry*, edited by W. F. Bynum, R. Porter, and M. Shepherd, 40–62. London and New York: Tavistock, 1985.

Bullough, Vernon. *Sexual Variance in Society and History*. Chicago and London: University of Chicago Press, 1976.

Bullough, Vernon. *Science in the Bedroom: A History of Sex Research*. New York: Basic Books, 1994.

Bullough, Vernon. "Introduction." In *The Homosexuality of Men and Women, Magnus Hirschfeld*, translated by Michael Lombardi-Nash. 11–17. New York: Prometheus Books, 2000.

Bullough, Vernon. "The Contributions of John Money: A Personal View." *Journal of Sex Research* 40, no. 3 (2003): 230–236.

Burke, Phyllis. *Gender Shock: Exploding the Myths of Male and Female.* New York: Anchor Books, 1996.

Burkitt, Ian. "Sexuality and Gender Identity: From a Discursive to a Relational Analysis." *Sociological Review* 46, no. 3 (1998): 483–504.

Butler, Judith. "Gendering the Body: Beauvoir's Philosophical Contribution." In *Women, Knowledge, and Reality: Explorations in Feminist Philosophy*, edited by A. Garry and M. Pearsall. New York: Routledge, 1989.

Butler, Judith. *Gender Trouble: Feminism and the Subversion of Identity.* New York: Routledge, 1990.

Butler, Judith. *Bodies That Matter: On the Discursive Limits Of "Sex".* New York: Routledge, 1993.

Butler, Judith. "Imitation and Gender Subordination." In *The Second Wave: A Reader in Feminist Theory*, edited by Linda Nicholson, 300–315. New York: Routledge, 1997.

Butler, Judith. "Sex and Gender in Simone De Beauvoir's Second Sex." In *Simone De Beauvoir: A Critical Reader*, edited by Elizabeth Fallaize, 29–42. London: Routledge, 1998.

Butler, Judith. *Undoing Gender.* New York: Routledge, 2004.

Cadden, Joan. *Meanings of Sex Difference in the Middle Ages: Medicine, Science, and Culture*, Cambridge History of Medicine. Cambridge and New York: Cambridge University Press, 1993.

Callon, Michael, and Bruno Latour. "Unscrewing the Big Leviathan: How Actors Macro-Structure Reality and Sociologists Help Them to Do So." In *Advances in Social Theory and Methodology: Toward an Integration of Micro and Macro Sociologies*, edited by K. Knorr-Cetina and A. Cicourel, 277–303. London: Routledge, 1981.

Cameron, Deborah, and Don Kulick. "Introduction: Language and Desire in Theory and Practice." *Language & Communication* 23, no. 2 (2003): 93–105.

Canguilhem, Georges. *On the Normal and the Pathological*, translated by Carolyn Fawcett. Dordrecht: Reidel Publishing, 1978.

Carpenter, Edward. *The Intermediate Sex: A Study of Some Transitional Types of Men and Women.* 5th ed. Manchester: Shadwell and Son, 1918.

Carter, Julian. "Normality, Whiteness, Authorship: Evolutionary Sexology and the Primitive Pervert." In *Science and Homosexualities*, edited by Vernon Rosario, 155–176. London and New York: Routledge, 1995.

"Census to Recognise Intersex Australians." Fairfax Digital, http://www.theage.com.au/news/national/census-to-recognise-intersex-australians/2006/03/01/1141095787949.html.

Chafetz, Mary Saltzman. *Masculine/Feminine or Human? An Overview of the Sociology of Sex Roles.* 1st ed. Itasca, IL: F. E. Peacock, 1974.

Chafetz, Mary Saltzman. *Masculine/Feminine or Human? An Overview of the Sociology of Sex Roles.* 2nd ed. Itasca, IL: F. E. Peacock, 1978.

Chase, Cheryl. *Hermaphrodites Speak!* San Francisco: Intersex Society of North America, 1997.

Chase, Cheryl. "Affronting Reason." In *Looking Queer: Body Image and Identity in Lesbian, Bisexual, Gay and Transgender Communities*, edited by Dawn Atkins, 205–219. New York: Haworth Press, 1998.

Chase, Cheryl. "Intersex Children: Comment on F. M. E. Slijper et al." *Archives of Sexual Behavior* 28, no. 1 (1999): 103.

Chau, P. L., and Jonathan Herring. "Defining, Assigning and Designing Sex." *International Journal of Law, Policy and the Family* 16, no. 3 (2002): 327–367.

Chodorow, Nancy. "Being and Doing: A Cross-Cultural Examination of the Socialization of Males and Females." In *Woman in Sexist Society: Studies in Power and Powerlessness*, edited by Vivian Gornick and Barbara K. Moran, 173–197. New York/London: Basic Books, 1971.

Chodorow, Nancy. "Family Structure and Feminine Personality." In *Woman, Culture, and Society*, edited by Michelle Zimbalist Rosaldo, Louise Lamphere, and Joan Bamberger, 43–66. Stanford, CA.: Stanford University Press, 1974.

Chodorow, Nancy. *The Reproduction of Mothering: Psychoanalysis and the Sociology of Gender*. Berkeley: University of California Press, 1978.

Chodorow, Nancy. "Feminism and Difference: Gender, Relation, and Difference in Psychoanalytic Perspective." *Socialist Review* 46 (1979): 42–69.

Chodorow, Nancy. "Feminism and Difference: Gender, Relation, and Difference in Psychoanalytic Perspective." In *The Gender and Psychology Reader*, edited by Blyth McVicker Clinchy and Julie Norem, 383–395. New York: New York University Press, 1998.

Clark, J. Michael. "The 'Third Gender': Implications for Men's Studies and Eco-Theology." *Journal of Men's Studies* 2, no. 3 (1994): 239.

Clausen, Jan. *Beyond Gay or Straight: Understanding Sexual Orientation*. Philadelphia: Chelsea House, 1996.

Cohen, Janine. "The Gender Puzzle." In *Four Corners*. Australian Broadcasting Corporation, 2005.

Colapinto, John. *As Nature Made Him: The Boy Who Was Raised as a Girl*. Sydney: Harper Collins, 2000.

Coleman, Eli, and John Money. *John Money: A Tribute*. New York: Haworth Press, 1991.

Collins, Patricia Hill. *Black Feminist Thought: Knowledge, Consciousness, and the Politics of Empowerment*. New York/London: Routledge, 2001.

Condorcet, A. *Sketch for a Historical Picture of the Progress of the Human Mind*. London: Weidenfeld and Nicholson, 1955.

Conrad, P., and J. W. Schneider. *Deviance and Medicalisation, from Badness to Sickness*. St. Louis: C. V. Mosby, 1980.

Consortium on the Management of Disorders of Sex Development. *Handbook for Parents*. Rohnert Park, CA: Intersex Society of North America, 2006.

Consortium on the Management of Disorders of Sex Development. *Clinical Guidelines for the Management of Disorders of Development in Childhood*. Rohnert Park, CA: Intersex Society of North America, 2006.

Cook, E. P. "Androgyny." In *The International Encyclopedia of the Social & Behavioral Sciences*, edited by Neil Smelser and Paul Baites, 496–500. Amsterdam: Elsevier, 2004.

Crasnow, Sharon. "Models and Reality: When Science Tackles Sex." *Hypatia* 16, no. 3 (2001): 138–148.

Crawford, M. "A Reappraisal of Gender: An Ethnomethodological Approach." *Feminism and Psychology* 10, no. 1 (2000): 7–10.

Creighton, Sarah. "Surgery for Intersex." *Journal of the Royal Society of Medicine* 94, no. 5 (2001): 218–220.

Creighton, Sarah. "Long-Term Outcome of Feminization Surgery: The London Experience." *British Journal of Urology International* 93, Supplement 3 (2004): 44–46.

Creighton, Sarah, and Catherine Minto. "Managing Intersex: Most Vaginal Surgery Should Be Deferred." *British Medical Journal*, 323, no. 7324 (2001): 1264–1265.

Creighton, Sarah, Catherine Minto, Lih Mei Liao, Julie Alderson, and Margaret Simmonds. "Meeting between Experts: Evaluation of the First Uk Forum for Lay and Professional Experts in Intersex." *Patient Education & Counseling* 54, no. 2 (2004): 153–157.

Creighton, Sarah, Catherine Minto, and Stuart Steele. "Objective Cosmetic and Anatomical Outcomes at Adolescence for Ambiguous Genitalia Done in Childhood." *Lancet*, no. 358 (2001): 124–125.

Curthoys, Ann, ed. *Gender in the Social Sciences in Australia*. Canberra: Australian Publishing Service, 1998.

Curthoys, Ann. "Gender Studies in Australia: A History." *Australian Feminist Studies* 15, no. 31 (2000): 19–38.

D'Emilio, J. "Capitalism and Gay Identity." In *The Gender Sexuality Reader*, edited by R. Lancaster and M. di Leonardo, 169–178. London: Routledge, 1997.

Daaboul, J., and Joel Frader. "Ethics and the Management of the Patient with Intersex." *Journal of Pediatric Endocrinology & Metabolism* 14, no. 9 (2001): 1575–1583.

Daniels, Arlene Kaplan. "Feminist Perspectives in Sociological Research." In *Another Voice*, edited by Marcia Millman and Rosabeth Moss Kanter, 340–380. New York: Anchor Press, 1975.

Darnovsky, M., B. Epstein, R. Flacks, eds. *Cultural Politics and Social Movements*. Philadelphia: Temple University Press, 1995.

Darwin, C. *The Origin of the Species by Means of Natural Selection*. London: Murray, 1897.

Darwin, Erasmus. *The Temple of Nature*. London: J. Johnson, 1803.

David. "I Am Not Alone!" *Hermaphrodites with Attitudes* 1, no. 1 (1994): 4–5.

Davis, Angela. *Women, Race, & Class*. 1st ed. New York: Random House, 1981.

de Beauvoir, Simone. *The Second Sex*, translated by H. M. Parshley. Middlesex: Penguin Books, 1972.

de Lauretis, Teresa. *Technologies of Gender: Essays on Theory, Film, and Fiction.* Bloomington: Indiana University Press, 1987.

Deaux, Kay. "Psychological Constructions of Masculinity and Femininity." In *Masculinity/Femininity: Basic Perspectives,* edited by June Reinisch, Leonard Rosenblum, and Stephanie Sanders, 289–303. New York: Oxford University Press, 1987.

DeCecco, J., and M. Shively. "From Sexual Identity to Sexual Relationships: A Contextual Shift." *Journal of Homosexuality* 9, no. 2/3 (1983): 1–26.

Dekker, Diana. "Intersexuals Demand Sole Choice on Deciding Gender." *Waikato Times,* June 23 1997: 1997, 7.

Denny, Dallas. "Sex Certainly Did Change!" *Journal of Sex Research* 40, no. 3 (2003): 316–317.

Devor, Holly. *Gender Blending: Confronting the Limits of Duality.* Bloomington and Indianapolis: Indiana Unversity Press, 1989.

Devor, Holly. *Ftm: Female-to-Male Transsexuals in Society.* Bloomington: Indiana University Press, 1997.

Devor, Holly. "Hermaphrodites and the Medical Invention of Sex." *Journal of Sex Research* 36, no. 4 (1999): 411.

Dewhurst, C., and R. Gordon. *The Intersexual Disorders.* London: Balliere, Tindall and Cassell, 1969.

Dewing, Phoebe, Tao Shi, Steve Horvath, and Eric Vilain. "Sexually Dimorphic Gene Expression in Mouse Brain Precedes Gonadal Differentiation." *Molecular Brain Research* 118, no. 1–2 (2003): 82–90.

di Leonardo, Micaela. "Margaret Mead Vs. Tony Soprano." *The Nation,* http://www.thenation.com/doc.mhtml?i=20010521&s=dileonardo.

Diamond, Michael. "The Shaping of Masculinity: Revisioning Boys Turning Away from Their Mothers to Construct Male Gender Identity." *International Journal of Psychoanalysis* 85, no. 2 (2004): 359–379.

Diamond, Morty. *From the Inside Out: Radical Gender Transformation, FTM and Beyond.* San Francisco: Manic D Press, 2004.

Diamond, Milton, and Keith Sigmundsen. "Management of Intersexuality: Guidelines for Dealing with Persons with Ambiguous Genitalia." *Archives of Pediatrics and Adolescent Medicine* 15, no.10 (1997): 1046–1050.

Diamond, Milton, and Keith Sigmundson. "Sex Reassignment at Birth: Long-Term Review and Clinical Implications." *Archives of Pediatrics and Adolescent Medicine* 151, no.3 (1997): 298–304.

Dickinson, Barry D., Myron Genel, and Carolyn B. Robinowitz. "Gender Verification of Female Olympic Athletes." *Medicine and Science in Sports and Exercise* [H. W. Wilson—GS] 34, no. 10 (2002): 1539.

Dinnerstein, Dorothy. *The Mermaid and the Minotaur: Sexual Arrangements and Human Malaise.* 1st ed. New York: Harper & Row, 1976.

Diprose, R. *The Bodies of Women: Ethics, Embodiment and Sexual Difference.* London: Routledge, 1994.

Diprose, R., and R. Farrell, eds. *Cartographies: Postructuralism and the Mapping of Bodies and Spaces.* Sydney: Allen and Unwin, 1991.

Dorland's Medical Dictionary. W. B. Saunders, http://www.merckmedicus. com/pp/us/hcp/thcp_dorlands_content.jsp?pg=/ppdocs/us/common/ dorlands/dorland/dmd-c-027.htm#951550.

Douglas, Mary. *Natural Symbols.* Middlesex: Penguin, 1970.

Downing, Lisa. "The Measure of 'Sexual Dysfunction': A Plea for Theoretical Limitlessness." *Transformations: Online Journal of Region, Culture and Society* (2004): 8. http://transformations.cqu.edu.au/journal/issue_08/article_02.shtml.

Dreger, Alice Domurat. "Doubtful Sex: The Fate of the Hermaphrodite in Victorian Medicine." *Victorian Studies* 38, no. 3 (1995): 335–370.

Dreger, Alice Domurat. "Hermaphrodites in Love: The Truth of the Gonads." In *Science and Homosexualities*, edited by V. A. Rosario, 46–66. New York: Routledge, 1997a.

Dreger, Alice Domurat. "Ethical Problems in Intersex Treatment." *Medical Humanities Report* 19, no. 1 (1997).

Dreger, Alice Domurat. "When Medicine Goes Too Far in the Pursuit of Normality." *New York Times*, July 28 1998, 4.

Dreger, Alice Domurat. "'Ambiguous Sex'—or Ambivalent Medicine?" *Hastings Center Report* 28, no. 3 (1998): 24–35.

Dreger, Alice Domurat. *Hermaphrodites and the Medical Invention of Sex.* Cambridge: Harvard University Press, 1998.

Dreger, Alice Domurat, ed. *Intersex in the Age of Ethics.* Hagerstown, MD: University Publishing Group, 2000.

Dreger, Alice Domurat. "Top Ten Myths About Intersex." *ISNA News* (2001): 3–5.

Dreger, Alice Domurat. "Why 'Disorders of Sex Development'? (on Language and Life)." http://www.alicedreger.com/dsd.html.

Dreger, Alice Domurat. "Footnote to a Footnote on Roving Medicine." *Bioethics Forum: Diverse Commentary on Issues in Bioethics*, October 10, 2008. http://www.thehastingscenter.org/Bioethicsforum/ Post.aspx?id=2484&terms=dreger+and+%23filename+*.html.

Dreger, Alice Domurat. "Shifting the Paradigm of Intersex Treatment." ISNA, www.isna.org/compare.

Dreger, Alice Domurat, Cheryl Chase, Aaron Sousa, Philip A. Gruppuso, and Joel Frader. "Changing the Nomenclature/Taxonomy for Intersex: A Scientific and Clinical Rationale." *Journal of Pediatric Endocrinology and Metabolism* 18, no. 8 (2005): 729–733.

Dreifus, Claudia. "Exploring What Makes Us Male or Female." *New York Times*, January 2 2001, F3.

Dreyfus, Hubert, and Paul Rabinow. *Michel Foucault: Beyond Structuralism and Hermeneutics.* 2nd ed. Chicago: University of Chicago Press, 1983.

Duberman, Lucile. *Gender and Sex in Society.* New York: Praeger, 1975.

Dunn, Robert G. "Self, Identity, and Difference: Mead and the Poststructuralists." *Sociological Quarterly* 38, no. 4 (1997): 687–705.

Eadie, Jo. "Activating Bisexuality: Towards a Bi/Sexual Politics." In *Activating Theory: Lesbian, Gay, Bisexual Politics*, edited by Joseph Bristow and Angelia R. Wilson, 139–170. London: Lawrence & Wishart, 1993.

Edwards, Anne. "Discussion. The Sex/Gender Distinction: Has It Outlived Its Usefulness?" *Australian Feminist Studies* 10, no. Summer (1989): 1–12.

Ehrhardt, Anke. "Sexual Orientation after Prenatal Exposure to Exogenous Estrogen." *Archives of Sexual Behaviour* 14 (1985): 57–77.

Anke Ehrhardt, "John Money, Ph.D. (Biography)." *The Journal of Sex Research* 44, no. 3 (2007): 223–224.

Elam, Diane, and Robyn Wiegman, eds. *Feminism Beside Itself.* New York: Routledge, 1995.

Elliot, Carl. "Why Can't We Go on as Three? (Intersexuality as a Third-Sex Category)." *Hastings Center Report* 28, no. 3 (1998): 36–39.

Ellis, Albert. "The Sexual Psychology of Human Hermaphrodites." *Psychosomatic Medicine* 7 (1945): 108–125.

Ellis, Albert. *Sex Beliefs and Customs.* London: Nerill, 1952.

Ellis, Albert, and Albert Abarbanel, eds. *The Encyclopedia of Sexual Behavior.* New York: Hawthorn Books, 1961.

Ellis, Havelock. *The Psychology of Sex: A Manual for Students.* London: William Heineman, 1933.

English, Jane. *Sex Equality.* Englewood Cliffs, NJ: Prentice-Hall, 1977.

Epstein, Barbara. "Political Correctness and Collective Powerlessness." In *Cultural Politics and Social Movements,* edited by M. Darnovsky, B. Epstein, and R. Flacks, 3–19. Philadelphia: Temple University Press, 1995.

Epstein, Julia. "Either/or—Neither/Both: Sexual Ambiguity and the Ideology of Gender." *Genders* 7 (1990): 99–142.

Epstein, Julia. *Altered Conditions: Disease, Medicine and Storytelling.* New York: Routledge, 1995.

Escoffier, J. "Community and Academic Intellectuals: The Contest for Cultural Authority in Identity Politics." In *Cultural Politics and Social Movements,* edited by M. Darnovsky, B. Epstein, and R. Flacks, 20–34. Philadelphia: Temple University Press, 1995.

Esterberg, Kristin. "The Bisexual Menace Revisited: Or, Shaking up Social Categories Is Hard to Do." In *Introducing the New Sexuality Studies: Original Essays and Interviews,* edited by Steven Seidman, Nancy Fischer, and Chet Meeks, 157–163. London: Routledge, 2007.

Fancher, Raymond E. "Terman and His Works." *Science* 244, no. 4912 (1989): 1596–1597.

Fausto-Sterling, Anne. *Myths of Gender: Biological Theories About Women and Men.* New York: Basic Books, 1985.

Fausto-Sterling, Anne. "Life in the Xy Corral." *Womens Studies International Forum* 12, no. 3 (1989): 319–331.

Fausto-Sterling, Anne. "The Five Sexes: Why Male and Female Are Not Enough." *The Sciences,* no. March/April (1993): 20–25.

Fausto-Sterling, Anne. "How to Build a Man." In *The Gender Sexuality Reader: Culture, History, Political Economy,* edited by R. N. Lancaster and M. di Leonardo, 244–248. New York: Routledge, 1997.

Fausto-Sterling, Anne. *Sexing the Body: Gender Politics and the Construction of Sexuality*. New York: Basic Books, 2000.

Fausto-Sterling, Anne. "The Five Sexes, Revisited." *The Sciences* 40, no. 4 (2000): 18.

Fausto-Sterling, Anne. "How Sexually Dimorphic Are We? Review and Synthesis." *American Journal of Human Biology* [H. W. Wilson—GS] 12 (2000): 151–166.

Fausto-Sterling, Anne. "The Bare Bones of Sex: Part 1—Sex and Gender." *Signs: Journal of Women in Culture and Society* 30, no. 2 (2005): 1491–1527.

Feinberg, Lesley. *Transgender Warriors: Making History from Joan of Arc to Dennis Rodman*. Boston: Beacon Press, (1996).

"The Feminist Chronicles." The Feminist Majority Foundation, http://www.feminist.org/research/chronicles/fc1974.html.

Fernandez-Cancio, M., M. Nistal, R. Gracia, M. Molina, J. Tovar, C. Esteban, A. Carrascosa, and L. Audi. "Compound Heterozygous Mutations in the Srd5a2 Gene Exon 4 in a Male Pseudohermaphrodite Patient of Chinese Origin." *Journal of Andrology* 25, no. 3 (2004): 412–416.

Findlay, Deborah. "Discovering Sex: Medical Science, Feminism and Intersexuality." *Canadian Review of Sociology and Anthropology* 32, no. 1 (1995): 25.

Fine, Gary A. "Public Narration and Group Culture: Discerning Discourse in Social Movements." In *Social Movements and Culture*, edited by Hank Johnstone and Bert Klandermans, 127–143. Minneapolis: University of Minnesota Press, 1995.

Firestone, Shulamith. *The Dialectic of Sex: The Case for Feminist Revolution*. New York: Morrow, 1970.

Flack, C., M. A. Barraza, and P. S. Stevens. "Vaginoplasty: Combination Therapy Using Labia Minora Flaps and Lucite Dilators – Preliminary Report." *Journal of Urology* 150 (1993): 654–656.

Ford, Clellan S., and Frank Beach. *Patterns of Sexual Behaviour*. New York: Harper, 1951.

Foucault, Michel. *Mental Illness and Psychology*. Berkeley: University of California, 1954.

Foucault, Michel. *Madness and Civilisation: A History of Insanity in the Age of Reason*. London: Tavistock, 1971.

Foucault, Michel. *The Birth of the Clinic*. London: Tavistock, 1973.

Foucault, Michel. *Discipline and Punish: The Birth of the Prison*. New York: Pantheon, 1977.

Foucault, Michel. *Herculine Barbin: Being the Recently Discovered Memoirs of a 19th Century French Hermaphrodite*. New York: Pantheon, 1980.

Foucault, Michel. *The History of Sexuality Volume 1. An Introduction*, translated by Robert Hurley. London: Penguin, 1990.

Foucault, Michel. *The Politics of Truth*, edited by S. Lotringer and L. Hochroth, Semiotext(e). New York: Columbia University, 1997.

Foucault, Michel. "The Abnormals." In *Ethics, Subjectivity and Truth: The Essential Works of Foucault 1954–1984*, edited by Paul Rabinow, 51–57. New York: The New Press, 1997.

Foucault, Michel. "Nietzsche, Genealogy, History." In *Michel Foucault: Aesthetics, Method, and Epistemology*, edited by James D. Faubion. New York: The New Press, 1998.

Frader, Joel, Dena Davis, Arthur Frank, and Paul Miller. "Health Care Professionals and Intersex Conditions." *Archives of Pediatrics & Adolescent Medicine* 158 (2004): 426–429.

Freud, Sigmund. *A General Introduction to Psychoanalysis; a Course of Twenty Eight Lectures Delivered at the University of Vienna, by Prof. Sigmund Freud*, translated by J. Riviere. New York: Liveright Publishing, 1935.

Freud, Sigmund. "Three Essays on the Theory of Sexuality." In *Standard Edition of the Complete Psychological Works of Sigmund Freud*. London: Hogarth Press, 1953.

Freud, Sigmund. *The Standard Edition of the Complete Psychological Works of Sigmund Freud*, translated by James Strachey. 24 vols. London: Hogarth Press, 1953.

Fried, Barbara. "Boys Will Be Boys Will Be Boys: The Language of Sex and Gender." In *Women Look at Biology Looking at Women: A Collection of Feminist Critiques*, edited by Ruth Hubbard, Mary Sue Henifin, and Barbara Fried, 37–59. Boston: G. K. Hall, 1979.

Friedan, Betty. *The Feminine Mystique*. London: Gollancz, 1963.

Fuss, D. *Essentially Speaking: Feminism, Nature and Difference*. New York: Routledge, 1989.

Gallagher, Catherine, and Thomas Laqueur, eds. *The Making of the Modern Body: Sexuality and Society in the Nineteenth Century*. Berkeley/London: University of California Press, 1987.

Gambs, Deborah. "Bisexuality: Beyond the Binary?" *Journal of Sex Research* 40, no. 3 (2003): 317–319.

Gamson, J. "Must Identity Movements Self-Destruct?: A Queer Dilemma." In *Queer Theory/Sociology*, edited by S. Seidman, 395–420. Oxford: Blackwell Publishers, 1996.

Garber, Marjorie. *Vested Interests: Cross-Dressing and Cultural Anxieties*. London: Routledge, 1992.

Garfinkel, Harold. *Studies in Ethnomethodology*. Englewood Cliffs, NJ: Prentice-Hall, 1967.

Garland-Thomson, Rosemary. "Introduction: From Wonder to Error—a Genealogy of Freak Discourse in Modernity." In *Freakery: Cultural Spectacles of the Extraordinary Body*, edited by Rosemarie Garland Thomson, 1–19. New York: New York University Press, 1996.

Garland-Thomson, Rosemarie. *Extraordinary Bodies: Figuring Physical Disability in American Culture and Literature*. New York: Columbia University Press, 1997.

Garton, Stephen. *Histories of Sexuality: Antiquity to Sexual Revolution*. London: Equinox, 2004.

Gatens, Moira. "A Critique of the Sex/Gender Distinction." In *Beyond Marxism?: Interventions after Marx*, edited by Paul Patton and Judith Allen, 143–160. Leichhardt, NSW: Intervention, 1983.

Gatens, Moira. *Imaginary Bodies: Ethics, Power and Corporeality*. London: Routledge, 1996.

Gatens, Moira. "Feminism as 'Password': Re-Thinking the " 'Possible' with Spinoza and Deleuze." *Hypatia* 15, no. 2 (2000): 59–75.

Geertz, Clifford. *Local Knowledge: Further Essays in Interpretative Anthropology*. New York: Basic Books, 1983.

Gerhardt, Uta E. *Talcott Parsons: An Intellectual Biography*. Cambridge: Cambridge University Press, 2002.

Germon, Jennifer. "Degrees of Freedom: Inscribing Gender on the Intersexed Body." Unpublished MA diss., University of Auckland, 1998.

Germon, Jennifer. "Generations of Gender: Past, Present, Potential." PhD diss., University of Sydney, 2006.

Germon, Jennifer. "Kinsey and the Politics of Bisexual Authenticity." *Journal of Bisexuality* 8, no. 3/4 (2008): 245–260.

Germon, Jennifer, and Myra Hird. "Women on the Edge of a Dyke-Otomy: Confronting Subjectivity." In *Lesbian Sex Scandals: Sexual Practices, Identities, and Politics*, edited by D. Atkins, 103–111. New York: Harrington Park Press, 1999.

Gilman, Charlotte Perkins. *Women and Economics: A Study of the Economic Relation between Women and Men*, Great Minds Series. Amherst, NY: Prometheus Books, 1898/1994.

Gilman, Charlotte Perkins. *Herland*. 1st ed. New York: Pantheon Books, 1915/1979.

Ginsberg, Ruth Bader. "Equal Opportunity, Free from Gender-Based Discrimination." In *Sex Equality*, edited by Jane English, 188–195. Englewood Cliffs, NJ: Prentice-Hall, 1977.

Goffman, Erving. *Stigma: Notes on the Management of Spoiled Identity*. Harmondsworth, England: Penguin, 1968.

Goffman, Erving. "The Arrangement between the Sexes." *Theory and Society* 4 (1977): 301–331.

Goffman, Erving, Charles C. Lemert, and Ann Branaman, eds. *The Goffman Reader*. Cambridge, MA: Blackwell, 1997.

Goldschmidt, Richard Benedict. *The Mechanism and Physiology of Sex Determination*, translated by William J. Dakin. London: Methuen, 1923.

Gordon, D. "Tenacious Assumptions in Western Medicine." In *Biomedicine Examined*, edited by M. Lock and D. Gordon, 1956. Dordrecht: Kluwer Academic Publishers, 1988.

Gornick, Vivian, and Barbara K. Moran. *Woman in Sexist Society: Studies in Power and Powerlessness*. New York: Basic Books, 1971.

Gough, Brendan, Nicky Weyman, Julie Alderson, Gary Butler, and Mandy Stoner. " 'They Did Not Have a Word': The Parental Quest to Locate a 'True Sex' for Their Intersex Children." *Psychology and Health* 23, no. 4 (2008): 493–507.

Gould, Meredith, and Rochelle Kern-Daniels. "Towards a Sociological Theory of Gender and Sex." *American Sociologist* 12 (1977): 182–189.

Grace, Victoria. *Baudrillard's Challenge: A Feminist Reading*. London and New York: Routledge, 2000.

Grace, Victoria, and Marion de Ras. *Bodily Boundaries, Sexualised Genders & Medical Discourses*. Palmerston North, N.Z: Dunmore Press, 1997.

Grafenberg, E. "The Role of the Urethra in Female Orgasm." *International Journal of Sexology* 3 (1950): 145–148.

Grant, Julia. "A 'Real Boy' and Not a Sissy: Gender, Childhood and Masculinity 1890–1940." *Journal of Social History* 37, no. 4 (2004): 829.

Green, Richard. *Sexual Identity Conflict in Children and Adults*. New York: Basic Books, 1975.

Green, Richard. *The "Sissy Boy Syndrome" and the Development of Homosexuality*. New Haven, CT: Yale University Press, 1987.

Greenburg, David. "Transformations of Homosexuality-Based Classifications." In *The Gender Sexuality Reader: Culture, History, Political Economy*, edited by Roger Lancaster and Micaela di Leonardo, 179–193. New York: Routledge, 1997.

Greenson, Ralph. "Dis-Identifying from Mother—Its Special Importance for the Boy." *International Journal of Psychoanalysis* 47 (1968): 396–403.

Greer, Germaine. *The Female Eunuch*. London: MacGibbon and Kee, 1970.

Greer, Germaine. *Sex and Destiny: The Politics of Human Fertility*. London: Secker and Warburg, 1984.

Greer, Germaine. *The Change: Women, Ageing and the Menopause*. London: Hamish Hamilton, 1991.

Greer, Germaine. *The Whole Woman*. 1st American ed. New York: A. A. Knopf, 1999.

Griffin, J. E., and J. D. Wilson. "Disorders of Sexual Differentiation." In *Campbells Urology*, edited by P. C. Walsh, A. B. Retik, T. A. Stamey, and E. D. Vaughan, 1509–1537. Philadelphia: Saunders, 1992.

Grosz, Elizabeth. *Volatile Bodies: Towards a Corporeal Feminism*. Bloomington: Indiana University Press, 1994.

Grosz, Elizabeth. "Intolerable Ambiguity: Freaks as/at the Limit." In *Freakery: Cultural Spectacles of the Extraordinary Body*, edited by Rosemary Garland Thomson, 55–66. New York: New York University Press, 1996.

Grosz, Elizabeth. *The Nick of Time: Politics, Evolution and the Untimely*. Crows Nest, NSW: Allen & Unwin, 2004.

Grumbach, Melvin. "Further Studies on the Treatment of Congenital Adrenal Hyperplasia with Cortisone: Iv. Effect of Cortisone and Compound B in Infants with Disturbed Electrolyte Metabolism, by John F. Crigler Jr, Samuel H. Silverman, and Lawson Wilkins, Pediatrics, 1952;10: 397–413." *Pediatrics* 102, no. 1 (1998): 215–221.

Haas, Kate. "Who Will Make Room for the Intersexed?" *American Journal of Law and Medicine* 30, no. 1 (2004): 41–68.

Hackney, Peter. "Census Caters for the Intersex and Androgynous." Evolution Publishing, http://evolutionpublishing.com.au/sxnews/index. php?option=com_content&task=view&id=103&Itemid=41.

Haig, David. "The Inexorable Rise of Gender and the Decline of Sex: Social Change in Academic Titles 1945–2001." *Archives of Sexual Behaviour* 33, no. 2 (2004): 87–96.

Halberstam, Judith. *Female Masculinity.* Durham, NC: Duke University Press, 1998.

Halberstam, Judith. *In a Queer Time and Place: Transgender Bodies, Subcultural Lives, Sexual Cultures.* New York: New York University Press, 2005.

Halperin, David. *One Hundred Years of Homosexuality: And Other Essays on Greek Love.* London: Routledge, 1990.

Halperin, David. "Homosexuality: A Cultural Construct. An Exchange with Richard Schneider." In *One Hundred Years of Homosexuality and Other Essays on Greek Love.* New York: Routledge, 1990.

Hampson, Joan. "Hermaphroditic Genital Appearance, Rearing and Eroticism in Hyperadrenocorticism." *Bulletin of the Johns Hopkins Hospital* 96, no. 3 (1955): 265–273.

Haraway, Donna. *Simians, Cyborgs, and Women: The Reinvention of Nature.* New York and London: Routledge, 1991.

Harding, Sandra. *Whose Science? Whose Knowledge?* Milton Keynes: Open University Press, 1991.

Hare-Mustin, Rachel, and Jeanne Marbeck. "The Meaning of Difference: Gender Theory, Postmodernism and Psychology." In *The Gender and Psychology Reader*, edited by Blyth McVicker Clinchy and Julie Norem, 125–143. New York: New York University Press, 1998.

Harper, Catherine. *Intersex.* Oxford: Berg, 2007.

Hausman, Bernice. *Changing Sex: Transsexualism, Technology and the Idea of Gender.* Durham, NC: Duke University Press, 1995.

Hausman, Bernice. "Sex before Gender: Charlotte Perkins Gilman and the Evolutionary Paradigm of Utopia." *Feminist Studies* 24, no. 3 (1998): 488–510.

Hausman, Bernice. "Do Boys Have to Be Boys? Gender, Narrativity, and the John/Joan Case." *NWSA Journal* 12, no. 3 (2000): 114–138.

Hausman, Ken. "Controversy Continues to Grow over DSM's GID Diagnosis." *Psychiatric News* 38, no. 14 (2003): 25–26.

Havranek, C. "The New Sex Surgeries." *Cosmopolitan*, November (1998) 1998, 146–150.

Hawkesworth, Mary. "Confounding Gender." *Signs: Journal of Women in Culture and Society* 22, no. 3 (1997): 649–685.

Haynes, Felicity, and Tarquam McKenna, eds. *Unseen Genders: Beyond the Binaries.* Vol. 12. New York: Peter Lang, 2001.

Hegarty, Peter, and Cheryl Chase. "Intersex Activism, Feminism and Psychology: Opening a Dialogue on Theory, Research and Clinical Practice." *Feminism and Psychology* 10, no. 1 (2000): 117–132.

Heidenry, John. *What Wild Ecstasy: The Rise and Fall of the Sexual Revolution.* Kew: William Heinemann, 1997.

Hekma, Gert. "'A Female Soul in a Male Body': Sexual Inversion as Gender Inversion in Nineteenth-Century Sexology." In *Third Sex, Third Gender: Beyond Sexual Dimorphism in Culture and History,* edited by Gilbert Herdt, 213–239. New York: Zone Books, 1994.

Hemmings, Clare. "Resituating the Bisexual Body: From Identity to Difference." In *Activating Theory: Lesbian, Gay Bisexual Politics,* edited by Joseph Bristow and Angelia R. Wilson, 118–138. London: Lawrence & Wishart, 1993.

Hemmings, Clare. "Locating Bisexual Identities: Discourses of Bisexuality and Contemporary Feminist Theory." In *Mapping Desire: Geographies of Sexualities,* edited by David Bell and Gill Valentine, 41–55. London: Routledge, 1995.

Hemmings, Clare. *Bisexual Spaces: A Geography of Sexuality and Gender.* New York: Routledge, 2002.

Hemmings, Clare. "What's in a Name? Bisexuality, Transnational Sexuality Studies and Western Colonial Legacies." *International Journal of Human Rights* 11, no. 1–2 (2007): 13–32.

Hendricks, Melissa. "Into the Hands of Babes." *Johns Hopkins Magazine* 52, no. 4 (September 2000). http://www.jhu.edu/~jhumag/0900web/.

Herdt, Gilbert. "Introduction: Third Sexes and Third Genders." In *Third Sex, Third Gender: Beyond Sexual Dimorphism in Culture and History,* edited by Gilbert Herdt, 21–81. New York: Zone Books, 1994.

Hester, J. David. "Intersex(Es) and Informed Consent: How Physicians' Rhetoric Constrains Choice." *Theoretical Medicine and Bioethics* 25, no. 1 (2004): 21–49.

Hines, Sally. "(Trans)Forming Gender: Social Change and Transgender Citizenship." *Sociological Research Online,* no. 1 (2007), http://www.socresonline.org.uk/12/1/hines.html.

Hinkle, Curtis. "Why the Intergender Community Is So Important to the Intersex Community." www.intersexualite.org.

Hinkle, Curtis. "Resisting Sexism from All Sides." www.intersexualite.org.

Hinkle, Curtis. "People without Faces." Intersex Pride, http://intersexpride.blogspot.com.

Hinkle, Curtis E. "Right to One's Self." OII, www.intersexualite.org.

Hird, Myra. "A Typical Gender Identity Conference? Some Disturbing Reports from the Therapeutic Front Lines." *Feminism & Psychology* 13, no. 2 (2003): 181–199.

Hird, Myra. "Gender's Nature: Intersexuality, Transsexualism and the 'Sex/Gender' Binary." *Feminist Theory* 1, no. 3 (2000): 347–364.

Hird, Myra, and Jennifer Germon. "The Intersexual Body and the Medical Regulation of Gender." In *Constructing Gendered Bodies,* edited by Katherine Backett-Milburn and Linda McKie, 162–178. Hampshire: Palgrave, 2001.

Hirschauer, S. "The Medicalisation of Gender Migration." *International Journal of Transsexualism* 1, no. 1 (1997).

Hirschauer, Stefan, and Annemarie Mol. "Shifting Sexes, Moving Stories: Feminist/Constructivist Dialogues." *Science, Technology & Human Values* 20, no. 3 (1995): 368–385.

Hirschfeld, Magnus. *The Transvestites: The Erotic Drive to Cross Dress*, translated by Michael Lombardi-Nash. Buffalo, NY: Prometheus Books, 1991.

Hirschfeld, Magnus. *The Homosexuality of Men and Women*, translated by Michael Lombardi-Nash. New York: Prometheus Books, 2000.

Hoenig, J. "Dramatis Personae: Selected Biographical Sketches of 19th Century Pioneers in Sexology." In *Handbook of Sexology: Volume 1: History and Ideology*, edited by John Money and Herman Musaph, 21–44. New York: Elsevier, 1978.

Hoenig, J. "The Development of Sexology During the Second Half of the 19th Century." In *Handbook of Sexology: Volume 1: History and Ideology*, edited by John Money and Herman Musaph, 5–20. New York: Elsevier, 1978a.

Holmes, Morgan. "I'm Still Intersexual." *Hermaphrodites with Attitudes*, Winter (1994): 5–6.

Holmes, Morgan. "Queer Cut Bodies: Intersexuality and Homophobia in Medical Practice." http://www.usc.edu/isd/archives/queerfrontiers/queer/papers/holmes.long.html.

Holmes, Morgan. "In(to) Visibility: Intersexuality in the Field of Queer." In *Looking Queer: Body Image and Identity in Lesbian, Bisexual, Gay and Transgender Communities*, edited by Dawn Atkins, 221–226. New York: Harrington Park Press, 1998.

Holmes, Morgan. "Rethinking the Meaning and Management of Intersexuality." *Sexualities* 5, no. 2 (2002): 159–180.

Holmes, Morgan. "Book Review. Intersex and Identity: The Contested Self." *Contemporary Sociology* 33, no. 4 (2004): 487–489.

Holmes, Morgan. "Locating Third Sexes." *Transformations*, no. 8 (July 2004), http://www.transformationsjournal.org/journal/issue_08/article_03.shtml.

Holmes, Morgan. "Mind the Gaps: Intersex and (Re-Productive) Spaces in Disability Studies and Bioethics." *Bioethical Inquiry* 5, no. 2–3 (2008): 169–181.

Holter, Harriet. *Sex Roles and Social Structure*. Oslo: Universitetsforlaget, 1970.

Hooker, Evelyn. "A Preliminary Analysis of Group Behavior of Homosexuals." *Journal of Psychology* 42 (1956): 217–225.

Hooker, Evelyn. "The Adjustment of the Male Overt Homosexual." *Journal of Projective Techniques* 21 (1957): 18–31.

Hooker, Evelyn. "Male Homosexuality in the Rorschach." *Journal of Projective Techniques* 23 (1958): 278–281.

Hooks, Bell. *Ain't I a Woman: Black Women and Feminism*. Boston: South End Press, 1981.

Hooks, Bell. *Feminist Theory from Margin to Center.* Boston: South End Press, 1984.

Hooks, Bell. *Talking Back: Thinking Feminist, Thinking Black.* Boston: South End Press, 1989.

Hoschchild, Arlie Russell. "A Review of Sex Role Research." *American Journal of Sociology* 78, no. 4 (1973): 1011–1029.

Hrabovszky, Z., and J. M. Hutson. "Surgical Treatment of Intersex Abnormalities: A Review." *Surgery* 131, no. 1 (2002): 92–104.

Hubbard, Ruth, Mary Sue Henifin, and Barbara Fried, eds. *Women Look at Biology Looking at Women: A Collection of Feminist Critiques.* Boston: G. K. Hall, 1979.

Hubbard, Ruth, and Marian Lowe. "Introduction." In *Pitfalls in Research on Sex and Gender. Genes and Gender; 2.*, edited by Ruth Hubbard and Marian Lowe, 154. New York: Gordian Press, 1979.

Hughes, Helen MacGill, ed. *The Status of Women in Sociology 1968–1972: Report to the American Sociological Association of the Ad Hoc Committee on the Status of Women in the Profession.* Washington, DC: American Sociological Association, 1973.

Hughes, Ieuan A. "Female Development—All by Default?" *New England Journal of Medicine* 351, no. 8 (2004): 748–750.

Hughes, Ieuan A., Christopher Houk, S. Faisal Ahmed, and Peter Lee. "Consensus Statement on Management of Intersex Disorders." *Archives of Diseases in Childhood* 90, no. 7 (2006): 554–562.

Hume, David. "Humes Ethical Writings: Selections Edited and Introduced by Alasdair Macintyre." New York: Collier, 1965.

"Intersex & Trans Demands." The Lesbian Avengers, http://www.geocities.com/gainesvilleavengers/intersextransdemands.htm.

Irvine, Janice. *Disorders of Desire: Sex and Gender in Modern American Sexology.* Philadelphia: Temple University Press, 1990.

ISNA. *Hermaphrodites with Attitude* Fall/Winter (1995–1996).

ISNA. *ISNA News* February (2001).

ISNA. *ISNA News* Fall (2002).

ISNA. "Tips for Parents." ISNA, http://www.isna.org/articles/tips_for_parents.

ISNA. *Hermaphrodites with Attitude* Spring (1995).

ISNA. *Hermaphrodites with Attitude* Summer (r 1995).

ISNA. *Hermaphrodites with Attitudes* 1, no. 1 (Winter 1994).

ISNZ. "Brochure: Intersex Society of New Zealand (Aotearoa)." Wellington, New Zealand, 1997.

Italiano, M., and Curtis Hinkle. "Ambiguous Medicine and Sexist Genetics: A Critique of the DSD Nomenclature." (2008), http://www.intersexualite.org/sexist_genetics.html.

Jaggar, Alison. "On Sexual Equality." In *Sex Equality*, edited by Jane English, 93–109. Englewood Cliffs, NJ: Prentice-Hall, 1977.

Jagose, AnnaMarie. *Queer Theory.* Dunedin: University of Otago Press, 1996.

Jenkins, Laura. "Corporeal Ontology: Beyond Mind-Body Dualism?" *Politics* 25, no. 1 (2005): 1–11.

JHU. *Transactions. Obstetrical Society of London.* Obstetrical Society of London, 1859–1907.

Joint LWPES/ESPE CAH Working Group. "Consensus Statement on 21-Hydroxylase Deficiency from the Lawson Wilkins Pediatric Endocrine Society and the European Society for Paediatric Endocrinology." *Journal of Clinical Endocrinology & Metabolism* 87, no. 9 (2002): 4048–4053.

Jones, James. *"We of the Third Sex": Literary Representations of Homosexuality in Wilhelmine Germany.* New York: Peter Lang, 1990.

Jones, Meredith. "Remembering Academic Feminism." PhD diss., University of Sydney, 2002.

Jost, Alfred. "Problems of Fetal Endocrinology." In *Recent Progress in Hormone Research*, edited by Gregory Pincus, 379–419. New York: Academic Press, 1953.

Kaldera, Raven. "Agdistis' Children: Living Bi-Gendered in a Single Gendered World." In *Looking Queer: Body Image and Identity in Lesbian, Bisexual, Gay and Transgender Communities*, edited by Dawn Atkins, 227–232. New York: Harrington Park Press, 1998.

Kant, I. *Critique of Pure Reason.* New York: St. Martins, 1933.

Kaplan, Alexandra G. "Human Sex-Hormone Abnormalities Viewed from an Androgynous Perspective: A Reconsideration of the Work of John Money." In *The Psychobiology of Sex Differences and Sex Roles*, edited by Jacquelynne E. Parsons, 81–91. Washington, DC: Hemisphere, 1980.

Karkazis, Katrina. *Fixing Sex: Intersex, Medical Authority and Lived Experience.* Durham, NC: Duke University Press, 2008.

Katz, Jonathan. *The Invention of Heterosexuality.* New York: Dutton, 1995.

Keane, Helen, and Marsha Rosengarten. "On the Biology of Sexed Subjects." *Australian Feminist Studies* 17, no. 39 (2002): 261–285.

Keir, John. "Yellow for Hermaphrodites: Mani's Story." In *"Private Lives"*, edited by John Keir. Green Stone Pictures, 2003.

Keller, Evelyn Fox. *Reflections on Gender and Science.* New Haven, CT: Yale University Press, 1985.

Kemp, Diane. "Sex, Lies and Androgen Insensitivity Syndrome." *Canadian Medical Association Journal* 154, no. 12 (1996): 1829.

Kenen, Stephanie. "Who Counts When You're Counting Homosexuals? Hormones and Homosexuality in Mid-Twentieth Century America." In *Science and Homosexualities*, edited by Vernon Rosario, 197–218. New York and London: Routledge, 1995.

Kennedy, Hubert. "Book Review. The Riddle Of 'Man-Manly' Love: The Pioneering Work on Male Homosexuality." *Journal of Homosexuality* 33, no. 2 (1997): 125–131.

Kennedy, Hubert. "Karl Heinrich Ulrichs, First Theorist of Homosexuality." In *Science and Homosexualities*, edited by Vernon Rosario, 26–45. New York and London: Routledge, 1997.

Kessler, Suzanne. "The Medical Construction of Gender: Case Management of Intersexed Infants." *Signs* 16, no. 1 (1990): 3–26.

Kessler, Suzanne. *Lessons from the Intersexed.* New Brunswick, NJ: Rutgers University Press, 1998.

Kessler, Suzanne, and Wendy McKenna. *Gender: An Ethnomethodological Approach.* New York: John Wiley, 1978.

King, Michael. "The Duke of Dysfunction." *NZ Listener,* April 4–10 1998, 18–21.

Kinsey, Alfred C. "Homosexuality: Criteria for a Hormonal Explanation of the Homosexual." *Journal of Clinical Endocrinology* 1, no. 5 (1941): 424–428.

Kinsey, Alfred C., Wardell B. Pomeroy, and Clyde E. Martin. *Sexual Behavior in the Human Male.* Philadelphia: Saunders, 1948.

Kinsey, Alfred C., Wardell B. Pomeroy, Clyde E. Martin, and Paul H. Gebhard. *Sexual Behavior in the Human Female.* Philadelphia: Saunders, 1953.

Kirmayer, L. J. "Mind and Body as Metaphors: Hidden Values in Biomedicine." In *Biomedicine Examined,* edited by M. Lock and J. Gordon, 57–93. Dordrecht: Kluwer Academic Publishing, 1988.

Kirsner, Douglas. "Unfree Associations. Inside Psychoanalytic Institutes." Academy for the Study of the Psychoanalytic Arts, http://www.academyanalyticarts.org/kirsner4.html.

Feder Kittay, Eva, and Ellen K. Feder, eds. *The Subject of Care: Feminist Perspectives on Dependency,* Feminist Constructions. Lanham, MD: Rowman & Littlefield, 2003.

Kitzinger, Celia. "Intersex and Identity: The Contested Self (Book Review)." *American Journal of Sociology* 109, no. 3 (2003): 802–804.

Klebs, Edwin. *Handbuch Der Pathologischen Anatomie.* Berlin: A. Hirschwald, 1876.

Klein, Fred. *The Bisexual Option.* 2nd ed. New York: Harrington Park Press, 1993.

Klein, Julia M. "A Sex of One's Own." *The Nation* 275, no. 19 (2002): 33.

Koopman, Peter. "The Genetics and Biology of Vertebrate Sex Determination." *Cell* 105 (2001): 843–847.

Koyama, Emi. "From 'Intersex' to 'DSD': Toward a Queer Disability Politics of Gender." Presented at the Translating Identity Conference. University of Vermont, Februrary 2006.

Koyama, Emi. "Suggested Guidelines for Non-Intersex Individuals Writing About Intersexuality and Intersex People." http://www.ipdx.org/articles/writing-guidelines.html.

Koyama, Emi. "Being Accountable to the Invisible Community: A Challenge for Intersex Activists and Allies." Intersex Initiative, http://www.ipdx.org/articles/invisible-community.html.

Koyama, Emi. "So, You Wanna Know About 'Hermaphrodites'?" Intersex Initiative, www.ipdx.org/articles/hermaphrodites.html.

Koyama, Emi, and Lisa Weasel. "From Social Construction to Social Justice: Transforming How We Teach About Intersexuality." *Women's Studies Quarterly* 30, no. 3/4 (2002): 169–178.

Krafft-Ebing, Richard. *Psychopathia Sexualis: With Especial Reference to the Anti-Pathic Sexual Instinct. A Medico-Forensic Study*, translated by Franklin Klaf. New York: Arcade, 1998.

Kuhn, Thomas. *The Structure of Scientific Revolutions*. 2nd ed. 2 vols. Vol. 2, International Encyclopedia of Unified Science. Chicago: University of Chicago Press, 1970.

Laqueur, Thomas. *Making Sex: Body and Gender from the Greeks to Freud*. Cambridge, MA: Harvard University Press, 1990.

Laqueur, T. "Orgasm, Generation, and the Politics of Reproductive Biology." In *The Gender Sexuality Reader: Culture, History, Political Economy*, edited by R. N. Lancaster and M. di Leonardo, 219–243. New York: Routledge, 1997.

Laramée, Joëlle-Circé. "Rejecting Assimilation within the GLBT Identity Movements." OII, www.intersexualite.org/English-Index.html#anchor_526.

Lashlie, Celia. *He'll Be Ok: Growing Gorgeous Boys into Good Men*. Auckland: HarperCollins, 2005.

Lashlie, Celia, and Katherine Pivac. *It's About Boys: The Good Man Project*. Nelson, N. Z.: Nelson College, 2004.

Lasky, Ella. *Humanness: An Exploration into the Mythologies About Women and Men*. New York: MSS Information Corp., 1975.

Laslett, Barbara, and Barrie Thorne, eds. *Feminist Sociology: Life Histories of a Movement*. New Brunswick, NJ: Rutgers University Press, 1997.

Lee, Peter, Christopher Houk, S. Faisal Ahmed, and Ieuan A. Hughes. "Summary of Consensus Statement on Intersex Disorders and Their Management." *Pediatrics* 111, no. 2 (2006): 753–757.

Liao, L. M. "Learning to Assist Women Born with Atypical Genitalia: Journey through Ignorance, Taboo and Dilemma." *Journal of Reproductive and Infant Psychology* 21, no. 3 (2003): 229–238.

Lillie, F. *Sex and Internal Secretions: A Survey of Recent Research*, edited by E. Allen. 2nd ed. Baltimore: Williams and Wilkins, 1939.

Lipset, David. "Rereading Sex and Temperament: Margaret Mead's Sepik Triptych and Its Ethnographic Critics." *Anthropological Quarterly* 76, no. 4 (2003): 693–713.

Lloyd, Barbara B., and John Archer, eds. *Exploring Sex Differences*. London and New York: Academic Press, 1976.

Lloyd, Elisabeth. *The Case of the Female Orgasm: Bias in the Science of Evolution*. Cambridge, MA: Harvard University Press, 2005.

Lloyd, Jillian, Naomi Crouch, Catherine Minto, Lih-Mei Liao, and Sarah Crieghton. "Female Genital Appearance: 'Normality' Unfolds." *BJOG: An International Journal of Obstetrics and Gynaecology* 112 (2005): 643–646.

Lock, Margaret. "Anomalous Ageing: Managing the Postmenopausal Body." *Body and Society* 4, no. 1 (1998): 35–61.

Lock, Margaret, and Deborah Gordon, eds. *Biomedicine Examined*. Dordrecht: Kluwer Academic Publishers, 1988a.

Lock, Margaret, and Deborah Gordon. "Relationships Between Society, Culture, and Biomedicine: Introduction to the Essays." In *Biomedicine Examined*, edited by M. Lock and D. Gordon, 11–16. Dordrecht: Kluwer Academic Publishers, 1988b.

Lopata, Helena. "Review Essay: Sociology." *Signs: Journal of Women in Culture and Society* 2, no. 1 (1976): 165–176.

Lopata, Helena, and Barrie Thorne. "Letters/Comments. On the Term 'Sex Roles'." *Signs* 3 (1978): 718–721.

Lorber, J. "Beyond the Binaries: Depolarising the Categories of Sex, Sexuality, and Gender." *Sociological Inquiry* 66, no. 2 (1996): 143–159.

Lorenz, Konrad. *King Solomon's Ring: New Light on Animal Ways*. London: Methuen, 1961.

Lottringer, S., ed. *Foucault Live: Collected Interviews, 1961–1984*. New York: Semiotext(e), 1989.

Lykke, Ninna. "Between Monsters, Goddesses and Cyborgs: Feminist Confrontations with Science." In *Between Monsters, Goddesses and Cyborgs: Feminist Confrontations with Science, Medicine and Cyberspace*, edited by Ninna Lykke and Rosie Braidotti, 13–29. London: Zed Books, 1996.

Maccoby, Eleanor. "The Varied Meanings of 'Masculine' And 'Feminine.' " In *Masculinity/Femininity: Basic Perspectives*, edited by June Reinisch, Leonard Rosenblum, and Stephanie Sanders, 227–239. New York: Oxford University Press, 1987.

Maccoby, Eleanor E. *The Development of Sex Differences*, Stanford Studies in Psychology. London: Tavistock Publications, 1967.

Maccoby, Eleanor E., and Carol Nagy Jacklin. *The Psychology of Sex Differences*. Stanford, CA: Stanford University Press, 1974.

Martin, Biddy. "Lesbian Identity/Autobiographical Difference[s]." In *The Lesbian and Gay Studies Reader*, edited by H. Abelove et al., 274–293. New York: Routledge, 1993.

Martin, Biddy. "Extraordinary Homosexuals and the Fear of Being Ordinary." *Differences* 6, no. 2 (1994): 100–125.

Martin, Patricia Yancey. "Gender as Social Institution." *Social Forces* 82, no. 4 (2004): 1249–1273.

Masters, William H., and Virginia E. Johnson. *Human Sexual Response*. Boston: Little, Brown, 1966.

Mayer, E. I., J. Homoki, and M. B. Ranke. "Spontaneous Growth and Bone Age Development in a Patient with 17alpha-Hydroxylase Deficiency: Evidence of the Role of Sexual Steroids in Prepubertal Bone Maturation." *Journal of Pediatrics* 135, no. 5 (1999): 653–654.

Mazur, Tom. "A Lovemap of a Different Sort from John Money." Review of Money's A Personal History 2003. *Journal of Sex Research* 41, no. 1 (2004): 115–116.

McIntyre, A., ed. *Hume's Ethical Writings: Selections from David Hume*. Oxford: Collier, 1965.

McKenna, Wendy, and Suzanne Kessler. "Afterword. Retropective Response." *Feminism and Psychology* 10, no. 1 (2000): 66–72.

McKhann, Guy M. "Neurology: Then, Now, and in the Future." *Archives of Neurology* 59, no. 9 (2002): 1369–1373.

McLaren, Angus. *Twentieth-Century Sexuality: A History.* Oxford: Blackwell, 1999.

McNay, Lois. *Foucault and Feminism.* Cambridge: Polity Press, 1992.

McRuer, Robert. "Compulsory Able-Bodiedness and Queer/Disabled Existence." In *Disability Studies: Enabling the Humanities*, edited by Sharon Snyder, Brenda Brueggemann, and Rosemarie Garland-Thomson, 88–99. New York: Modern Language Association of America, 2002.

Mead, Margaret. *Sex and Temperament in Three Primitive Societies.* New York: Morrow, 1963.

Mead, Margaret. *Male and Female: A Study of the Sexes in a Changing World.* Harmondsworth: Penguin, 1962.

Mein-Smith, P. *Maternity in Dispute: New Zealand 1920–1939.* Wellington: Historical Publications, Dept of Internal Affairs, 1986.

Melton, Lisa. "New Perspectives on the Management of Intersex." *Lancet* 357, no. 9274 (2001): 2110.

Melucci, Alberto. "The Process of Collective Identity." In *Social Movements and Culture*, edited by Hank Johnston and Bert Klandermans, 41–63. Minneapolis: University of Minnesota Press, 1995.

Meyer-Bahlburg, Heino F. L. "Intersexuality and the Diagnosis of Gender Identity Disorder." *Archives of Sexual Behavior* 23 (1994): 21.

Meyer-Bahlburg, Heino F. L., Rhoda S. Gruen, Maria I. New, Jennifer J. Bell, Akira Morishima, Mona Shimshi, Yvette Bueno, Ileana Vargas, and Susan W. Baker. "Gender Change from Female to Male in Classical Congenital Adrenal Hyperplasia." *Hormones and Behavior* 30, no. 4 (1996): 319–332.

Meyerowitz, Joanne. "Sex Research at the Borders of Gender: Transvestites, Transsexuals, and Alfred C. Kinsey." *Bulletin of the History of Medicine* 75 (2001): 72–90.

Meyerowitz, Joanne. *How Sex Changed: A History of Transsexuality in the United States.* Cambridge, MA: Harvard University Press, 2002.

Migeon, Claude, Wisniewski Amy, Brown Terry, Rock John, Meyer-Bahlburg Heino, Money John, and Berkovitz Gary. "46, Xy Intersex Individuals: Phenotypic and Etiologic Classification, Knowledge of Condition, and Satisfaction with Knowledge in Adulthood." *Pediatrics* 110, no. 3 (September 2002), http://www.pediatrics.org/cgi/content/full/110/3/e32.

Migeon, Claude, Amy Wisniewski, John Gearhart, Heino Meyer-Bahlburg, John Rock, Terry Brown, Samuel Casella, Alexander Maret, Ka Ming Ngai, John Money, and Gary Berkovitz. "Ambiguous Genitalia with Perineoscrotal Hypospadias in 46,Xy Individuals: Long-Term Medical, Surgical, and Psychosexual Outcome." *Pediatrics* 110, no. 3 (September 2002), http://www.pediatrics.org/cgi/content/full/110/3/e31.

Millett, Kate. *Sexual Politics.* London: Granada, 1971.

Millman, Marcia, and Rosabeth Moss Kanter, eds. *Another Voice.* New York: Anchor, 1975.

Mills, C. Wright. *The Sociological Imagination*. London: Oxford University Press, 1959.

Minto, Catherine, Julie Alderson, Adam Balen, and Sarah Creighton. "Management of Intersex—Specialists Reply." *Lancet* (North American edition) 358, no. 9298 (2001): 2085–2086.

Mitchell, Juliet. *Psychoanalysis and Feminism*. England: Pelican, 1974.

Mitchell, Juliet, ed. *Selected Melanie Klein*. Harmondsworth: Penguin, 1986.

Modleski, Tania. "On the Existence of Women: A Brief History of the Relations between Women's Studies and Film Studies." *Women's Studies Quarterly* 30, no. 1/2 (2002): 15–24.

Money, John. "Hermaphroditism: An Inquiry into the Nature of a Human Paradox." PhD diss., Harvard University, 1952.

Money, John. "Hermaphroditism, Gender and Precocity in Hyper-Adrenocorticism: Psychologic Findings." *Bulletin of the Johns Hopkins Hospital* 96, no. 3 (1955): 253–263.

Money, John. *The Psychologic Study of Man*. Springfield, IL: Charles C. Thomas, 1957.

Money, John. "Psychosexual Differentiation." In *Sex Research New Developments*, edited by John Money, 3–23. New York and London: Holt, Rinehart and Winston, 1965.

Money, John, ed. *Sex Research New Developments*. New York and London: Holt, Rinehart and Winston, 1965.

Money, John. "Bisexual, Homosexual, and Heterosexual: Society, Law, and Medicine." *Journal of Homosexuality* 2, no. 3 (1977): 229–231.

Money, John. "Determinants of Human Gender Identity/Role." In *Handbook of Sexology: History and Ideology*, edited by John Money and Herman Musaph, 57–79. New York and Oxford: Elselvier, 1978.

Money, John. *Love and Love Sickness: The Science of Sex, Gender Difference, and Pair-Bonding*. Baltimore: John Hopkins University Press, 1980.

Money, John. "To Quim and to Swive: Linguistic and Coital Parity, Male and Female." *Journal of Sex Research* 18, no. 2 (1982): 173–176.

Money, John. "Sexual Reformation and Counter-Reformation in Law and Medicine." *Medicine and Law* 4 (1985): 479–488.

Money, John. "Gender: History, Theory and Usage of the Term in Sexology and Its Relationship to Nature/Nurture." *Journal of Sex and Marital Therapy* 11, no. 2 (1985): 71–79.

Money, John. "The Conceptual Neutering of Gender and the Criminalisation of Sex." *Archives of Sexual Behaviour* 14, no. 3 (1985): 279–291.

Money, John. *Lovemaps: Clinical Concepts of Sexual/Erotic Health and Pathology, Paraphilia, and Gender Transposition in Childhood, Adolescence, and Maturity*. New York: Irvington, 1986.

Money, John. *Venuses Penuses: Sexology Sexosophy, and Exigency Theory*. Buffalo, NY: Prometheus Books, 1986a.

Money, John. "A Conspiracy Against Women." In *United States of American Vs. Sex: How the Meese Commission Lied About Pornography*, edited by P. Nobile and E. Nadler, 339–342. New York: Minotaur Press, 1986b.

Money, John. "Propaedeutics of Deicious G-I/R: Theoretical Foundations for Understanding Dimorphic Gender-Identity/Role." In *Masculinity/Femininity: Basic Perpectives*, edited by June Reinisch, Leonard Rosenblum, and Stephanie Sanders, 13–28. New York: Oxford University Press, 1987.

Money, John. *Gay, Straight, and In-Between: The Sexology of Erotic Orientation*. New York: Oxford University Press, 1988.

Money, John. *Biographies of Gender and Hermaphroditism in Paired Comparisons: Clinical Supplement to the Handbook of Sexology*, edited by John Money and Herman Musaph. Amsterdam and New York: Elsevier, 1991.

Money, John. *The Adam Principle: Genes, Genitals, Hormones and Gender: Selected Readings in Sexology*. Buffalo, NY: Prometheus Books, 1993.

Money, John. *Reinterpreting the Unspeakable. Human Sexuality 2000: The Complete Interviewer and Clinical Biographer, Exigency Theory, and Sexology for the Third Millenium*. New York: Continuum, 1994.

Money, John. *Gendermaps: Social Constructionism, Feminism and Sexosophical History*. New York: Continuum, 1995.

Money, John. *Sin, Science, and the Sex Police: Essays on Sexology and Sexosophy*. New York: Prometheus Books, 1998.

Money, John. *The Lovemap Guidebook: A Definitive Statement*. New York: Continuum, 1999.

Money, John. *A First Person History of Pediatric Psychoendocrinology*, edited by Richard Green. New York: Kluwer Academic/Plenum Publishers, 2002.

Money, John. "History Causality, and Sexology." *Journal of Sex Research* 40, no. 3 (2003): 237–239.

Money, John. "Once Upon a Time I Met Alfred C. Kinsey." *Archives of Sexual Behavior* 31, no. 4 (2003): 319–322.

Money, John, J. E. Cawte, G. N. Bianchi, and B. Nurcombe. "Sex Training and Traditions in Arnhem Land." *British Journal of Medical Psychology* 47 (1970): 383–399.

Money, John, and Anke Ehrhardt. *Man and Woman Boy and Girl: The Differentiation and Dimorphism of Gender Identity from Conception to Maturity*. Baltimore: Johns Hopkins University Press, 1972.

Money, John, Joan Hampson, and John Hampson. "Hermaphroditism: Recommendations Concerning Assignment of Sex, Change of Sex, and Psychologic Management." *Bulletin of the Johns Hopkins Hospital* 97, no. 4 (1955a): 284–300.

Money, John, Joan Hampson, and John Hampson. "An Examination of Some Basic Sexual Concepts: The Evidence of Human Hermaphroditism." *Bulletin of the Johns Hopkins Hospital* 97, no. 4 (1955b): 301–319.

Money, John, Joan Hampson, and John Hampson. "Sexual Incongruities and Psychopathology: The Evidence of Human Hermaphroditism." *Bulletin of the Johns Hopkins Hospital* 98, no. 1 (1956): 43–57.

Money, John, Joan Hampson, and John Hampson. "Imprinting and the Establishment of Gender Role." *AMA Archives of Neurology and Psychiatry* 77 (1957): 333–336.

Money, John, and M. Lamacz. *Vandalized Lovemaps: Paraphilic Outcome of Seven Cases in Pediatric Sexology.* Buffalo, NY: Prometheus Books, 1989.

Money, John, and Patricia Tucker. *Sexual Signatures: On Being a Man or a Woman.* London: Sphere Books, 1977.

Moore, Henrietta. *A Passion for Difference: Essays in Anthropology and Gender.* Cambridge: Polity, 1994.

Moore, Henrietta L. *Feminism and Anthropology*, Feminist Perspectives. Cambridge and Oxford: Polity Press, B. Blackwell, 1988.

Morland, Iain. "Management of Intersex." *Lancet* (North American edition) 358, no. 9298 (2001): 2085.

Morland, Iain. "The Glans Opens Like a Book: Writing and Reading the Intersexed Body." *Continuum: Journal of Media & Culture Studies* 19, no. 3 (2005): 335–348.

Morland, Iain. "Narrating Intersex: On the Ethical Critique of the Medical Management of Intersexuality, 1985–2005." PhD, University of London, 2005.

Morris, Jenny. "Impairment and Disability: Constructing an Ethic of Care That Promotes Human Rights." *Hypatia* 16, no. 4 (2001): 1–16.

Mulkay, M. *Sociology of Science: A Sociological Pilgrimage.* Milton Keynes: Open University Press, 1991.

Murphy, Timothy. "Redirecting Sexual Orientation: Techniques and Justifications." *Journal of Sex Research* 29, no. 4 (1992): 501–523.

Nagle, Jill. "Framing Radical Bisexuality." In *Bisexual Politics: Theories, Queries, Visions*, edited by Naomi Tucker, 305–314. New York: Harrington Park Press, 1995.

Natarajan, Anita. "Medical Ethics and Truth Telling in the Case of Androgen Insensitivity Syndrome." *Canadian Medical Association Journal* 154, no. 4 (1996): 568–570.

Nelson, Hilde Lindemann, and James E. Lindemann. *Meaning and Medicine: A Reader in the Philosophy of Health Care*, Reflective Bioethics. New York and London: Routledge, 1999.

Nestle, Joan, Clare Howell, and Riki Wilchins. *Genderqueer: Voices from Beyond the Sexual Binary.* Los Angeles: Alyson Books, 2002.

Nicholson, Linda. "Interpreting Gender." *Signs: Journal of Women in Culture and Society* 20 (1994): 79–105.

O'Connell, Agnes. "The Social Origins of Gender." In *Female and Male: Psychological Perspectives*, edited by Rhonda Unger. New York: Harper and Row, 1979.

O'Connell, Helen E., and John O DeLancey. "Clitoral Anatomy in Nulliparous, Healthy, Premenopausal Volunteers Using Unenhanced Magnetic Resonance Imaging." *Journal of Urology* 173 (2005): 2060–2063.

OAC. "Stoller (Robert J.) Biography." http://www.oac.cdlib.org/findaid/ark:/13030/tf5s2006mg/bioghist/639277564.

Oakley, Ann. *Sex, Gender and Society.* New York: Harper Colophon, 1972.

Oakley, A. *The Captured Womb: A History of the Medical Care of Pregnant Women.* Oxford: Basil Blackwell, 1984.

Oliver, Michael. *The Politics of Disablement: A Sociological Approach.* New York: St. Martin'ss, 1990.

Oliver, Michael. *Understanding Disability: From Theory to Practice.* Houndmills, Basingstoke: Macmillan, 1996.

Onions, C. T., ed. *The Shorter Oxford English Dictionary of Historical Principles.* 3rd ed. Oxford: Clarendon Press, 1973.

Oosterhuis, Harry. "Richard Von Krafft-Ebing's 'Step-Children of Nature': Psychiatry and the Making of Homosexual Identity." In *Science and Homosexualities,* edited by Vernon Rosario, 67–89. London and New York: Routledge, 1995.

Ormrod, Susan. "Feminist Sociology and Methodology: Leaky Black Boxes in Gender/ Technology Relations." In *The Gender-Technology Relation: Contemporary Theory and Research,* edited by Rosalind Gill and Keith Grint, 31–47. London: Taylor and Francis, 1995.

Ortner, Sherry. "Is Female to Male as Nature to Culture?" In *Woman, Culture, and Society,* edited by Michelle Zimbalist Rosaldo and Louise Lamphere, 67–87. Stanford, CA: Stanford University Press, 1974.

Ounsted, Christopher, and David Charles Taylor. *Gender Differences: Their Ontogeny and Significance.* Edinburgh: Churchill Livingstone, 1972.

Padgug, Robert. "Sexual Matters: On Conceptualizing Sexuality in History." In *Culture, Society and Sexuality: A Reader,* edited by Richard Parker and Peter Aggleton, 15–28. London and Philadelphia: UCL Press, 1999.

Pagon, R. A. "Diagnostic Approach to the Newborn with Ambiguous Genitalia." *Pediatric Clinics of North America* 34, no. 4 (1987): 1019–1031.

Parasnis, Ila. *Cultural and Language Diversity and the Deaf Experience.* Cambridge and New York: Cambridge University Press, 1996.

Parker, I., E. Georgaca, D. Harper, T. McLaughlin, and M. Stowell-Smith. *Deconstructing Psychopathology.* London: Routledge, 1995.

Parker, I., and J. Shotter, eds. *Deconstructing Social Psychology.* London: Routledge, 1990.

Parker, Richard, and Peter Aggleton, eds. *Culture, Society and Sexuality: A Reader.* London and Philadelphia: UCL Press, 1999.

Parsons, James. *A Mechanical and Critical Enquiry into the Nature of Hermaphrodites.* London: Printed for J. Walthoe, 1741.

Parsons, Talcott, and Robert Freed Bales. *Family: Socialization and Interaction Process.* Glencoe, IL.: Free Press, 1955.

Paul, Jay P. "The Bisexual Identity: An Idea Without Recognition." *Journal of Homosexuality* 11, no. 2–3 (1984): 45–63.

Paul, Jay P. "Bisexuality: Reassessing Our Paradigms." In *Bisexuality in the United States: A Social Sciences Reader,* edited by Paula C. Rodriguez Rust, 11–23. New York: Columbia University Press, 2000.

Penelope, Julia. *Speaking Freely: Unlearning the Lies of the Father's Tongues.* New York: Pergamons, 1990.

Perlmutter, A. D., and M. D. Reitelman. "Surgical Management of Intersexuality." In *Campbell's Urology,* edited by P. C. Walsh, A. B. Retik,

T. A. Stamey, and E. D. Vaughan, 1951–1966. Philadelphia: Saunders, 1992.

Petersen, Alan. "Biofantasies: Genetics and Medicine in the Print News Media." *Social Science & Medicine* 52, no. 8 (2001): 1255–1268.

Philips, Helen. "The Gender Police." *New Scientist* 170, no. 2290 (2001): 38–40.

Porter, R. *The Enlightenment*. London: Macmillan, 1990.

Porter, R. "Barely Touching: A Social Perspective on Mind and Body." In *The Languages of the Psyche: Mind and Body in Enlightenment Thought*, edited by G. S. Rousseau, 45–80. Berkeley: University of California, 1990.

Porter, R. *Disease, Medicine and Society in England, 1550–1860*. 2nd ed. London: Macmillan, 1993.

Porter, R. *The Greatest Benefit to Mankind: A Medical History of Humanity from Antiquity to the Present*. London: Harper Collins, 1997.

Preves, Sharon. "Negotiating the Constraints of Gender Binarism: Intersexuals' Challenge to Gender Categorization." *Current Sociology* 48, no. 3 (2000): 27–50.

Preves, Sharon Elaine. "Sexing the Intersexed: An Analysis of Sociocultural Responses to Intersexuality." *Signs* 27, no. 2 (2002): 523–557.

Price, Janet, and Margrit Shildrick. "Uncertain Thoughts on the Dis/Abled Body." In *Vital Signs: Feminist Reconfigurations of the Bio/Logical Body*, edited by M. Shildrick and J. Price, 224–249. Edinburgh: Edinburgh University Press, 1998.

Pringle, Rosemary. "Absolute Sex? Unpacking the Sexuality/Gender Relationship." In *Rethinking Sex: Social Theory and Sexuality Research*, edited by Robert Connell and Gary Dowsett, 76–101. Philadelphia: Temple University Press, 1993.

Probyn, Elspeth. *Blush: Faces of Shame*. Minneapolis: University of Minnesota Press, 2004.

Prosser, Jay. "Transsexuals and the Transsexologists: Inversion and the Emergence of Transsexual Subjectivity." In *Sexology in Culture: Labelling Bodies and Desires*, edited by Lucy Bland and Laura Doan, 116–131. Cambridge: Polity, 1998.

Prosser, Jay. *Second Skins: The Body Narratives of Transsexuality*. New York and Chichester: Columbia University Press, 1998.

Queen, Carol. "Sexual Diversity and Bisexual Identity." In *Bisexual Politics: Theories, Queries, and Visions*, edited by Naomi Tucker, 151–160. New York: Harrington Park Press, 1995.

Queen, Carol, and Lawrence Schimel, eds. *Pomosexuals: Challenging Assumptions About Gender and Sexuality*. San Fransisco: Cleis Press, 1997.

Rabinow, P., ed. *Michel Foucault: Ethics, Subjectivity and Truth. The Essential Works of Foucault 1954–1984 Vol. 1*. New York: The New Press, 1997.

Rado, Sandor. "A Critical Examination of the Concept of Bisexuality." *Psychosomatic Medicine* 2 (1940): 459–467.

Rado, Sandor. *Psychoanalysis of Behavior: The Collected Papers of Sandor Rado*. New York: Grune and Stratton, 1956.

Rapp, Rayna. "Margaret Mead's Legacy: Continuing Conversations." The Scholar and Feminist Online, http://www.barnard.edu/sfonline/mead/rapp.htm.

Raymond, Janice. "Transsexualism: An Issue of Sex-Role Stereotyping." In *Pitfalls in Research on Sex and Gender*, edited by Ruth Hubbard and Marian Lowe, 131–142. New York: Gordian Press, 1979.

Raymond, Janice. *The Transsexual Empire: The Making of the She-Male*. New York: Teachers College Press, 1994.

Reed, Matt. "Historicizing Inversion: Or, How to Make a Homosexual." *History of the Human Sciences* 14, no. 4 (2001): 1–29.

Reiner, William G. "Sex Assignment in the Neonate with Intersex or Inadequate Genitalia." *Archives of Pediatrics & Adolescent Medicine* 151, no. 10 (1997): 1044–1045.

Reiner, W. G. "Mixed-Method Research for Child Outcomes in Intersex Conditions." *British Journal of Urology International* 93, no. Supplement 3 (2004): 51–53.

Reinisch, June, Leonard Rosenblum, and Stephanie Sanders. "Masculinity/Femininity: An Introduction." In *Masculinity/Femininity: Basic Perpectives*, edited by June Reinisch, Leonard Rosenblum, and Stephanie Sanders, 3–10. New York: Oxford University Press, 3–10, 1987.

Reiter, Rayna R. *Toward an Anthropology of Women*. New York: Monthly Review Press, 1975.

Rich, Adrienne. *Of Woman Born: Motherhood as Experience and Institution*. Toronto and New York: Bantam Books, 1977.

Richardson, D. "Sexuality and Gender." In *International Encyclopedia of the Social & Behavioral Sciences*, edited by Neil J. Smelser and Paul B. Baltes, 14018–14021. Amsterdam and New York: Elsevier, 2001.

Ritchie, James, and Jane Ritchie. "Beaglehole, Ernest 1906–1965." In *Dictionary of New Zealand Biography Volume Five (1941–1960)*, 42–43. Wellington: Ministry for Culture and Heritage, 2000.

Robinson, Paul A. *The Modernization of Sex: Havelock Ellis, Alfred Kinsey, William Masters, and Virginia Johnson*. 1st ed. New York: Harper & Row, 1976.

Rodriguez Rust, Paula C. "Alternatives to Binary Sexuality: Modeling Bisexuality." In *Bisexuality in the United States: A Social Sciences Reader*, edited by Paula C. Rodriguez Rust, 33–54. New York: Columbia University Press, 2000.

Rodriguez Rust, Paula C. "The Biology, Psychology, Sociology, and Sexuality of Bisexuality." In *Bisexuality in the United States: A Social Sciences Reader*, edited by Paula C. Rodriguez Rust, 403–470. New York: Columbia University Press, 2000.

Rodriguez Rust, Paula C. "Popular Images and the Growth of Bisexual Community and Visibility." In *Bisexuality in the United States: A Social Sciences Reader*, 537–553. New York: Columbia University Press, 2000.

Roen, Katrina. "Queerly Sexed Bodies in Clinical Contexts: Problematizing Conceptual Foundations of Genital Surgery with Intersex Infants." In *Sex and the Body,* edited by Annie Potts, Nicola Gavey, and Ann Weatherall, 89–106. Palmerston North: Dunmore Press, 2004.

Roen, Katrina. "Editorial. Intersex Embodiment: When Health Care Means Maintaining Binary Sexes." *Sexual Health* 1 (2004): 127–130.

Roen, Katrina. " 'But We Have to Do Something': Surgical 'Correction' of Atypical Genitalia." *Body and Society* 14, no. 1 (2008): 47–66.

Rosaldo, Michelle Zimbalist, and Louise Lamphere. *Woman, Culture, and Society.* Stanford, CA: Stanford University Press, 1974.

Rosario, Vernon. "Inversion's Histories/History's Inversion: Novelising Fin-De-Siecle Homosexuality." In *Science and Homosexualities,* edited by Vernon Rosario, 89–107. London and New York: Routledge, 1995.

Rosario, Vernon. "Homosexual Origins: Theories and Research." *The Harvard Gay & Lesbian Review* 3, no. 4 (1996): 42.

Rosario, Vernon. ed. *Science and Homosexualities.* London and New York: Routledge, 1997.

Rosario, Vernon. "The Science of Sexual Liberation." *The Gay & Lesbian Review Worldwide* 9, no. 6 (2002): 37.

Rosario, Vernon. "From Hermaphrodites to Sox9: The Molecular Deconstruction of Sex." Paper presented at the Presentations in the History of Medicine Series, Royal Australasian College of Physicians, Sydney, August 1 2005.

Rosario, Vernon. "This History of Aphallia and the Intersexual Challenge to Sex/Gender." In *A Companion to Lesbian, Gay, Bisexual, Transgender, and Queer Studies,* edited by G. Haggerty and M. McGarry, 262–281. Oxford: Blackwell, 2007.

Rose, Jacqueline. *Sexuality in the Field of Vision.* London: Verso, 1986.

Rose, N. *Inventing Ourselves.* Cambridge: Cambridge University Press, 1996.

Rosen, G. "Evolution of Social Medicine." In *Handbook of Medical Sociology,* edited by J. Freeman, S. Levin, and L. Reeder, 23–50. Englewood Cliffs, NJ: Prentice-Hall, 1979.

Rosen, Ismond, ed. *Sexual Deviation.* 2nd ed. New York: Oxford University Press, 1979.

Ross, Michael W. "Homosexuality and Social Sex Roles: A Re-Evaluation." *Journal of Homosexuality* 9, no. 1 (1983): 1.

Roszak, Betty, and Theodore Roszak. *Masculine/Feminine: Readings in Sexual Mythology and the Liberation of Women.* New York: Harper and Row, 1969.

Roughgarden, Joan. *Evolution's Rainbow: Diversity, Gender, and Sexuality in Nature and People.* Berkeley: University of California Press, 2004.

Rousseau, G. S. *Enlightenment Borders: Pre- and Post-Modern Discourses: Medical, Scientific.* Manchester: Manchester University Press, 1991.

Rousseau, G. S., and R. Porter. "Introduction: Toward a Natural History of Mind and Body." In *The Languages of the Psyche: Mind and Body in Enlightenment Thought,* edited by G. S. Rousseau, 3–44. Berkeley: University of California Press, 1990.

Rowold, Katharina. "A Male Mind in a Female Body: Sexology, Homosexuality, and the Woman Question in Germany, 1869–1914." In *From Physico-Theology to Bio-Technology: Essays in the Social and Cultural History of Biosciences: A Festschrift for Mikulas Teich*, edited by Kurt Bayertz and Roy Porter, 153–179. Amsterdam and Atlanta: Rodopi, 1998.

Rubin, Gayle. "The Traffic in Women: Notes on the 'Political Economy' of Sex." In *Toward an Anthropology of Women*, edited by Rayna R. Reiter, 157–210. New York: Monthly Review Press, 1975.

Rubin, Gayle. "Thinking Sex: Notes for a Radical Theory of the Politics of Sexuality." In *The Lesbian and Gay Studies Reader*, edited by Henry Abelove, Michele A. Barale, and David Halperin, 3–44. New York: Routledge, 1993.

Rubin, Gayle, and Judith Butler. "Sexual Traffic." In *Coming out of Feminism?* edited by Mandy Merk, Naomi Segal, and Elizabeth Wright, 36–73. Oxford: Blackwell, 1998.

Rye, B. J. "Teaching About Intersexuality: A Review of Hermaphrodites Speak! And a Critique of Introductory Human Sexuality Textbooks." *Journal of Sex Research* 37, no. 3 (2000): 295.

Sawhney, Sabina. "Authenticity Is Such a Drag." In *Feminism Beside Itself*, edited by Diane Elam and Robyn Wiegman, 197–215. New York: Routledge, 1995.

Sax, Leonard. "How Common Is Intersex? A Response to Anne Fausto-Sterling." *Journal of Sex Research* 39, no. 3 (2002): 174–178.

Saxton, P., A. Hughes, H. Worth, A. Reid, E. Robinson, and C. Aspin. "Male Call/Waea Mai, Tane Ma Report No.5: Sexual Identity." Auckland: New Zealand AIDS Foundation, 1997.

Schatzki, T. R. "Practiced Bodies: Subjects, Genders, and Minds." In *The Social and Political Body*, edited by T. R. Schatzki and W. Natter, 49–77. New York: Guilford Press, 1996.

Schatzki, T. R., and W. Natter, eds. *The Social and Political Body*. New York: Guilford Press, 1996.

Schatzki, T. R., and W. Natter. "Sociocultural Bodies, Bodies Sociopolitical." In *The Social and Political Body*, edited by T. R. Schatzki and W. Natter, 1–28. New York: Guilford Press, 1996.

Schiebinger, Londa. *The Mind Has No Sex? Women in the Origins of Modern Science*. Cambridge, MA: Harvard University Press, 1988.

Schiebinger, Londa. *Nature's Body: Gender in the Making of Modern Science*. Boston: Beacon Press, 1993.

Schur, E. *The Politics of Deviance: Stigma Contests and the Uses of Power*. Englewood Cliffs, NJ: Prentice Hall, 1980.

Scott, Joan Wallach. *Gender and the Politics of History*. New York: Columbia University Press, 1988.

Scott, Joan W. "Gender as a Useful Category of Historical Analysis." In *Culture, Society and Sexuality: A Reader*, edited by Richard Parker and Peter Aggleton, 57–75. London and Philadelphia: UCL Press, 1999.

Sedgwick, Eve Kosofsky. *Between Men: English Literature and Male Homosocial Desire*, Gender and Culture. New York: Columbia University Press, 1985.

Sedgwick, Eve Kosofsky. *Epistemology of the Closet*. Berkeley: University of California Press, 1990.

Sedgwick, Eve Kosofsky. "Gender Criticism." In *Redrawing the Boundaries: The Transformation of English and American Literary Studies*, edited by S. Greenblatt and G. Gunn, 271–302. New York: MLA, 1991.

Sedgwick, Eve Kosofsky. *Tendencies*. Durham, NC: Duke University Press, 1993.

Sedgwick, Eve Kosofsky, Adam Frank, and I. E. Alexander. *Shame and Its Sisters: A Silvan Tomkins Reader*. Durham, NC: Duke University Press, 1995.

Segal, Lynne. *Slow Motion: Changing Masculinities, Changing Men*. London: Virago, 1990.

Seidman, Steven. *Contested Knowledge: Social Theory in the Postmodern Era*. Oxford: Blackwell, 1994.

Seidman, Steven. ed. *Queer Theory/Sociology.*,Cambridge and Oxford: Blackwell, 1996.

Seidman, Steven. *Difference Troubles: Queering Social Theory and Sexual Politics*. Cambridge: Cambridge University Press, 1997.

Seidman, Steven, and Linda Nicholson, eds. *Social Postmodernism: Beyond Identity Politics*. Cambridge: Cambridge University Press, 1995.

Seidman, Steven, and Linda Nicholson. "Introduction." In *Social Postmodernism: Beyond Identity Politics*, edited by Steven Seidman and Linda Nicholson, 1–35. Cambridge: Cambridge University Press, 1995.

"Sex Testing at the Beijing Olympics." Radio Interview. *The Hack*, 10m. Australia: Triple J, Australian Broadcasting Corporation, 2008.

Seymour, Wendy. *Bodily Alterations: An Introduction to a Sociology of the Body for Health Workers*. Sydney: Allen and Unwin, 1989.

Shakespeare, Tom. *The Disability Reader: Social Science Perspectives*. London: Cassell, 1998.

Shakespeare, Tom, and Mairian Corker. *Disability/Postmodernity: Embodying Disability Theory*. London: Continuum, 2002.

Sherfey, Mary Jane. *The Nature and Evolution of Female Sexuality*. New York: Random House, 1972.

Sherman, Julia. *On the Psychology of Women: A Survey of Empirical Studies*. Springfield, IL: Charles C. Thomas, 1971.

Shildrick, Margrit. *Leaky Bodies and Boundaries: Feminism, Postmodernism and (Bio)Ethics*. London and New York: Routledge, 1997.

Shopland, A. "Trapped between Sexes." *New Zealand Herald*, November 15 1997, 1997, G2.

Simon, William. *Postmodern Sexualities*. London: Routledge, 1996.

Singer, June. *Androgyny: Toward a New Theory of Sexuality*. New York: Anchor, 1976.

Slijper, Froukje M. E., Stenvert L. S. Drop, Jan C. Molenaar, and Sabine M. P. F. de Muinck Keizer-Schrama. "Long-Term Psychological Evaluation of Intersex Children." *Archives of Sexual Behavior* 27, no. 2 (1998): 125–144.

Slocum, Virginia. "Letter to Suzanne Kessler." *Hermaphrodites with Attitude* Summer (1995): 6–7.

Smith, Dorothy. "Women's Perspective as a Radical Critique of Sociology." *Sociological Inquiry* 44 (1976): 7–13.

Smith, Glenn, Annie Bartlett, and Michael King. "Treatments of Homosexuality in Britain since the 1950s—an Oral History: The Experience of Patients." *British Medical Journal* 328, no.7437 (2004): 427–430.

Snitow, Ann, Christine Stansell, and Sharon Thompson, eds. *Desire: The Politics of Sexuality.* London: Virago, 1984.

Socarides, Charles. "A Provisional Theory of Aetiology in Male Homosexuality." *International Journal of Psycho-Analysis* 49 (1968): 27–37.

Somerville, Siobhan. "Scientific Racism and the Invention of the Homosexual Body." In *Sexology in Culture: Labelling Bodies and Desires,* edited by Lucy Bland and Laura Doan, 60–76. Cambridge: Polity, 1998.

Spanier, Bonnie. " 'Lessons' From 'Nature': Gender Ideology and Sexual Ambiguity in Biology." In *Body Guards: The Cultural Politics of Gender Ambiguity,* edited by Kristina Straub and Julia Epstein, 329–350. New York: Routledge, 1991.

Spender, Dale. *Man Made Language.* London: Routledge & Kegan, 1980.

Steakley, James. "*Per Scientiam and Justitiam*: Magnus Hirschfeld and the Sexual Politics of Innate Homosexuality." In *Science and Homosexualities,* edited by Vernon Rosario, 133–154. London and New York: Routledge, 1995.

Stein, Arlene. "Sisters and Queers." In *The Gender Sexuality Reader: Culture, History, Political Economy,* edited by R. N. Lancaster and M. di Leonardo, 378–391. New York: Routledge, 1997.

Stein, Arlene, and Ken Plummer. " 'I Can't Even Think Straight': 'Queer' Theory and the Missing Sexual Revolution in Sociology." In *Queer Theory/ Sociology,* edited by Steven Seidman, 129–144. Cambridge and Oxford: Blackwell, 1996.

Stein, Atara. " 'Without Contraries Is No Progression': S/M, Bi-Nary Thinking, and the Lesbian Purity Test." In *Lesbian Sex Scandals: Sexual Practices, Identities, and Politics,* edited by Dawn Atkins, 45–59. New York: Harrington Park Press, 1999.

Stein, Edward. *The Mismeasure of Desire: The Science, Theory, and Ethics of Sexual Orientation.* New York: Oxford University Press, 1999.

Stevenson, Michael. "Ken from Mars, Barbie from Venus: What on Earth Has Happened with Sex?" *Journal of Sex Research* 34, no. 4 (1997): 411–414.

Stockard, Charles R. "Developmental Rate and Structural Expression: An Experimental Study of Twins, 'Double Monsters' and Single Deformities and Their Interaction among Embryonic Organs During Their Origins and Development." *American Journal of Anatomy* 28 (1921): 115–225.

Stoller, Robert. "Gender-Role Change in Intersexed Patients." *Journal of the American Medical Association* 188, no. 7 (1964): 164–65.

Stoller, Robert. "A Contribution to the Study of Gender Identity." *International Journal of Psychoanalysis* 45 (1964a): 220–226.

Stoller, Robert. *Sex and Gender: On the Development of Masculinity and Femininity*. London: Karnac Books, 1968.

Stoller, Robert. "The 'Bedrock' of Masculinity and Feminity: Bisexuality." *Archives of General Psychiatry* 26 (1972): 207–212.

Stoller, Robert. "Psychoanalysis and Physical Intervention in the Brain: The Mind-Body Problem Again." In *Contemporary Sexual Behaviour: Critical Issues in The 1970s*, edited by Joseph Zubin and John Money, 339–350. Baltimore and London: Johns Hopkins University Press, 1973.

Stoller, Robert. *Presentations of Gender*. New Haven: Yale University Press, 1985.

Stoller, Robert. "Patients' Responses to Their Own Case Reports." *Journal of the American Psychoanalytic Association* 36 (1988): 371–392.

Stoller, Robert, and Gilbert Herdt. "Theories of Origins of Male Homosexuality." *Archives of General Psychiatry* 42 (1985): 399–404.

Stone, Sandy. "The Empire Strikes Back: A Post-Transsexual Manifesto." In *Body Guards: The Cultural Politics of Gender Ambiguity*, edited by J. Epstein and K. Straub, 280–304. New York: Routledge, 1991.

Storr, Merl. "Transformations: Subjects, Categories and Cures in Krafft-Ebing's Sexology." In *Sexology in Culture: Labelling Bodies and Desires*, edited by Lucy Bland and Laura Doan, 11–26. Cambridge: Polity, 1998.

Strathern, Marilyn. "An Anthropological Perspective." In *Exploring Sex Differences*, edited by Barbara B. Lloyd and John Archer, 49–70. London and New York: Academic Press, 1976.

Sulloway, Frank. *Freud, Biologist of the Mind: Beyond the Psychoanalytic Legend*. New York: Basic Books, 1979.

Suppe, Frederick. *From the Semantic Conception of Theories and Scientific Realism*. Champaign: University of Illinois Press, 1989.

Swain, John, Sally French, and Colin Cameron. *Controversial Issues in a Disabling Society*, Disability, Human Rights, and Society. Philadelphia: Open University Press, 2003.

Swartz, David. *Culture & Power: The Sociology of Pierre Bourdieu*. Chicago: University of Chicago Press, 1997.

Szacki, Jerzy. *History of Sociological Thought*. London: Aldwych Press, 1979.

Szasz, T. *The Manufacture of Madness*. New York: Harper and Row, 1970.

Tauchert, Ashley. "Beyond the Binary: Fuzzy Gender and the Radical Center." In *Unseen Genders: Beyond the Binaries*, edited by Felicity Haynes and Tarquam McKenna, 181–191. New York: Peter Lang, 2001.

Tauchert, Ashley. "Fuzzy Gender: Between Female-Embodiment and Intersex." *Journal of Gender Studies* 11, no. 1 (2002): 29–38.

Taylor, V., and N. Whittier. "Analytical Approaches to Social Movement Culture: The Culture of the Women's Movement." In *Social Movements and Culture*, edited by Hank Johnstone and Bert Klandermans, 163–187. Minneapolis: University of Minnesota Press, 1995.

Teifer, Lenore. *Sex Is Not a Natural Act and Other Essays*. Boulder and San Fransisco: Westview Press, 1995.

Terman, Lewis M., and Catherine C. Miles. *Sex and Personality: Studies in Masculinity and Femininity*. New York: Russell and Russell, 1936/1968.

Terry, Jennifer. "The Seductive Power of Science in the Making of Deviant Subjectivity." In *Science and Homosexualities*, edited by Vernon Rosario, 271–295. New York and London: Routledge, 1995.

Terry, Jennifer. *An American Obsession: Science, Medicine and Homosexuality in Modern Society*. Chicago: University of Chicago Press, 1999.

Terry, Jennifer, and Jacqueline Urla, eds. *Deviant Bodies: Critical Perspectives on Difference in Science and Popular Culture*. Bloomington: Indiana University Press, 1995.

Thomas, Barbara. "Report on Chicago Consensus Conference October 2005." XY-Frauen; AISSG UK, 2006, aissg.org/PDFs/Barbara-Chicago-Rpt.pdf.

Thomas, Carol. *Sociology of Disability and Illness: Contested Ideas in Disability Studies and Medical Sociology*. New York: Palgrave, 2007.

Tolman, Deborah L., and Lisa M. Diamond. "Desegregating Sexuality Research: Cultural and Biological Perspectives on Gender and Desire." *Annual Review of Sex Research* 12 (2001): 33–74.

Toomey, Christine. "Hidden Genders." *The Weekend Australian Supplementary Magazine*, 8–9 December 8–9, 2001), n.p.

Trebilcot, Joyce. "The Argument from Nature." In *Sex Equality*, edited by Jane English, 121–129. Englewood Cliffs, NJ: Prentice-Hall, 1977.

Tresemer, David. "Assumptions Made About Gender Roles." In *Another Voice*, edited by Marcia Millman and Rosabeth Moss Kanter, 308–339. New York: Anchor, 1975.

Triea, Kira. "Untitled." http://www.qis.net/~triea/kira.html.

Turner, Bryan. *Medical Power and Social Knowledge*. London: Sage, 1987.

Turner, Bryan. *Regulating Bodies: Essays in Medical Sociology*. London: Routledge, 1992.

Turner, Stephanie. "Intersex Identities: Locating New Intersections of Sex and Gender." *Gender & Society* 13, no. 4 (1999): 457–479.

Ukia Homepage. UKIA, www.ukia.co.uk/index.htm#list.

Ullian, Dorothy. "The Development of Conceptions of Masculinity and Femininity: Development of Gender Concepts." In *Exploring Sex Differences*, edited by Barbara B. Lloyd and John Archer, 25–47. London and New York: Academic Press, 1976.

Unger, Rhoda. *Female and Male: Psychological Perspectives*. New York: Harper and Row, 1979.

Unger, Rhoda. "Toward a Redefinition of Sex and Gender." *American Psychologist* 34 (1979): 1085–1094.

Urla, Jacqueline, and Jennifer Terry. "Introduction: Mapping Embodied Deviance." In *Deviant Bodies: Critical Perspectives on Difference in Science and Popular Culture*, edited by Jennifer Terry and Jacqueline Urla, 1–18. Bloomington: Indiana University Press, 1995.

Valentine, David. " 'I Went to Bed with My Own Kind Once': The Erasure of Desire in the Name of Identity." *Language & Communication* 23, no. 2 (2003): 123–138.

Vance, Carol. "Anthropology Rediscovers Sexuality: A Theoretical Comment." In *Culture, Society and Sexuality: A Reader*, edited by Richard Parker and Peter Aggleton, 39–54. London and Philadelphia: UCL Press, 1999.

Vasseleu, C. "Life Itself." In *Cartographies: Poststructuralism and the Mapping of Bodies and Spaces*, edited by R, Diprose and R, Ferrell, 65–76. Sydney: Allen and Unwin, 1991.

Vilain, Eric. "Genetics of Sexual Development." *Annual Review of Sex Research* 11 (2000): 1–24.

von Neugebauer, Franz. "Hermaphrodism in the Daily Practice of Medicine Being Information Upon Hermaphrodism Indispensable to the Practitioner." *British Gynaecological Journal* 19 (1903): 226–263.

Walker, Peter, ed. *Chambers Science and Technology Dictionary*. Edinburgh: Chambers, 1991.

Wallace, Christine. *Greer, Untamed Shrew*. Sydney: Macmillan Pan, 1997.

Wark, McKenzie. "Bisexual Meditations: Beyond the Third Term." In *Sex in Public: Australian Sexual Culture*, edited by Jill Julius Matthews, 63–77. Sydney: Allen & Unwin, 1997.

Warnke, Georgia. "Intersexuality and the Construction of Sex." *Hypatia* 16, no. 3 (2001): 126–137.

Weatherley, Amanda. "Intersexuality: Breaking the Silence." *Contact*, May 15 1997, 3.

Weeks, Jeffrey. *Coming Out: Homosexual Politics in Britain from the Nineteenth Century to the Present*. London: Quartet Books, 1977.

Weeks, Jeffrey. *Sexuality and Its Discontents: Myths, Meanings and Modern Sexualities*. London: Routledge and Kegan Paul, 1985.

Weeks, Jeffrey. *Sex, Politics, and Society: The Regulation of Sexuality since 1800*. 2nd ed. London and New York: Longman, 1989.

Weeks, Jeffrey. "The Construction of Homosexuality." In *Queer Theory/ Sociology*, edited by Steven Seidman, 41–63. Cambridge and Oxford: Blackwell, 1996.

Weigman, Robyn. "Object Lessons: Men, Masculinity and the Sign Women." *Signs* 26, no. 2 (2001): 355–375.

Weigman, Robyn. "The Desire for Gender." In *A Companion to Lesbian, Gay, Bisexual, Transgender, and Queer Studies*, edited by George Haggerty and Molly McGarry, 217–236. Oxford: Blackwell, 2007.

Weiner, D. B. "Mind and Body in the Clinic: Philippe Pinel, Alexander Crichton, Dominique Esquirol, and the Birth of Psychiatry." In *The Languages of the Psyche*, edited by G. S. Rousseau, 331–402. Berkeley: University of California Press, 1990.

Weiss, Jillian Todd. "GL Vs. BT: The Archaeology of Biphobia and Transphobia Within the U. S. Gay and Lesbian Community." In *Bisexuality and Transgenderism: Intersexions of the Others*, edited by Jonathan Alexander and Karen Yescavage, 25–55. New York: Harrington Park Press, 2003.

Weisstein, Naomi. "Psychology Constructs the Female." In *Sex Equality*, edited by Jane English, 205–215. Englewood Cliffs, NJ: Prentice-Hall, 1977.

Welch, D., B. Ansley, M. White, M. Revington, M. Philp, and T. Watkin. "Unsung Heroes: Ten New Zealanders Who Should Be Famous, but Aren't." *New Zealand Listener*, January 10 1998, 1998, 18–22.

West, Candice, and Don Zimmerman. "Doing Gender." In *The Gender and Psychology Reader*, edited by Blyth McVicker Clinchy and Julie Norem, 104–124. New York: New York University Press, 1987/1998.

West, Louis Jolyon, Richard Green, and Peter Loewenberg. "Robert J. Stoller, Psychiatry and Biobehavioral Sciences: Los Angeles 1924–1991 Professor of Psychiatry." University of California, http://dynaweb.oac.cdlib.org:8088/dynaweb/uchist/public/inmemoriam/inmemoriam 1993/3502.

Whisman, Vera. *Queer by Choice: Lesians, Gay Men and the Politics of Identity.* New York: Routledge, 1996.

White, M. "Deconstruction and Therapy." In *Experience, Contradiction, Narrative and Imagination: Selected Papers of David Epston & Michael White 1989–1991*, edited by D. Epston and M. White. Adelaide: Dulwich Centre Publications, 1992.

Whittier, Nancy. *Feminist Generations: The Persistence of the Radical Women's Movement*, Women in the Political Economy. Philadelphia: Temple University Press, 1995.

Wikan, Unni. "Man Becomes Woman: Transsexualism in Oman as a Key to Gender Roles." *Man* 12 (1977): 304–319.

Wilchins, Riki Anne. "A Continuous Nonverbal Communication." In *Genderqueer: Voices from Beyond the Sexual Binary*, edited by Joan Nestle, Riki Anne Wilchins, and Clare Howell, 11–17. Los Angeles: Alyson Books, 2002a.

Wilchins, Riki Anne. "A Certain Kind of Freedom: Power and the Truth of Bodies—Four Essays on Gender." In *Genderqueer: Voices from Beyond the Sexual Binary*, edited by Joan Nestle, Riki Anne Wilchins, and Clare Howell, 21–63. Los Angeles: Alyson Books, 2002b.

Wilchins, Riki Anne. "Gender Rights Are Human Rights." In *Genderqueer: Voices from Beyond the Sexual Binary*, edited by Joan Nestle, Riki Anne Wilchins, and Clare Howell, 289–297. Los Angeles: Alyson Books, 2002c.

Wilkins, Lawson, M. Grumbach, J. Van Wyck, T. Shepherd, and C. Papadatos. "Hermaphroditism: Classification, Diagnosis, Selection of Sex and Treatment." *Pediatrics* 16, no. 3 (1955): 287–302.

Williams, Carolyn. " 'Sweet Hee-Shee-Coupled-One': Unspeakable Hermaphrodites." In *Indeterminate Bodies*, edited by Naomi Segal, Lib Taylor, and Roger Cook, 127–138. New York: Palgrave Macmillan, 2003.

Wilson, Angelia R. "Which Equality? Toleration, Difference or Respect." In *Activating Theory: Lesbian, Gay, Bisexual Politics*, edited by Joseph Bristow and Angelia R. Wilson, 171–189. London: Lawrence & Wishart, 1993.

Wilson, Elizabeth Ann. *Neural Geographies: Feminism and the Microstructure of Cognition*. New York: Routledge, 1998.

Wilson, Elizabeth Ann. "Biologically Inspired Feminism: Response to Helen Keane and Marsha Rosengarten, 'On the Biology of Sexed Subjects'." *Australian Feminist Studies* 17, no. 39 (2002): 283–285.

Wilson, Elizabeth Ann. "Gut Feminism." *Differences: A Journal of Feminist Cultural Studies* 15, no. 3 (2004): 66–94.

Wilson, Elizabeth Ann. *Psychosomatic: Feminism and the Neurological Body*. Durham, NC: Duke University Press, 2004.

Wilton, Karen. "The Third Sex." *Next*, November 1997, 54–58.

Wisniewski, A. B., and C. J. Migeon. "Gender Identity/Role Differentiation in Adolescents Affected by Syndromes of Abnormal Sex Differentiation." *Adolescent Medicine* 13, no. 1 (2002): 119–128.

Wittig, M. "One Is Not Born a Woman." In *The Lesbian and Gay Studies Reader*, edited by H Abelove, M. H. Burdle, and D. Halperin, 103–109. New York: Routledge, 1995.

Wolff, Charlotte. *Magnus Hirschfeld: A Portrait of a Pioneer in Sexology*. London and New York: Quartet Books, 1986.

Woolhouse, R., ed. *George Berkeley: Principles of Human Knowledge/Three Dialogues*. London: Penguin, 1988.

Wright, P., and A. Treacher, eds. *The Problem of Medical Knowledge: Examining the Social Construction of Medicine*. Edinburgh: Edinburgh University Press, 1982.

Yolton, J. W. *John Locke: An Introduction*. Oxford: Basil Blackwell, 1985.

Young, Iris Marion. *Justice and the Politics of Difference*. New Jersey: Princeton University Press, 1990.

Young, I. M. *Intersecting Voices: Dilemmas of Gender, Political Philosophy and Policy*. Princeton, NJ: Princeton University Press, 1997.

Zeitlin, I. M. *Ideology and the Development of Sociological Theory*. Englewood Cliffs, NJ: Prentice Hall, 1968.

Zita, Jacqueline. "Male Lesbians and the Postmodernist Body." In *Adventures in Lesbian Philosophy*, edited by Claudia Card, 112–132. Bloomington: Indiana University Press, 1994.

Zola, Irving. "Medicine as an Institution of Social Control." *Sociological Review* 20 (1972): 487–504.

Zondek, B. *Clinical and Experimental Investigations on the Genital Functions and Their Hormonal Regulation.* Baltimore: Williams and Wilkins, 1941.

Zucker, Kenneth J. "Intersexuality and Gender Identity Differentiation." *Annual Review of Sex Research* 10 (1999): 1–69.

INDEX